M

BLOOD

of the

LIBERALS

ALSO BY GEORGE PACKER

The Village of Waiting

The Half Man

Central Square

◆

BLOOD

of the

LIBERALS

◆

GEORGE PACKER

Farrar, Straus and Giroux

New York

Farrar, Straus and Giroux
19 Union Square West, New York 10003

Copyright © 2000 by George Packer
All rights reserved
Distributed in Canada by Douglas & McIntyre Ltd.
Printed in the United States of America
Designed by Abby Kagan
Interior collages by Eric Fuentecilla
First edition, 2000

Library of Congress Cataloging-in-Publication Data

Packer, George.
    Blood of the liberals / George Packer. — 1st ed.
      p. cm.
    ISBN 0-374-25142-8 (alk. paper)
    1. Packer, George — Family.   2. Novelists, American — 20th century — Family rela-
tionships.   3. Liberalism — United States — History — 20th century.   4. Journalists —
United States — Family relationships.   5. Progressivism (United States politics)
6. Huddleston, George, 1869–1960.   7. Packer, Herbert L.   I. Title.

PS3566.A317 Z465 2000
813'.54 — dc21
[B]   00-027743

Portions of this work originally appeared, in different form, in *Dissent, DoubleTake, Harper's, Mother Jones,* and *The New York Times Magazine.*

"I'm Still Here" by Stephen Sondheim © 1971 Range Road Music Inc., Quarter Music Inc., Rilting Music Inc., and Burthen Music Company, Inc. All rights administered by Herald Square Music Inc. Used by permission. All rights reserved.

Photographs not from the collection of the author were provided by UPI/CORBIS–BETTMANN, Reuters/Win McNamee/Archive Photos, and Culver Pictures.

For my mother and sister

and in memory of my father

Contents

BLOOD

of the

LIBERALS

Blood of the Liberals

In early 1969 my father suffered a stroke that paralyzed his right side and left him a cripple who had difficulty speaking whole sentences. He was forty-three and about to leave his position as an academic administrator at Stanford to return to the rational world of teaching law. Throughout 1968 he had been battling sit-ins and firebombings at the university, while the country was torn apart by riots, assassinations, and the endless war in Vietnam. After these upheavals, the year ended with the election of Richard Nixon, the politician my father had hated all his life.

At the time of his stroke I was eight years old. I didn't know why my father got sick; I knew still less why students shouted at him on the campus radio, why the Democratic convention in Chicago turned into a pitched battle as we watched on television, why the word "assassination" put such a spell on me. But I understood with a child's clarity that the world, which not long before had been a delightful place of caterpillars and basketball, was suddenly full of danger, that the adults had lost control and were helpless to protect me. Even then I sensed my father's fragility, not just in his body but in his manner of thinking and living—that his commitment to the life of reason stood no chance against the world going mad.

He was a liberal. He once called himself "a nineteenth-century liberal," but it would be more precise to say that he was a procedural, civil-libertarian, John Stuart Mill, Adlai Stevenson, Eugene McCarthy liberal—and he believed in liberalism with a confidence that would be impossible to muster today. In 1968 this species was under assault from two directions: on its left, radical students denounced their teachers as apologists for imperialism or, even worse, irrelevant; on its right, the Nixon-Agnew backlash professed to speak against the elitists and for the great silent majority who wanted law and order. Between intolerable pressures and the suppressed rage of his response, my father's brain, the instrument of his life's work, was flooded with blood from a burst vessel one night as he slept. He lived for three more years, struggling to walk again, thick of speech, increasingly despondent, until he committed suicide on December 6, 1972.

I never knew him well, and I spent the first twenty years after his death trying to escape the shadow of the man in the wheelchair. The face of his illness—pallor, the dark beard, the stammering mouth, and the deep black eyes that shone with fear—blotted out every other memory. Of the man who had studied, gone to war, practiced law, loved, married, fathered, taught, written, argued, and reasoned in the forty-three years before the stroke, I knew little and remembered nothing.

A few years ago, I found myself wondering about him again. All through the autumn of 1992, as the Democrats closed in on the presidency and conservatism finally looked defeated, I kept thinking about 1968, the year my father's liberalism collapsed. Six weeks after Clinton's victory, I flew back to California to spend Christmas at my mother's, in the house where I'd lived my first eighteen years. I asked my mother if she had any papers of my father's. She mentioned some boxes in the garage. I found them up in a loft, five cardboard boxes that had sat moldering and untouched for the twenty years since his death. I dragged them into the house and stayed up late every night for a week reading everything my father had left behind, hundreds and hundreds of pages, drafts of speeches, articles, reassuring letters to his parents handwritten aboard a destroyer during World War II, an angry resignation he never submitted, the blue carbons of letters written to colleagues in the last desperate weeks of his life. I read without knowing what I was looking for—simple facts, evidence of his other life apart from the wheelchair and me, and of the kind of life it had been. I suppose I was digging for an answer to the question buried under the intervening years: Why did it happen? And the related question, unanswerable when I asked it at eight and unanswerable now: Will it happen to me?

For twenty years my mother, my sister, and I had seldom spoken of my father. If he happened to come up in conversation, pain and embarrassment entered the room and stayed until he disappeared back into the silence with which we all felt more at ease. But during those nights in the family room with the cardboard boxes, my father came back. While I read, I imagined him at the end of the dark hall that led past the kitchen to the living room, leaning on his cane in just the spot where as a boy I'd fantasized an intruder bent on murder. But his eyes were fixed on me with warmth and a strange insistence. I found that I wanted to know him again. I wanted to share the good news of the Democrats' victory, and to find out what had gone wrong a quarter century earlier for my father and his politics. But now he was silent.

My mother seemed disturbed by the way I was spending my holiday.

"You were up late," she said one morning. "What are you doing anyway?"

"Just . . . reading stuff. I need to ask you some things about Dad."

My mother and I had always talked freely—except about my father. After his death she didn't remarry but instead rebuilt her life around her children and her work in the creative writing program at Stanford. Students revered her, younger women looked to her as a model of strength and independence. Now she was nearing seventy and retirement. She had willed her own peace with the past, and she could only regard my intrusion as a threat.

"I would prefer not to," she said, and then she resigned herself, knowing that, however unwelcome to her, this was necessary for me.

One night we sat down at the 1960s-style round white-laminate kitchen table where as a family of four we had endured so many tense dinners after my father's stroke. My mother waited with patient resentment for the interrogation to begin.

What was he like in the last weeks of his life? Did he leave a note before he went away that Monday twenty Decembers ago? What did it say? Did it mention me? Had he tried to kill himself before, talked about doing it before? Exactly what caused the stroke? What were the early years of their marriage like? Did he ever discuss his parents, his childhood? What happened to him in 1968? What was she going through that year? What was I like then?

Some of the questions made her grimace or groan, and once her eyes filled, a rare thing. "Do you have to ask this? Why do you want to know?" But she answered every question that night. She answered some questions I didn't even ask. Over the following months and years, through many other conversations, she kept nothing from me, without ever relinquishing her right to let me know what it cost her. She told me about not just my father but hers as well: her politician father, my namesake, George Huddleston, who represented Birmingham, Alabama, in Congress for twenty-two years in the early part of the century. He fought countless lonely fights on behalf of those he called "the plain people" until, in the 1930s, the coal miners and ironworkers and dirt farmers back in his district finally rejected their small, passionate, maverick of a congressman. She told me about her childhood in a large unhappy family with hopelessly mismatched, warring parents. She told me stories that she herself had chosen to omit from her own writings about her family, out of a desire not to wound *her* mother, who was still alive then. "Loyalty is my favorite virtue," she said in the middle of one of our conversations, as if to warn me: "Handle with care." On the continuum between loyalty and disclosure—perhaps this was generational as much as personal—we came down at widely different points. And yet she placed in my hands all the instruments of her own pain.

The search for my father that began that week in December 1992 eventually took me far back before the 1960s, beyond Stanford, beyond my father. It sent me down to Alabama and Tennessee, deep into the family past, where some secrets awaited me, and eventually into the country's past, from Jefferson through the Civil War and into the bloody century that, as I write, is coming to an end.

At twenty I thought I was the author of my own life and could go on willing it into any shape I wanted—being myself had nothing to do with being my father's son. In my thirties I discovered how much had been fixed by the accidents of birth. Not just the twisting chains of nucleic acids that gave me the broad mouth of a long-dead Jewish grandmother, the freckles of southern cousins, my mother's temper and flair for rhetoric, the listening gesture of cupping chin in hand that came from my father along with high cholesterol and a tendency toward depression. Along with these, I also inherited a history that went in one direction back to the Jews who came to New York City around 1900, and in another down into the defeated and impoverished South. I was born, like everyone, into the legacy of a genetic makeup, a family tree, a historical moment—even a worldview.

Call it liberalism. A notoriously elusive term: like "irony" and "culture," it has multiple nuances and shifting emphases, sometimes meaning opposite things. Goethe said that there are no liberal ideas, only liberal sentiments. But sentiments and ideas are more closely related than we usually think. Few people reach a political opinion by deduction from an abstract system of philosophy; most feel their way into the opinions they hold, often contradictory ones, and are hardly aware of the forces within and without that drive them. Among the liberal sentiments that run in my family are a tendency to side with the underdog, to feel that society imposes mutual obligations from which no one is excused. The rational mind, unconstrained by religion or tradition or authority, has the capacity to solve our problems. Progress is possible, if not inevitable; reason is the means, human happiness the end. Politics is lifeblood, an arena of moral choice, and more often than not a place of pain. Each generation has prided itself on being practical, yet found its own way to avoid the worldly success that might have come with compromise—the temptation to lose on principle has seldom been resisted. In general, the men in my family have been defeated and the women have endured.

But the ideas that these sentiments produce can clash between the generations, or even within a single individual. Personal troubles change the color of beliefs. Historical tides go out and leave people stranded with convictions that no longer have any way of being realized. The meaning of key words like "freedom," "equality," "democracy," "truth" can be turned inside out. The story of each generation of my family is in a way the story of an inherited idea crashing up against the hard rock of new circumstance.

In Jefferson's century, to be a liberal meant to believe in political liberty and freedom of thought. In the twentieth century, in this country, it has meant more narrowly a belief that government should take an active part in solving society's problems. It has also implied membership in a sector of the educated middle class, with a distinctive way of life. For many decades—the span of my father's life—it was the reigning view. But the twentieth century has not been kind to the notion that human reason can control human fate. Since I was a boy, "liberal" has been a political weapon, a name no one answers to, the initial consonant drawn out in contempt. The word underwent a transformation over the course of the century; its traces show up like the white glow of a barium test through the high events in the lives of my forebears. A family's history can be the history of an idea.

The liberalism I inherited is made up of these two strands: one Jewish, immigrant, academic, modern; the other Gentile, southern, populist, backward-looking. Over three generations—my grandfather's, my parents', and mine—the strands that entwined biologically to produce me were coming apart politically, weakening liberalism at the very moments when it seemed to have reached its greatest strength. To understand what happened to my father in the late '60s, when he was so embattled and isolated, I had to go back to my grandfather's career half a century before. To appreciate the context of my own boyhood, a university campus where the postindustrial future was being invented, I had to see the older face of industrialism when fortunes were hammered out of minerals and sweat in places like Alabama. I found that in pulling at the thread of a speech my father gave in 1968, a large area of the American fabric started to unravel, and in intricate ways the same thread connected that man to a different man, my grandfather, and a speech he gave in 1912. It wasn't possible to stay within one person or generation, or within one family's private affairs. A hundred years of liberalism had led up to the moment when I found the cardboard boxes in my mother's garage.

Since liberalism rejects blood in favor of mind, refusing the commands of the tribe and instead taking the free individual to be supreme, there's irony if not outright contradiction in an effort to find the sources of my own life and times in bloodlines that lead back into the distant and dead past. I've been given more freedom than my forebears had—enough to spend the past few years exploring the forces that made me and my world. I didn't choose either of my two names—and yet each of them represents a range of limits and possibilities within which I have to make my own way. Neither my grandfather nor my father figured out how to make a happy marriage of abstract ideals and concrete realities: the first lost his career, the second his life. Coming after them, I was born into an age of liberal decline, with few outlets for whatever impulses survive in this latest generation. It became a matter, if not of my own life, at least of my pursuit of happiness, to learn how this came about, and to see where those impulses might lead in a new century.

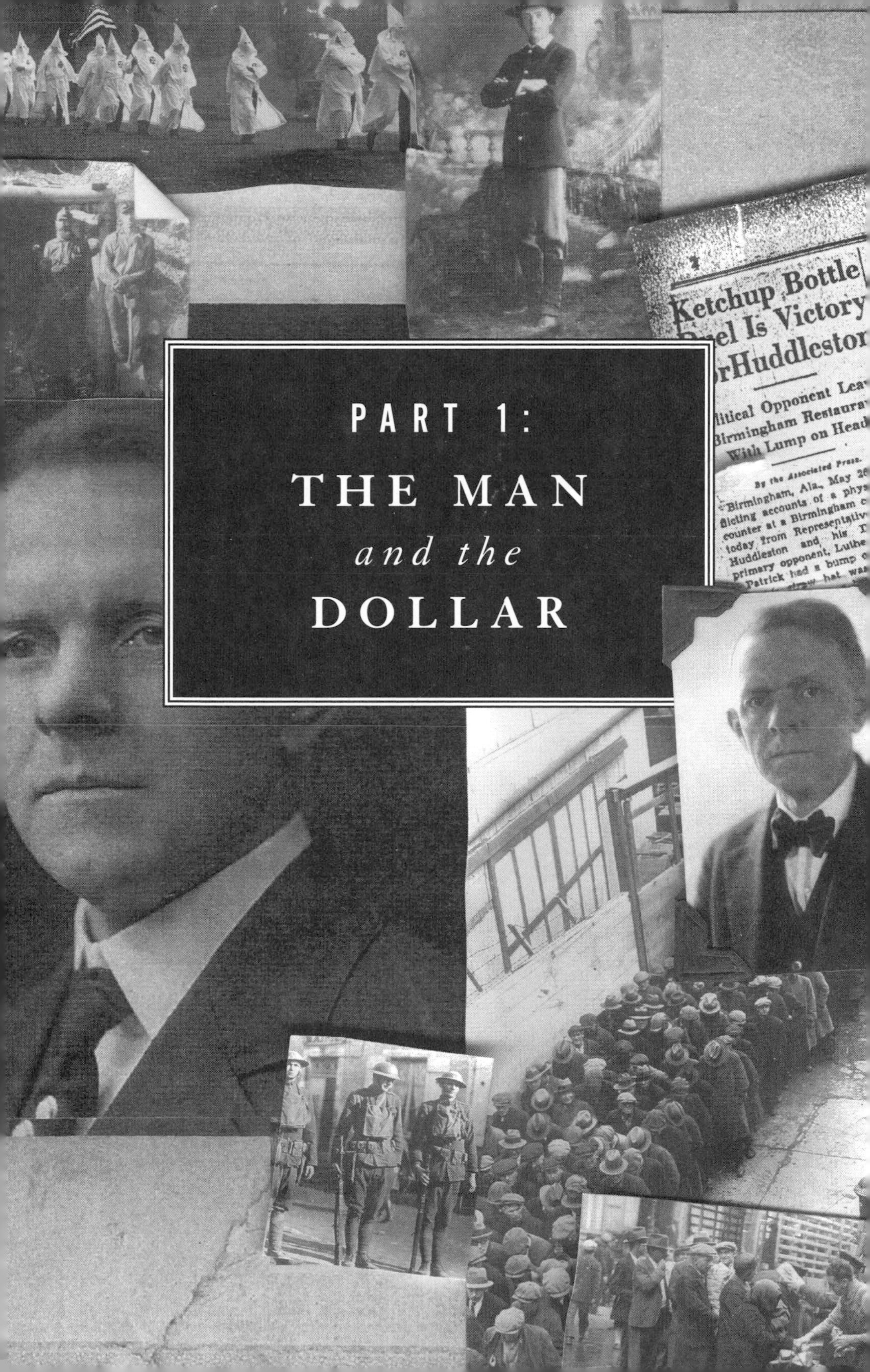

PART 1:
THE MAN *and the* DOLLAR

CHAPTER 1

◆

A Thomas Jefferson Democrat

In the year of my grandfather's birth, 1869, Ulysses S. Grant became President and General Nathan Bedford Forrest (CSA) resigned as Grand Wizard and dissolved the recently formed Invisible Empire of the Ku Klux Klan, fifty miles south of my grandfather's birthplace in Tennessee. On the day of my grandfather's death in 1960, John F. Kennedy was campaigning for the Democratic nomination for President and Martin Luther King, Jr., was holding a strategy session in Montgomery, Alabama, on the new student sit-in movement. The year 1869 is almost as close to 1776 as to 1960. Born in the nineteenth century, dying in the twentieth, George Huddleston lived mentally in the eighteenth, the century of yeoman farmers and revolutionary democrats. His congressional career stretched from 1915 to 1937, and his views won him, at various turns, the labels Bolshevik, socialist, liberal, and finally "the conservative gentleman from Birmingham, Alabama," and "the darling of Wall Street." But at the most difficult moments, when his political life was on the line, he always called himself "a Thomas Jefferson Democrat." To him the meaning was self-evident; in fact, the term encompassed a set of complications, even contradictions, that originate in Jefferson himself and the revolutionary age, when the new republic was working out what kind of society it wanted to be. By our standards, George Huddleston ended his career repudiating everything he had stood for at the start. By his own lights, he remained true to a core of belief—the heartwood within the rings of modern interpretation, something old and hard and knotty. He believed in the right and ability of ordinary people to run their own lives, and he distrusted any concentration of wealth or power that threatened to take that right away. This core sustained him until the age moved on, and then it brought him to grief, public defeat added to private misery, leaving him with not much more than his fierce pride.

When I was a boy my grandfather meant little to me. He was the Solomonic figure at the center of my mother's tales about a raucous household of five children. The stories always followed the same path—from civil war or rebellion to gruff, essentially good-humored restoration. These were comedies, and to me their moral was that a big family, with lots of children and dogs, was happier than my own. The dogs made a far deeper impression on me than my grandfather, especially the heroic Great Dane, Duke, whom a cop shot through the neck as the dog chased a bicycle. Duke survived, but the cop, whose bullet just missed hitting my mother, was suspended from the force on orders of Representative Huddleston. He was the unquestioned authority who only had to utter a name to quiet the thousand petty disputes that broke out daily among his offspring. I knew that he was nearly twice as old as my grandmother when he married at age forty-eight, and ninety when he died, and though he died just six months before my birth I always assumed that he'd been dead for decades. My main impression was that he was old, impossibly old. When I was thirteen and my grandmother died, I inherited my grandfather's pocket watch, a pair of Civil War muskets, his infantryman's sword from the Spanish-American War, and a set of brass knuckles, all of which deepened my sense that he and I belonged to different civilizations.

A few years ago I asked my mother if her father's family had owned slaves. She sighed, as if I'd finally raised the subject she'd always dreaded. Only a dozen, she said, and not on a cotton plantation but on a hardscrabble farm in the bluegrass country of middle Tennessee, all of them freed (by defeat in the Civil War) several years before my grandfather was born. Still, slave owners. The stain of the South, even a small one, lay upon us. The news shocked me, though it seemed to implicate her rather than me, as if the sins of the fathers have a statute of limitations at the third generation. Instead of personal culpability or the heavy hand of ancestral guilt, I felt mildly excited to learn of the family's connection to the great American crime. History, any history, confers meaning on a life.

The truth is, I already should have known. My mother had published a collection of essays about her father, most of them written when I was a boy. In "Lee's Lieutenants" she wrote: "My father said that before the Civil War his grandfather had a fairly large farm worked by ten or twelve hands." I read this sentence several times over the years without stopping to consider just who those "hands" were—I'd always pictured young white hires, like the ranch hands on *Bonanza*. Perhaps some scruple had kept my mother from using the word "slaves."

When she was twelve, eager to assert her regional pride among classmates at a new school, she announced that she wished the South had won the war, slavery or no slavery. That night she boasted of her rebel stand to her father.

"Don't talk like an ass," he told her. "Slavery is a terrible evil. It degrades both sides."

"The Confederates must have believed it was all right," she said.

"I'm sorry to say that at that time most Southerners did think it was all right. And the South paid for it."

"I thought you would have been a Confederate," she said.

"No doubt I would have been with my people," her father admitted, "right or wrong, foolish or wise."

She absorbed both lessons, about slavery and loyalty—"and I would be forever escaping the ambivalence toward love and conscience that trapped me then."

The father in her book is not without faults, too forbidding to be lovable, but an admirable man of the crotchety, set-in-his-ways sort, whose role is to teach integrity to the children, tease his volatile wife, and impose his law on the house with a quick clearing of the throat. "None of it is false," my mother once told me, "but it isn't the whole truth." She placed kin ahead of candor and spared both her parents the pain of exposure—for, as I would come to learn, there was plenty of pain to expose, stories she didn't write, ones she's since told me or I've discovered on my own, leaving me to work out my own ambivalence toward love and conscience.

Reading my grandfather's speeches in crumbling red-leather-bound volumes of the *Congressional Record*—alive all these years later with his quick wit, his love of a righteous fight—I often heard my mother's voice. She's my link to him, his values and his world, and in searching for my grandfather, dead before I was born, I came to know a woman who's been there since my birth.

When I went down to Lebanon, Tennessee, and browsed through the Wilson County archives, I discovered that at the start of the Civil War the Huddlestons owned a total of thirty-four slaves, lodged in six slave houses, which made them one of the country's larger slave-owning families. On June 16, 1860, my grandfather's grandfather—also George Huddleston—was deeded a "negro woman Martha and 5 children" by his oldest son. A year later that son joined the 7th Tennessee Infantry; a year after that he was killed at Antietam, one of 23,000 casualties on the single bloodiest day in U.S. military history. Another of my grandfather's uncles, Billy, lost a leg in a Yankee prison camp. But my grandfather's father, Joseph Franklin, a twenty-six-year-old merchant at the outbreak of war, didn't fight. He drew up a list of names for a company that he would lead into action, but the company never materialized. Instead he stayed home and married a woman named Nancy Sherrill. The war raged back and forth in large battles and guerrilla skirmishes and marauding banditry across middle Tennessee for three long years, and at its end the region was devastated.

"Mourning in every household," wrote one contemporary, "desolation written in broad characters across the whole face of their country, cities in ashes and fields laid waste, their commerce gone, their system of labor annihilated and destroyed. Ruin, poverty, and distress everywhere, and now pestilence adding to the very cap sheaf to their stack of misery; her proud men begging for pardon and appealing for permission to raise food for their children; her five million of slaves free, and their value lost to their former master forever." So observed William Tecumseh Sherman—the man the South held personally responsible for a good deal of its misfortune.

The Huddlestons were financially ruined, their slave labor gone, their acreage diminished. The store my grandfather's grandfather had owned since the 1820s closed, and the place known as "Huddleston's Cross Roads" ceased to exist. "After the War," my mother wrote, "most of the land was sold for taxes and my great-grandfather was hard put to feed his family. He got mighty little help from his many sons, my father said, for they were so ashamed of working the fields that whenever a carriage or horse passed by they ducked below the level of the corn to protect their honor from the view of ex-slaves and scalawags and social inferiors.

" 'Protect their honor?' my father repeated, outraged, gazing around the dinner table at each of us as if we had called it honor. 'Bosh. Honor would have set to work and amounted to something and got the land back.' "

My grandfather was born in a clapboard house, on a dirt road off the pike between Lebanon and Murfreesboro down which Sherman had marched just five years before. "My earliest memories are of the poverty which in the seventies fell upon the people of the Triangle" between Nashville, Franklin, and Murfreesboro, he wrote near the end of his life. "Poverty and privation did what war with all its horrors could not do. The people were conquered at last; their spirits were broken; they were in despair." His father's wealth had been reduced to half its level at the start of the decade. Joseph Franklin tried farming but abandoned it. He moved his family to Nashville and opened a store that failed. The hardships, his general fecklessness, his failure to serve in the Lost Cause, left his son George with a sense of shame and quite possibly hatred, which he repressed into an unpretentious family pride. In later years the ties of blood would lead him to take in countless long-lost cousins who needed a place to stay, send them to school or find them a job, force his children to pay regular visits to their hick relations in Tennessee, and compile a volume called *Huddleston Family Tables* that traced his forebears back to pre-Norman Yorkshire. He said that he wanted to make the book as uninteresting as possible. "What he honored was not the romance of family riches or accomplishment or derring-do, but the simple country fact of kinship," my mother wrote. "It is a book of begats, not of celebration." When a man named Huddleston sent him a commercially prepared family tree that claimed to prove descent from Saxon royalty, my grandfather wrote back: "If you believe this you should immediately lay claim to the British throne."

With the Huddlestons there were no trappings or displays. My grandfather grew up among defeated, unsmiling people. In a family reunion photograph taken in 1931, several generations of Huddlestons are lined up all wearing the same grim jaw, even the toddlers. His father and cousins were followers of Alexander Campbell—Church of Christers, so austere they didn't allow music in services, so unforgiving they believed members of all other denominations were hellbound. When my grandfather was old enough to become a skeptic—which he remained for the rest of his life—he asked his father whether this law of damnation would include a baby born on a ship that then shipwrecked. "Well, I don't really know," Joseph Franklin Huddleston replied, "but I don't hold out much hope."

"Huddlestons don't gush," my grandfather liked to say. "And they don't marry either," my grandmother would answer. "They just dry up and blow away." Of ten children in one branch of the family, four never married, two married cousins, two married when they were almost fifty, and just three had offspring. Only my grandfather's eccentric uncle G. Perk Huddleston, who fathered a mulatto daughter, who rode a horse into church one day, who raised regionally famous gamecocks and peddled his patented "Chicken Powder" ("puts life and vigor in your flock giving them red combs and beauty of plumage, while as an egg producer it is unequaled")—only Uncle G. Perk seems to have had any pleasure in life.

The Huddleston graveyard lies alongside the Murfreesboro–Lebanon Pike, now Highway 231, where it crosses the dry bed of Hurricane Creek—the original Huddleston's Cross Roads, where my great-great-grandfather had built his store. On a trip South not long ago I went in search of my dead kin one warm spring evening. This part of middle Tennessee is Bible Belt and horse-farm country, bluegrass fields and rolling limestone hills. Around a bend in a backcountry road, a tin-roof church appeared with a glaring marquee: "THE WAGES OF SIN IS DEATH." The graveyard is so plain that I drove by three times before noticing it next to a pasture where three horses were browsing. A stone wall about 150 by 200 feet, with a chain-link gate, surrounded a grove of tall cedar trees wrapped in vines. It was seven o'clock and the sun was going down behind the graveyard. Golden light slanted through the branches, and the air was full of the burnt smell of cedar needles. The gravestones tilted crookedly in the dirt. The more recent ones near the front were rather large and polished, but the deeper into the plot I walked, the older and humbler they became. "He died as he lived an honest man," said one-legged Uncle Billy's, but this was relatively flamboyant. Most of them were on the order of "Mary (wife)—1846–1935." Along the back wall stood a row of little foot-and-a-half-by-one-foot markers that said nothing at all, the names worn away. As the sun went down a gloom settled over the headstones. Nothing moved. A dog was barking in the pasture. The stillness in the Huddleston family graveyard seemed deeper than the silence of the dead. These ancestors of mine had never had much to say.

The next day I found the Sherrill plot on a road a couple of miles west. The difference was striking. My great-grandmother's family had erected little obelisks and scrolls and medallions to catch the eye of a passerby—their last chance to make a favorable impression. They were handsome and sophisticated people—flighty spendthrifts, according to my grandfather—who scattered after the war. His mother was the main, maybe the only, source of warmth in his early life. Nancy Sherrill Huddleston felt that her third child was destined for greatness, and she told him, "You'll be President someday." In January 1882 she drank bad water from their contaminated well in Nashville and died of typhoid fever at age forty-two. Her unsentimental husband buried her in the Sherrill plot, to leave room among the Huddlestons for his next wife, who turned out to be a hard country woman named Miss Betty Barrett.

So at the vulnerable age of twelve my grandfather lost the most important person in his life. Decades later he still got depressed in January and talked about his mother in lugubrious terms. Her death seemed not to have drained all the feeling out of him, but to have blocked it far down in dark pools, where it grew morbidly romantic.

Not long ago his oldest child, my aunt Mary, gave me a thin brown booklet labeled "Students' Note Book.—EXTRA FINE PAPER," with George Huddleston's signature on the cover. Its ruled pages are filled with poems he wrote between fourteen and twenty, in pencil or brown ink in a looping old-fashioned script. One of them is called "A Dead Mother":

> *Close her eyes for she is dying.*
> *Lightly tread around the bed where she is lieing.*
>
> *Gently fold her hands upon her breast.*
> *Softly speak around her now for she's at rest . . .*
>
> *Sing sweetly spirits unto a brother*
> *Unto a sad and sorrowing son, that's lost a mother.*

Most of the others are gloomy love poems, under the influence of Burns, about cruel girls named Mary, Jane, and Nancy, the names he would give his daughters—likely pseudonyms for a cousin improbably named Mordante Chenault, with whom he was in love and who broke his heart. His mother's ambition for him when she was alive, combined with the unhappy romanticism brought about by her death, made this barely schooled young man want to become a poet. A colored tintype shows him as an ancient-looking boy standing in a waistcoat and britches and porkpie hat, with his right hand placed flat on a thick volume on a table, a solemn little country boy striking a literary pose—but his feet are bare. He wrote poems throughout his teens and read "all of the books left in our family and all that I could borrow from neighbors within a radius of miles." He took volumes of Shakespeare and Dickens from the Nashville library and pored over them in the attic. "At thirteen a neighbor lent me a copy of *Paradise Lost*. I was routed horse and foot, after the first few pages." The writing stopped in his twenties but the reading never did, "quite without system and undirected."

His early literary fantasies found a second life when he entered politics and eventually became one of the renowned speakers in Congress. His favorite writers remained the masters of Victorian rhyme, Swinburne and Tennyson, and at eighty-two he took the unwise step of self-publishing a collection of his own lovelorn doggerel. In the way of most rigid and repressed men, he carried on a sort of shadowy emotional life that mainly found expression in sentimentality.

With his mother's death, existence went from hard to grim. His father, having failed at his Nashville store, returned to the family farm in Wilson County. George stayed behind and tried to continue in school while selling newspapers on the street, but he too failed. He dropped out of school after sixth grade and got a position working in a country store for five dollars a month. But when he saw the owner making money peddling goods, George quit the store and, now fourteen years old, struck out on his own. He became an itinerant peddler, selling chickens and eggs, beeswax, hides, tallow, feathers, lead shot, and snuff from a secondhand wagon drawn by a blind horse that he'd bought on credit.

All around the bluegrass country of middle Tennessee the boy and the blind horse plodded, from farm to farm and market to market. The rural South was falling into even deeper poverty as agricultural prices collapsed to starvation levels during the 1880s. George Huddleston had gone into business at the bleakest moment since the end of the war. Acreage reduced, mules and equipment in short supply, crops mortgaged at interest rates reaching 50 percent under the crop lien system, poor farmers were leaving the land altogether for the new industries in the cities. Some of the fields my grandfather rolled past were abandoned, corn and sorghum replaced by tall grass and weeds, houses collapsing in on themselves. The farmers who stayed behind were slipping into "a fatal lethargy," one contemporary wrote—"our minds become benumbed, deadened."

My grandfather willed himself to persist, save his money, and pull himself up toward the greater things his mother had imagined for him. The price this austere self-discipline exacted on his character was paid in a stunted affective life that would strain all of his most important relationships. He was incapable of easy bonhomie, prone to quick and severe judgment of others. But hardship also shaped the growth of his moral consciousness, in a way that's revealed by this story from when he was seven, published years later in a Birmingham newspaper:

Little George wanted some money all his own—money that he could spend just as he pleased. A neighbor had a cotton field. All but fifteen rows had been hoed. This fifteen rows of cotton looked like a job. He approached the owner: "I will hoe out those fifteen rows of cotton for a nickel," he said.

"It is a trade," replied the neighbor farmer.

George sailed in, and at the end of the first half day he had hoed seven rows. He had realized also that he had made a bad trade. But he did not back down. This has been a characteristic of his life. When he begins a job he finishes it. But this was about the first and last bad job he ever took. It was certainly the first and last bad trade he ever made.

He worked all next day on the cotton patch, and finished it.

Then he got his nickel. He kissed the nickel and swore that from that time on he would be a friend to the poor and oppressed.

It begins like a typical tale from the Horatio Alger age, another poor but plucky boy who impressed adults with his diligence and cleverness, learned from mistakes, and worked tirelessly toward his deserved reward on top of a mountain of cash—until the last phrase. The Horatio Alger novels were set in the victorious, industrializing North. My grandfather, growing up in the defeated, rural South, discovered at an early age that even American stories don't always have happy endings, family pride is mingled with shame, and life can grind people down until they lose the will to strive.

As it happened, Huddleston's biography bears some resemblance to the rags-to-riches legend—he would make his fortune practicing law and then go on to public office. He could have adopted the self-made man's smug view: if I can do it, anyone can. In another version of the story, the poor boy learns business shrewdness and swears that one day he'll buy out the neighbor's farm and pay someone else a nickel to hoe it. This would be Little Richard Nixon's version. Both boys worshiped their mothers, had failures of fathers, suffered early humiliations. Psychologically, two reactions are possible—one that resents and rejects poverty, the other that embraces it as a virtue.

My grandfather once said, "I have come in contact with a few great men and quite a few 'near' great ones. But I consider the contacts which I made as a lad when engaged in buying and selling as the basis of my knowledge of and love for what Abraham Lincoln called the 'plain people,' and this is the secret of my ability, if I have any, to mix and mingle with them, for in so doing I am not playing a part, but simply acting naturally along lines which give me my greatest joy."

Whenever one of his children would put on airs or groan at having to attend another Sunday picnic with their father's poor Alabama constituents, he would snap, "Quit posturing," and then quote his favorite lines of verse, from Goldsmith's "The Deserted Village":

Ill fares the land, to hastening ills a prey,
Where wealth accumulates, and men decay:
Princes and lords may flourish, or may fade;
A breath can make them, as a breath has made;
But a bold peasantry, their country's pride,
When once destroyed, can never be supplied.

For George Huddleston, the "bold peasantry" of the eighteenth-century English poet was simply the American common man—the "plain people" whom he came to know as an itinerant peddler. It's important to realize what this did not mean. His was not a modern, quasi-Marxist view of economic class conflict involving ceaseless struggle for wealth and power between the haves and the have-nots. His thinking was not "scientific." He disliked elites on moral, and maybe even aesthetic, grounds—because he loathed "posturing," had an instinctive sense of justice, and believed that democracy depended on a rough equality of conditions. He once gave a speech called "The New Americanism—and the Old," in which he said, "There can be no abiding democracy among a people separated into social classes and economic groups, in which all the advantage, all the hope, and all the opportunity rests with the few, and all the labor and all the burdens are imposed upon the many." The "Old Americanism," he believed, was a republic of free equals. And this is what my grandfather meant when he called himself a Thomas Jefferson Democrat.

As a young man he poured all his hardships and pride into the romance of the plain people. He would redeem his family's fall and his mother's ambition by raising his voice for those who had none. But the world into which he was born gave him no models. America in the late nineteenth century had corrupted democracy into a stampede for wealth, while the plain people were no longer independent yeomen but farmers and tenants locked into perpetual debt, their lives owned by merchants, railroads, and banks. Anyone who comes of age feeling that his own time is evil will look forward or back. My grandfather's utopia lay not in the millennial future of a classless society governed by the machine, but a hundred and more years in the past. A youthful poem expressed the idea in quaintly sentimental terms:

Back at the farm, the dear old farm
And the house beneath the hill
Far from the city's ways that harm
And the city's sins that kill
From where corruption holds its sway
From the haunts of vice and sin
Back to the father stooped and gray
And his arms that fold me in.

Compare these lines from Benjamin Franklin's almanac:

O happy he! happiest of mortal Men!
Who far remov'd from Slavery, as from Pride,
Fears no Man's frown, nor cringing waits to catch
The gracious Nothing of a great Man's Nod;

Tempted nor with the Pride nor Pomp of Power,
Nor pageants of Ambition, nor the Mines
Of grasping Av'rice, nor the poison'd Sweets
Of pamper'd Luxury, he plants his Foot
With Firmness on his old paternal Fields,
And stands unshaken.

In the eighteenth century, republicans held that when men depended for their livelihood on other men, corruption followed and democracy decayed. This was why Jefferson distrusted the manufacturing economy and disliked cities, where "men eat each other." "Those who labour in the earth are the chosen people of God," he wrote in *Notes on the State of Virginia.* "Dependence begets subservience and venality, suffocates the germ of virtue, and prepares fit tools for the designs of ambition." For this reason, his draft constitution for Virginia established a fifty-acre property qualification for voting but also appropriated up to fifty acres for the propertyless so that they might become voters. His original wording of the Declaration of Independence read: "All men are created free & independent."

Independence—fifty acres and a public education—ensured the kind of personal qualities on which a republic depended. Hierarchical societies like the one the revolution overthrew were held together by obedience and patronage ("the gracious Nothing of a great Man's Nod"). But self-government, Jefferson argued, demanded much more of citizens: they had to act out of a concern for the common good—a natural "love of others, a sense of duty to them, a moral instinct, in short, which prompts us irresistibly to feel and to succor their distresses." This moral instinct did away with distinctions between men, leveled the high and the low. In Jefferson's words: "State a moral case to a ploughman and a professor; the former will decide it as well, and often better than the latter." The principle of moral instinct, which the eighteenth century called "benevolence" or "sympathy," was as revolutionary as the related idea of democracy. It replaced obedience to divine or worldly command with the dictates of the individual conscience acting out of a sense of common humanity. The leading historian of the republican period, Gordon Wood, calls it "the basis for all reform movements of the nineteenth century, and indeed for all subsequent modern liberal thinking. We still yearn for a world in which everyone will love one another."

In eighteenth-century republican thought, there was an intimate connection between property, virtue, and self-government. Economic arrangements don't only create wealth—they also form character, which determines the fate of a republic. Widespread ownership and cultivation of the land, Jefferson believed, would create a citizenry "tied to their country and wedded to its liberty and interests by the most lasting band." Even the Federalist Noah Webster said, "An equality of property, with a necessity of alienation, constantly operating to destroy combinations of powerful families, is the very *soul of a republic*."

In the 1780s, as the new republic's first ambassador to France, Jefferson saw inequality on a scale that even American slavery had not prepared him for. He made a practice of disguising himself as a traveler among the French poor, getting himself invited into their hovels, eating their food and sleeping in their beds, and recording everything in his insatiably curious way. In a letter to James Madison, Jefferson described a country walk near Fontainebleau, where the French court repaired every fall so the King could hunt (in 1785 Louis XVI had four such Octobers left). Meeting a poor woman on the road, Jefferson pretended to be lost and wheedled out of her the details of her miserable existence. Upon parting he gave her a sum of money that amounted to three days' pay for labor and reduced the woman to tears. His letter goes on to muse about the fact of great poverty and vast tracts of idle land coexisting in the same country.

> I am conscious that an equal division of property is impracticable. But the consequences of this enormous inequality producing so much misery to the bulk of mankind, legislators cannot invent too many devices for subdividing property, only taking care to let their subdivisions go hand in hand with the natural affections of the mind. . . . Another means of silently lessening the inequality of property is to exempt all from taxation below a certain point and to tax the higher portions of property in geometrical progression as they rise.

Over a century before it became national policy, Jefferson is proposing progressive taxation (and on property, where progressivity is still unheard of). This might seem a strange idea from the man who most famously believed that government governs best which governs least. Between individual freedom and the common good there was an unresolved tension in Jefferson's thought that runs all through the history of American liberalism. But Jefferson, the apostle of small government, feared government's threat not to property but to the rights of common people. His experience of the swollen state was George III's England,

and Jefferson imagined that the manufacturing and military power Alexander Hamilton wanted America to become would only benefit the well-connected few. Limited government, like private property, wasn't an end in itself but a safeguard of self-rule and ultimately a means to human happiness—which was why the Declaration substituted "the pursuit of happiness" at the end of Locke's "life, liberty, and property." Confronted with the flagrant inequality of France in the last rotten years before the French Revolution, Jefferson was quite prepared to see government intervene on the side of the poor woman on the road near Fontainebleau.

In his own country he never had to work out the conflict between the ideals of equality and small government. That problem would be left to his heirs, including my grandfather. It has resisted most of their efforts and continues to haunt us today. But it's worth wondering how much inequality and how little government Jefferson would have accepted had he known that the America of fifty-acre freeholders would, within a hundred years, be transformed into Andrew Carnegie and ten thousand half-starved steelworkers. Jefferson predicted that within a generation we would be a republic of Unitarian farmers. He believed in small government because he didn't understand the direction in which the country was moving.

We honor Jefferson as the philosophical architect of our democracy, and yet in some ways he was a historical loser. When the ink on the Constitution dried, the republican idea of public virtue had lost out to the more hardheaded understanding of human nature that Madison and Hamilton enshrined at the Philadelphia convention while Jefferson was away in France: the idea that people are largely driven by private interests, which government must control through a system of checks and balances. "The most common and durable source of factions," Madison wrote in *Federalist* X, "has been the various and unequal distribution of property." The anti-Jeffersonian solution was not more equal distribution of property but "the regulation of these various and interfering interests." Human beings were more selfish than virtuous, more in competition and conflict with one another than joined together by the common good. At the beginning of American history psychological realism won out over idealism, and this turn in political attitudes shaped our institutions and set us on the course we've pursued ever since.

In the early years of the republic, the triumph of democracy over hierarchy released the massive energy of a free people—not into the pursuit of the public good, but into the individual scramble for private happiness. Property ceased to be the safeguard that made you virtuous and became what it is today: the commodity that made you rich. Equality meant that everyone had an equal chance to make money. "The market house, like the grave," wrote the revolutionary poet and satirist Philip Freneau, an ally of Jefferson, "is a place of perfect equality." When commercial activity replaced sympathy as the principle of social cohesion in the decades after the revolution, America was launched on the noisy, gaudy, unrestrained traveling show that would astonish and appall and seduce the world.

It wasn't the republic of Jefferson's lofty agrarian dreams, but for most of a century it was a country in which, if you were white, the platitudes about opportunity and hard work were basically true. Even as America began to industrialize and urbanize, to become the society of classes and interests that Jefferson believed was fatal to self-government, there was enough available land and wealth to create the most free and equal country the world had ever seen, the first one in history where the accident of your birth did not automatically determine your fate. The myth of the self-made man rested on enough truth for common people to believe that the unfettered market worked on their behalf and that the role of government was simply to secure equal rights for all and special privileges for none—to interfere on no one's behalf. In 1832 Andrew Jackson, who began his career in the part of Tennessee where my grandfather grew up, a region fertile with champions of popular democracy, vetoed the rechartering of the Bank of the United States, declaring: "It is to be regretted that the rich and powerful too often bend the acts of government to their selfish purposes. . . . If it would confine itself to equal protection, and, as Heaven does its rains, shower its favors alike on the high and the low, the rich and the poor, it would be an unqualified blessing." It's difficult for a modern liberal to grasp that in the nineteenth century government was seen by ordinary Americans—Jackson's "farmers, mechanics, and laborers"—as an ally of the rich and an obstacle to equality. During the first half of the nineteenth century, unrestrained capitalism liberated common people as never before or since.

By the 1860s, the decade of my grandfather's birth, this was ceasing to be true. Lincoln became the century's pivotal figure. His life and thought embodied the idea of equal opportunity that made a career like his possible in the first half of the century, while as President he moved national government and the industrial economy in a direction that would render America increasingly hierarchical in the second half. He took the Democratic Party to task for abandoning freedom and equality and embracing the cause of a caste society built on slavery. "The Jefferson party was formed upon its supposed superior devotion to the *personal* rights of men, holding the rights of *property* to be secondary only, and greatly inferior," he wrote in 1859. Slavery had rendered that devotion hollow. "Republicans, on the contrary, are for both the *man* and the *dollar*," Lincoln went on, "but in case of conflict the man *before* the dollar."

The irony of this claim became clear within a few years of Lincoln's death, as his Republican Party committed the reunified nation to the task of industrial growth. Private fortunes of unprecedented wealth would be accumulated, and the kind of small-scale competition that had made Abraham Lincoln would be crushed. The age of monopoly was beginning.

Not Golden, Mark Twain quipped, but Gilded: an age of whiskered pygmies in the White House, ruthless visionaries at the head of corporations, whole legislatures bought by railroads, the two parties fighting over spoils instead of ideas, cheap labor, immigrants packed in squalid tenements, hired strikebreakers, moralistic bombast and nocturnal vices—an age when democratic politics was subsumed by vast economic and technological change, the difference between success and failure sharpened, and the pursuit of private gain drowned out talk of the public good. In other words, an age not unlike our own.

"The man and the dollar" is one of those slogans, like "All men are created equal" and "Big Government," that contain a whole era. Everyone is born into a given historical constellation of ideas, formulations, alternatives, and for most people they become the four walls of available thought. Beliefs are shaped by the accident of birth as much as nose and hair and temperament. One era thinks in terms of private interest and public virtue, another in terms of rights and responsibilities. For over half a century after the Civil War, the conflict between the man and the dollar framed political thinking in America, the phrase and its variations appearing again and again. Among the Americans who would have occasion to use it was George Huddleston.

My grandfather inherited—along with family failure, regional defeat, and an exploitative age—a set of beliefs that went back a century to Jefferson. By the time he grew up in the 1880s, they had decayed almost out of recognition. Freedom meant the freedom, guaranteed by the Supreme Court, to hire children. Equality meant that in theory anyone could become Andrew Carnegie. In 1886 Carnegie summed up the spirit of the time in *Triumphant Democracy*, a long hymn of praise to the adopted country in which he had grown rich, dedicated to "the beloved republic under whose equal laws I am the peer of any man." A few years later, hired Pinkertons massacred the striking steelworkers at Carnegie Steel's Homestead mill. "A fair field and no favor," declared the lone Democratic President of the Gilded Age, Grover Cleveland, in the finest Jacksonian vein; then he sent federal troops to crush the Pullman strike of 1894. Jefferson's republic of "free and independent" men, Jackson's "equal protection and equal benefits," Lincoln's "man before the dollar," provided rhetorical cover while a vast robbery took place.

"The Jeffersonian conviction that political liberty was safe only where no man was economically beholden to any other died hard in America," the historian Daniel Rodgers wrote. By 1891 it seemed a cold corpse. Yet the ghost of the eighteenth century haunted the close of the nineteenth, and it haunts us today at the end of the twentieth, like a memory of youthful idealism that occasionally disturbs the torpid compromises and evasions of our middle-aged afternoons. We may have grown fat in the waist and acquired a lot of bad habits that we don't particularly want to give up, we may even be able to justify this state of affairs as our right and due, but we can't help remembering an earlier time when we swore it wouldn't happen to us. The vague sense that there's something wrong, some perversion of the original American spirit, in an arrangement in which people can work hard all their lives and never crawl out of poverty while others spin millions from pieces of paper—this sense won't quite leave us alone, as if we've failed to live up to our youthful promise and may yet pay the price. We still yearn for a world in which everyone will love one another. We don't expect it ever to arrive, but we can't afford to give up on it either, for that would mean resigning ourselves to our own moral flabbiness.

Countries, like individuals, bear the marks of their birth for the rest of their natural lives. And history's losing ideas don't always die out; they can go underground and carry on a sort of phantom existence, shadowing the prevailing ideas, sometimes coming to corporeal life in strange and disturbing manifestations. Perhaps this is true of Jefferson's republic where no one owned anyone else and everyone acted according to the common good. Perhaps this idea that lost when America was born has survived as an unconscious ideal. From time to time—not much more than once a century—it suddenly reappears, and our slackness produces a wave of self-disgust, and we hurl ourselves into reform.

One such moment came around the time that George Huddleston, having peddled goods from a horse-drawn wagon for six years, scraped together his earnings of $500 and put himself through nine months of law school at Cumberland University in Lebanon, Tennessee. Then, degree in hand, he left his old paternal fields like every other ambitious young man of the nineteenth century and went off to seek his fortune, down in boomtown Birmingham, in the county of Jefferson. He began his career there just in time for the political revolt that gave modern American liberalism its birth. The year was 1891; he was twenty-one.

CHAPTER 2

◆

Iron and Flesh

Birmingham was two years younger than George Huddleston, and they came of age together. From its beginning, the city that Martin Luther King, Jr., and Bull Connor would later make world-famous concentrated all the American ills of race and class. It held up a fun-house mirror to the country's face, magnifying every ugliness, mocking its liberal optimism about justice and progress. Birmingham's brutal rise in the late nineteenth century, when my grandfather began his career there as a lawyer, explains the reform impulse that would propel his political career in the early twentieth.

In 1871 the proposed crossing of two railroad lines in Jones Valley, where the Appalachians peter out in the scrub-pine hills of northern Alabama, gave an engineer named John Milner and a real estate speculator named Colonel James Powell the idea of establishing a new town and naming it after England's capital of industry. The lots they carved out of a cornfield and a rabbit-infested swamp and put up for public sale were surrounded by vast deposits of coal, iron ore, and limestone. Birmingham had everything necessary for the making of pig iron and steel except capital and labor, and those weren't far behind. Even before the town was chartered, an old Swedish sea captain bought the first lot for $400 and immediately built a three-story brick bank dubbed "Linn's folly." Two years later, cholera and a Wall Street panic hit Birmingham, leaving it "practically a graveyard." The pattern of boom and bust was set at the start. Birmingham's arriviste pretensions would be forever infected with a kind of hysteria—panics, depressions, revivals, rallies, crusades, lynchings. The grab motive and the sense of sin made it a city of raw nerves, easily inflamed or undermined.

Within a few years coal and iron barons arrived, breathing life into prostrate Birmingham through blast furnaces. Then it grew so fast that civic boosters coined the name "Magic City." But beneath the spectacle of New South capitalism, a precarious feeling ran deep among the superstitious farmers and miners of the hills, expressing itself in a gloomier motto that also stuck: "Hard times come here first and stay longest."

The city fathers were unsentimental men whose only aim was wealth. "I like to use money as I use a horse—to ride!" declared Colonel Henry DeBardeleben, whose coal and iron company in the 1880s owned most of Birmingham and Red Mountain, the iron-ore ridge overlooking it from the south. More than anyone else, the Alabama-born DeBardeleben, with his poker player's instincts and insatiable lust for minerals, made Birmingham the center of commercial fever in the last quarter of the century. "His aquiline nose and a certain arch of brows," a contemporary wrote, gave him "a hawk-like look . . . There is that in him, indeed, the urge, the verve—born between the dark and the dawn—to which men give the name of genius." "I wanted to eat all the craw-fish I could," this bird of prey crowed, "swallow up all the little fellows, and I did it!" But up North there were far bigger hawks with names like Morgan. DeBardeleben gambled disastrously on stock, made and lost his fortune several times over, and in the end saw his mine shafts and blast furnaces fall into the hands of Wall Street financiers. "They cut my claws, and you can't fight without claws," he said near the end of his life. "When my money went I came to hear men's voices change, see their expression change . . . And I clawed the rocks." He died in a mining camp south of Birmingham, nearly seventy and still hunting minerals like some coal-maddened Ahab.

In Chicago, Pittsburgh, and New York, robber barons were molting into philanthropists, Andrew Carnegie was spreading the Gospel of Wealth, but in Birmingham one industrialist swore, "Before God, I will be damned before I will put my hand in my pocket for anything!" The city's leading citizens didn't even have to pay lip service to public-spiritedness. In an age that celebrated "verve" and "gumption" as virtues in themselves, the mine owners and pig-iron manufacturers took on the aura of industrial Jeffersons and Madisons. "At times, when the life and death of Birmingham had been hanging on the deals," Ethel Armes, their enthusiastic chronicler, admitted, "nobody stopped to think of the place as a city. It ran wild, grew any old way."

Birmingham grafted the worst of the industrial urban North onto a racial caste system that had risen again from the ashes of war. In the New South, late-nineteenth-century capitalism brought tuberculosis, child labor, the company town, the factory whistle, the seventy-hour work-week, the twelve-family privy, and the ten-person room to a society of the Bible and the whip. When cotton fell to eight cents a bale, white and black sharecroppers abandoned their fields and flocked to the company-owned mining villages, where pigs snuffled through garbage within shitting distance of public wells whose water became too dirty to drink whenever it rained. Downtown, in an alley between Fifteenth and Sixteenth streets, plantation shacks without light or air were built on top of each other. Fifty thousand people lived in close quarters without sewers.

It was a frontier town hard by genteel cotton plantations. In neighborhoods with names like Buzzard's Roost, Scratch Ankle, Hole-in-the-Wall, and Beer Mash, miners came down from the hills to get drunk on Saturday night and shoot each other dead. Everyone except fools and women carried a gun. The murder rate was far higher than in any other city Birmingham's size, and a good deal of the killing was done by the law. A policeman shot a thirteen-year-old black girl named Lizzie for picking up coal near a railroad car. Needless to say, the vast majority of those killed were black, so many that one white lawyer was moved to write: "Cruel, brutal, inexcusable murders of Negroes do not even excite public comment much less conviction, and we have thus had our sense of justice blunted until it is almost destroyed, and wonder that things can be so. It is manifest that we have carried our own, the white people's interest too far. Nothing else seems to have concerned us and by the inevitable law we are reaping our reward."

At the heart of the scramble for wealth, deep down in the mines, lay a legalized crime. Birmingham's marriage of traditional bigotry and new greed was consummated in the system known as convict lease. The hiring out of state prisoners to the coal and iron companies was the pin that held together the political economy of Alabama and much of the South in the years after Reconstruction. Convict labor— 90 percent black—brought in as much as 30 percent of the state budget. The profits allowed the state to keep taxes low without sacrificing the spending that fueled industrial growth. Conservative "Bourbon" Democrats ruled on a platform of small government, business expansion, and white supremacy—which, in one form or another, was the South's political program for the next century.

Slave owners had been reluctant to send slaves down into the mines because the work was so dangerous. Industrialists, whose capital was invested in machinery and minerals, not human flesh, were unburdened by such scruples. Henry DeBardeleben caught the unpoetic spirit of the Gilded Age when he explained to a legislative committee: "Convict labor competing with free labor is advantageous to the mine owner. If all were free miners they could combine and strike, and thereby put up the price of coal, but where convict labor exists the mine owner can sell coal cheaper." Mine operators also favored the convicts' regularity compared with the constant loafing of free laborers, especially the incorrigible black ones. "There are no picnics, no general laying off to attend funerals of fellow workers, no excursions."

Convict lease solved so many problems (today we would call it a "win-win situation") that it must have seemed like a stroke of genius. Everyone made out except the convicts. Their daily quota was four tons of hand-cut coal, and if they failed to meet it they received fifteen lashes with a thick leather strap five feet long. The rate of convict death in the mines—from disease or overwork, from gas or cave-ins or fire, from fights among themselves—was about one in ten. When they died, their bodies were hauled out of the mines and buried in shallow graves in the woods. One convict who made the dangerous but understandable decision to escape was hunted down by dogs and mauled to the point of begging for death. Instead, his pursuers interrogated and whipped him, then tied him to the back of a mule and carried him back to the mine, but he died on the way. In 1911 an explosion killed 128 convicts at the Banner mine of the Pratt Consolidated Coal Company. Most of the dead had been convicted of offenses so slight— drinking (Jefferson County voted dry in 1907), gambling, vagrancy— that they lost their lives while serving sentences of twenty or thirty days because they couldn't pay their fines.

Here convict lease dovetailed with another innovation of the law, the fee system. Instead of receiving salaries, sheriffs and court officers were paid on piecework, by the warrant served or arrest made. This created such an incentive to perform their duties that every year 30 percent of Birmingham's population was arrested. The fee system fed off Christian piety, which made not just drinking and gambling but "the playing of any baseball, or football, or tennis, or golf on Sunday in any public place" a misdemeanor in Alabama, subject to a $50 fine— or, if the golfer couldn't pay up, work in the mines. On Sundays, the Jefferson County sheriff sent provocateurs into the mining camps to entice workers (mostly black) into gambling on cards or dice. In the middle of the game, sheriff's deputies appeared out of nowhere and placed the miners under arrest. The sheriff pocketed his fee, the state collected its lease money, and Tennessee Coal and Iron or Pratt Consolidated put another batch of convicts to work, at a third the cost of what they'd been paid as "free" workers a day before they were foolish enough to roll dice with a stranger.

Convict lease and the fee system made exploitation in Birmingham pathological, involving the entire political, economic, and legal establishment in an arrangement so brutally corrupt that it became a kind of social condition. The sense of justice in Birmingham wasn't so blunted that these scandals went unremarked. In fact they occasioned a steady flow of mine inspectors' reports, grand jury investigations, legislative committee hearings, and published outcries from conscience-stricken citizens. Even George Gordon Crawford, president of the Tennessee Company, admitted, "I really don't think we ought to have this club over the unions." But the system, like campaign finance today, rewarded too many too well, and it wasn't until 1928 that Alabama became the last state in the country to abolish convict lease.

George Huddleston arrived in this pitiless city in the summer of 1891, bearing letters of introduction from his professors at Cumberland Law School and a maternal uncle. He knew no one in Birmingham. He was, he later said, "just from the backwoods and without money or friends" and "had to fight the battle of life alone." In his first year in Birmingham he rented a desk in another lawyer's office and slept on it at night. He would walk ten miles to the nearby town of Woodlawn, collect a bill, and earn 10 percent commission. He made $37 that year, and $118 the next. He felt that his poor education left him unprepared for the work and he stayed up late nights reading Gibbon, the classics of American political debate, legal texts, the poems of Sidney Lanier, and "whatever I could get, much of which was trash."

As a practical matter he could have read less and gotten more sleep, because Gibbon was no longer a professional requirement. Throughout the nineteenth century, the legal profession had carried eighteenth-century traces of classical learning and public-spiritedness—not an expert's trade but a gentleman's profession open to young men with brains and ambition but no money. "It is at the bar or the bench that the American aristocracy is found," Tocqueville said, and law was the only institution able to "neutralize the vices inherent in popular government." But by the time my grandfather set up his practice in Birmingham, law had gone the way of everything else at the end of the century and become a business increasingly dominated by corporations. The lawyer-gentleman whose devotion to precedent and reason reined in mob passions had given way to the hired gun who felt responsibility to nothing but his well-paying corporate client, like the Wall Street lawyers who helped J. P. Morgan's U.S. Steel buy the city of Birmingham. Small, independent practitioners were losing work to large firms and finding themselves reduced to ambulance chasing (this was how Hugo Black, George Huddleston's rival in Alabama politics and future Supreme Court justice, got his start in Birmingham as a poor boy from the hills). By the turn of the century few lawyers could say with Jefferson that law practice "qualifies a man to be useful to himself, to his neighbors, and to the public." The Progressive impulse found some of its leading spokesmen in socially insecure, morally troubled lawyers, some of whom left practice altogether for public service or else the rising field of legal education, which restored their sense of professional purity and provided a platform for reform ideas—a course my father would follow half a century later.

It might have been the panic of 1893 that turned my grandfather to bankruptcy practice. In Birmingham this proved a promising branch of the law, and within a few years he was earning a comfortable living. Whenever the city's iron industry underwent one of its frequent shake-ups, often precipitated by stock manipulation on Wall Street, a whole new wave of fortune hunters required his help in protecting their assets. His clients were small businessmen, many from Birmingham's tiny community of German Jews. Money admitted him into the circles of the successful, which in turn brought in more business. "Self-made" men are men who make the most of connections they weren't born with.

He was single-minded enough in pursuing his career as a lawyer that the record of his progress is practically nonexistent. These two decades of his life, which transformed him from a country boy with a sixth-grade education and a law degree to a well-known and prosperous man, left behind no letters, no newspaper clippings, few anecdotes.

When I went to Alabama, I learned that the trunk containing his papers and letters, professional and personal, didn't survive the closing up of the Huddleston house after my grandmother Bertha died in 1974. In the distractions of a funeral and a housecleaning, no one thought them worth giving to his law school alma mater or the Birmingham Public Library. My only lead was a warehouse next to a lumber yard on the seedy edge of Montgomery, where the business partner and drinking buddy of my late uncle John, who was my grandfather's executor, had storage space. Unsurprisingly, I found no trunk. The records of George Huddleston's life were gone—lost.

No one from the 1890s survives, and he was not given to the southern habit of tale-telling; so I know little for sure. I know that after one courtroom dispute he exchanged pistol shots with another lawyer on a downtown street; fortunately for me and their other descendants, neither man seems to have been competent with his weapon. I know that he became romantically linked with a gaunt, unlovely older woman named Kate Earle for about a decade without any intention of marrying her, perhaps so that he wouldn't be bothered by other prospectors. Before his papers were thrown out, one of my cousins found among his possessions a letter from a prospective date, apologizing for making him wait while she got ready but also gently chiding him for going home before she could come downstairs. Beyond this, I can only say that he must have worked very hard.

Just a few years before, he'd written:

Far from the city's ways that harm
And the city's sins that kill
From where corruption holds its sway
From the haunts of vice and sin . . .

Now he was making a living off some of that corruption. Fresh from the "backwoods," not far removed from his horse-drawn-wagon days, his head stuffed with random pieces of literature, he was seeing all the open sores of industrialism at their ugliest in a city whose population had grown almost tenfold in its twenty years. He had known only the society of "plain people," and now he was brushing against general managers and bank presidents in starched collars who dealt in sums of money ten thousand times his peddler's earnings. The roaring blast furnaces, the air so choked with smoke that breathing blackened people's nostrils, the slag heaps piled on downtown streets, the filthy privies and casual violence—gargoyles of injustice leered on every corner like figures from a vision of hell. But under the surface a great change was about to erupt in Alabama, the South, and throughout the country. These years that left almost no personal trace were decisive in the making of the public man. My grandfather got his political education in a time of upheaval, when the meaning of American democracy was suddenly up for grabs.

In his old age, my grandfather, himself a son of the decayed gentry, recalled sitting down to a meal in 1890 with a farm family that had fallen on hard times. "The food though well cooked was plain; potatoes, greens with bacon and cornbread with buttermilk was the fare. But despite the poverty, the hospitality was unstinted. The father in his patched clothes presided at the table with all dignity. Only one sign of more prosperous days remained in evidence. It was the massive ladle of solid silver with which the potatoes were served. Gone the big house, the broad acres; gone the old life of dignity, comfort and leisure; gone everything, but the battered old ladle, the relic of happier days."

By 1891 the small farmers—Jefferson's "chosen people of God"—had seen crop prices fall, freight rates rise, and debt increase for almost two decades, and they had seen enough. The losses weren't just financial: their lives had fallen under the control of legislatures, railroads, and banks as far afield as England. Pride and self-respect were reduced to a silver serving ladle.

Beleaguered country folk poured into the company towns of Jefferson County and got their first look at the face of industrialism. A system of withheld wages, high-interest loans, and commissary price-gouging kept the miners, like their tenant-farming brothers, constantly in debt, and they were routinely shortchanged when their daily output of coal or iron ore was placed on the scales. One miner's wife wrote to the governor: "The company has not give the poor Men Worke enough to hardly Maintain his family for they sell things so high in the comasary, and When the Men pay house rent out of that they had but little to live on . . . Why isent one Man as free as a nother."

During the last two decades of the century a number of futile wildcat strikes broke out and were inevitably put down by the arrival of imported black strikebreakers and convicts. This sometimes strained race relations among the workers to the point of mob violence. Yet in the years after Reconstruction, the most integrated place in the state was a coal mine. The strikes achieved remarkably high degrees of black and white cooperation. The companies employed tactics calculated to enrage the whites while cowing the blacks into giving in, but again and again black strikers proved their loyalty by staying out of the mines and shooting at trainloads of black strikebreakers from Tennessee or Kansas. The unity between black and white workers wasn't a threat just to company control but to the ideology by which Alabama was governed under the Bourbon Democrats. For white supremacy was the indispensable adhesive. It held together what vast economic change was beginning to rip apart, and as the social system cracked under industrial pressure the racial system hardened. The year 1891, when my grandfather arrived in Birmingham, saw the passage of Alabama's first Jim Crow law enforcing segregation. It saw twenty-four lynchings, the state's all-time high.

That year also saw the stirrings in Alabama and throughout the South and West of a movement known as Populism, which threatened the rule of class and caste as nothing would again for over half a century. Three years later, in 1894, Alabama Populism reached its height and then met its fate, in a stolen election and a broken strike.

Less an ideology than a mood, Populism put up the first serious challenge to the corrupt consensus of the Gilded Age and in doing so drew on old and deeply felt democratic values. Its weakness lay in its incoherence, in contradictions between belief and program, program and action. The Populists represented a peculiarly American type whose longing for the Golden Age of the past makes them radicals. Mentally of the eighteenth and nineteenth centuries, they laid down the first trestles for the great liberal reforms that would come in the twentieth. Archindividualists, they formed cooperatives and acted for a few brief years with surprising collective discipline. Conscious heirs of Jefferson—in Alabama they called their splinter party the "simon-pure Jeffersonian Democratic Party" in opposition to the corrupted version of the Bourbons—they abandoned the party gospel of small government and advocated federal interventions like railroad regulation, farm credits, ownership of communications, and a graduated income tax. Confederate veterans and sons, they wrote into their platforms the protection of Negro rights.

The Populists were parochial men of the earth, but their Agricultural Wheel and Farmers' Alliance dispensed, along with practical advice on farming methods, a rhetoric of universal justice that borrowed the apocalyptic moral fervor of the Bible Belt. The spirit was both narrow-minded and visionary, crankishly paranoid and bravely humanistic. The publication in 1888 of Edward Bellamy's *Looking Backward,* a dream of the cooperative commonwealth set in Boston in the year 2000, which sold half a million copies, inspired a large crop of utopian novelists such as Alabama's Populist Representative Milford W. Howard, author of *If Christ Came to Congress* ("unwillingly and without permission dedicated to Grover Cleveland, President of the United States, and his drunken, licentious cabinet and certain members of Congress"). Today, after a century of totalitarianism, the word "utopia" suggests feckless romanticism or a blueprint for terror. But to the reformers of the late nineteenth century, an image of utopia seems to have been psychologically necessary for them to think their way beyond the overwhelming facts of industrial capitalism. Utopias have always cut both ways: taken literally, they inspire fanaticism or disbelief; but they also carry the imagination of hope, without which no reform movement is likely to survive its own inevitable defeats and the corrosive power of the status quo.

Many of the southern Populist leaders were, like my grandfather, members of the landed gentry who wanted to restore this marginalized class to the moral center of American politics, where Jefferson had once put them. In doing so they never noticed that they were turning the basic assumptions of American political thought upside down. Democracy had become plutocracy, the rule of wealth; equality by right had created inequality in fact, and this called into question the very meaning of freedom. The freedom to pursue individual self-interest had resulted in conditions that prompted the Birmingham miner's wife to ask, "Why isent one Man as free as a nother." Roscoe Pound of Harvard Law School, writing nine months later, explained her plight in different language but just as directly: "Necessitous men are not, truly speaking, free men." The Populists grasped what Jefferson didn't anticipate: that a society of free equals could become a society of entrenched classes. But they continued to think as Jeffersonians, demanding merely a return to individualism and popular rule even while they were seeking an expansion of government beyond Hamilton's biggest dreams. They saw the federal government as the instrument of the people's will. This last gasp of agrarianism was also the first tremor of modern liberalism.

The southern Populists carried their banner into the teeth of the most entrenched social codes. Men who had never ventured out of their home county defied the sacred Democratic Party of their Confederate fathers. Farmers made common cause with urban industrial workers who had alien ways and sometimes spoke alien languages. Nothing, though, asked more of the Populists in places like Alabama than their willingness to embrace the cause of black political equality. They didn't do it consistently, they sometimes did it opportunistically, and eventually some of them, like Tom Watson of Georgia and "Pitchfork" Ben Tillman of South Carolina, became more viciously racist than the conservative Democrats. But for a few years in the early 1890s poor Southerners turned their backs on the most rigid orthodoxy of their world and reached out to their brethren among Negro Farmers Alliancemen and black coal miners. For a rare moment in southern history, class mattered more than race. It amounted to a revolution, and if it had succeeded, the twentieth century might have looked very different in America.

In their 1892 platform, Alabama's Jeffersonian Democrats called for "the protection of the colored race in their political rights"; also the end of convict lease. Before mixed crowds their speakers frankly proposed an alliance of white farmers and black sharecroppers. "I had rather see Mobile Bay filled with Pinkerton's detectives," the Populist orator Peyton Bowman told a black crowd, "the banks of every river and creek in Alabama lined with Federal bayonets and crimson with blood, rather than see you deprived of the privilege of voting for whom you please." This kind of talk exposed the Populists to the grave charge that they were dividing the white electorate and allowing an opening for blacks to become their social equals (which not even the Populists dared advocate). The *Birmingham News* called the "Negro plank" "a slap in the face of every white Democrat in the state."

But the conservatives had a trick card up their sleeve, and ironically it was the black vote. Down in the Black Belt cotton counties of southern Alabama, where the black population ran higher than 75 percent and remained in a state of utter peonage, white planters rigged a black sweep in favor of white supremacy even if it meant raising the dead for phantom votes. In this way the Democratic candidate for governor stole the 1892 election from the Jeffersonian Democrats' Reuben Kolb, who won the largely white hill counties up north.

The panic of 1893, which plunged the country into its worst economic crisis to date, deepened the farmers' anger and began to draw small-town businessmen and industrial workers to their cause. The following year, 1894, looked like the reformers' year. This time, to avoid fraud, the Jeffersonian Democrats called for an all-white gubernatorial primary while keeping their plank for black political rights. The Bourbons refused and proceeded to rig a second election. That same year, in Jefferson County, black and white coal miners of the newly organized United Mine Workers of Alabama staged the state's first large-scale strike, over low wages. Allied with the Populists, they held on from April until August, maintaining remarkable solidarity in the face of continuous race-baiting from mine owners like Henry DeBardeleben and the Birmingham papers. Ultimately the combination of imported black strikebreakers, state militiamen, and the stolen election forced them to settle on poor terms and go back to work.

Electoral fraud, the race card, and the hired gun meant the beginning of the end for Populism in Alabama. Thereafter it fell into disorder and the instinctive fatalism of the southern poor. The last act was played out in 1896, the year the Democratic presidential candidate, William Jennings Bryan, adopted the least useful reform idea—free coinage of silver—and rode it to defeat against William McKinley. In Alabama, the Populists, desperate with a foreboding of defeat, encouraged their black allies more explicitly than ever. The Bourbons warned, "Their children shall sit side by side with children with white faces and straight hair," and they won again, hands down. It was the end of southern racial unity for the next hundred years.

As an organized political entity Populism was finished, having risen and crashed in meteoric American fashion. The Populists themselves never saw the full implications of their uprising—the men weren't as large as their ideas. Among those who actually got elected to office, some wandered half asleep back to the old Democratic lair, voting against the very things they had once championed. But the spirit of opposition to rapacious business and corrupt government that Populism unleashed would dominate the politics of the new century. For the next forty years, its heirs in liberal reform would be locked in a fitful debate over whether they wanted to restore individual competition or enlarge the collective state—to go back to Jefferson or forward to Roosevelt. The most perceptive admitted the impossibility of doing both; others zigzagged back and forth across the line. For his part, my grandfather would emerge as a late-blooming populist two decades after the movement itself had officially expired. He would fight his main political battles over freedom and equality, and lose for good when the contradictions finally caught up with him.

In 1898, at age twenty-eight, George Huddleston put aside his law practice and enlisted as a private in the 1st Alabama Volunteer Infantry Regiment. Under President McKinley, the country, having put down a political rebellion among its marginal citizens, turned to the more uplifting experience of war—Theodore Roosevelt's friend John Hay called it "a splendid little war"—against Spain. What looked to some Populists like a crusade in the name of humanity turned out to be America's first imperial adventure just before the start of the American Century. Black and white Southerners joined in droves to prove their loyalty to the Union.

No doubt my grandfather volunteered out of a characteristic sense of duty—and perhaps to honor his Confederate uncles and redeem his noncombatant father's shame. But military service seems to have had a fairly devastating effect on him. Recently my mother dug up his records and sent them to me. They tell a strange tale. He spent six miserable months encamped in Mobile and Miami, never getting to see action in Cuba, appearing regularly on the Register of Patients for "jaundice," "acute posterior nasal catarrh—not severe," "slight rheumatic trouble in both legs," "intermittent malarial fever," "diarrhea," and "acute constipation." In August he asked to be furloughed home to Tennessee for thirty days, saying, "I am still unfit for duty being weak and greatly troubled with diarrhea and have not yet recovered from my illness with jaundice." The regiment's surgeon approved: "He needs a change of climate & complete rest from duties for a month, at least."

After the war ended in September, my grandfather led a protest of enlisted men who demanded to be mustered out faster than the Army was going about it. But at his discharge examination, a Captain Charles Ledbetter declared that he saw no reason to believe Private Huddleston's claim of suffering any health disability incurred during service. Was he malingering as part of the protest? Or did the months of military discipline in a steamy sinkhole in southern Florida undermine him, leading to a sort of breakdown? In later years he would repudiate this war as imperialistic and unnecessary, and he would speak with bitterness about military life as "the antithesis of equality," with all the privilege resting with officers and the sacrifice with enlisted men. Military hierarchy and the unquestioning obedience it demanded affronted his political values. "Molded by democracy, man is reasonable, kind, and just; shaped by militancy, he is machinelike, emotionless, and severe," he would warn in 1917 as America prepared to throw itself into the European bloodbath. But his deepest feelings—anger at military authority and the "undemocratic classes" who supported it, together with compassion for the common soldier—had painful personal sources, in those months in uniform when he learned "what a soldier must encounter even in camp, the privation, the hardships, the homesickness, the discouragement, the disease, perhaps even death."

Honorably discharged, he resumed his law practice in Birmingham. After the depression of the early 1890s, prosperity was returning. But the turbulent decade had exposed a serious problem for the ruling Democrats in Alabama and the South: when whites were divided along class lines, blacks held the balance of power. This threatened nothing less than "negro domination," which in turn made it necessary for the ruling party to cheat. But cheating was supposed to be for Tammany Hall and the Republican machines up North.

Fortunately, a solution was at hand: Alabama could rewrite its constitution to take the vote away from blacks. Washington appeared ready to receive the South back into the national fold, "traditions" and all. In 1896 the Supreme Court sanctioned Jim Crow in *Plessy* v. *Ferguson*. In 1898 the acquisition of Puerto Rico and the Philippines in the Spanish-American War, which suddenly brought millions of brown-skinned people under American rule, made the North more sensitive to the complexities of the "race problem." President McKinley took his message of capitalist triumph to Montgomery, where enormous crowds heard the Republican President sing "Yankee Doodle" and "Dixie" in the birthplace of the Confederacy. The message was clear: the federal government wouldn't stand in the way if Alabama decided to solve its problem.

The constitutional convention opened in Montgomery on May 21, 1901, in the domed antebellum statehouse. In case any of the 155 delegates didn't understand why they had come to Montgomery, John B. Knox, Esq., spelled it out in his keynote speech. "What is it that we want to do? Why, it is, within the limits imposed by the Federal Constitution, to establish white supremacy in this State."

The federal constitution raised a pair of obstacles in the form of the Fourteenth and Fifteenth amendments, but the delegates were confident in their task. "This is a practical question," one of them said, "to be dealt with by practical men." A humble petition from Booker T. Washington and other leading black citizens, asking only that the "tenderness, good will and sympathy existing between the two races in this State . . . not be disturbed," must have sounded like a benediction when it was read aloud.

But the work of disfranchisement turned out to be not at all simple for these practical men. The trouble came down to this: they couldn't decide what they thought about blacks, or about democracy. The convention sweltered for three and a half months through the heat of summer, as the effort to square constitutional principle with their stated purpose produced marathons of southern oratory from ex-Confederate planters and industrialists sweating in starched collars. The more they talked, the more they disagreed. Was voting a right or a privilege? Who should enjoy it? Should it be hereditary? Did education and property guarantee good citizenship? Were blacks capable of becoming citizens or not? The delegates had inadvertently opened up the basic questions of republican government, and the great constitutional debates from just over a century before rose up again, in grotesquely distorted echoes, on behalf of a white oligarchy.

The proposed suffrage article disqualified from voting—along with tramps, vagrants, idiots, insane persons, sodomists, and other criminals—any man between twenty-one and forty-four who had failed to pay his cumulative $1.50 poll tax; or any man who couldn't read and write an article of the U.S. Constitution; or any man who owned neither forty acres of land nor $300 of personal property. Taxation, literacy, and property became the southern way of ridding blacks from politics without running afoul of the Constitution. The old Jeffersonian idea of a property qualification resurfaced, now down to forty acres — this time not to ensure the citizen's independence, but to keep out the black poor. But everyone knew that these very standards would disqualify a good many poor whites as well. As a compromise, the Suffrage Committee inserted the "Fighting Grandfather Clause," which gave southern veterans and their descendants (by definition all white) who couldn't pass the other tests one year to register; then the loophole would close.

The "Solid South" turned out to be deeply split along class and generational lines. Former governor William Oates, white-headed and -mustached, his empty sleeve a badge of Confederate honor, epitomized the older Bourbon conservative. He had benefited personally from electoral fraud in 1894, and now he wanted to make amends. But "I am for eliminating from the right to vote all those who are unfit and unqualified, and if the rule strikes a white man as well as a negro, let him go. There are some white men who have no more right and no more business to vote than a negro and not as much as some of them." Believing education, wealth, and virtue synonymous, this planter-general became the convention's unlikely advocate for black rights and abilities. The wounds of the Populist wars were fresher than Gettysburg's, and patricians like Oates were more appalled by the thought of poor voters than black voters. "It is not a racial question," he insisted — throwing the entire project into confusion.

This was too much for the younger delegates. Having abandoned paternalism for the harder ideology of social Darwinism, they didn't dwell on tender memories of slave mammies and faithful servant boys. Their racial reference points were the federal bayonets of Reconstruction and black crowds at polling places. Linen-suited, long-winded J. Thomas Heflin, a prototype for the modern race demagogue of the George Wallace variety, argued for starving black schools of tax money. "Some day when the two separate and distinct races are thrown together, some day the clash will come and the survival of the fittest, and I do not believe it is incumbent upon us to lift him up and educate him and put him on an equal footing that he may be armed and equipped when the combat comes." These protofascists wanted the franchise for all white men, rich and poor—not because of economic populism or democratic principle, but for power and control. If the choice came down to republican virtue or racial solidarity, they knew where their interest lay. Oates belonged to the past; Heflin spoke for the South of the new century.

Throughout the summer, the convention was haunted by the ghost of Thomas Jefferson. Speakers on every side cited him for authority. And yet the Jeffersonian principle that self-government is an inalienable human right had so withered that by 1901 it dwindled to a single delegate among the 155 in Montgomery—one Newton B. Spears. The son of a Union general, he had come down from Tennessee to Alabama like my grandfather just in time to catch the Populist fever, and somehow he didn't lose it when Populism failed. Of all the delegates only Newton B. Spears could say unequivocally, "I have planted my feet upon the rock of universal manhood suffrage, and I am not afraid." Someone tried to answer, but for sixty-six days Spears had scarcely spoken and now he would not be interrupted, as if he had no illusion of persuading anyone but simply wanted to have his say. "I stand where Jefferson stood when he declared in the face of kings and tyrants that all men are created equal and endowed with certain inalienable rights . . . Have we in this Convention a greater statesman, a greater lover of liberty, a greater publican, a greater Populist than Thomas Jefferson? If so, point him out that I may go and touch the hem of his garment."

Having taken the last breath of Populism in Alabama, Newton B. Spears stepped down into obscurity. No one even bothered to rebut him; the convention moved on. But he left hanging in the air a question that would come to torment Alabama and the South half a century later: "Do you want to pursue a course and a policy that will make the negro look to Washington and not to Montgomery for protection?"

By September 3 the work was finally done. Two months later, a surprisingly narrow majority of voters approved the new constitution. Alabama's was now the longest in the country, the suffrage article alone (which doesn't mention "black" or "white") nine byzantine pages—the same constitution under which the state labors to this day. And for all the philosophical tangles it had stumbled into, the convention achieved its original purpose. Within five years only 2 percent of the state's adult black men were voting. A quarter of the whites lost their vote because of the poll tax alone.

Alabama's poor whites never again organized themselves into a political force. Its blacks, now noncitizens in the state where they continued to live and work and pay taxes, fell into official subordination and endured silently for half a century. It wasn't until the early spring of 1965, when blacks and whites from around the country marched from Selma to the steps of the very building in Montgomery where the delegates had held forth in the summer of 1901, that the federal government, answering Newton B. Spears's prophecy, restored what the convention had taken away.

The political problem solved, Birmingham went back to making money. The "Big Mules," Birmingham's business elite, retreated from the cauldron of race and class to count their money in houses they built up on Red Mountain. The first generation of pioneer barons yielded to managerial executives in pince-nez, and while they mastered the open-hearth process of converting high-phosphorus iron into basic steel, the reins slipped out of their hands. Speculation fever, a top-heavy economy, and the cyclical collapses these provoked brought more and more of Birmingham's wealth under the control of Wall Street finance. Then came the panic of 1907, when, for the good of the country and with the blessing of the "trustbuster" President Theodore Roosevelt, J. P. Morgan's U.S. Steel Corporation agreed to buy its main competitor, Tennessee Coal and Iron, the Birmingham district's largest company and only steelmaker, with a billion in mineral rights alone, for less than a fiftieth of its potential value. Suddenly

Birmingham had become an economic colony of northern monopoly.

In the summer of 1911 a New York philanthropic journal sent a team of investigators down to study the quality of life in the New South's capital of industry. "Birmingham," *The Survey* summed up in its special issue, "a city with no public library, no public recreation, no regulation of housing, no meeting-hall for her citizens, no civic center, no city plan for growth; a city which lets railroads cut her in two, which is only beginning to be ashamed to have chain gangs cleaning her streets, which, in spite of her wealth, cannot pay for the most ordinary municipal service, which nevertheless undertakes to provide such service in duplicate, which allows her streets to be piled high with slag from an iron furnace, and which has given away in perpetuity priceless franchises for public utilities." Twenty years after he'd arrived, George Huddleston's adopted hometown was still a democrat's hell.

By 1911 my grandfather had made enough money to sell his practice to a Jewish lawyer named Leo Oberdorfer. He would later claim that he retired from the law because his clients were crooks, hiding their assets from creditors—to which Oberdorfer replied that those crooks were their bread and butter. Huddleston bought 50,000 acres down in the dirt-poor pine hills of Shelby County, which he never bothered to develop but enjoyed in the spirit of amateur yeomanry. He spent a year looking at paintings and cathedrals in Europe; Georgian England and the Kaiser's Germany did nothing to diminish his bias for American democracy. Upon his return he decided to enter politics. On the strength of legal work he'd done against industry and the utilities on behalf of a civic group, he won election as alderman. Immediately he established his Progressive credentials, fighting to bring the city's water and light franchises to a popular vote and forcing Sloss Furnace to clean up the slag it had dumped on Second Avenue and to shut down coke ovens that belched smoke and dust. Progressivism in Birmingham, as in the eastern cities, was largely a movement of middle-class professionals and businessmen in the early 1900s who mourned the old days of individual opportunity, watched the age of the self-made man give way to giant corporations and equally menacing labor unions, and felt the tug of Protestant guilt at the evils bred by industrialism, "the shame of the cities." They saw the country's problems in moral rather than structural terms. Their reforms were real but limited by self-interest and a belief in the essential rightness of the social order. Less alienated and more respectable than the Populists, in the short term the Progressives got more done.

It soon became clear, though, that Huddleston was no mild reformer.

In July 1912 he traveled down to Montgomery to address the Alabama Bar Association, which was gathering to discuss legal reform in the same state capitol chamber where in 1901 the constitutional convention had restricted the franchise to the intelligent, virtuous, and propertied. On the first day of the meeting, Huddleston went to the podium where Newton B. Spears had spoken eleven years before. In his first recorded political speech, he sounded nothing like a deferential newcomer. "I would like to call the attention of the lawyers here, who represent the progressive and leading elements of society," he began, "to the fact that the voters of Alabama compose, in round numbers, five per cent of the population . . . Our suffrage laws—whether so designed or otherwise—operate to suppress the common and the ignorant man."

He put his argument in the old republican terms that had been stood on their head at the convention. Perfect government by 5 percent of the people—"an honest oligarchy"—was not democracy. Democracy derived its powers from the consent of the governed, and it required citizens. Self-government made people better. "I submit that when you take away a man's ballot, you have degraded him; when you take away his right to govern himself, you take away the possibility of making a man worthy of the name of citizen. So I say, it is unfortunate for the people of Alabama that they have denied the right of suffrage to so large a part of our population."

He was getting to the heart of the matter now, and he didn't flinch from its implications. "We have the negro here with us, we cannot kill him, we cannot deport him, we have got to make him a citizen. How are you going to do it so long as you deny him the right to vote? The right of manhood's expression is the greatest incentive he can have to make himself a man."

In two minutes he had scotched the 1901 state constitution and undermined the foundation of the Alabama Democratic Party, whose symbol was a gamecock under the slogan "White Supremacy for the Right." While the Bar Association was still reeling, Huddleston took it even further. "The right of suffrage should be extended regardless of race and sex," he declared. Then he went back to his seat. Governor Emmet O'Neal, a proud veteran of 1901, jumped up and denounced "the startling, revolutionary and indefensible doctrines" of the young gentleman from Jefferson County.

I read my grandfather's speech sitting at a conference table in the businesslike offices of the Alabama Bar Association, just down Dexter Avenue from the state capitol, where Jefferson Davis took the oath of office as President of the Confederacy in 1861, where the constitutional convention met to restore white supremacy in 1901, and across Dexter Avenue from the church where Martin Luther King launched the Montgomery bus boycott and the civil rights movement in 1955. Closing the Bar Association's annual report, I momentarily fell under the delusion that in 1912 my grandfather could have stretched across the divide between 1861 and 1955. Geometrically, the state capitol and the Dexter Avenue Baptist Church formed a triangle with the Bar Association building. The building housed a book, the book contained a speech, the speech closed the triangle. The sins of the slave South, which lay on the heads of Huddlestons, the new caste system called Jim Crow, the horrors of convict lease, the disfranchisement of poor black and white alike, all of it cleansed with the universal waters of democracy in the words of an obscure alderman from Birmingham.

Who was about to launch a career in southern politics. The next year my grandfather threw his hat in the ring to replace Birmingham's revered congressman Oscar W. Underwood, who was running for the Senate. Inevitably, an opponent dug up the Bar Association speech and accused Huddleston of favoring black equality. "If you qualify women to vote, then there will be hundreds of negro women voting in

Birmingham," Jere King said, throwing the volatile mix of race and sex into his attack. "I do not believe that our white women want to face negro women at the polls . . . We have 1,000,000 negroes in Alabama, and this new doctrine with race questions involved is repellent to the people of the south." "Mr. Huddleston wants the negro to be a political factor," another candidate added in even rawer terms—"wants kinky-headed Sambo and thick-lipped Dinah to vote and each to count as much as your vote, or yours, or yours."

My grandfather did what politicians have always done: backtracked, claimed he was quoted out of context, changed the subject. "I deplore the persistent efforts of two of my opponents to inject race prejudice into this campaign," he huffed. "It has no proper place here. I am as much opposed to putting the negro back into politics as any other southern man could be . . . The speech was taken down in part by a stenographer who reported it inaccurately," he claimed, sounding uncharacteristically defensive and lame. As for woman suffrage, he said that it was a matter of states' rights and he would oppose any meddling by Congress.

George Huddleston's career as a stubbornly independent and often radical congressman was about to begin. But on the race question it had already ended. The line was drawn there, and after 1912 this man who would go on to court unpopularity in so many other matters never again made the mistake of defying the regional orthodoxy and sticking his neck across that line for black people.

In 1917, when America entered the European war and Huddleston proclaimed the loyalty of his district's 100,000 blacks, a congressman from Indiana asked why these black Alabama patriots were denied the right to vote. "Oh, the gentleman juggles with political questions," Huddleston answered. "It would not be well to give the vote indiscriminately to the negroes. That would not be well. I have not the time to explain why this is true." He promised vaguely that "the door of hope must be held open . . . some time in the future—when they shall have been fully fitted and qualified to receive all the rights of citizenship."

In 1922, when an antilynching bill came up before the House, he voted against it.

In 1929 he told the Jefferson's Birthday Dinner of the Women's Democratic Club in Birmingham: "In striving for white supremacy we battle against social equality between the races and for the purity of the blood which flows in our veins. The real issue is whether the people of the South shall be degraded mongrels of mixed and polluted blood."

In 1931, when nine black youths were arrested on charges of raping two white women on a freight train in northeastern Alabama, a young woman from the ACLU named Hollace Ransdall came to his Birmingham office two weeks later and asked him, as a "liberal friend of labor," to represent the Scottsboro boys at trial. "He rared up out of his chair and nearly hit the ceiling," she reported back to Washington. " 'I don't care whether they are innocent or guilty. They were found riding on the same freight car with two white women, and that's enough for me . . . You can't understand how we Southern gentlemen feel about this question of relationships between negro men and white women.' "

It is difficult for his surviving children—my mother and my aunts—to accept these things. The words don't sound like the man who raised them. All three daughters simply refused to believe the Scottsboro outburst, and when I sent a copy of the ACLU confidential report to my aunt Jane she wrote back on a postcard: "A woman convinced against her will / Is of the same opinion still." Their father had always treated black people with respect. "It might not sound like much," my mother said, "but he always shook hands with them, which wasn't done in those days." When Alabama politics fell under the influence of the resurgent Klan in the 1920s, George Huddleston was almost alone in defying it; his life was threatened on campaign stops out in the hills, and miners who often were themselves Klansmen but devoted to him volunteered as bodyguards.

And when the Supreme Court finally overturned Jim Crow in *Brown* v. *Board of Education*, my grandfather, aged eighty-four and long since out of politics, seemed to go back to the speech he had made half a lifetime before. "Well," he told my mother, "the South's been getting away with it for a long time, and it's about time we got caught."

But for the most part he simply avoided the subject of race—which

Birmingham's silenced blacks made easy. I might wish that the speech in Montgomery had marked the first of many courageous stands, instead of just a footnote. But as my grandfather himself once told my mother when, at twelve, she was trying to figure out her own relation to the South, race, and the Lost Cause: "Nanny, you mustn't judge one time in history by the conscience of another. Lee did what he thought was honorable and right for him at that time. I hope you do as well. It isn't all that simple and easy."

By the accident of birth, George Huddleston's too long life fell in the years between Civil War and civil rights, which meant that he was practically, if not morally, exempt from the vexations of race, as his children would not be. And this freed him to fight the battles of class.

When he won the Democratic primary for Congress in 1914 (which in single-party Alabama was tantamount to winning the election, the November ballot being known as "the complimentary poll"), George Huddleston was forty-four years old. He was fully formed as a man and a politician. A newspaper figured him at 130 pounds, about five foot five, "including a rather thin crop of auburn hair," and said he was one of the smallest men in Congress. His campaign photograph shows a young-looking man with a broad forehead and thin lips gazing into the distance, earnest and quietly confident. "His face wore a student's air," a reporter wrote, "and his attire was as simple and plain as his manner." He was one of those people who didn't care what others thought of him and made sure they knew it. He drew notice on Capitol Hill for walking to his office on rainy days with newspapers wrapped around the bottoms of his trousers. He wore one-dollar shirts, he said, because he couldn't get them for fifty cents. He dressed and lived as if any display of style was immoral, and his personal austerity expressed his politics as well.

In my mother's words: "My father made an odd politician. He was small and shy and introverted. There was nothing hail fellow about him. He seldom complimented and never flattered. He was too proud to lie or trim." Huddleston did not suffer fools and could seem severe. In public he was verbally aggressive and often wittily caustic. Unsystematic but intense reading, together with a love of argument, a sense of drama, and a deep bass voice, gave him a rhetorical skill that compensated for his small size. He would use this skill to effect in Washington.

He was still a bachelor and in no hurry to change his status. "A true bachelor," he told a reporter, drawing a self-portrait, "is a man who is sensible of his defects and deficiencies and refuses to mar another's life, possibly, by asking anyone to put up with him. To be true to type, he must lack the desire to lose his personality, to alter his cranky ways and to adjust his peculiarities to a new system." Yet he also believed, unusual for his time, that "the day is coming when woman will be just as free as man to decide this and live up to it. Her political enfranchisement will help much, and her economic independence will be a large factor in shaping the new conditions." Though fanatical about independence in personal and political life, he felt an abiding obligation to his stepmother and assorted Tennessee kin, to whom he sent money and whom he often lodged in his miser's quarters on the slightest acquaintance. He later said that he entered politics because he owed it to his family's honor.

He built his career on universal ideals, but his pride was stubbornly parochial. He called slavery a terrible evil, but he revered Lee. He swore his allegiance to the public good, but individualism remained his watchword. He had an old-fashioned liberal's faith in self-rule, in the ability of the poorest men to reason out their own destiny, but he also harbored a conservative's skepticism about human nature, a secular idea of original sin. He supported the most progressive programs of the day, but his utopia was in the past. It was the modest utopia of the eighteenth-century revolutionaries, the small-scale utopia of virtuous citizens and self-made men, of no one owning anyone else, of equal rights and roughly equal conditions. It was the democrat's utopia that regarded wealth and power as threats to liberty and the brotherhood of man.

By 1914 this utopia had already ceased to exist, and nowhere more completely than in Birmingham. But because he genuinely believed in it, because it still hovered within the reach of historical memory, and because he had grown up poor, my grandfather was able to speak of these things with a passionate conviction not often heard in America today—least of all in the city where he would spend the next twenty-two years. His speeches of that 1914 campaign echoed Jefferson and Lincoln. "I am independent and owe no man anything," my grandfather said, "but I have never ceased to be a friend to the poor. I have a due regard for the rights of property, but I have never come to regard it is of as much importance as the rights of man. In any case in which a choice must be made between men and dollars, my choice will be on the side of humanity."

He won by campaigning in the industrial quarters and mining villages and farms, among the kind of people who had bought his wares when he was a youthful peddler with a horse-drawn wagon. He could say, "I belong to the plain people. They are my friends, my kinfolks, and my associates. I am proud to call thousands of men who toil with their hands my personal friends. I eat at their tables and sleep in their beds. I love them."

◆

CHAPTER 3

The Little Bolsheviki

When I was ten, I stood on a beach in Normandy and listened as my father told me about the greatness of Woodrow Wilson. "Fourteen Points" and "League of Nations" were meaningless phrases to me, but I understood that Wilson had once dreamed of an international body that would secure peace and freedom for all countries. If not for the opposition of small-minded men, my father said, Wilson's dream might have prevented the beach where we stood from becoming a scene of the next terrible war, in which my father had fought as a young man. We looked out at the English Channel and my father clutched his cane in his left hand and shed tears. It seemed to me as if the League of Nations might have freed him too, his longing and grief were so intense. From that moment, I associated the failure of Wilson's dream with the unhappy man standing next to me. Wilson and my father seemed bound together in defeat.

What my father didn't tell me was that, in the middle of the fight over the League of Nations, Wilson suffered a massive stroke and lived out his last years paralyzed on the left side.

He also didn't mention that Wilson had tried to bring about the political defeat of a fellow Democrat who happened to be my grandfather. I would later learn that the President who loved humanity had little but contempt for most human beings, George Huddleston among them. "Perhaps it is better to love men in the abstract," Wilson once said, "than to love them individually."

The difference between my grandfather's and my father's attitude toward Wilson is one marker of the difference between the two men, and of the change in the liberal temperament during the first half of the century. For years I held on to my father's idealized view, until the story of the clash between Wilson and my grandfather made me take a closer look. Then Wilson became impossible to love or even like—and yet his life has the quality of a tragedy, and his fate was so like my father's that I can't help thinking of Wilson with grief.

He was a Presbyterian preacher's horse-faced son, with a prim mouth and piercing steely eyes. Born in Virginia, raised in Georgia, he grew up during the Civil War yet remembered little of it, had no southern loyalties—almost none of any kind except to his father, his father's God, and the divine mission to bring light on earth. Wilson was plagued all his life by digestive troubles, headaches, and other classic symptoms from the fin de siècle Age of Neurosis. Freud, who seems to have hated Wilson for his part in forcing the Versailles Treaty on Europe, co-authored a book-length psychological study with the diplomat William C. Bullitt, who had broken with Wilson over Versailles. Freud provided the conceptual weaponry, Bullitt the ammunition, and together they reduced much of early twentieth-century American history to the twenty-eighth President's unconscious hatred of his father. "His early relationship to his father doomed him to expect of himself all his life more than his body or mind could give," they wrote. "A considerable portion of the human race had to suffer for the overwhelming love which the Reverend Joseph Ruggles Wilson had inspired in his son."

The conventional idea of Wilson as a sort of marbleized schoolmaster doesn't do him justice. He was a passionate prig. The frieze of his face betrayed an effort to command visceral turmoil. His early letters to his first wife show him desperate for love, doubting his abilities, physically and mentally at the edge of breakdown. "I am too sensitive," he warned her, "too intense, too anxious, too selfish, too open to any influence that stirs anywhere near me, to escape having a great deal of suffering at every turn of my life." As President in 1914, he analyzed himself before the members of the National Press Club in more self-revealing terms than any politician would dare in our supposedly confessional age: "My constant embarrassment is to restrain the emotions that are inside of me. You may not believe it, but I sometimes feel like a fire from a far from extinct volcano, and if the lava does not seem to spill over it is because you are not high enough to see into the basin and see the cauldron boil."

All this turbulence and self-control made Wilson unappealing in flesh and blood. He struck almost everyone who met him as aloof and cold. He made few friends and kept none. Initially taking them fiercely to his heart, which was a dangerous place for a man, Wilson invariably ended up casting them out for minor acts of disloyalty. (His relations with women were warm and stable.) He claimed to prefer "government by discussion" to "government by control," but Wilson never discussed anything with anyone, and he often took disagreement or even gentle advice as betrayal. Many of the contradictions and reversals in his remarkable career came from a tension between the conservatism of an overprotected, small-town Southerner (he segregated the federal government, feared immigration, opposed woman suffrage) and the moral fervor of a high Presbyterian, which would carry him to the verge of visionary greatness and then destroy him. In the end, belief in God and his own righteousness was all that held Wilson's being together.

His scholarly writing, focused on American and English systems of government, did not suggest a natural candidate to lead Progressive America into the modern world. By 1909 Wilson was, if anything, the unlikely hope of conservative Democrats trying to free their party from the death grip of the thrice-defeated William Jennings Bryan. Yet he was a powerful orator, had a brilliant mind for ideas, and felt that "this is what I was meant for, anyhow, this rough and tumble of the political arena." In three meteoric years he went from being president of

Princeton to governor of New Jersey, where he defied the party bosses who had gotten him there and enacted sweeping political and economic reforms; and then, in 1912, he became the Democratic Party's presidential nominee in one of the most significant elections in American history. As far as Wilson was concerned, it was all part of a Calvinist God's predestined will. Since he was a little boy he had known that he would be a great statesman like his hero Gladstone.

The year 1912 was the tipping point in American political history, when the first great phase of our politics was coming to an end and the second was beginning. The shift was seismic, and it would take several decades to play out. By the 1930s many people who had stood on one side were now standing, or appeared to stand, on the other, George Huddleston among them. The two parties exchanged each other's rhetoric and some of the underlying convictions. The meaning of liberalism itself was thrown up for grabs. It came back down in roughly the same shape that we know today, set on the course of its triumph and defeat.

The literature of the Progressive era is full of anxiety about the rise of organization—"the curse of bigness," Justice Louis D. Brandeis called it in the title of his collected writings. In the 1890s William Dean Howells had written, "The struggle for life has changed from a free fight to an encounter of disciplined forces, and the free fighters that are left get ground to pieces." By 1908 Robert La Follette of Wisconsin announced on the floor of the Senate that the interlocking directorates of the major corporations left the country's business interests in the hands of a cabal of one hundred men. The Morgan interests alone, having just swallowed the Birmingham steel industry whole, held 341 directorships in 112 corporations, capitalized at over $22 billion—more than double the value of all the property in the South.

These facts reflected more than just social problems calling for legislation. The rise of bigness brought a crisis of identity to a people who had inherited a century's belief in the moral value of individualism. My grandfather the self-employed lawyer gave it voice in the 1914 campaign when, mixing the language of Jefferson and Progressivism, he said, "I am absolutely free and independent. I wear the cap of no corporation nor other selfish interest. I am lined up with no clique. I will not be any man's tool or dupe."

The corporation was distasteful and suspect (as was the labor union to middle-class professionals and businessmen), but it was a fact: an efficient, sometimes brutal, perhaps inevitable form of economic progress. Meanwhile, the small-town doctor and the shop owner felt increasingly like losers in the new arrangement; the steelworker and the railroad man were interchangeable industrial parts. The psychological difference between success and failure began to seem vast and permanent.

In 1914 twenty-five-year-old Walter Lippmann, in transit from socialism to liberalism and about to help launch *The New Republic*, paused to take stock: "We are unsettled to the very roots of our being. There isn't a human relation, whether of parent and child, husband and wife, worker and employer, that doesn't move in a strange situation. We are not used to a complicated civilization, we don't know how to behave when personal contact and eternal authority have disappeared . . . The modern man is not yet settled in his world. It is strange to him, terrifying, alluring, and incomprehensibly big."

Bigness gave the election of 1912 its overarching theme. That year—which saw the first presidential primaries, a Progressive reform— ex-President Theodore Roosevelt the Bull Moose and Woodrow Wilson the Democrat both ran as Progressives against the conservative Republican incumbent William Howard Taft and the Socialist Eugene V. Debs. Yet Roosevelt seemed no more like a modern liberal than Wilson. He was a New York aristocrat who feared the violence of working-class mobs as much as he loathed the moral shabbiness of big business. A childhood weakling, he was in love with physical action, with the cult of power, which sometimes brought him close to the spirit of fascism that was soon to appear in Europe.

For two terms as President in the early 1900s, Roosevelt had spoken loudly against the trusts while carrying a fairly small stick. But once out of the White House, he laid down how far he was prepared to go in battling corporate power. In Osawatomie, Kansas, in 1910, before a crowd of Union Army veterans, he echoed his hero Lincoln. "Whenever the alternative must be faced, I am for men and not for property." Roosevelt was promising to take "the man before the dollar" much farther than Lincoln ever had. He wasn't talking about equal rights and opportunity; nor was he proposing to break up the trusts and return to individualism. Combination was inevitable and often good, he thought, but a strong national government had to control the trusts "completely"—not so much for the sake of justice, but for national greatness. "Every man holds his property subject to the general right of the community to regulate its use to whatever degree the public welfare may require it."

This from a man who hated socialism. The era of big government had begun, and Roosevelt understood perfectly well the consequences. "This, I know, implies a policy of a far more active governmental interference with social and economic conditions in this country than we have yet had, but I think we have got to face that such an increase in governmental control is now necessary."

Roosevelt's theoretical champion was Herbert Croly, soon to found *The New Republic*. Croly was born in 1869, the same year as my grandfather, but this son of two New York City journalists had no connection to the agrarian individualism of the nineteenth century, no Jeffersonian inheritance. He was well placed to smash it to pieces and hammer out a new framework for liberalism's modern shape. More influentially than any other political writer of the twentieth century, Croly laid down a philosophy of large-scale government intervention in American life. After years of leisurely study and writing for the *Architectural Record*, he emerged fully armed in 1909 with a dense and massive argument against most of American history called *The Promise of American Life*. Its heroes are Hamilton, Lincoln, and Roosevelt himself (who loved the book). Its singular villain is Jefferson. Croly convicted Jefferson of every political crime that the Progressive generation inherited: plutocracy, national drift, sectionalism, mediocrity, confusion.

"Jefferson sought an essentially equalitarian and even socialistic result by means of an essentially individualistic machinery," Croly wrote. "His theory implied a complete harmony both in logic and in effect between the idea of liberty and the idea of equality." In other words, set people free, let them run their own affairs, and power and wealth will be spread among them roughly equally. By 1909 things had manifestly not worked out that way. Liberty and equality appeared to be pulling in opposite directions. To Croly, J. P. Morgan was the inevitable descendant of Jefferson, the incarnation of American individualism. Bigness was inescapable. You couldn't repeal corporations with legislation like the Sherman Antitrust Act, any more than you could repeal the wind. Jeffersonian reformers like the Populists who talked about restoring "free competition" were trying to keep their philosophy and change the historical facts. Croly characterized William Jennings Bryan in shrewd terms: "a curious mixture" of traditional democracy and modern radicalism, "he can, perhaps, be best understood as a Democrat of both Jeffersonian and Jacksonian tendencies, who has been born a few generations too late." The same words could be used to describe my grandfather.

Croly replaced Jeffersonian liberalism with a far-reaching vision of the modern nation under a powerful central government. The heroes of his democratic nationalism were not the "plain people" of the nineteenth century or the proletarian masses of the early twentieth, but a rising class of technicians, experts, intellectuals. Human nature, Croly believed, can be limitlessly improved by political institutions—but citizenship in a democracy demands an extremely high standard of public virtue. It demands "disinterested human action" and solidarity between strangers. Croly quoted the French historian Emile Faguet: "Liberty and equality are therefore contradictory and mutually exclusive; but brotherhood reconciles them." Brotherhood, mending what individualism had torn asunder, was the key to Croly's vision—yet he was too modern to speak in the old moral terms and replaced the eighteenth century's "sympathy" with the unsentimental "national purpose."

But brotherhood—even "national purpose"—is not a demand that

Americans often respond to, especially when it comes from the federal government. Individualism turns out to be a value we won't surrender quite so easily; lately the ghosts of Jefferson and Jackson have come back to haunt their party. A new crop of journalists has recently turned to Croly for inspiration in reviving liberalism, but Croly more than any other writer set liberalism on the course of its ultimate debacles. We aren't selfless enough for him.

Roosevelt and Croly would go on to win the argument over the future of liberalism in the twentieth century; but they lost the election of 1912. The winner, Woodrow Wilson, had to confront a historical dilemma: how could he remain a good Democrat—that is, a Jeffersonian—in the modern era? On September 25, 1912, campaigning in New Haven, he addressed the dilemma directly. In the twentieth century, he said, life had become tremendously complex, and the size of corporations threatened individual freedom in a new way. He reminded his audience that Jefferson had warned against excessive government interference in the activities of citizens, a warning that had been gospel to the Democratic Party ever since. By raising the spirit of Jefferson, Wilson was admitting what is true for every new generation: that current conditions posed a conflict with inherited values—in this case, that the rise of trusts presented a hard knot for Democrats. Then he proceeded rhetorically to untie it:

> But I feel confident that if Jefferson were living in our day he would see what we see: that the individual is caught in a great confused nexus of all sorts of complicated circumstances, and that to let him alone is to leave him helpless against the obstacles with which he has to contend; and that, therefore, law in our day must come to the assistance of the individual. It must come to his assistance to see that he gets fair play; that is all, but that is much . . . Freedom today is something more than being let alone.

Thus a Progressive could remain a Jeffersonian. Government would intervene, not to check the individual but to free him, thereby "unfettering his energies, and warming the generous impulses of his heart." Wilson saw monopoly as he saw everything, in moral terms, with blame falling on individuals rather than on an economic system. In the name of moral regeneration, the "New Freedom" would restore the old fair play. Instead of "regulating monopoly," as Roosevelt proposed, under Wilson government would "regulate competition." On this slender distinction the momentous election of 1912 hung. In practice it turned out to be illusory.

Wilson was the last Jeffersonian elected President. Two years later, in 1914, the inaugural issue of *The New Republic* appeared, with Croly as its guiding hand and the two German-Jewish Walters, Weyl and Lippmann, completing the editorial triumvirate. One article drew a caustic analogy between the third and twenty-eighth Presidents: "Agrarian democracy was the goal of Jefferson's analysis, just as the equally unreal and unattainable democracy of small business is Wilson's goal." But Wilson ceased to be a Jeffersonian almost as soon as he entered the White House. His first term enacted the Federal Reserve System, the Federal Trade Commission, work regulation for railroad employees and seamen, farm credits, child-labor law. Wilson called them New Freedom reforms, but their effect was to regulate monopoly and not competition. In his second, wartime term, the War Industries Board attempted central economic planning for the first time in our history and provided the model for the early New Deal. By 1917 *The New Republic* had changed its tune about Wilson: his policies were building "far more nearly the morale of a cooperative commonwealth than of a nation in arms." Meanwhile big business kept getting bigger, fattened on war contracts, barely irritated by legislation like the Clayton Antitrust Act. Wilson's reforms ended up rationalizing industrial combinations rather than breaking them up. Within four years the New Freedom had become the New Nationalism.

When George Huddleston arrived in Washington in 1915 and moved into his rooms on the top floor of the House office building, Europe was slaughtering its youth for a second year. President Wilson was in the White House for his third. The modern world was busy being born. The telephone, the automobile, the airplane, the corporation, and the slum were established facts of life. Around 1915, according to Alfred Kinsey, premarital sex and the female orgasm first began to appear in America. Social forces set in motion during the last frenetic years of the nineteenth century were taking clear shape by the second decade of the twentieth. The frontier tradesman became the robber baron and the robber baron became U.S. Steel; the urban mechanic became the Knight of Labor and the Knight of Labor became the A.F. of L. The age of the individual was over; the organization age had begun.

Huddleston won a seat on the House Foreign Affairs Committee. The first bill he got passed was for the pension of a "poor, paralyzed, blind veteran who was a cook in our company kitchen in the Spanish War." He was lucky to start his career under the first Democratic President in a generation, whom he admired. But when my grandfather began to be heard as a junior member of the Alabama congressional delegation, he sounded like an apostle of neither the New Freedom nor the New Nationalism, though his ideas sometimes resembled aspects of one or the other. Instead he was far more radical than either. "I am no Socialist," he had insisted in his first campaign. "I do not believe in a single principle of Socialism. I never made a Socialist speech in my life. I am a real Democrat." But when, a week after his reelection to Congress in 1916, he traveled from Birmingham to Chattanooga and addressed a theater overflowing with members of the Central Labor Union, the distinction between his language and the Socialist leader Eugene Debs's was subtle at best.

"I have come to the state of my birth to talk to you as a friend," he told the assembly of men in overalls and caps, who kept interrupting with cheers and applause, "for I believe with all my heart that the cause of organized labor is the cause of humanity. I believe that the future of the country depends upon the solidarity of the working classes."

Neither Theodore Roosevelt nor Wilson liked unions any more than trusts; in their equations of bigness, labor organizations were on the same side of the ledger as corporations. Both Presidents considered sweatshops, strikes, tenements, and dark-skinned Europeans as social threats. Both regarded the cause of humanity as the cause of the middle class—the only disinterested Americans, the true citizens. But my grandfather never even used the term "middle class"; instead, he divided Americans into "the few" and "the common people." He told the workers in Chattanooga that the economic individualism of the nineteenth century was past, that employees could no longer go it alone. He urged class-consciousness on them.

"We are confronted with conditions never before experienced and which are getting worse daily. The wealth of the nation is in the hands of the few and everything is monopolized, resulting in trusts which levy heavy tolls on the masses in the shape of unreasonable and unjust profits. I do not know what the future will bring—I hope for the best—but the greatest safeguard for the toiler is organization.

"I am well versed in the race question which has hung like a dark pall over the South," he went on, gingerly returning to the subject that had bedeviled his first campaign in 1914, "and being a Southerner I know how it feels to have a negro placed alongside of you at your work, but I want to say to you that economical conditions make it more important that you give more consideration to the condition of your black co-laborer than you do your employer."

Class was more basic than race. From this apostasy he moved on to another. "We often boast of this land of the free, where they say there are no classes. I wish that this was true. But the workers had nothing to do with bringing about a condition where the people are broken up into classes. We are not one people and it is useless for us to delude ourselves on this question any longer. When you touch one capitalist you touch them all. Why, in the last Congress there was a little amendment up for consideration which prevented the use of stopwatches in government plants, and you would be surprised at the number of employers who appealed to the Congress to kill this legislation.

"The future of the country—peace, prosperity and liberty, depend on organization of labor. You might sweep away the employing class and the great heart of the country would not be touched"—in closing he seemed to paraphrase his favorite lines, from Goldsmith's "The Deserted Village"—"but destroy the laboring class and you would wreck the nation."

His language was, in a word we can't use anymore, heartwarming. It was confident and simplistic and uplifting, like the rhetoric of the homegrown radicals of the 1910s, like the oratory of Debs, who was known as "lover of mankind," not in the way of Wilson, who abstracted individuals from his chilly heights, but in a way that made each man who listened feel the worth of his own humanity. This language put men on one side and stopwatches on the other. Even when using stock phrases, it had the potency to stir deep individual feelings and rouse mass actions on the part of poor people who had never imagined themselves capable of anything except meager survival. Today we smile when we read it. Too many people in the twentieth century abused the words to death, and we know better now, and the one thing we want not to be is naive. The cause of organized labor has not turned out to be the cause of humanity. But without this language and the feeling it voices, we've cut ourselves off from the main source of reform. Irony never got anyone to go to a meeting.

The Chattanooga speech and others like it put Huddleston in the radical wing of the Progressive movement, now in its last phase. He became a staunch defender of organized labor during its weakest years (in 1915 the total number of United Mine Workers in Alabama fell to twenty-eight). At times his only ally in Congress was the New York Socialist Meyer London. Socialist newspapers claimed him as a friend, and the red flag became a weapon in the hands of his increasingly numerous enemies. And yet his self-description was apt. His idea of class conflict was neither scientific nor socialist. He never stopped thinking of the "masses" as Jefferson's "chosen people of God," Lincoln's "plain people." He saw the struggle between capitalists and workers as a struggle for democracy, not power, continuous with the fight between Tories and revolutionaries, between Federalists and Republicans, between the two schools of political thought that prevailed everywhere at all times:

> On the one side are the antidemocrats, those who hold that men have no natural right to order their own lives and that the wealthy, the cultured, and those of birth are best qualified to rule and hence should hold the political power. A tenet of the faith of these is that property and property rights are sacrosanct as the instrumentality through which their positions of influence may be assured. On the other hand are the humanitarians, those who value men per capita, those who feel that the right to life, liberty, and the pursuit of happiness is equally the natural and moral right of all men, whether great or small. These hold that God never made any man wise enough or good enough to be the ruler of another man.

In this simple worldview, economic tyranny and political tyranny always went together. Alexander Hamilton was the ancestor of Andrew Mellon, Thomas Jefferson of Eugene Debs. The difference between a Democrat and a Socialist mattered far less than the difference between a humanitarian and an antidemocrat. The people who passed laws against free speech were the same ones who wanted to increase profits. Unlike Herbert Croly, he still believed that freedom and equality were always on the same side. In 1916 he hadn't yet seen the tyranny that went under the name of "the solidarity of the working classes," nor the concentration of political power that justified itself by the values of humanitarianism. What he saw, and what he felt in his rural southern bones to be unjust, was a society whose lines of caste and privilege were still hardening after a decade of Progressive reform. "A nation may be a powerful imperialism," he once said, "but it cannot be truly great, it cannot be a truly democratic nation, if typical of its life is the gilt and splendor of Fifth Avenue and the squalor and hunger of the slums."

As America began its slide into the European war, this democratic radicalism deepened and ultimately set the junior member of the House Foreign Affairs Committee on a collision course with the leader of his party and country.

When I was a boy World War I held absolutely no interest for me. What was the use of a war in which the front lines never moved, every offensive was stopped after three miles, and there was no clear side to hate? World War II, sweeping across Europe and the Pacific in great mechanized battles, was thrilling; trench warfare was incomprehensibly dull. Only an adult could find the stagnant Western Front more compelling than Stalingrad or Midway—for the trenches were the scene of a moving and terrible change. The Great War destroyed a generation of young men not only through death and mutilation but in the explosion of their mental world. In the mud of a broken landscape the individual ceased to matter. Honor and patriotism were mocked by the endless slaughter. Under bombardment and poison gas, the worldview of the Great War's soldiers left them as helpless as their weapons did. This crisis produced a much greater literature among combatants than World War II, poignant in the attempt to convey an unprecedented and shattering experience within the conventions of nineteenth-century verse. Ezra Pound, who escaped the fighting, afterward declared in the muscular language of modernism:

> *There died a myriad,*
> *And of the best, among them,*
>
> *For an old bitch gone in the teeth,*
> *For a botched civilization.*

But for the war's pathos you have to turn to the Georgian rhymes of Wilfred Owen, who was killed in its last week:

If in some smothering dreams you too could pace
Behind the wagon that we flung him in,
And watch the white eyes writhing in his face,
His hanging face like a devil's sick of sin . . .
My friend, you would not tell with such high zest
To children ardent for some desperate glory,
The old Lie: Dulce et decorum est
Pro patria mori.

Woodrow Wilson led America into the European slaughterhouse with the highest possible motives. They were not the motives of the young Europeans who went off to die *pro patria*. Patriotism hardly entered his justifications. In the early years of the war, America was "too proud to fight." After German U-boats sank the *Lusitania* and over one hundred Americans perished with it, Wilson's note to the German Foreign Minister demanding reparation payments put the man before the dollar: "The United States is contending for something much greater than mere rights of property or privileges of commerce. It is contending for nothing less high and sacred than the rights of humanity." Three months before declaring war, he called for "peace without victory" among the belligerents, founded on a "universal covenant" of self-determination and equality among the "community of nations," saying that he was "speaking for liberals and friends of humanity in every nation." John Dos Passos later wrote that this speech made Wilson the hero "of collegebred idealists throughout the Englishspeaking world," including for a short time Dos Passos himself. When Germany resumed unrestricted submarine warfare in February 1917, Wilson called the arming of American merchant ships one of "those rights of humanity without which there is no civilization." With each speech he raised the cause higher, carrying America toward war on the sheer sweep of his words.

On the evening of April 2, Wilson was driven up Pennsylvania Avenue to address a joint session of Congress. The galleries were packed, and the assembled congressmen waved little American flags.

My grandfather sat amid the cheers from the benches and heard a war message that had all the high-minded magnanimity of Lincoln's Second Inaugural. "The world must be made safe for democracy," Wilson declared. "Its peace must be planted upon the tested foundations of political liberty. We have no selfish ends to serve. We desire no conquest, no dominion. We seek no indemnities for ourselves, no material compensation for the sacrifices we shall freely make. We are but one of the champions of the rights of mankind. We shall be satisfied when those rights have been made as secure as the faith and the freedom of nations can make them."

Wilson's rhetoric—the "glittering generalities" an opponent once derided—made it a war for the man and not the dollar, except that the man was now completely abstracted into "humanity" and "mankind." The Great War would universalize the New Freedom. In the name of extending Jeffersonian principles around the world, Jefferson's warning against foreign entanglements would be ignored. America would become a world power in order to end the bloody game of power. Force would create freedom. The moral restlessness of Progressivism would have its ultimate fulfillment in the trenches of France.

"If this war had not come, we should all have been rotten!" the Progressive journalist and future Wilson biographer Ray Stannard Baker wrote in his diary. "At moments I fear this war be over too soon—before the people are scourged into an awakening."

But Wilson himself had not wanted war. He foresaw with amazing clarity the social psychosis that war would release and that his speeches suppressed. On the night before his war message, he had told an old friend visiting the White House: "It would mean that we would lose our heads along with the rest and stop weighing right and wrong. It would mean that a majority of people in this hemisphere would go war mad, quit thinking, and devote their energies to destruction . . . Conformity will be the only virtue. And every man who refuses to conform will have to pay the penalty . . . Once lead this people into war and they'll forget there ever was such a thing as tolerance . . . If there is any alternative for God's sake let's take it." And after returning to the White

House from his triumphant appearance before the joint session of Congress, he told the cabinet, "My message today was a message of death for our young men. How strange it seems to applaud that."

But the lonely misgivings only fed Wilson's self-righteousness. His goals were so lofty that failure would make the destruction an unforgivable waste. Wilson became the type of liberal that later generations of Americans so admired and despised. He was an idealist with no dirt under his nails. His mankind didn't have an individual human face. His moral passion seemed cold-blooded, impersonal. He urged Americans "not to think about me personally at all, but merely to think of me as the expression for the time being of the power and dignity and hope of the United States." But when the war failed to bring the peace Wilson had called its true and only purpose, the reaction against him would be all the more vehemently personal.

Modern liberalism did not originate in the New Deal. The concentration of state power, the use of government for humanitarian ends, the rise of the expert, all began with Wilson's high-minded decision to take America into World War I (a war much of the country and the Congress didn't want). The word "liberal" first came into wide political usage in America during this period, when the editors of *The New Republic* began to substitute it for "Progressive," which was now tarnished by their former hero Roosevelt's political defeats and increasingly crankish jingoism. They were importing the word from England, where it referred both to the nineteenth-century European idea of enlarging individual freedom against the power of the state and to the Liberal Party's activist program of using government to address modern social ills. In nineteenth-century America few people spoke of being politically "liberal" because almost all Americans were liberal in their belief in self-government and freedom. It was during the second decade of the twentieth century that the word came to mean a specific attitude toward government's role in industrial society.

The declaration of war galvanized *The New Republic*'s New Liberals to claim Wilson as their own, his war as their war. "Mr. Wilson is today the most liberal statesman in high office," the magazine editorialized, "and before long he is likely to be the most powerful. He represents the best hope in the whole world." The war would join "the forward liberal movement in American national life." It would be a collectivist war, involving industry, labor, economic central planning, nationalization of railroads, the first large-scale conscription in American history, the most draconian suppression of dissenting speech since the Alien and Sedition Acts of 1798, and a nationwide propaganda campaign waged by the new Bureau of Public Information. The population of Washington, D.C., would grow by 40,000 in one year. It would be America's first truly national war.

A new term was about to come into use: "Americanism." In its name, pacifists, socialists, labor radicals, German aliens, and other questionables would be hunted down, threatened, jailed, tarred, publicly humiliated, and driven out of towns across the land. Wilson would protest rather feebly against "the mob spirit," but he would also enforce the only test of Americanism: unqualified support for his war effort. Those who opposed making the world safe for democracy would be morally and perhaps legally arraigned on charges of disloyalty.

One of the most brilliant was *The New Republic*'s hunchbacked young education writer, Randolph Bourne. Unlike his more famous colleagues at the magazine, Bourne grasped that war wouldn't consummate the years of Progressive reform but would end them. "Willing war means willing all the evils that are organically bound up with it," he wrote (but not in *The New Republic*, which banned his criticism). "A good many people still seem to believe in a peculiar kind of democratic and antiseptic war. The pacifists opposed the war because they knew this was an illusion, and because of the myriad hurts they knew war would do the promise of democracy at home. For once the babes and sucklings seem to have been wiser than the children of light." Liberals like his old Columbia professor and idol John Dewey, he said, were too rational to understand war. They didn't want to know that they were killers.

Isolated and ill, harassed by the police, hobbling through Greenwich Village in his black cape, Bourne nursed his scorn into an attack on the American state itself. "War is the health of the state," he wrote, and his fury drove him back to the origins of the republic, which now, in the grim light glowing from Europe, seemed "no bright and rational creation of a new day . . . but the last scion of an ancient and hoary stock." Other than a few years of self-government under the Articles of Confederation, American democracy had always served the propertied classes. War and disillusion turned Bourne away from optimistic liberalism, toward "a more skeptical, malicious, desperate, ironical mood" that anticipated the moral rebellion of the 1920s. He was abandoning Dewey for Nietzsche. But Bourne didn't have time to shape the mood into a new politics. A month after the Armistice, just as unimaginable happiness was materializing for him in the form of a beautiful ballet dancer named Esther Cornell, Bourne died at thirty-two of influenza, which was a legacy of the war and by the end of 1918 killed twice as many people. Unfinished, "The State" was published posthumously in the bitter year of 1919, when the editors of *The New Republic* began to realize that their misshapen and rejected young comrade had been right.

Wilson's war made a number of its critics more eloquent, George Huddleston among them. He never went as far as Bourne — unlike the Greenwich Village radical, he felt attachments of region, party, and ancestral democracy as rich sustenance rather than fetters on a free mind. But in 1917 and 1918, as the whole nation mobilized for war, his vision of democracy and justice came into focus and my grandfather gave the greatest speeches of his career. When Birmingham's establishment concentrated all its fire on him in the primary summer of 1918, he relished his role as lonely tribune of the people and refused to bend. The ultimate tribute came from President Wilson himself, who personally intervened to try to bring about this obscure second-term congressman's defeat.

My grandfather saw the war as a racket foisted upon the country by eastern bankers, industrialists, publishers, armchair jingoes from the Yale and Harvard clubs—"the natural enemies of democracy." The House of Morgan wanted to recoup its hundreds of millions in loans to Great Britain. U.S. Steel, Birmingham's largest employer, wanted to fatten its profits on government contracts. As for making the world safe for democracy: "War is a hideous nightmare," he said. "It is never justified except in a clean-cut, single-hearted defense of national honor. It is never to be waged to vindicate abstract rights or technical principles."

For Wilson, democracy was a worldwide crusade on the part of politicians and social experts, backed by military force. For Huddleston, it had a human face—the living aspirations of common people, the miners and farmers and factory workers in his district, backed by the Declaration of Independence and the Bill of Rights. Having suffered through the Spanish-American War as an enlisted man, he hated "the military system, with its manifold gradations, with its iron discipline, which has as its ideal the making of a senseless human machine with which the superior may work his absolute will; where the dangers and hardships are borne by the inarticulate men in the ranks and the honors and rewards are enjoyed by the wearers of gold lace and epaulets." He ardently opposed Wilson's conscription bill—the country's first ever—because "by compulsory military service they will teach the masses to obey and to respect their masters. They will break the spirit of the people. They will teach labor its proper place and make order and industry the supreme law and habit of the man who toils." When conscription became law, he called for equal pay and pensions to officers and men. He feared American imperialists more than European ones because "they have no spirit of noblesse oblige. They are merely the newly rich Wall Street gamblers, the taskmasters, and profiteers. Their only restraints are those of selfishness, egoism, and class instinct." Like Bourne and the Socialists, he saw the war as a reaction against the period of reform:

> These selfish interests have viewed with growing dissatisfaction the trend of affairs during the past dozen years. The people have been getting harder to control. There has been too much evi-

dence of democratic spirit, too much idealism and brotherhood. They are displeased by the swing toward amelioration
and the recognition of the rights of common men; they long for
the former era of unrestrained combination, monopoly, and
exploitation; they are determined to seize out of the present
world crisis some means of ending such foolishness once and
for all.

Opposition to the war united the populists and Socialists, rural and
urban radicals, agrarians steeped in American tradition and urban immigrants at ease with European isms—all those who spoke for the voiceless
and disfranchised. After the war these two groups, which needed each
other for legitimacy and coherence, would split apart and never really
come back together, even coming to fear and despise each other.

Huddleston opposed every measure leading up to the declaration of
war. But at the moment of truth in the early hours of April 6, 1917, when
the House took its roll call, my grandfather voted with the "yeas." Fifty
representatives went against the war (there were just two after Pearl Harbor), so he would hardly have been alone in opposition. But he had
decided that the U-boat attacks and the German secret plan to subvert
America through Mexico threatened "national honor"—a conclusion
explained in none of his speeches, so that it seems more like acquiescence before the inevitable rush of events. Was his vote expedient? Did
he flinch from challenging a Democratic President and the feeling that
was beginning to sweep the country, which almost overnight switched
from hesitation to hysteria? Huddleston wasn't a pacifist or dissenter in
the tradition of Thoreau. Duty to individual conscience wasn't absolute
with him; there was also the sometimes conflicting duty to country. Perhaps, paraphrasing his revered Lee, Huddleston would have said,
"There is no sacrifice I am not ready to make for the preservation of
peace save that of honor." Perhaps, as with Lee, the decision was less
simple and glorious than honor.

Huddleston would give the war critical support, careful to distinguish Wilson from the "profiteers and patrioteers," opposing a handful
of key administration policies such as the Espionage and Explosives

Acts, and never ceasing to insist that "no man should be allowed to come out of this war richer than he went into it." If his position now seems equivocal, in the wartime mood of intolerance it struck the patrioteers as a clear case of disloyalty, and they went after him with venom.

By World War I, outlaw Birmingham had begun to present itself as a respectable American city whose leading citizens—business executives, corporate attorneys, Protestant ministers, newspaper publishers—would not be outdone in patriotic display. On April 9, 1918, a group of them met for lunch at the Tutwiler Hotel, built downtown so that U.S. Steel executives visiting their southern satellite would have first-class lodgings—"that splendid hostelry," Huddleston called it, "the center of extravagance and display of the swagger and fashion in my city." For over a year his rhetoric had infuriated these patriots and, as far as they were concerned, disgraced their young city in the nation's eyes. When he began to denounce the tenfold increase in wartime profits enjoyed by U.S. Steel and to call for higher taxes on income and capital to pay for the war, the indignation came to a head. Over lunch at the Tutwiler, an Episcopal minister spoke about the need to conscript factory workers for war production. Suddenly he exclaimed, "Let us conscript a congressman!"

"The great dining room of the Tutwiler instantly rang with the loudest applause," the *Birmingham News* editorialized the next day. "Mr. Huddleston does not represent this district effectively, sympathetically, satisfactorily. He is a narrow, shallow, vain, self-sufficient, self-opinionated man, who has an inadequate vision of his opportunities and responsibilities. Elected as a Democrat, he has preferred from the outset to follow the dictates of his own erratic judgment, instead of the duly constituted Party leadership . . . He is a pacifist, a socialist."

The writer, the paper's editor-in-chief, was a Princeton classmate of President Wilson's named Frank Glass. The *News* was the more responsible of Birmingham's two leading dailies, following the new style of "objective" reporting and espousing a mild probusiness Progres-

sivism; the *Age-Herald* was the crude mouthpiece of corporate interests. The papers' editors hated each other, but through the spring and
summer of 1918 they found common cause in demonizing George
Huddleston—the *News* through Glass's editorials, the *Age-Herald*
through front-page cartoons. One cartoon, published five days after the
Tutwiler luncheon, caricatured my grandfather as a diminutive figure
with a big head, dressed in pinstriped trousers with an iron cross on
his jacket, declaring, "At the very time America needs my support, I
always refuse to give it." The caption above the drawing read: "The
Little Bolsheviki From Birmingham Desires to Address the House."

As the August 13 primary drew near, the barrage intensified. An
organization of leading citizens calling itself the Jefferson County
Patriotic League suddenly appeared with the sole purpose of defeating
the "mutineer." "If we vote against the President," one of their ads said,
"there will be 'extras' on the streets of Berlin and rejoicing in the heart
of every German snake in America." In early August my grandfather's
caricature graced the *Age-Herald*'s front page every day under headlines reporting great battles in France: Huddleston throwing a tantrum
and shaking toys labeled "Sabotage," "Socialism," "Made in Germany," while doughboy Wilson points toward Europe and the sinking
Lusitania: "This way!" (caption: "Too Little to Lead and Not Big
Enough to Follow"); Huddleston kicking over the Statue of Liberty
while the Kaiser applauds (caption: "Comfort to the Enemy"). A *News*
editorial headline demanded: "Let Mr. Huddleston Prove His Loyalty." Rallies and counter-rallies spilled through the downtown streets,
ending in fistfights and near riots. Soldiers marching through the city
sang, "We'll hang George Huddleston to a sour apple tree!" Speakers
charged that Huddleston had used nonunion labor to build his house,
that he had spent a summer in Prague and was fluent in German. His
two opponents were a manufacturer and a Baptist minister, but newspaper coverage was so relentlessly negative that neither of the con-
scripts could match the visibility of Huddleston, who remained in
Washington until the campaign's last five days.

Meanwhile, the moral history of the war period was being written in the corners of the inside pages. "Two Birmingham Negroes Lynched in Lowndes County," read the headline above one small article.

> Will and Jesse Powell, negroes, who were arrested here early this morning, tonight were taken from deputies in Lowndes County, near here, where they were wanted, and lynched to a nearby tree. The mob numbered about 100. The deputies endeavored to protect the negroes, but the mob overpowered them and forcibly took possession of their prisoners . . . The negroes had brushed against [a] white man's horse, and when the latter remonstrated, they drew their revolvers and threatened him . . . Both freely admitted holding their pistols on the man, but claimed the white man had struck one of them and they tried to protect themselves.

> . . .

> Horace Bryan, negro, was bound over to await the action of the Federal Grand Jury, following a preliminary hearing before Judge Kenneth Charlton, United States Commissioner, Wednesday afternoon, charged with having violated the espionage act. His bond was fixed at $300. He is alleged to have made seditious remarks about the government.

> . . .

> A loafer will be about as popular in Birmingham from now until the end of the war as a prohibitionist in a German brewery or a pacifist in the French trenches. You may be armed with a registration card, but that will not lock you out of the workhouse if you can give no satisfactory explanation of your present idleness . . . It is not believed that many failed to register. Those that did not may find themselves in the clutches of a blue clothes man before nightfall, and, in that event, tomorrow will likely find them earning an honest meal pounding rock or shoveling sand for the city.

A secret society called the Vigilantes told four men with German names to leave Birmingham. A man accused of disloyalty was tied to a post and jeered for several hours. And small groups of self-appointed guardians of public decency were beginning to march in bedsheets and masks. Half a century after General Nathan Bedford Forrest shut it down, the Invisible Empire had risen from the dead and was riding into Birmingham on the back of "Americanism." The Robert E. Lee Klan No. 1 Klavern's first act was to burn down a Catholic church and school. Within a few years the Birmingham Klan would rule Alabama politics and elect one of its own to the Senate—future Supreme Court justice Hugo Black.

It was the ultimate irony of Progressivism that Wilson's war made America safe for the Ku Klux Klan. Floggings, arson, and lynchings were not what the editors of *The New Republic* had in mind when they hailed wartime America's "morale of a cooperative commonwealth," but as Bourne had foreseen, "war determines its own end" and "it is difficult to see how the child on the back of a mad elephant is to be any more effective in stopping the beast than is the child who tries to stop him from the ground." The New Liberals in New York and Washington had no grasp of the forces war had set in motion in cities like Birmingham. The spirit of reform was metamorphosing into its terrifying twin, the muckraker into the night rider, child labor law into the grotesque crusade for Prohibition, as if idealism and irrationality are not opposites but related in some intimate and disturbing way. Wilson deplored the "organizations in this country whose object is anarchy and the destruction of law," but the Jefferson County Patriotic League was only carrying out his will: "The enemies of the President," it claimed, "are the enemies of America." In the last week of the 1918 campaign, the President made sure that it came down to "Wilson or Huddleston?"

Five days before the election, my grandfather was finally due in Birmingham on an evening train. For several days friends had been advertising his arrival in the same papers that were calling him a traitor:

George Is Coming Home
THURSDAY NIGHT AT 7:30
Let's meet him at the Terminal Station.

We will go from there to Capitol Park,
where he will speak to the folks.
EVERYBODY BRING A FLAG

But the train stalled on a hill ten miles outside the city. Afterward, it was suggested that his opponents had soaped the tracks. Three hours late, he was met at the station by several thousand supporters who had converged from the mining villages and industrial quarters and stayed up to greet "the Little Bolsheviki." "All was noise and confusion," he remembered later. "A multitude of torches were burning and cheers of welcome came from thousands of friendly throats." He was lifted into a chair on a platform and carried like some Siamese prince in a torchlight parade. "When the crowd passed the Birmingham News building," the *News* evenhandedly reported the next day, "the cheering began and lasted until after the Age-Herald building was passed." At Capitol Park, he told 15,000 people that he supported the President but would not be a "phonograph."

"It was 1 o'clock when I reached my hotel. A dozen strong-armed friends stuck close to the very last. I did not understand at the time. They feared I would be assassinated."

Late the next day, a Western Union telegram reached the office of Frank Glass at the *Birmingham News*. It was from the White House, Glass's old friend from Princeton '79. By nightfall the telegram was spread across a special edition of the paper: "Your message received. I do not feel at liberty to make any discrimination between candidates equally loyal, but I think I am justified in saying that Mr. Huddleston's record proves him in every way an opponent of the Administration."

For a month Wilson had resisted Glass's efforts to get him to intervene. But now, three days before the election, he violated the rule against picking sides in his own party's primary—apparently his righteous conviction that anyone who disagreed with him was at best a fool had won out. The telegram was reprinted across the front pages of both Birmingham papers in the campaign's final days, and my grandfather's opponents declared victory. "Wilson or Huddleston? America or Germany? The choice is simple. Your duty is clear."

Huddleston was stung by this rejection from a President he had mainly supported and genuinely admired. He sent his own telegram to Wilson: "Your telegram coming at the last moment before the election does a cruel injustice." Wilson replied with characteristic detachment. "I certainly have no wish to do any injustice. Let the record speak for itself."

On August 13 the electorate finally got to speak for itself. In spite of presidential intervention and the disfranchisement of most of the district's poor by the 1901 constitution, Huddleston defeated his two opponents with 60 percent of the vote. He won big in all the rural and working-class precincts. Then, feeling that his honor had been affronted but no longer willing to settle such things with an exchange of pistol shots, he sued both Birmingham papers for libel. This time his initial victory was overturned by an appeals court, and he had to settle for a front-page apology.

In their postmortems on the campaign of 1918, Frank Glass and George Huddleston came close to agreeing for the first time. "Huddleston's campaign throughout was a systematic undertaking to arraign class against class," the editor concluded. "Unfortunately conditions favored his undertaking and there were no recognized representatives of the mass of people, of the laboring man and the farmer, who consciously opposed Huddleston in this outrageous demagogy."

"In its controlling features," my grandfather said later, "the campaign for the Democratic nomination for Congress became finally a fight of classes."

Three months after the Birmingham election, the war in Europe finally ended after four years and ten million corpses. The year 1919 began with high hopes for the peace that would justify such a catastrophe, but it became a year of nightmare. At home, it was the period of America's first Red Scare. Strikes by workers whose wages hadn't risen with wartime profits were put down with force; in Seattle a general strike met with vigilante violence. Agents of Wilson's Attorney General, A. Mitchell Palmer, raided, jailed, and summarily deported thousands of immigrants suspected of subversion—a more flagrant abuse of civil liberties than anything during the McCarthy era. Race riots in northern cities left hundreds dead, and in the South the number of lynchings surged, with eight in Alabama, including a certain Cicero Cage, who was cut to pieces in Tuscaloosa. The pressures of war, immigration, black demands and migration, Bolshevik revolution in Russia, and anxiety among small-town Americans about the alien modern world, combined into a kind of national psychosis.

Wilson arrived in Europe as a liberator and peacemaker, hailed by war-exhausted crowds that regarded him as their only hope of relief from the madness of blood. But in Paris Wilson's grand Fourteen Points were nibbled to death by power politics. The document he eventually signed became a notorious example of victor's justice. He came home with nothing in hand to show for 116,000 American deaths but the hope of a League of Nations, and soon it ran into opposition in the Senate. Refusing to compromise in Washington with Senator Henry Cabot Lodge as he had in France with Clemenceau, Wilson set out on a futile train trip across the country, trying to summon his old internationalist and humanitarian rhetoric on behalf of the flawed treaty.

But Americans had grown weary of crusades. The reaction against Wilsonian idealism was setting in, a revulsion all the more fierce and visceral for the failure of history to live up to his lofty proclamations. Wilson became the prototypical liberal who is hated for being high-minded—the original egghead. And suddenly the President who had urged his countrymen "not to think about me personally at all" was an exhausted but still inflexible human being on the verge of a terrible defeat. John Dos Passos, who had participated in the war and come back with a whole generation of disillusioned liberals hating Wilson, captured the mood in 1919, the second volume of his U.S.A. trilogy:

From the day he landed in Hoboken, he had his back to the wall of the White House, talking to save his faith in words, talking to save his faith in the League of Nations, talking to save his faith in himself, in his father's God.

He strained every nerve of his body and brain, every agency of the government he had under his control (if anybody disagreed he was a crook or a red; no pardon for Debs).

In Seattle the wobblies whose leaders were in jail, in Seattle the wobblies whose leaders had been lynched, who'd been shot down like dogs, in Seattle the wobblies lined four blocks as Wilson passed, stood silent with their arms folded staring at the great liberal as he was hurried past in his car, huddled in his overcoat, haggard with fatigue, one side of his face twitching.

In Pueblo, Colorado, Wilson stumbled on the step leading up to the auditorium where he was to speak. "Germany must never be allowed . . . ," he started to tell the large crowd, and then he stopped and fell silent. "A lesson must be taught to Germany . . ." He couldn't finish this sentence either. The left half of his face was jerking, a massive headache moving in. "The world will never allow Germany . . ." He stopped again. The mental powers of the scholar President were breaking down before the country's eyes, and by the end of the speech this supposedly unfeeling man was weeping.

The next morning the left side of his body was paralyzed from a stroke, saliva drooled from the corner of his mouth, his words were mumbled. The whistle-stop trip was canceled. His doctor told the world, "The President has suffered a complete nervous breakdown." The train sped back to Washington, where Wilson was driven to the White House past empty sidewalks and doffed his hat for the cheering crowds he imagined there. Two weeks later, a second stroke nearly killed him, leaving the President bedridden and incapable of carrying out his duties. Petitioners came to the Lincoln bedroom and begged Wilson to accept the Senate's compromise on the League of Nations. "Let Lodge compromise," he snapped, and turned away. The treaty on which he'd staked everything went down to defeat. His congressional opponents celebrated their victory with such vindictiveness that Alice

Roosevelt Longworth, T.R.'s daughter and no admirer of Wilson, said, "Some of the comments were noticeably lacking in the Greek quality of Aidos—the quality that deters one from defiling the body of a dead enemy."

"If I were not a Christian," Wilson said, "I think I should go mad."

He grew a white beard, and gave his doctor's son rides on his wheelchair, and wept often. In the East Room he watched a silent movie of his triumphant postwar tour of Europe. He fantasized running for a third term, until his aides discreetly squelched the possibility. When he was well enough to be taken for a drive, the crowds didn't cheer but stared to see if it was true that the President had become insane. The drives stopped.

For the rest of his second term he was a ghost President, entirely dependent on his second wife, Edith, a widow and former jewelry shop owner, who took over presidential responsibilities, her looping childish script covering the official documents that reached the Lincoln bedroom. Franklin Roosevelt, the Democrats' vice presidential nominee in 1920, visited the White House and came away stunned by the sight of the wasted President. Within a year Roosevelt would be paralyzed, too, but his character was different and he would do more than survive. Eugene Debs, an old man himself and still in prison for opposing the war—the President steadily refused to pardon him—called Wilson "the most pathetic figure in the world." Wilson watched helplessly as the Progressive ideals in whose name he had justified entering the war degenerated into violent frenzy, and then into the frank embrace of hedonism that marked the election of the handsome, genial, submediocre Warren G. Harding to succeed him.

Unfortunately, Wilson, though irrational, was not insane. He understood what it all meant, and the day after Harding's victory he said, "There is nowhere to go now."

If there is a comparison to be made with Wilson, it might be with the presidency of Lyndon Johnson. Complete opposites in temperament and career, they both used a lofty humanitarian rhetoric to forge triumphs in domestic reform, only to overreach, out of idealism and arrogance, in a foreign war that destroyed their lives and the great societies they had painstakingly tried to build. It can hardly have been lost on Wilson's formidable though damaged mind that he had foreseen it all the night before he delivered his war message to Congress: "Once lead this people into war and they'll forget there ever was such a thing as tolerance."

On Inauguration Day in 1921 Wilson presided over his last cabinet meeting. He found himself unable to articulate an answer to the tributes, and as his lips quivered and tears rolled down his cheeks he said, "Gentlemen, it is one of the handicaps of my physical condition that I cannot control myself as I have been accustomed to do. God bless you all." Three years after leaving office he was dead.

My father was born the year after Wilson's death, in 1925. He would become one of the "collegebred idealists throughout the Englishspeaking world" who revered Wilson for his dream of international peace. He saw in Wilson a fellow intellect, a man who had placed all his faith in ideals of human progress. I wonder now if Wilson also seemed to my father, standing on Omaha Beach in the summer of 1971, like a comrade in suffering, his brain unequal to the demands of his mind and will. Stroke seems to me the fate of a certain kind of liberal.

Unlike the President who had tried to defeat him, my grandfather survived the bruising war years. He hadn't staked everything on "some eternal principles of right," hadn't run his moral supply lines far into nebulous ideals. When political crisis came in the summer of 1918 he fell back on the working men whose hard lives represented his own standard of right. It was a solid standard on a human scale, founded not on a new world order but in a specific place, based on a few elemental ideas about democracy, and it would sustain him in the politically lonely years ahead, when the business of America became business.

But he was no longer alone. When his train had pulled into the Birmingham station three hours late on the night of the torchlight parade, his pregnant wife was on board with him.

Bertha Baxley was twenty-six when they married—barely half his age. She was auburn-haired, lively, quick-tempered, fond of dancing, and soon to like gin. She came from a family of hard-luck drinkers in the gritty industrial town of Bessemer. Her father, a carpenter at an ironworks, lost an eye to a chip of wood, quit, and started a store, and was ultimately run over by a Tin Lizzie—he had gone deaf and didn't hear the driver calling, "Watch out, Mr. Jim." Her mother was a hard, snuff-dipping woman named Nina Antoinette Cosper, who judged everyone harshly except her future son-in-law. Bertha, who didn't finish high school, feared her mother and worshiped her father.

She found a replacement for him when she went to work in 1914 as the Birmingham congressman's secretary. Before laying eyes on him she fell in love with his deep voice when she heard it on an elevator at his office. Their courtship began in the way their marriage would play out, when he charged her with some clerical mistake that she hadn't made. She fumed for a while, then went into his office, and threw her steno pad in his face: "I quit." He followed her home, apologized, and begged her to come back to work. The fight stirred something in the self-described "lifelong bachelor."

The proceedings could not have been less romantic. On Thanksgiving Day 1917 they wed in semi-secrecy, after which the bridal couple dined with an old locksmith friend of my grandfather's named Abromson. The next day work resumed. When reporters got wind of the marriage, they confronted the new husband in a Birmingham restaurant. "The Congressman, small of frame, who stands unblinkingly in the spotlight of a nation's criticism," said the News, "hid behind a menu card and blushed."

"She was always my advisor, you know," Huddleston told reporters, "and we decided that we might as well make it a permanent contract, giving her power to execute as well as suggest."

If three years as his secretary hadn't clarified what kind of man she was marrying, Bertha quickly found out. "He had married her for her high spirits and spent the next forty years trying to curb them," my mother later wrote, "and she had married him for his reserve and dignity and spent the next forty years trying to get him to change." George Huddleston told his young wife that he wanted to pass on the family name, and the children came one after another, a daughter, then two sons, then two more daughters—five in six and a half years. As the marriage filled with strife, the first four would be conscripted, two on either side. By the time the fifth, my mother, Nancy, arrived, the battle lines were drawn.

◆

CHAPTER 4

No Is Always Right

The 1920s put George Huddleston and his generation of liberals in a dilemma for which they never found a solution. How could they fight for justice when half the country was dizzy making money and the other half was turning to virulent fundamentalism? Younger radicals thought they had the answer: the Communist Party, curator of history. But this was no alternative for a democrat, though Huddleston continued to defend the right of "Reds" to free speech and collective bargaining. Instead of riding any of the available historical currents, he spent the '20s along with a handful of congressional allies fighting hopeless rearguard battles against the ever-increasing power of corporate wealth and its Republican partners in Washington.

The great themes of freedom and equality no longer seemed to move his working-class supporters. Many of them fell under the spell of the Ku Klux Klan, led by its Grand Cyclops, James Esdale, which was carrying on a rule of terror in Birmingham and creating a statewide political machine. During the Klan's rise to power, the Big Mules regarded it as a friendly movement: anti-immigrant, anti-union, pro-white supremacy, pro-"Americanist." But by the mid-'20s, in the absence of a labor movement—President Harding and his Secretary of

Commerce, Herbert Hoover, had strangled the coal and railroad strikes of the early '20s with federal injunctions, over Huddleston's ardent protests—the Klan was the only organization in the South left to carry the flag for the common people. The Birmingham Klan fused violent intolerance (Catholics shot and their churches burned, suspected adulterers kidnaped and flogged) with a half-baked economic program that recalled the Populist dreams of the 1890s. By 1926 the Klan represented the "left" in Alabama. When its own Hugo Black won a Senate seat against an establishment candidate, the Big Mules realized that the Invisible Empire was a threat and began to deplore vigilante justice. The Alabama Democratic Party split open just as it had in the 1890s.

Throughout the 1920s national Democrats quarreled over Prohibition, immigration, and the Klan, while the ruling Republicans stole from the Treasury and divided the pie of federal largesse among corporate friends. In 1924 my grandfather urged William Jennings Bryan to put his name up for the Democratic nomination one last time as the only hope for Progressives: "As I see the situation, you are the only available man." But in the heat of Madison Square Garden the Great Commoner couldn't bring himself to condemn the Klan. "My friends, it requires more courage to fight the Republican Party than it does to fight the Ku Klux Klan," he said to applause and jeers. The party was hopelessly divided between wet and dry, Catholic and Protestant, urban and rural, eastern and southern-western. Bryan's effort to unite it against the old enemies, monopoly and privilege, collapsed. In the 1920s, as in more recent years, class conflict was smothered by cultural antagonisms. Deadlocked until the 103rd ballot, the Democratic convention finally compromised on a conservative Wall Street attorney from West Virginia named John W. Davis to run against Calvin Coolidge.

This left Progressives of both parties with no one to support, and Wisconsin's Senator Robert La Follette ran on a third-party ticket. With La Follette, George Huddleston had helped create an alliance of congressional liberals called the People's Legislative Service, and in

1924 his name was floated as a running mate for La Follette. He declined, perhaps not wanting to end his own career in a doomed cause. The Progressive Party won five million votes, but this was the decade of Republicans and Big Money. Within a year both La Follette and Bryan were dead. The spirit of reform they had embodied for three decades seemed to have died too. Bryan's life ended amid the mockery of H. L. Mencken at the Scopes trial—a trial that pitted a liberal of one sort against a liberal of another in the worst guise of each type, caustic sophistication against ignorant fundamentalism, each made harsh and unlovely by the antagonism of the other, both far too narrow to embrace "the cause of humanity." Bryan became known as the buffoon of the Scopes trial and one of history's comic losers. But the real loser at the trial was wholehearted liberalism.

In the fulminations of racists, nativists, and other malcontents of the 1920s, the first signs of cleavage in the old Populist-Progressive forces begin to appear. Liberalism, a relatively new term, suddenly took on the taint of un-American elitism from which it has never really recovered. Hiram Evans, Imperial Wizard and Emperor of the Ku Klux Klan, writing for the sophisticated readership of the *North American Review*, called the urban reformers "intellectually mongrelized 'Liberals.' " You can almost hear George Wallace snarling about "pointy-headed bureaucrats who can't park a bicycle straight" in Imperial Wizard Evans' complaint: "The average Liberal idea is apparently that those who can produce should carry the unfit, and let the unfit rule them. This aberration would have been impossible, of course, if American Liberalism had kept its feet on the ground. Instead it became wholly academic, lost all touch with the plain people, disowned its instincts and common sense, and lived in a world of pure, high, groundless logic." The Klan view would become the Republican view and, eventually, the popular view. All the accusations we now know so well appeared already full-grown in an essay written by a Klansman in 1926.

Huddleston's district kept sending him back to Congress. Somehow he could defend imprisoned labor radicals, argue against Jewish immigration quotas, oppose the Prohibition amendment on states' rights grounds, defy both the Big Mules and the Klan, denounce the invasion of Nicaragua as imperialism, campaign for the wet Catholic Al Smith in 1928 amid rumors that his own wife, Bertha, was a Catholic herself, and continue to be reelected, often unopposed. He had earned his constituents' respect in 1918, and though his oratory was far more impressive than his legislative record, he worked hard on behalf of individual petitioners. When another congressman once asked him why he exhausted himself over petty drudgery, Huddleston replied, "I make a slave of myself in my office in order that I may be free when I get over in the House. You make a slave of yourself in the House so that you can be free when you get back to your office."

In the 1920s a tone of skepticism entered his voice, and as the decade staggered on it grew more harsh. It's as if the smell of too many bad bills haggled over in too many airless committee rooms started to sour him. He took to calling himself "a natural-born conservative" with a "hidebound distrust of new things. Not long ago I remarked to a fellow member of my committee, who is also an ironclad conservative, that the reason why he and myself were not oftener together in our views was that he threw back to 1890, whereas I threw back to about 1820."

The liberal language of humanitarianism, the radical language of economic justice, began to go underground in his speeches. He didn't stop speaking out against concentrations of money and power, but after a decade and a half in Congress the message was entirely negative. "I have sometimes felt that a Member might come into the Chamber and without knowing what was going on vote 'no,' 'no,' 'no' on every proposal and his batting average would be about 900." The reason why " 'no' is nearly always right," he said, was that "every measure that comes here comes because some great selfish interest stands behind it."

In an exchange on the floor of the House in 1928, a fellow Democrat asked him whether the A.F. of L. wasn't an interest "organized for the public good."

Huddleston answered sharply: "The American Federation of Labor is organized to protect the interests of wage earners."

"Is not that a good purpose?" asked the other congressman, astonished at his prolabor colleague's apparent change of heart.

"Not more so, perhaps, than an organization of employers of labor. Those organizations do not represent the public. How is it possible for a man of the gentleman's intelligence to ask such a question?"

"I think the wage earners are organized naturally for their own good," the other man said, "and that in the long run that will be for the good of the whole country, for the good of the people generally."

Huddleston wearily brushed the argument aside. "I have had entirely too much experience and have too much knowledge of life and of human nature to be willing to intrust the common good to any particular class or calling, much less any organization formed to promote the interest of any group."

In Chattanooga in 1916 he had told a theater full of workers that "the cause of organized labor is the cause of humanity." Now there were only special interests—no one spoke for the public, or for democracy. Before, he had described the two schools of political thought as humanitarians and anti-democrats. Now he began to make a new distinction—between individualists and collectivists.

> The individualist holds that man has a natural moral right to govern himself, to order his own actions, to live his own life, and that no restrictions should be placed upon the individual except for the protection of the rights of other men. The collectivist is not interested in the individual and feels that he has no natural or moral rights inconsistent with the welfare of the mass.

He went on: "It is undoubtedly true that our civilization is developing toward collectivism, and that the rights of the individual are held in diminishing regard." Nor was this only the case in Europe, where Mussolini and Stalin had come to power and Hitler was on the horizon. In America, too, the unseemly alliance of business and government threatened the rights of states, localities, individuals. Earlier in his career he had advocated government ownership of utilities and railroads, on the theory that "if I must take the choice between the monopolies owning the Government and the Government owning the monopolies, I shall not hesitate to accept the latter." By 1930 he was saying, "I believe in competition. I am an old-fashioned man. I believe in the old-fashioned political system and the old-fashioned economic system. They are tied up with each other and cannot exist independently. When one goes, the other goes."

Humanitarians vs. antidemocrats, individualists vs. collectivists: when my grandfather shifted from one dichotomy to another something important was lost, for good. In pronouncing himself an individualist, he was giving up the hope of justice and equality in modern society. A humanitarian could call for publicly owned electric power and see no danger of excessive government, because to him government meant the people. This was the assumption of the Populists, of Bryan, of La Follette. But an individualist saw a move toward collectivism and a threat to democracy. In an age of centralized organization, individualism is bound to be an essentially negative, even reactionary idea. It implies a sense of strict limits to social improvement—to human nature itself.

My grandfather always insisted that history changed while he stood fast. The truth is more nearly that history forced him to choose between principles that he had always held simultaneously. In 1916 he was a humanitarian and an individualist without any sense of contradiction. Each tendency put him on the side of the common man. But by 1930 it was no longer possible to be both. As America succumbed to the Great Depression, the seismic political shifts that had begun with the Populists and accelerated after 1912 played themselves out, the two parties seemed to exchange core principles, humanitarians became collectivists, antidemocrats became individualists—and a Thomas Jefferson Democrat who "threw back to about 1820" became a historical anomaly, a seemingly impossible creature, like the duck-billed platypus.

Not long ago I came into possession of a studio portrait of my grandfather, made in 1929, when he was sixty. It had turned up, by coincidence, in a San Francisco photo archive owned by the husband of one of his ten granddaughters. The seven-by-ten glossy shows my grandfather from the chest up, wearing a dark woolen jacket, vest, and bow tie. The photographer has created so little depth of field that the nose and ears are slightly out of focus. But the rest of the face is clear enough to betray every freckle, every line of strain around the eyes and mouth and across the forehead. He's so drawn and pale that life seems to have drained from his features along with blood. The tightened lips seem incapable of ever smiling again. Seeing the picture, my aunt Jane exclaimed, "He looks so desolate!"

Glued to the back there is a press release on Underwood and Underwood paper that must have been accompanied by the studio photograph. Headlined "CONGRESSMAN WINS SUIT AIMED TO MAKE HIM LIABLE FOR WIFE'S DEBTS," the press release announces:

> A descision [sic] which may have an important bearing on credit transactions by married women, was rendered in Washington today in the case of Rep. George Huddleston, Dem, of Alabama, who was sued by a local merchant for payment for a 245 dollar fur coat and scarf, purchased by Mrs. Huddleston without his permission. The court ruled the Legislator not responsible and the case was appealed by the store, and the descision of the lower court was upheld.
>
> An especially posed portrait of Rep. Huddleston.
>
> Dec. 5, 1929

He had been married twelve years.

By 1929 the man in the portrait and his much younger wife — now the parents of five brawling children, my mother the newest at four — were married in name only. She revered her congressman husband

like a father; and like a daughter she revolted against his rule. As the
'20s spilled into the '30s she drank more and stayed out longer—with
other men. The dynamic of the marriage drove her to destructive reck-
lessness when, with a different husband, ordinary self-indulgence
might have satisfied her.

In the middle of the day one of the children would call the house
where they knew Bertha had gone. "When are you coming home?"
"Half an hour," she would lie. Sometimes she missed dinner, returning
at midnight. Then her husband would find out, and there would be a
drama of anger and contrition and household misery. One night Bertha
came home drunk and picked my mother up. "I'll take her," George
said. "No you won't," his wife answered, and he slapped her—the only
time the children saw this happen. On another occasion she and my
mother, age six or seven, missed a train from Washington to Birmingham because Bertha had been somewhere with a man. My mother was
so angry that Bertha finally took her in her lap and rocked her and said
sweet things until my mother stopped crying. Her mother was capable
of soothing the pain she herself inflicted, the children's main source
of love as well as anguish—but they wanted their mother to behave.

Their father evoked neither anguish nor love. Around the house he
was a sort of Old Testament deity. "Mary," he would tell his oldest
child at the dinner table, "you're hugging Nanny too much. You're disturbing the table. Nanny, go sit next to your mother." In his presence
the children were absolutely respectful; when he was at work and
Bertha off with her drinking friends, all hell broke loose. Then one of
the children would get on the phone to the House of Representatives,
NAtional 3120, extension 746.

"Miss Sudie, let me talk to Daddy."

"He's on the floor of the House."

"What's that extension?"

Or: "He's in Interstate and Foreign Commerce Committee."

"What's that extension?"

And George Huddleston would be called from the floor or the
committee room to his office phone.

"What is it?"

"John's hitting me."

"Let me speak to John. John, stop hitting Nancy."

"Yes sir."

And the hitting would stop. This conversation happened almost every day.

My mother was in the thick of it all, "as the youngest and a tomboy," she later wrote, "with a volatile temper and a craving for prestige and notice." Her political blood was roused at a very early age. In 1928, when Governor Al Smith of New York was nominated by the Democrats as the first Catholic candidate for President, and Alabama's Klan-ridden Democratic Party almost tore itself apart over the issue, my grandfather toured the state for Smith and told one crowd, "My little girl of three marches around wearing a Smith button and, with a swagger, declares, 'I don't like old Hoover.'" During that election year her passions ran so high that, when her mother teased her by announcing that she would vote Republican, three-year-old Nancy reached up from her perch in her mother's lap and gave her a black eye. A family friend made the same mistake and my mother ripped the strand of pearls off the astonished woman's neck. Four years later, at age seven and sensing the shift in the political wind toward FDR, she carried a sign around the neighborhood that gloated, "Be Kind to Dumb Animals — Pity Hoover the Elephant."

Competition with four older siblings was useful training for political combat. The fights were constant at the Huddleston house, my mother wisely aligning herself with one or another of her brothers. As the children grew older, fistfights turned to arguments around the dinner table, in which the object was not enlightenment of the subject matter but destruction of the opponent in whatever way possible. As the voices grew heated, their mother would retreat with her plate to the kitchen. At some point their father, who often triggered the arguments with baiting questions and then sat back to watch the parliamentary effects, would declare the debate closed by slapping the tabletop. If things didn't die down, he picked up a corn biscuit and threw it at one of his children.

Neither George nor Bertha hesitated to expose the children to their cross fire. "Jane, you will never know what I have had to go through," he told my aunt, age twelve, on a trip to Tennessee, as if she hadn't been absorbing it all along. Jane, the fourth child, was his darling, but when the third, John, was eighteen months old, Bertha came into the room and heard her husband telling his son, "You're Daddy's boy. George is Mama's boy." So George and John grew up in their own small sideshow of the main war.

It was, of course, the oldest child, Mary, who carried the heaviest portion of her parents' unhappiness. Bertha made her a confidante early on, asking six-year-old Mary whether it was wrong to dance with other men when she went out. The father's coercions were less subtle. On winter days in Washington he obliged his pretty daughter to wear long johns to school under her skirt. He spent hours combing out the permanent her mother had inflicted on Mary's hair. When he was campaigning in Birmingham, he essentially left his "dear sweet Mary" in charge of the household. His letters made demands she was never able to live up to:

> I want to remind you to try to form the habit of orderliness and system. It is your most serious fault but is one which you can correct with proper effort. Try to train yourself to do things in a regular way—have a place for everything and put it in its place—hang your clothes up in a regular place or put them in a drawer—keep your shoes, coat etc each in its place—don't leave your books and other things lying around. By practicing and care you can build up such habits and they will be a great help to you in future.
>
> With a kiss from
Daddy

Give the check to Ida—she should sign it on back

The check to Ida—their Negro maid, and Mary's truest friend—was conveyed through a child because George Huddleston didn't trust his wife. With the same letter he enclosed a second check, $45 for household expenses. "I hope mother can get along on it. Tell her to send any bills that come to the house on to me at once." By 1929 money was the only means my grandfather could find to control his young wife. The legislator who had once spoken up for women's empowerment and raised his three daughters in the same spirit didn't hesitate to use Bertha's economic dependence on him as a weapon.

He hated the decade that Dos Passos called "the Big Money." He saw the flaunting of wealth the way he saw the tight connection between big business and government: as a threat to democracy itself. "This bill is in thorough harmony with the spirit of the times," he said of a proposal to raise judges' salaries. "It assumes that there is nothing worth while except money and that money will buy everything. Thank God all of the people do not feel that way about it. When all do feel that way, America will be lost, and judges cannot save it." And he went on to quote Senator George Norris of Nebraska, the only member of Congress who retained his complete admiration now that his friend La Follette was dead: "No man can stick his legs under the tables of the idle rich every night and be fit the next day to sit in judgment on those who toil."

"No"—nearly always right in Congress—became nearly all he said at home. Public virtue turned into private cruelty. When he posted his wife's debts in the newspaper, then forced litigation on the department store that was trying to collect $245 for the fur coat, domestic conflict turned into a high-stakes game of humiliation, with my grandmother's extravagance ending up on the front page of *The New York Times*.

So Bertha retaliated. In the midst of "the greatest, gaudiest spree in history," she spent ever more freely, plunged deeper into the pleasures of illegal liquor, made bathtub gin in her own home. By the end of the 1920s Prohibition had become a national farce. Bootleggers hid their stock in the privet hedge around the White House, or in the bushes at the base of the Alexander Hamilton monument, directly under the windows of the Treasury Department's Prohibition enforcement chief.

At the Government Printing Office orders for type-cleaning fluid doubled. At the Smithsonian Institution reptile exhibits decayed when the alcohol in which they were pickled started to disappear. The drink of choice, and my grandmother's favorite, was bathtub gin — 50 percent alcohol, 49 percent water, plus essence of juniper berries, glycerine, and orange-water compound. Clear and thus more likely to betray impurities, it killed fewer people than rye or corn whiskey. However much she enjoyed drinking and spending for their own sakes, Bertha knew how to torment her dry and miserly husband. But the ultimate power was his.

She bought herself a Chevy and took her children on high-spirited excursions with their Great Dane, Duke. Her husband stopped the allowance she was using to pay for it. She fell behind on the installments. The car was repossessed. The day she lost it, Bertha came into the kitchen, where the coal stove was burning. Ida, the maid, was there with a couple of the children, and Bertha began crying. Losing the car, my mother recalled, "was a kind of killing blow in their relationship." My grandmother responded with the worst incident of the marriage and its most public disgrace.

She was having an affair with a Washington salesman three years her senior named Mark Middleton Penn — the man who had made her miss the train to Birmingham. All my mother remembers about him is that he wore a fedora. On the night of June 8, 1932, a car containing the man in the fedora and the congressman's wife swerved across West Virginia Avenue in northeastern Washington and struck the parked car of a Mrs. J. K. Moore. Bertha was driving; she and Penn were both drunk, and both were arrested at the scene. I see it as a period movie, one of the early talkies like *It Happened One Night* — the couple singing and laughing in the front seat against a filmed background of nighttime city streets, a cut to the automobile careening across the avenue and into the parked car, the couple again in the front seat rather gently jolted, the laughter dying on the faces of the man in the fedora and the beautiful woman at the wheel: "Did we hit something?" Then laughter again, wilder than before, until a policeman's face appears at the window.

My grandmother was brought to the Ninth Precinct, where, the arresting officer later testified, she "reeked with the fumes of liquor and talked foolishly." Her husband was summoned to the station and paid the $500 bond that sprang his wife—twice the cost of the fur coat. Later that night, at home, my mother remembers sitting on a footstool near her father when Bertha, now sober in every sense, came into the room and said, "I'm sorry."

She was sorrier the next day when the story, released by the Associated Press, was picked up on the front pages of *The Washington Post, Chicago Tribune,* and *Los Angeles Times,* as well as the *Birmingham News.* On the *Post's* front page, three columns to the right of the article titled "Representative's Wife Arrested After Crash," there is an account of the Republican Party's debate over Prohibition repeal. The representative whose drunken wife smashed into a parked car had voted against national Prohibition in 1917 on states' rights grounds, and in 1932 he opposed its repeal for the same reason—ever on the principled and losing side, ever saying no. At the very least, his wife's scandal complicated his position with the constituents back home in one of the country's driest districts.

"I'm sorry about your mother's accident," a girl in my aunt Jane's class said the next day.

"What accident?"

Two weeks later the corporation counsel for the District of Columbia interceded, the drunk driving charge was reduced, and Bertha was fined a mere $50 in Police Court. The Washington columnist Drew Pearson published a book later that year in which the incident involving the "dashing young wife of Representative George Huddleston" became an example of political influence undermining the Prohibition laws. "Despite the testimony of the police, Mrs. Huddleston was allowed to plead guilty only of reckless driving. All she had to face after that was the threat of Mrs. Penn for a damage suit for the alienation of her husband's affections."

The suit never materialized. The husband's affections continued to be alienated. It wasn't until 1936, when her mother lay on her deathbed, calling out to Bertha's beloved father, "I'm coming, Jim!" that Bertha vowed to stop drinking and straying. And she was sentimental enough to keep a promise to a dying mother, though the spending went on unabated, food for strife and loan sharks for two and a half more decades, the one form of rebellion left her other than smoking. The debts dried up only after George Huddleston's death, when his sixty-eight-year-old widow, no husband-father to rebel against, at last became the luncheoning, utterly conventional Bertha Huddleston who made preserves in her basement instead of gin in her bathtub, who was nominated Birmingham's Woman of the Year for 1968, and whom I remember with great fondness as my grandmother.

Rumor of a long-ago drunk driving incident circulated among the grandchildren—but in our generation the extent of George and Bertha's unhappiness remained unknown. My mother and aunts and uncles kept it quiet. I knew that the family had had its battles, that the children were intensely competitive, the parents mismatched in age and in some vague way unsuited for each other. Most of my mother's reminiscent essays show her parents entangled in some tense but not particularly explosive conflict—over her smoking, his driving—with the children fighting their own local battles and sometimes delicately intervening in the parents' central one with the hope of a peaceful settlement. George teases, rebukes, withdraws; Bertha defies, pouts, even weeps once when George refuses to participate in the surprise birthday party she's thrown for him. She has to swallow her hurt and go outside to persuade him to come back and join the guests. "My sisters and I went to the window. We could see him across the street in the shadow of a large elm. He looked like a sentry. We saw our mother go up to him and put her hand on his arm . . . And so they became friends again, or at least no longer foes, occupying the fluid middle ground that marked the major portion of their life together. Relief and irritation sighed through us. How could she? Thank God she did."

There are no devastating blows or unforgivable humiliations, no final victories or defeats. The occasions are inherently comic and the denouements full of tense laughter. Perhaps this "fluid middle ground" stands closer to the daily truth of the marriage than the crises that loom large in retrospect. Most family memoirs exaggerate pain—"the revenge of the repressed," my mother called it. But she chose not to mention what any memoirist of my generation would harp on—alcohol, debts, love affairs, newspaper scandals. She made Bertha less destructive and George less harsh. The reckless young wife of the Prohibition era and her miserable congressman husband never appear. My mother once told me, "I wanted funny stories."

A few years ago, I was at the Boston Public Library, looking through *The Washington Post* index for articles on George Huddleston when I found my grandmother's name listed alongside his. The article was headlined "Representative's Wife Arrested After Crash." By then, my mother and aunts were willing to answer my questions. At a family reunion in Birmingham the three sisters and I sat around a table by the hotel pool, and once they began they kept adding to one another's recollections as if talk finally brought some relief. My aunt Mary—the oldest child, who took the heaviest load of her mother's confidences and her father's demands—simply said, "George, it was a horror."

Two images from my mother's childhood stick in my mind. In one, the family is having a dinnertime discussion and she is so overcome with the righteousness of her position that she climbs up on the table and continues to orate amid the plates of food. A freckled and red-headed tomboy, stick-legged and knob-kneed, her face aflame with the heat of polemic, she declaims down at her four older brothers and sisters, her mortified young mother, and her dryly amused old father, who finally orders, "Nanny, get down off the table."

In the other, it's late at night and she's lying in her mother's bed, in the room they share. She's waiting for the sound of the front door to tell her that her mother has come home. She sniffs the air in the dark room, to find out by child's magic if her mother has been drinking and will come back smelling of gin and have a fight with her husband. She exercises all the telepathic force of her will to make her mother be good.

For a long time the first of these pictures—mixing Bertha's volatility with George's love of a fight for the just cause—had fixed my idea of my mother's childhood. The picture showed her public self, an early version of the woman who, while keeping her seat at dinner, would transmit to me her father's political passion and firm moral sense. I had always understood her protectiveness about the past—about my father as well as her parents—in terms of the code she had inherited from her father, one of loyalty and integrity. But over the course of our conversations the second picture, the girl lying in her mother's bed, took its place alongside the first. It's a more private image, and it suggests the woman who would endure loss and try to head off disaster through a tremendous effort of will, even a will to silence. I imagine my mother growing up between these two scenes—determined to win, and desperate for people to behave.

If liberalism implies a faith that people can be better than they are, conservatism often springs from a wound as personal and damaging as the domestic humiliation George Huddleston underwent in the late 1920s and early 1930s. The relationship between politics and home is impossible to pin down, and impossible to ignore.

The worst years of his private life coincided with his loss of faith in Congress, the Democratic Party, labor unions, the public, the republican character of America itself. All around he saw self-interestedness, indulgence, corruption; he called it "government by organized selfishness." As his pessimism about American institutions deepened, the language of radical idealism fell out of his speech. His political principles—which he once summed up as the Declaration of Independence, the Preamble to the Constitution, and the Bill of Rights—remained the same, but their emphasis grew dark and bitter, backward-looking, even reactionary. My grandfather seemed to be saying "no" to the modern world.

Then that world produced the Great Depression, and at first it had a clarifying effect on him. Birmingham's brittle, heavily mortgaged prosperity crumbled faster than ever before, and the city where hard times came first and stayed longest found itself utterly incapable of feeding and housing its 25,000 or 50,000 unemployed and their families. The wretched condition of the Jefferson County almshouse, wrote the *Birmingham News*, "signifies that our civilized society is not quite stony-hearted enough to execute its aged poor or to let them starve to death, but that it doesn't care to be bothered about them one mite more than it is absolutely necessary." And yet city and county were the only levels of government legally entrusted with the care of the poor. So the job was left to private charity—Herbert Hoover called it "the spiritual responses of the American people." But Birmingham was largely owned by men in New York and Pittsburgh whose spiritual response was limited in radius as well as generosity and didn't extend to their southern dependency, despite its official status as "the worst-hit city in the nation."

In 1932 Huddleston appeared before a Senate subcommittee to lay out his district's plight. He had recovered his old indignation. "My people are desperate. They are not in a condition to reason about things," he warned. "Any thought that there has been no starvation, that no man has starved, and no man will starve, is the rankest nonsense. Men are actually starving by the thousands today . . . I do not mean to say that they are sitting down and not getting a bite of food until they actually die, but they are living such a scrambling, precarious existence, with suffering from lack of clothing, fuel, and nourishment, until they are subject to be swept away at any time, and many are now being swept away."

Starvation made things morally simple—as simple as the nineteenth century. The desperation of men lining up for ditch-digging jobs did not induce any agonizing in Huddleston over the principle of limited government. "No honest American should be allowed to starve," he told the packed opening session of Congress on the night of December 9, 1931. The Democrats had been returned to the majority after twelve years of Republican rule, and they chose Huddleston to deliver their response to President Hoover's blandly optimistic State of the Union message.

"We are reaping the harvest of the collectivism," Huddleston said from the front of the chamber, "which you gentlemen of the Republican side of the aisle have sown with your special favors and group discriminations." The cause of the Depression was not old-fashioned individualist free enterprise, but its abuse by fifty years of corporate collusion with government. He called it private socialism and said it was worse than state socialism.

"The thoughtful American would not try to remedy this situation by rushing on to rash experiments in a new and more radical collectivism. He would return rather to the purity of individualism, in which there should be some real chance for private initiative and for individual effort upon a fairly equal basis. He would destroy the monopolies which you have fostered," he told the Republicans. "He would scatter by lawful and legitimate means the vast concentrations of wealth which it has been your pride to encourage."

Then Huddleston introduced a bill authorizing the administration to spend $100 million in direct federal relief to individuals—the first such bill in American history—knowing that Hoover would reject it, for Hoover had rejected his $50 million bill for relief to the states the year before.

"The State is not in a situation to help," he said of his own Alabama. "Uncle Sam can help, but the man at Uncle Sam's helm will not help." The Democratic benches and the gallery burst into applause. "He hears our cry unmoved. Starving women and children appeal to him in vain, his answer is, 'A dole for business, more time to pay for Germany, but not a cent for you.'" Federal aid to needy individuals was not a threat to the moral character of America, as Hoover warned; it was a matter of simple justice in a national emergency. "Speaking on the state of the Union and expressing my opinion, I should say it is bad, and one of the worst things about it is that we have a man in charge of the Government who is more interested in the pocketbooks of the rich than he is in the empty bellies of the poor."

He stepped down to an ovation.

A Massachusetts congressman rose to give the Republican

response. "This great Democratic Party has abandoned entirely the principles of Jefferson, its founder," he proclaimed, "for the principles of Karl Marx."

This night marked the last time that George Huddleston would use the old moral language, the old populist language of anger on behalf of "the toiling masses." It would never again be so clear as "the man and the dollar" in the old days had been. Hoover and the Republicans' tone-deaf response in the face of unprecedented suffering made things simple—but within a year Franklin Roosevelt was elected President; within two years the American landscape was radically altered by the New Deal. And then, for my grandfather and those of his generation, nothing was simple again. The ghost of Jefferson was invoked on all sides. It was invoked by business conservatives, by older Progressives and southern Democrats, by the protofascist William Randolph Hearst, who tried to launch yet another Jeffersonian Democratic Party, by FDR himself, even by the Communists, who made Birmingham their southern headquarters. And over and over it was invoked by my grandfather, as if he was trying to find some solid ground on which to stand with everything around him in flux.

Liberalism itself was hotly contested in those first years of the New Deal. In the 1930s, the L-word was not the word everyone ran from but the word everyone claimed. The most ardent and bewildered claimants were men who today would be called conservatives. Hoover claimed it: after being turned out of office he took to the stump and wrote books in which he denounced Roosevelt for abandoning "true liberalism." Hoover's Treasury Secretary, Ogden Mills, claimed it in a book called *Liberalism Fights On*, and so did Lewis Douglas, FDR's first budget director, who quit the New Deal and wrote an attack called *The Liberal Tradition*. To these men, liberalism meant laissez-faire individualism.

But the most persuasive claim on the word was made by Roosevelt. Adopting it from Croly and the New Nationalists, Roosevelt used "liberal" in place of "Progressive" to distinguish himself from those old Progressives like Al Smith who turned violently against the growth of

federal power in the '30s. By liberalism Roosevelt meant, in the words
of his great acceptance speech at the 1936 convention, the belief that
"government in a modern civilization has certain inescapable obligations to its citizens." This is the claim that stuck, and sticks, for better
and worse, to this day.

What's striking about the vitriolic fight over liberalism that broke
out in Roosevelt's first term is how little separated the sides, at least
rhetorically. Roosevelt and Hoover alike spoke for liberty, individualism, equal opportunity, old-fashioned competition—the whole package
of Jeffersonian values. Both sides opposed undemocratic concentrations of power. Both pointed to rising totalitarianism in Europe as a
threat to "Americanism." The terms of debate disguised profound differences over the role of government in American life. But the fact that
each side in one of the great ideological battles of our history, while
maintaining that the other was out to destroy the country, employed the
same set of clichés, shows the consensus about ultimate values that
underlies the disagreements in American politics.

Yet the New Deal *was* a break with the past, the one great excep-
tion to the American story of self-interested pursuit backed up by the
Bill of Rights; and never more so than in its early days. The "first New
Deal"—one of government-business partnership, with the ubiquitous
blue eagle of the National Recovery Administration, the acceptance of
monopoly, the fixing of wages and prices, the large-scale public works,
the control of agricultural production, the plowing under of fields and
wholesale slaughter of piglets—saw a native form of economic collectivism that not even the War Industries Board of World War I could
begin to rival. It was the triumph of the central planners, the brain trust
from Columbia, and it looked nothing like Jeffersonian democracy or
the New Freedom or anything else that the Democratic Party had ever
stood for.

So it's strange that George Huddleston went along with these
"Hundred Days" measures, in fact helped shepherd them through the
vital Interstate and Foreign Commerce Committee, on which he was
the ranking Democrat after his old friend, Chairman Sam Rayburn of

Texas. Huddleston had welcomed Roosevelt's election (Alabama had been the first delegation pledged to FDR, back in 1931), and he wasn't about to oppose the brand-new Democratic President, the first in twelve years. At the end of the Hundred Days he received a personal letter of thanks for his efforts from the Postmaster General, Jim Farley, Roosevelt's lieutenant from Albany. Maybe the White House already sensed that the Alabama congressman's loyalty was in doubt.

It soon became clear. The Roosevelt recovery acts "are steps towards collectivism," Huddleston warned the Birmingham Real Estate Board in the summer of 1933. "What we must keep in front of us is a return to our ancient trust in individualism." In committee that winter he fought the most draconian elements of the stock-market reform bill. On the House floor he spoke against abandoning the gold standard and devaluing the dollar. He disparaged the homestead communities that Eleanor Roosevelt envisioned for West Virginia miners. The Depression would correct itself, he said; the government should simply pay its debts and balance the budget. "We have had our dance; now then it is 'pay the fiddler.' And the awful pity of it is that so many of the innocent, and those least responsible, have the heaviest price to pay." He had begun to sound like a fiscal conservative—like a man bruised by fiddling and dance and debt.

The 1934 primary gave him a scare. He won in a runoff, but some of his old labor allies were beginning to turn against him. Not coincidentally, he now found himself praised for his newly acquired maturity (at sixty-five) in the editorial columns of the *News* and *Age-Herald*, the hometown papers that had once called him a socialist and traitor.

When he finally broke with Roosevelt and the New Deal, it came in the stifling Washington summer of 1935, over an obscure economic entity called a public utility holding company.

For three decades, electric power had been the central metaphor in the struggle over control of America's new industrial economy. The philosopher John Dewey called power "the most weighty single issue in the political field." As the country rushed headlong from the age of coal and steam and gas to the electric age, who should own the immense potential of its rivers and lakes, its dams and turbines and generators?

When electric power was young the federal government all but gave away the rights to its distribution. Then the Progressive era saw the rise of the municipal franchise, the Federal Power Commission, and the first calls for government control. In 1917 George Huddleston took to the floor of the House and demanded that hydroelectric power at Niagara Falls not be sold to a private corporation but be taken over by a public commission — the first legislative proposal for federal control of electric power. As usual, he lost.

In the 1920s the debate focused on a small Alabama town a hundred miles northwest of Birmingham called Muscle Shoals, where the Tennessee River grew turbulent as it dropped a hundred thirty feet across forty miles of farmland. Muscle Shoals was the site of the Wilson Dam, built to power a federal nitrate plant during World War I. Successive Republican administrations wanted to sell the plant on the cheap to private electric utilities. Senator George Norris, the austere Nebraska visionary, had a different idea: "This is a property which belongs to all of us, a source of human happiness." He wanted the federal government to take over Muscle Shoals for the common good of the region. The two sides neutralized each other throughout the 1920s in a debate that consumed more congressional hours than any other issue. Muscle Shoals sat idle, while ownership of electric power was concentrated in fewer and fewer hands.

In the first year of the New Deal, the Tennessee Valley Authority Act realized Senator Norris' idea beyond his dreams and began to revolutionize the lives of impoverished southern farmers — not just through electrification but with fertilizer, soil conservation, flood prevention, agricultural tools. In the dirt farms along the Tennessee River, in the wretched homesteads of hollow-eyed men and women and children deformed by rickets, Roosevelt saw a community of yeomen farmers straight out of the eighteenth century. A socially controlled Tennessee Valley would keep people close to the land in the interests of "a balanced civilization" and, by Jefferson's alchemy, turn the rural poor into property-owning American stakeholders, defenders of democracy. Hamiltonian means to Jeffersonian ends: big government would create local initiative and save individualist capitalism. "Is this socialistic?" the President asked *The New York Times*'s Anne O'Hare McCormick, throwing his head back in the Roosevelt laugh.

The TVA's first chair was an engineer of land, water, and human beings named Arthur E. Morgan, who spent years on a biography of the utopian writer Edward Bellamy. Morgan saw the TVA as an exercise in the social transformation of human nature. "There is no traditional line at which men must stop in their efforts to bring order out of a chaos; no limits need be set on our hopes for a more inclusive and masterly synthesis." For him, the aim of this great experiment was nothing less than "the improvement of that total well-being, in physical, social, and economic condition."

My grandfather voted for the TVA but he never said a good word about it. The utopian schemes of bureaucrats and academics made the Southerner in him, the localist, the skeptic, far more suspicious than the possible benefits to Alabama farmers made the humanitarian in him hopeful. Throughout the 1920s he had taken an active role in the debates over Muscle Shoals; when the issue was simply electric power, he was on the side of public ownership. But the TVA, he said, wanted to "be clothed with the authority not only to save men's bodies but to take care of their souls," and he began to smell a new wave of meddlers and carpetbaggers, following on the heels of Yankee soldiers who laid waste to the South, Radical Republicans who punished it, missionaries who reformed it, and New York financiers who bought it. Since the 1890s the federal government had carried the dreams of Populists, Progressives, and other reformers as the singular agent of the people's will. Now, in Huddleston's eyes, Washington became something alien from the people, a burden on them, a threat to freedom and custom even while its bureaucrats "are able to draw around their shoulders the cloak of patriotism — 'I am the defender of the people.' "

By the summer of 1935 my grandfather was in open revolt against Roosevelt. And he drew the line at a now-forgotten piece of New Deal legislation called the Public Utility Holding Company Bill.

"A holding company," said Will Rogers, "is a thing where you hand an accomplice the goods while the policeman searches you." By the 1930s most of the private electric power in America was controlled by thirteen of these elaborate pyramids, some stacking half a dozen layers of investment on top of one another. Almost half the private power was controlled by just three. Holding companies were set up to water stocks and siphon off profits; otherwise they had no managerial function, and many of them yoked together operating companies from halfway across the country. Roosevelt, who had championed public ownership of power as governor of New York, regarded them as parasites on the consumers, archvillains of the business empire. Through interlocking directorates, he believed—echoing La Follette in 1908— eighty men controlled the fate of every American. In the spring of 1935 he called on Congress to end this "system of private socialism."

Quarrels over large principle often turn on minute differences— the narrower the difference, the more fundamental the principle. Huddleston tried to stop the Roosevelt juggernaut over a single section in the hugely complicated Wheeler-Rayburn bill regulating holding companies. Roosevelt supported the Senate version, which in fact had been written by two administration lawyers. This version contained the "death sentence," which would abolish altogether the broadest, least integrated holding companies. Here is how Walter Lippmann described its difference from the House bill, which by June had become the Huddleston bill: "Under the Senate bill the holding company must prove to the [Securities and Exchange] commission and to the courts that it ought not to be dissolved eventually, and under the House bill the commission must prove to the court that the company ought eventually to be dissolved. Either way nothing much can happen until after two new Congresses have been elected. Even then nothing much must happen until a batch of complicated lawsuits have made their weary way through the courts. The struggle has turned upon whether something must, or whether something may, happen five or ten years from now."

But in the summer of 1935 this thimble's worth of difference contained a half century's battle over the regulation of business. The power industry marshaled its vast resources in a propaganda campaign that flooded Congress with telegrams "written" by electricity consumers. Senator Hugo Black, my grandfather's old Alabama nemesis, responded with a very public inquisition into industry lobbyists. Roosevelt threw all the charm and influence he owned into the fight for the "death sentence." For the first time in his presidency, Congress rebelled. And the rebellion was led by the twenty-year veteran from Birmingham, who took his stand on this square inch of hallowed ground, from which he gave two of his greatest speeches in a final doomed cause.

It was a strange choice of cause on which to stake everything. The administration bill, inspired by Brandeis and Frankfurter as part of the "second New Deal," meant a return to the philosophy of smallness, to the antitrust fervor of the Progressive era, to the New Freedom. It sought to break up the largest concentration of economic power in America and restore local control. Lippmann, no friend of the New Deal, called it "the spirit of American individualism in its original form." But Huddleston, fastening on the "death sentence," saw a new threat of political power in Washington that now exceeded even the dangers of economic power. Concentrated power itself was the enemy.

"You would take vengeance, you say, by destroying the holding companies," he told administration supporters in Congress on June 28. "Take vengeance upon whom? On the corporations who are inanimate creatures and without souls? Would you take vengeance upon the corporation officials who were guilty of the misdeeds and wrongs of which you complain? Some of these you would have to pursue into the Great Beyond, and I would suggest that you clothe yourselves with asbestos before you start on the quest . . . What have the hapless investors done that you should take vengeance upon them? What have those who have put their savings of a lifetime into these securities done? What is their offense? What is their crime for which you are seeking to punish them?"

Having raised his voice for the widows whose lives depended on the share price of Commonwealth & Southern, he trained his fire on the two young lawyers sent to Washington by their Harvard law professor, Roosevelt's close advisor, Felix Frankfurter.

"This bill was written by Mr. Benjamin Cohen and Mr. Thomas Corcoran, two bright young men brought down from New York to teach Congress 'how to shoot.' Some of us were here when both were yet in short pants. But these are days when experience and fidelity in public service or in business life are exceedingly 'disqualifying.' I pay them a tribute for the exceeding skill which they have shown in weaving in and weaving out, piling words upon words, phrase upon phrase, clause upon clause, until a Philadelphia lawyer would get down on his knees and pray to be delivered from the task of interpretation."

It was 1918 again. He was taking on his own party's immensely popular President, risking his career in the cause of justice, this small man relishing the role of Goliath slayer—"and neither the imps of darkness nor those who have seen a new light shall move me the breadth of a hair." Now, though, "the little Bolsheviki" had become the champion of the utility industry.

Why did Cohen and Corcoran—"those two 'brain trusters,' those envoys extraordinary, those ambassadors and plenipotentiaries, this firm of 'Cohen & Corcoran,' late of New York, now operating in Washington, telling Congress what to do"—come in for so much of Huddleston's wrath? They represented a profound generational and cultural shift, especially Cohen. He understood the philosophical circle that the New Deal was trying to square: increase individual freedom by increasing central power. "[F]ar-reaching reforms are necessary to preserve that individualism which was achieved in a simpler and less complicated society through laissez-faire." But Cohen understood it in the way of a young Harvard-trained intellectual destined for Washington power—abstractly. His "simpler and less complicated society" was the world that shaped my grandfather, his biases and instincts and values. "Individualism" and "laissez-faire" were ideas to Cohen; but to my grandfather they meant driving a horse-drawn wagon through the Tennessee bluegrass. They meant a world that "far-reaching reforms," intended to preserve it, might actually destroy.

Cohen was an early example of the modern liberal—born into a sophisticated society, wholly identifying with the beneficent power of government, more comfortable with ideas than with "the toiling masses." As such, he was very like the man my grandfather's youngest child, my mother, Nancy, would marry. And as such, he was an alien creature to a man like George Huddleston. After two decades of continuous battle against powerful interests, to be handed a bill written by this young man, to be told that anyone who opposed it was a pawn of the utility industry, was more than my grandfather could endure.

One can almost point to these weeks in Washington, these attacks and counterattacks in Congress over the Holding Company Bill, as the moment when liberalism, reaching the peak of its New Deal heyday, lost its connection to something vital from the past. In the summer of 1935, to the harm of both, liberalism and populism, the brain truster with his briefcase and the one-gallused dirt farmer, parted ways.

The day after his speech, Huddleston was ridiculed on the floor of the House by several members of his own party. The exchange has the bitter flavor of a culmination and an ending, and at its heart lies a fight over the meaning of liberalism itself. When I found the passage in the *Congressional Record*, I felt torn between sympathy for both sides—for my embattled grandfather and for the opponent who asked him all the questions that I would have liked to ask.

With Huddleston strenuously trying and failing to interrupt, Knute Hill of Washington read from the 1917 *Congressional Record* Huddleston's remarks in favor of public ownership of electric power at Niagara Falls.

"This evidently gets under the skin of the gentleman from Alabama," Hill said.

"I want to tell the gentleman from Washington that I stand by every word I said then," Huddleston answered, "and I believe now what I said then, and I stand by it now."

Hill was not to be deterred. "Yesterday he said he was a Thomas Jefferson Democrat. What kind of a Thomas Jefferson Democrat? An Al Smith–Thomas Jefferson Democrat, a Hoover–Thomas Jefferson Democrat, a reactionary Republican Thomas Jefferson Democrat?" Hill read a few more lines from the 1917 speech, then put it aside.

"When shall we follow this Dr. Jekyll and Mr. Hyde of the Democratic Party? When he is a real Thomas Jefferson Democrat? Is it in 1917, when he is pleading the cause of the common people, or is it in 1935, when he is defending the uncontrollable Power Trust?

"Yesterday a large part of the House Membership rose and applauded the gentleman from Alabama when he concluded his remarks. I could not. I sat with bowed head, ashamed and grievously disappointed." The congressman from Washington was moving in for the kill. "The great liberal—yes, the radical of 1917—and I ask Members to judge of this by his own speeches of 20 years ago—George Huddleston, of the United States, was closing his great career as the conservative gentleman from Birmingham, Ala. He has sung his swan song. And how pathetic!"

Finally the floor belonged to George Huddleston. Though his reply was philosophical, he had never endured insult easily and his small frame must have been trembling with rage.

"Men have called me a liberal," he began, "and I was glad to be called that. But always I have called myself a 'Democrat,' an old-fashioned, southern, Jeffersonian Democrat. I claimed that when first I came to the House. I claim that today. It is not my fault if, in the light of the actions and words of men like the gentleman from Washington . . . principles which at one time were considered liberal should now be considered as conservative. My principles and myself remain unchanged—it is the definition of 'liberalism' which has been changed. It is not my fault that I am unable to accompany these courteous gentlemen to the extremes of radicalism and that variety of 'liberalism'—spurious and false liberalism—the 'liberalism' of Mussolini and of Stalin and of Hitler, which they support upon the floor of the House."

So ended the Thomas Jefferson Democrat's swan song.

In the short run, Huddleston emboldened the growing congressional opposition to Roosevelt's heavy-handedness, and the Senate version failed to pass the House. *The New York Times* called it "the most decided legislative defeat dealt to President Roosevelt since he assumed office." The battle dragged on through the heat of July and August. FDR was rumored to be in a state of mental collapse. The bill's Senate sponsor, Burton Wheeler of Montana, wanted Benjamin Cohen to sit in on conference committee sessions. Huddleston was vehemently opposed. In 1924 Wheeler had been La Follette's running mate on the Progressive Party ticket, a spot my grandfather had been considered for as well. Wheeler and Huddleston were longtime allies in the People's Legislative Service, and they shared and admired each other's streak of stubborn independence, which in both carried more than a little vanity. Within five years Wheeler, too, would turn against Roosevelt, but in 1935 he and Huddleston became enemies. My grandfather was now under intense pressure, and when Wheeler promised to campaign against him in the next election they nearly came to blows in the presence of reporters outside the conference committee room.

"You know the utilities don't want an agreement on this bill," Wheeler said. "They want it to die right here."

Huddleston reddened with anger. "They never told me that."

"You know it just the same, and furthermore, you know I know it."

"You are nothing but a grandstander."

Huddleston's wife and children were on vacation in Birmingham, but the Holding Company Bill kept him sweating in Washington all summer. My mother, ten years old now and as fanatically partisan as ever, wrote him: "When are you come down. I hate for you to work when we're having a good time. Some men I hate are up there. For instins Wheeler, Rayburn, and *Rosevelt*. I need (I mean I want) some money about $5.00. I hate to ask for money when you are up there working you're fingers to the bone. I heard Wheeler is going to fight against you next year. Your Loving Daughter, Nancy Huddleston."

But her father was reaching the end of the road.

In late August, after two defeats of the Wheeler-Rayburn bill in the House, Roosevelt finally brought his enormous influence to bear and secured passage of a "compromise" authored by Felix Frankfurter that gave the administration almost everything it wanted. That night FDR celebrated his latest victory at Marwood, Joe Kennedy's estate fourteen miles up the Potomac. Missy LeHand, Roosevelt's secretary-mistress, was there, and after dinner, a movie, and a number of mint juleps, Thomas Corcoran took out his accordion and the President joined in singing "Old George Huddleston ain't what he uster be, ain't what he uster be, ain't what he uster be." The names of other opponents of the Holding Company Bill were filled in. The singing died, and someone said, "Did you know Huddleston once posted his wife for debt?" Cries of horror from the women. The singing started again, Kipling's "Gentleman Rankers." FDR launched into college memories, sailing stories. The party broke up well after midnight.

My parents were members of the generation that grew up knowing no other President. My mother would eventually outgrow her young hatred of "*Rosevelt*," and my father, a thorough product of the New Deal, uncharacteristically slugged another sailor onboard a destroyer in the Pacific when the lout cheered the news of Roosevelt's death. In our house he was an unquestioned hero, and, in my private ranking, the greatest President of all, followed by Lincoln. At eleven I named our new pug puppy after him. I worshiped Roosevelt, partly because I knew that he was crippled and had triumphed spiritually over his crippling—unlike Woodrow Wilson, and unlike my father. Even at eleven I felt that his will to live was stronger, and that this was why the New Deal had succeeded. Not long ago, while I was reading Schlesinger's three-volume history of the Roosevelt years, this feeling returned to me in a dream. I was at a cabinet meeting, and FDR was listening to whatever I had to say with sympathetic attention, but without committing himself. At some point he got up and walked along the table, and I watched closely to see whether he had to support himself (as he did throughout his presidency, at great physical cost, to keep his crippling from the public) against the chair backs and the wall. But he was walking under his own power. His legs were good. This discovery filled me with happiness.

But there was also Roosevelt the aristocrat who bantered with the press about Franklin Jr.'s rowing career at Harvard, the Roosevelt of the merry party at Joe Kennedy's, gloating happily over the defeat of a bypassed southern congressman who had dared to oppose him on principle. And for this Roosevelt—arrogant in his privileges—I can feel, along with my mother at age ten, a little hatred.

My grandfather knew that he would lose in 1936. He had opposed not just the Holding Company Bill but Social Security (on states' rights grounds) and a piece of coal-mining legislation dear to the heart of labor. The administration was against him, the Democratic Party was against him, John L. Lewis of the United Mine Workers was against him. Lewis' lieutenant in Birmingham, an Indiana socialist named William Mitch, was rallying organized labor to oppose their old stalwart who had inexplicably deserted them. This time around, Huddleston's support was strongest in Birmingham's wealthier precincts. As in 1918 he was fighting for his political life, but now everything had been reversed.

It was a nasty campaign, and my grandfather, facing oblivion, contributed his share to the nastiness. For the first time since his original campaign in 1914, race prejudice made an entrance—but this time it came from his side. Huddleston called Mitch a carpetbagger and allowed a prominent supporter to Red-bait and race-bait him. Photographs were published showing an integrated meeting of Mitch's Alabama Federation of Labor and his black colleague Walter Jones. Huddleston's campaign speeches sounded like southern boilerplate. "I am opposed to centralization of authority in Washington, and I am opposed to the robbery of our states. My father fought for the rights of these states to live their lives, and to be free from a central autocracy in Washington, or any Summer resort," he said. "I am an old fogey that the young scorn to fight, although they do not hesitate to insult. But I would bare my thin and ancient breast to die for these principles."

My grandfather had made a crucial slip. Carried away by rhetoric, he put his father in the Confederate gray that he had never worn. Under the pressure of imminent defeat, he revised the family past and redeemed his father's shame.

Huddleston's opponent in the June runoff was an amiable pro–New Deal lawyer and "poet-entertainer" named Luther Patrick, who had a radio program called *Good Mornin' Neighbor*. Patrick wisely refused to engage Huddleston in debate; instead, he said folksy things like "I've been thinking about Old George calling me a jackass. It really ain't so bad, when you take a long view in the matter. For 6000 years this animal has been carrying burdens for the meek and lowly of the earth. And that is all I am asking to do in Congress for the people of my district."

In the final days of the campaign, facing rejection from the "thousands of men who toil with their hands," the "personal friends" who had opened their homes to him and supported him for twenty-two years, my grandfather snapped.

He was eating dinner at a downtown Birmingham restaurant when Luther Patrick came in with several other men. Patrick either thrust a finger in Huddleston's face or else extended his hand to shake. According to my grandfather, he grabbed Patrick's finger ("I naturally assumed he was there for trouble"). According to Patrick, he asked Huddleston why he'd denied boasting that he would win the race with superior money. What happened next is not in dispute: My grandfather, who had exchanged shots over an insult outside a courtroom forty years before, this time chose for his weapon the bottle of Worcestershire sauce sitting on his table. He brought it down on his opponent's straw boater, crushing the hat and his own chances of victory.

The next morning, back in Washington, my mother grabbed the *Post* off the front steps, started searching for the funnies, and instead saw her father's name on the front page. The news of his showdown made her swell with pride. But when Bertha read the article—four years almost to the day after her driving incident was publicized in the same place—she assumed that her reserved and rational husband had had a nervous breakdown.

Within two weeks, at age sixty-six, his career was over.

The family returned to Birmingham in time for the start of the school year. The drive from Washington, according to my aunt Jane, felt like doom. "Our father was defeated," my mother said, "and our mother was tamed." Huddleston sold some of his scrub-pine land and bought property downtown for income. He gave up his simple suits and bow ties and took to wearing old shirts with frayed collars and cuffs; he looked like a hobo. He played hours of solitaire, and at night sometimes he roamed the house with a revolver, imagining prowlers. Once a week he went downtown to the bank and the real estate office and visited friends. His name disappeared from the local press. He didn't lose interest in politics entirely: in 1940 he supported Wendell Willkie, former head of the Commonwealth & Southern utilities corporation, against Roosevelt; by 1948 he was a Dixiecrat. But he had no desire to reenter public life. The wound of political rejection was too personal.

"I had to vote against you," an acquaintance told him one day on the street, "because you'd just gotten out of touch with the world."

"That's your right."

"How does it feel to be out of office after so long?"

"It feels good to be able to tell people like you to go to hell."

Richard Hofstadter wrote of a type of American in whom "the progression from one political position to another" is actually "the continued coexistence of reformism and reaction; and when it takes the form of a progression in time, it is a progression very often unattended by any real change in personal temper." Hofstadter named politicians like the western and midwestern progressives Burton Wheeler, Gerald Nye, and William Lemke, the southern populists Tom Watson, Pitchfork Ben Tillman, and Huey Long, the publisher William Randolph Hearst, the writer Jack London (and he might have added John Dos Passos). George Huddleston's temperament was more restrained than these others', without the demagogic hatreds that disfigured most of them (and his influence was smaller); but in a less spectacular way he fits the type. The difference between attacking J. P. Morgan in the name of labor and Franklin Roosevelt in the name of the individual is not as large as we might think. The unhappy Tennessee boy who swore to be a friend to the poor and oppressed was the same person as the unhappy husband and father who tried to stop the New Deal. His vulnerable pride in family and place, his kinship with common people, his belief in self-rule, his suspicion of every form of concentrated power, his unease with the modern world, his moral strictness, his personal severity, his love of the lonely, honorable, losing cause—these produced large dreams of human brotherhood, and a sharp sense of human failing. Idealism and disbelief sprang from the same source.

One by one the Huddleston children left home. My mother stayed longest, caring for her father until she was thirty-two. By then he was eighty-eight, a very old man who was beginning to lose his wits. But near the end they had what my mother called the most honest conversation of their lives.

"Mary only loves me," he said, "because I'm her father."

"That's not true," she said. "Do you only love her because you're her father?"

"Yes, I love her because she's my daughter."

"And George?"

"Same."

"John?"

"Same."

"Jane?"

"No, I really love Jane."

"Me?"

"Yes, I love you because you're my daughter."

He had told her what she already knew, and she was grateful.

Then she decided to marry a Jewish man who had just begun teaching law across the country at Stanford University, in California. Her father warned her against it. A mixed couple would have problems, he said, especially in the South; there would be places where they would not be welcome.

His campaign against his daughter's marriage was George Huddleston's last fight. Like most of the other fights in his career, he lost it, and lost his last daughter with it. This, of course, had been his real objection all along. But he was about to slip away into senility. My mother and father were married in the house on Birmingham's South Side. Then they left to start a life together out on the West Coast.

George Huddleston finally died, at age ninety, on February 29, 1960. Six months later I was born and given his name.

PART 2:

THE SUNLIGHT
of
REASON

CHAPTER 5

◆

A Modern Jew

I have my father's childhood pictures spread out before me. His mouth is full-lipped, and he wears his belt too high up his chubby belly; he looks handsome but physically graceless. He is a shy dark-featured little boy who seems to age thirty years in a dozen. By his early teens he has already become the steady-eyed intellectual he remained for most of his life. In some ways he seems older at thirteen than at forty-three, after his stroke, when fear widened and moistened his eyes so that they began to resemble once again the little boy's, looking out on a world they hadn't mastered. In family snapshots his stout mother is always smiling, her arm linked in her son's, her hands on her little daughter's shoulders; but neither father nor son smiles.

My mother's lineage ran back to the South, the Civil War, the early republic, strongly printed by regional character and national history. My father's is lost in the mud near the Polish-Ukraine border, one of the world's geographically doomed places, in the Jewish ghetto of Zhitomir. It begins to emerge into historical light around the time that Populism was catching fire in Alabama, when the first generation left for steerage and New York. The second generation worked hard and obscurely to climb into the lower middle class. The third generation, my father's, cut itself off at the roots to live by the free uses of the mind. And for many years, he needed nothing else.

His father, Abraham, was an immigrant milk peddler's son, born in 1896 in Hell's Kitchen, New York, and raised among Jewish gangsters, including one bank robber who died in a shoot-out with police. Abraham was a small, quiet, depressed man with spectacles perched on a large balding head. He took a degree in veterinary medicine but, without enough money to set up a practice, he had to go to work for the Department of Agriculture as a meat inspector. Instead of caring for live animals, he spent long hours going from slaughterhouse to slaughterhouse, approving or rejecting suspended carcasses. Education hadn't freed him from the coarse world of his ancestors, the old trade of kosher inspection transplanted to a secular government job, the same smell of fresh blood and cold meat. Abraham's line of work turned his son's complexion green on the rare occasions when my father accompanied him.

With the Depression, Abraham had to uproot the family from the New York area and found meat inspection work in a series of New England towns where there were few other Jews. The isolation and constant moving oppressed his wife, Lillian. She had been born in Lithuania into a family of rabbis, intellectually and socially superior to her husband, and in these New England towns she tried to set up Hadassah groups and reading clubs. But she poured most of her energy into her son, with a sickly and frustrated woman's anxiety and ambition. He seemed to remain a lonely only child even after his sister came along when he was seven.

My father read and read. His mother gave him the taste for books, and to escape her suffocating embrace and his father's fleshbound misery he fled into them. By age eleven, he once told my mother, he had reached almost his maximum height and done almost all his important reading. Once, when his mother and sister showed up at his summer camp with blueberry muffins, they couldn't find young Herb participating in any of the group activities. They finally came upon him sitting by himself behind a tree with a sack of books, and took him home.

My father's early pictures speak of loneliness. The loneliness of a family of Jews who left the teeming New York metropolis for tree-lined towns in New Hampshire and Vermont and Connecticut where their community was sparse; the loneliness of the studious boy who grew up without stickball and soapboxes and Yiddish and PS 123.

But really the pictures are silent. They tell no story. In the mother and father—my grandparents—I see nothing of myself except in my grandmother's mouth, feel not even a faint pulse of connection. They are strangers who died a decade before my birth. My mother's family left behind written records, a store of anecdotes about their loud and battling clan, tombstones with names like Andrew Jackson Huddleston; I don't remember my father mentioning his parents, not once, as if the silence shrouded some deep family shame. But there was no shame—only, perhaps, the shame of particulars. My father inherited from his forebears a dark complexion, vulnerable arteries, and the Talmudic habit of study, and discarded the rest. Far more real to him than the leafy clapboarded lower-middle-class house in Hamden or the smell of his mother's hair or the Hebrew words of his Bar Mitzvah was the tradition that he willed to be his own: the tradition of the mind, of Locke and Madison and Mill and Dewey. He rushed into the embrace of the twentieth century bearing the texts of enlightenment. He cast his own and his ancestral past into oblivion. For him, ideas were the ultimate reality.

For all these reasons—because he told no stories, because his parents were buried in deep silence, because ethnicity and region and faith had no claim on him, because I was too young to ask, and because he is dead—my father, at heart, remains unknowable to me. So I have to piece together words and actions and contexts. As the 1930s give way to the '40s and then the '50s, he starts to emerge in letters and scraps of anecdote, fading in from the blur of his past, then growing more corporeal in the '60s, in dim fragmentary memories, a sort of background noise of my early childhood; finally, after his stroke, he arrives directly before me with sudden and terrible vividness. But the inner man continues to elude me.

No one is completely free, and those who live as if they are can be most ruled by the accident of birth. We don't choose our parents, our biology, or our history. Stroke was a part of my father's inheritance, coded into his brain by some gene on the depressive Y chromosome. So was the twentieth century. His future father-in-law, George Huddleston, was shaped by the nineteenth, the century of self-made men. My father was born into an age of large institutions, none larger or more significant than the federal government. Through economic depression and world war, Washington was no longer a remote rumor but a given, its hand felt in almost every important passage of his life. It had replaced the Protestant church and the republican meetinghouse as the seat of reason, the main expression of liberal democracy and the human aspiration toward perfection. The world that my grandfather ended his career trying to turn back was the world that my father grew up accepting.

In an interview just before his stroke in 1969, he contrasted his own generation with that of the student radicals: "My generation, by and large I think, is composed of people who believe in the power of the human mind to cope with problems. We take a very operational view. We don't think that slogans are really going to solve anything, and we think that the patient, slow, steady, one-step-at-a-time approach in the end gets results. That, I think, is largely the result of the fact that we grew up during a depression and a war, and we're much less used to instant solutions to problems."

The postwar sociologist C. Wright Mills, who would become a hero to the generation of 1960s radicals, gave liberalism as short and comprehensive an account as any I know: he called it "the control through reason of man's fate." My father's faith in "the power of the human mind to cope with problems" came out of the Enlightenment and had lain at the heart of the democratic revolution in America. But by the time his generation came of age, it no longer meant what it had meant to Jefferson and his heirs. They had located this power in the common man—in the plowman who could solve a moral case as well as or better than a professor. Jefferson, himself the most abstract-minded of politicians, nonetheless held a deep conviction that the virtues required of citizens in a democracy were available to the lowest-born. This allowed him to bridge the great American divide between intellectuals and common people. But in the twentieth century, as intellectuals became a powerful social class, the divide split wide open, putting men like my father on one influential but isolated side. He believed in the power of the mind—believed in little else—but he meant the educated mind. He belonged to a meritocratic age, became its beneficiary, and put his faith in special knowledge, in expertise—"a very operational view." The implications of this change from my Jeffersonian grandfather would be profound.

My father's faith in rational human progress took hold early. A letter from a teenaged Marxist friend named Ray, written April 4, 1941, preached the virtues of the Soviet Union and exhorted fifteen-year-old Herb to oppose Roosevelt's war policy: "You said, 'It would be taking at base a pessimistic view of mankind to state that more advanced forms of government should be brought in by sudden revolutionary means.'—When you find an insect on your arm, do you spend a long time getting rid of it? It makes no difference if the insect is a mosquito or capitalism." Two months later, Hitler would invade Russia and Ray, in a party-line about-face, would have to embrace his liberal gradualist friend's position on the war. Within three years my father would enlist to fight in it.

Fall of 1941: a few months before Pearl Harbor, and just sixteen, my father entered Yale. As a Jew and a local boy (by then he lived in Hamden, just east of New Haven, in a house on Ridge Road that I passed without knowing, without wanting to know, dozens of times on runs when I was in college), he had to clear the highest obstacles to gain admission. The meritocratic idea hadn't yet become an article of elite faith; Yale was still dominated by the old-boy connections that had led George Huddleston during World War I to lump the university with the country's "natural enemies of democracy." In the early 1940s Yale and the other top universities were still enforcing unofficial quotas on Jewish students that dated back to the '20s, when Ivy League presidents began to notice that their Jewish enrollment was rising alarmingly—at Yale, to a high of 13.3 percent in 1927.

In 1922 President Abbott Lawrence Lowell of Harvard made the mistake of raising the Jewish problem publicly, and the bad press that followed taught the other presidents to solve it quietly, behind the scenes. At Yale the job was left to the chair of the Admissions Board, Robert Corwin, who reported in a 1922 memorandum: "The opinion is general in the Faculty that the proportion of those in college whose racial elements are such as not to permit of assimilation has been exceeded and that the most noticeable representatives among those regarded as undesirable are the Jewish boys, especially those of local origin." Corwin's solution, which remained secret for decades, was called the "Limitation on Numbers" policy. In a strange way it echoed some of the arguments and strategies that had arisen in 1901 when delegates to Alabama's constitutional convention were trying to figure out how to disfranchise the state's black voters. At Yale, as in Montgomery, the authorities had a problem: how to justify doing something that couldn't be done under its rightful name. At Yale the problem was PR, not the Fourteenth and Fifteenth Amendments (a private university had no constitutional constraints on admission; the Alabama delegates had no constraints on what they dared to say), but in both cases the solution drew on the eighteenth century and the republican idea of citizenship to justify excluding a minority.

"While many of these Hebrew boys are fine students, I think the general effect on the scholastic standing is bad," the college dean observed in 1922. Jews ("the 'greasy grind' ") performed so well that they devalued academic achievement in the eyes of the beanies and raccoon-skin coats. In the words of one Yale psychologist, Jews "are more or less in the nature of a foreign body in the class organism." They could be brilliant students but their "characters" were often doubtful, and in determining its student body under the new numerical limits Yale's administration chose to put the education of the citizen of good character on a higher level than scholarship.

In 1923 Yale announced a general restriction on the number of entering freshmen. The top qualifiers would still get in on the basis of academic strength, but the borderline candidates would now be subject to a character test: such virtues as "manliness, uprightness, cleanliness, native refinement, etc.," would go into the admissions mix, guaranteeing that Jews and other undesirables would be weeded out without any declared policy of anti-Semitism. There would even be something like Alabama's "Fighting Grandfather Clause": a provision that the "limitation on numbers shall not operate to exclude any son of a Yale graduate who has satisfied all the requirements for admission."

So a little over a century after the founding of Jefferson's University of Virginia, the country's leading universities invoked the old republican virtues in order to keep out the "brain specimens" and "greasy grinds" swarming across the Ivy League from Eastern Europe. By 1923 civic character meant being a good Yale man. Six years earlier, when the Yale Club of New York—"We men of Yale"—had demanded war and conscription, my Alabama grandfather (BA nonexistent, LlB Cumberland University, 1891) had called them "the most reactionary sources in the United States." Two decades later, my Jewish father would seek to join them.

The hypocrisy of Yale's public stance on its Jewish problem could be taken as a sign of social progress in the decades since the Montgomery convention. No one announced openly that the purpose of the Limitation on Numbers policy was "to establish Christian supremacy in this university." In private, though, Yale's leaders expressed their feelings without constraint. President James Angell wrote in a letter to Corwin just a few weeks before Hitler took power in 1933: "If we could have an Armenian massacre confined to the New Haven district, with occasional incursions into Bridgeport and Hartford, we might protect our Nordic stock almost completely."

Eight years later my father was the most undesirable of Jewish applicants: educated in the local public schools, relatively poor, a scholarship boy who passed the entrance exam at a precocious age. Socially, he had everything going against him. He was short, plump, dark, handsome against the prevailing WASP type, and brilliant enough to be admitted in spite of everything. The interwar Yale of George Bush, Skull and Bones, social successes who "exuded shoe," was still a snob's stronghold. President Roosevelt, who presided from his wheelchair like a benign divinity over my father's youth, was widely hated among the Yale elite: author of the "Jew Deal," his administration filled with Hebrews, rumored to have a strain of tribal blood himself. Yale was near the bottom of the Ivy League in Jewish enrollment. Three-quarters of its student body came from private schools. Jews were automatically housed together. The college faculty had not one tenured Jewish professor (and wouldn't until 1950). Under the "gentleman's agreement" Jews weren't openly shunned, but the price of a limited equality was the submergence of Jewish identity and the acceptance that certain elite domains remained off-limits. By this time Yale had gone public with a new policy that would result, unacknowledged, in more anti-Jewish restrictions. It raised enrollment from states outside the Northeast where Jews were few, in the name of "geographical balance"—which we now call diversity.

But the atmosphere was about to change. Within a few months of my father's entrance, war was declared against Japan and Germany, and soon after that the campus was overrun with soldiers in training whose presence effected a rapid democratization. Waiter service gave way to cafeteria lines, military uniforms leveled distinctions of dress, the number of boys admitted from public schools surged. The common fascist enemy and the need for fighting men made the old social connections seem comparatively trivial—at least, less vital to success. The great wartime rise of meritocracy was underway.

How did this Jewish boy, still in his teens, pass through an elite bastion in those years? By studying hard; by joining the highbrow Elizabethan Club and the eating club Mory's; by making friends with Gentiles as well as Jews; by writing an essay called "The Perfect State," a survey of utopian philosophy, in which he exulted, "It commands us to blend emotion and intellect into one glowing creative unity, into a Moral Absolute which will blaze over and illuminate the future by the light of its flaming torch." He didn't embrace the WASP world, but he didn't reject it either. Reason was the universal solvent of differences.

And yet, among his papers I found a letter written in the last year of his life to an old college friend that suggests a world of slights: "I have a good deal more affection for Yale Law School, which really gave me a good education. I don't mean that Yale College did not, but the scars of that exposure to anti-Semitism remain." Other than this passing reference, the scars remained hidden. My father shunned not only religious belief but a sense of group identity or grievance or memory.

On April 10, 1944, eighteen years old and just short of graduation, my father resigned from Yale College and applied for a commission in the U.S. Navy (he would only rise as high as petty officer). He was 4-F because of a knee injury and had to have surgery before he could qualify.

I have his dog tags, which hung around his neck for almost two years—a pair of thin metal wafers tied to an orange-and-blue braided plastic strap, stamped: "Herbert Leslie Packer, 899-00-37, T5/44TYPE-O, USNR-SV/H." And I have his letters home, written on U.S. Navy letterhead from training camps and bases in upstate New York, the Gulf Coast, California; and then, starting in December 1944, from the Pacific onboard the destroyer USS *Bailey*, overcrowded with 15 officers and 300 men. He wrote dozens of them, most addressed to his mother. He worries about losing touch with the world and asks for subscriptions to *Partisan Review, Harper's, Foreign Affairs, The New Republic*, and a dozen other magazines. June 21, 1944: "Dear Mother, If all you can manage is 5 subscriptions, O.K. Don't worry about my not having enough time to devote to them. My evenings are completely free. After all, I can't let my mind rot completely. It's all I've got to get along on, you know . . . I'm damned if I want the war to get in my way any more than it has to, and I consider it a real setback to give in on anything like that." (In April 1944, the month my father enlisted, Saul Bellow's first novel, *Dangling Man*, appeared, in which the diarist-narrator says of the war for which he's waiting to be called up: "I would like to see it as an incident. . . . A very important one; perhaps the most important that has ever occurred. But, still, an incident. Is the real nature of the world changed by it? No. Will it decide, ultimately, the major issues of existence? No. Will it rescue us spiritually? Still no.")

October 19, 1944, from Shoemaker Naval Base near San Francisco, after receiving news of an unstable cousin's discharge from war service into a VA hospital: "I'm sorry to hear about [him], but not particularly surprised. He always struck me as having a very weak character, enfeebled all the more by his mother's excessive pampering. It was only natural that when he was cast upon his own resources, he wasn't quite up to it. Liquor, I suppose, seemed the handiest way out of his troubles. Needless to say, you don't have to have any fears on my account. It has always seemed to me that alcoholism and similar maladies rise out of an individual's inability to cope with the conditions of his environment, and the consequent need for a method of escape. Thanks to my upbringing, I don't worry about that. Without being a prig, I do think that I have a sufficiently strong sense of what is befitting to a gentleman to safeguard me from any such easy way out as I gather [he] has taken. As difficult as things get, I am confident of my ability to face up to them and see them through. And you ought to know that what gives me that confidence is a good education, good friends, and—above all—good parents. With such a mother and father, such friends, and such a university to live up to, I can hardly go wrong."

He sounds like a prig; like a son reassuring his parents on the eve of going to war; like a newly appointed quartermaster in the U.S. Navy; like a young man who doesn't know himself. In his Navy snapshots— posing in cramped quarters with his shipmates, sleeves rolled up, a corncob pipe stuck jauntily in the corner of his mouth—he looks bored and tough. He would not let the rigors and ennuis of the Pacific undermine him any more than Yale had. The war, and the military's inanities (the most vivid letter describes several days without sleep spent scraping barnacles off the *Bailey*'s hull and polishing its brass under the western Pacific sun after months at sea and in combat), forced a premature and self-protective hardness on teenagers. The bookish Jews perhaps had more to protect themselves from than the Southerners and Irish Catholics with whom they were thrown together in an alien masculine world. After the war my father wrote a short story with the Forsterian title and theme "The Undeveloped Heart," about the thwarted relationship between an admiring younger sailor and an older one who spurns him. Even with its hard-boiled naturalistic prose, the story betrays its author's sense of being unloving and unloved. When this little fish gets put back in water, just watch him swim!" The wartime generation of Jews acquired a certain tone of voice—dry, tough-minded, analytically aggressive, sometimes arrogant—that marked them as they aged, a tone born of the ambitions and hidden wounds of this famously self-confident generation of immigrants' children, hungry to lay their claim on the vast postwar American possibilities.

Unlike my grandfather, my father seems to have suffered no physical or emotional breakdown in uniform, even after enduring months of combat in a war he later called "the last of the just wars, maybe." "Mentally I'm sort of hibernating, these days," my father wrote home after seeing action off Zamboanga and Legaspi in the Philippines. "Less wear and tear that way. Don't worry about it, though."

The only part of my father's life that interested me as a boy was his war experience, but the subject never came up unless I asked about it. He obliged me with so little embellishment that I came away with just two pieces of information: that his hand had been wounded during a Japanese aerial attack (this in answer to a direct question about war wounds) and that when word of President Roosevelt's death reached the ship and another sailor cheered the news, my father punched him. The hand wound came as a disappointment—not his face or guts? How could an air attack wound someone's hand? And the punch seemed and still seems so out of character that I wonder whether I've remembered it wrong. He was much more forthcoming about the nature of fascism, or the importance of the Anglo-American alliance, or the legal charade of the Nuremberg trials, or, even farther afield, the tragedy of Woodrow Wilson's League of Nations, than he was with his own war stories. Here was his best chance to impress his ten-year-old, World War II–obsessed son, and he passed it up. By then he was crippled and volatile, and I didn't press him.

John Stuart Mill was one of my father's early heroes—liberalism's great philosopher, high priest of the nineteenth-century faith in freedom. My father's whole legal framework was based on Mill's famous dictum that the only justifiable use of coercive power is "to prevent harm to others." Mill was educated by two philosophers—his father, James Mill, and Mill's friend Jeremy Bentham—according to Utilitarian principles. He was raised to be a perfectly rational man. He was reading Greek at three; at eleven (the age when my father was devouring the New Haven public library), Mill was assigned to read out loud his father's *History of India* and compare the account of Indian and English societies, while critiquing England's as it was and should be. And at twenty—the age when my father was scraping barnacles off the *Bailey*—John Stuart Mill had a nervous breakdown.

In his *Autobiography* he describes it as "one of those moods when what is pleasure at other times, becomes insipid or indifferent." In this gloom Mill asked himself a nearly fatal question: " 'Suppose that all your objects in life were realized; that all the changes in institutions and opinions which you are looking forward to, could be completely effected at this very instant: would this be a great joy and happiness to you?' And an irrepressible self-consciousness distinctly answered, 'No!' At this my heart sank within me: the whole foundation on which my life was constructed fell down."

Mill considered suicide. His entire life up to that point had been shaped by the Utilitarian principle that happiness lay in working toward social reforms that would benefit the greatest number of people along rational lines. Instead, his education had brought him to a dead end, seemingly incapable of feeling. He confided this "crisis in my mental history" to no one—least of all his philosopher father, who "had no knowledge of any such mental state as I was suffering from." Mill doesn't acknowledge that it was his father who had led him to this dark place, but the implication is clear. "I now saw, or thought I saw, what I had always before received with incredulity—that the habit of analysis has a tendency to wear away the feelings."

This passage in the *Autobiography*, where Mill applies all of his analytical power to understand the failure of analysis to make him happy, concludes with a redemptive moment: "a small ray of light broke in upon my gloom. I was reading, accidentally, Marmontel's Memoirs, and came to the passage which relates his father's death, the distressed position of the family, and the sudden inspiration by which he, then a mere boy, felt and made them feel that he would be everything to them—would supply the place of all that they had lost. A vivid conception of the scene and its feelings came over me, and I was moved to tears. From this moment my burthen grew lighter. The oppression of the thought that all feeling was dead within me, was gone. I was no longer hopeless: I was not a stock or a stone."

In order to feel again, young Mill had to kill off his father. Utilitarianism had nearly killed him, and with this crisis he began to break from his father's and Bentham's doctrine. Happiness, he decided, couldn't be an end in itself, but only the by-product of other pursuits: the happiness of others, poetry, music, the cultivation of the feelings. One outcome of his nervous breakdown, thirty-three years later, was *On Liberty*, the most important book in my father's intellectual development.

Why does this story make me think of my father?

Because his education, though directed from within, was almost as precocious as Mill's. Because he believed with Mill in "unchecked liberty of thought, unbounded freedom of individual action in all modes not hurtful to others; but also, convictions as to what is right and wrong, useful and pernicious, deeply engraven on the feelings by early education and general unanimity of sentiment, and so firmly grounded in reason and in the true exigencies of life, that they shall not, like all former and present creeds, religious, ethical, and political, require to be periodically thrown off and replaced by others." Because, as with Mill, these convictions brought enormous pressure to bear on his mind ("It's all I've got to get along on, you know"), the pressure to figure things out without the help of any "former and present creeds," without givens. Because it made them both unhappy young men. Because he was alienated from his father. And because I wish that the long months at sea on the *Bailey*, the boredom and fear and the intellectual void, had produced a crisis in my father's mental history when he was Mill's age, twenty—when an "undeveloped heart" could have survived it and grown.

After the war my father's trail goes cold.

He disappeared into the great reverse migration of veterans (some, like him, barely into their twenties) who returned to school on the GI Bill. He entered Yale Law School, which had long been more open to Jews than the college—there was no such thing as a "Yale Law Man." Academic achievement determined admission and law review positions; half the members of the *Yale Law Journal* were Jews, and there were three Jewish tenured law professors. Since the days of Brandeis, law schools had generally functioned as meritocracies, and so they became pathways to Jewish success before medical schools and English departments opened their doors.

My father was admitted to the New York bar, clerked for a year in the 2nd Circuit, then joined Lloyd Cutler's liberal firm in Washington. When he moved to D.C. he left behind a young woman named Barbara who was studying medieval literature at Brown. In breaking off with her he must have expressed unhappiness about his capacity for love; in a letter, Barbara took the blame on herself, referring to her own "clinging femininity." She reassured him about his skills as a lover and joked that she'd never had a chance to give him the tie she'd made. Her letter has the tone of the postwar years, striving to be grown-up and ironic about a tangle of emotions she could hardly sort out.

When I turned twenty-four I had just come back from service in West Africa with the Peace Corps and was working on a construction crew in Boston, having no idea about my future. By twenty-four my father had fought in a war, earned a law degree, and begun a career. His name was on the masthead of Cox, Langford, Stoddard & Cutler. No prolonged adolescence for this generation—the course of his professional life was set. The young men posing in coats and ties for his law school class photo look freighted with responsibility. They've gone through depression and war and now cold war and world power, and there isn't much playfulness in their faces, or cockiness either. They wear heavy black shoes and charcoal suits and their mouths are set and their eyes strained. They are trying terribly hard to be men, and perhaps for this reason their faces don't betray any obvious age. Twenty-five? Forty? Maybe both, because the war and the GI Bill scrambled higher education and threw it wide open. And unlike George Huddleston, who took his law degree in nine months at age twenty-one and then ventured forth to set up his own practice in raw young Birmingham, my father followed the pattern of his generation by joining the world of big institutions: a Washington law firm, the federal government (he became a consultant to the Wage and Price Stabilization Board), and a large foundation (he worked on projects funded by an offshoot of the Ford Foundation).

The mental atmosphere of the late 1940s: the sense of having been thrust too young under too many burdens, of life being a serious business with no time for "finding yourself," of the world situation as one endless crisis with the constant threat of dire consequences. You see it in the black-and-white newsreels showing Communist advances across Europe and Asia, cartoon lightning bolts jagging across an illuminated sky and the creeping black oil of Soviet conquest, narrated by an unrelievedly grim announcer's voice over a harsh score, with none of the whimsy of those newsreels Dos Passos ran in *U.S.A.*: "STARS PORTEND EVIL FOR COOLIDGE," "BROADWAY BEAUTY

BEATEN." You hear the harsh new voice in political campaign slogans—no more folksy anecdotes about "Little George" and "the man
and the dollar"; now candidates accuse their opponents of softness and
treason. You find the new moral style in the turn Hollywood takes
toward "message" pictures—movies like *All the King's Men,* about
political corruption; *The Men,* about paralyzed GIs; *The Lost Weekend,*
about alcoholism; and *Gentleman's Agreement,* about anti-Semitism.
The wisecracks of screwball comedy have mostly died, and the studio
movies that continue to keep the formula alive, like Frank Capra's
political comedy *State of the Union* with Tracy and Hepburn, seem
badly dated. When there's humor in the message movies, it's tense;
repression is the operative psychological mode, alcohol the chief outlet. The men have buried the trauma of the war, the women have married them and settled down too fast.

These movies try hard to treat the audience like grown-ups. The
world-renowned physicist Professor Lieberman informs Gregory Peck
and Dorothy McGuire in *Gentleman's Agreement* that he is going to
launch a "crusade" to declare that he isn't Jewish, because he has no
religious belief and Jews aren't a race. "There must be millions of people nowadays who are religious only in the vaguest sense. I've often
wondered why the Jewish ones among them still go on calling themselves Jews. Can you guess why, Mr. Green?" Gregory Peck can't guess
why. "Because the world still makes it an advantage not to be one.
Thus for many of us it becomes a matter of pride to go on calling ourselves Jews. So you see, I will have to abandon my crusade before it
begins. Only if there were no anti-Semites could I go on with it." Moss
Hart's lines expressed almost exactly what Jean-Paul Sartre was saying
at much greater length in *Réflexions sur la question juive,* which was
being serialized in *Partisan Review* and *Commentary* that same year.

Gentleman's Agreement is a revealing marker of the postwar mood,
weighted with a dark sense of the possibility of justice. Gregory Peck is
a magazine writer who can't find an "angle" on an assignment to write
about anti-Semitism—until he remembers how he once wrote about
Okies and coal miners: by becoming one. Now he'll become Jewish, to

see how it plays in Darien. It doesn't play well, and Peck is such a "solemn fool" about what ought to be a "practical matter" that he jeopardizes his engagement to a nice divorcée from Darien who doesn't quite have the social courage of her convictions. Peck's Jewish friend, played by John Garfield (né Julius Garfinkle), brings the postwar news to the fiancée: "Lots of things are pretty rough, Kathy. This is just a different kind of war." And yet the Holocaust, barely two years past, is never mentioned—just as Saul Bellow's novel about anti-Semitism, *The Victim*, which appeared the same year as the film, doesn't mention it. The liberal mind could not accept, let alone explain, its enormity, and so for years the Holocaust remained fragmentary and unfocused in the numbed consciousness of even the most alert American Jews. "The great psychological fact of our time which we all observe with baffled wonder and shame," Lionel Trilling wrote in those years, "is that there is no possible way of responding to Belsen and Buchenwald." It took almost two decades for the Holocaust to be approached head-on in American culture.

Perhaps as a kind of displacement, the subject of *Gentleman's Agreement* is anti-Semitism among the kind of attractive and moneyed society people who filled the screen in the 1930s without having their prejudices scrutinized. But Gregory Peck won't let them get away with it anymore. It's hard to imagine a more morally earnest leading man (by contrast, he seems rather easygoing fifteen years later confronting another kind of prejudice in *To Kill a Mockingbird*). Every scene of the movie shows the world that took shape after the war: the pull of the suburbs for veterans with young families; the cocktail party; the politics of the large Manhattan office (Peck would incarnate the 1950s corporate type a few years later in *The Man in the Gray Flannel Suit*). The change in Peck's journalistic assignment from his Depression-era ones is also telling: from life among the down-and-outs to social prejudice in the suburbs. Popular Front-era perorations to the common man have gone the way of the Soviet myth. Professor Lieberman's speech with all its nuances lacks the blunt passion of Henry Fonda's "Wherever there's a fight so hungry people can eat, I'll be there" at the end of

The Grapes of Wrath. The burning issue is no longer class. Half a century of political combat between the haves and have-nots—from Populism and Progressivism to the New Deal and Truman's Fair Deal—was coming to a close. The presidential election of 1948 was the last in almost half a century to be fought along lines of economic interest.

By mid-century the central issues had changed, and the election of 1952 began what we can now see as an era in which class gave way to social issues. The political age in which most Americans alive today grew up began with the first Eisenhower-Stevenson race, which pitted the politician my father loathed, Richard Nixon, the Communist hunter, against the one he loved, Adlai Stevenson, a new kind of liberal. It was characteristic of my father that the hatred got more passionate airtime than the love.

Perhaps because the New Deal proved so successful that not even the Republicans in power could undo it, and perhaps because the eruptions of working-class politics in the 1930s went the way of agrarian Populism, by the 1950s liberalism had lost its hard edge. It had become a governing ideology, which guaranteed abundance to all players who accepted the rules of the twenty-year Democratic reign: labor-management consensus, the Keynesian policies of spending and growth, the concentration of power in large institutional hands, the fact of the welfare state. The postwar boom was on, fueled by the "permanent war economy," and it appeared endless. The New Deal bureaucracies were in place to manage it. In other words, by 1950 the bread-and-butter issues had been decided and liberalism began to sing other, softer songs. Populism was long dead; socialism had lived a short and feverish life, but it too lay exhausted with self-inflicted wounds. The early century's utopian flames were adjusted to low on a million new Westinghouse stovetops.

What remained was corporate liberalism, the creed of foundation presidents and labor union bosses. The whole premise of Arthur

Schlesinger, Jr.'s three-volume history of the New Deal—a kind of imperial chronicle from a late-coming court sympathizer—is that the welfare state solved so many human problems that nothing imaginable could replace it. The only requirement was skillful management from the centers of power. Schlesinger was aware of the risks of complacency, and he wrote a book—*The Vital Center* (1949)—and a number of articles arguing for ways to revitalize liberalism. Unfortunately, he was never able to make the case convincingly—perhaps because he was prone to complacency himself. *The Vital Center*, for all its talk of "the revival of American radicalism," was basically a manifesto of the status quo, advocating "limited state power," with neither too much nor too little class conflict, claiming "a moderate pessimism about man" that fell philosophically somewhere between Dark Age conservatism and Communist utopianism. Schlesinger tried to draw a straight line between his Democratic heroes, connecting Jefferson and Jackson to FDR and Truman, without realizing that, in the name of the people, the welfare state had already created a new establishment in Washington that couldn't quite speak on behalf of the "humble members of society—the farmers, mechanics, and laborers" with the same ringing conviction as Old Hickory. He didn't even seem to grasp that he himself was a leading member of this new establishment.

A few years later, in an article in *The Reporter*, Schlesinger contrasted the old "quantitative liberalism" with the new "qualitative liberalism": "Today we dwell in the economy of abundance—and our spiritual malaise seems greater than before. As a nation, the richer we grow, the more tense, insecure, and unhappy we seem to become. Yet too much of our liberal thought is still mired in the issues, the attitudes, and the rallying cries of the 1930's." The concern of liberalism in the new era should be "the *quality* of civilization to which our nation aspires in an age of ever-increasing abundance and leisure." This vague notion of "quality" encompassed civil rights and civil liberties, urban planning and rural beautification, mass media and popular culture—but not jobs, poverty, or the old war against bigness.

If quality of civilization had replaced equality of wealth and power as the main task of liberalism, the need for intellectuals became obvious. This change of emphasis put in their hands a claim of potentially great value that they would cash in during the Kennedy years, with Schlesinger himself leading the way. By the early 1950s intellectuals were coming into their own as a privileged class, no longer living on air in cold-water Greenwich Village walk-ups, but scattered and comfortably ensconced in research universities and think tanks and laboratories and government agencies. Many former radicals were beginning to make their peace with American capitalism. Like any upwardly mobile group, they wanted their share of social distinction. And they had their own brand of politics. "After twenty years," Richard Hofstadter wrote in 1954, "the New Deal liberals have quite unconsciously taken on the psychology of those who have entered into possession."

The overriding issue of the postwar era for these liberal arrivistes, and for my father, was not economic justice but civil liberties. The Communist hunts of the late '40s and early '50s forced the issue on them, and it became a matter of principle and decency to defend not just the innocent and the "guilty by association" but even those guilty of onetime membership in the Communist Party from destruction by congressional investigation, press sensation, and criminal trial. Though the question of, say, Alger Hiss's guilt or innocence of espionage drove the public debate, it was the vicious manner of his relentless pursuit by Congressman Richard Nixon and the House Un-American Activities Committee that infuriated people like my father—the same way Nixon would conduct his political campaigns in those years, as in later years.

But as an issue, civil liberties also suited the temperament and self-interest of liberal intellectuals, and it exposed the weakness of their rising position. In demanding virtues like restraint, sophisticated judgment, distinction-making, adherence to abstractions, it divided intellectuals from their original allies in the New Deal coalition, those farmers and workers who were less likely to see why some Harvard-trained professor with alien ideas and dubious masculinity ought to be allowed to use his well-paid position to attack the American way of life.

Civil liberties had no plebeian appeal. Intellectuals had to look for allies elsewhere, in some cases among the patricians, with whom they were culturally more comfortable anyway. The old antagonism toward Wall Street now paled in comparison with the fear of Senator McCarthy's mob rule. A new crop of scholars traced McCarthyism with its demagogic excesses directly back to the Populist revolt of the 1890s.

My father's idea of liberty—the modern liberal's—differed from my grandfather's in a crucial way. George Huddleston understood it in eighteenth-century terms, as self-government. Liberty had value in the context of a republic, and it implied the duties as well as rights of citizenship. But my father's liberty was procedural, taking the individual in isolation. A modern liberal looked to the courts for liberty, just as he looked to the federal government for equality. A Jeffersonian like my grandfather had looked to the popular will for both. So in the late '40s and early '50s, when defenders of civil liberties claimed that the Communist investigations violated the First and Fifth Amendments, they still had no substantive answer to the right-wing charge that they were weakening American democracy by defending its opponents.

As part of his new Washington law practice my father defended, pro bono, government employees—accused Communists and fellow travelers—charged under the Truman administration's 1947 loyalty-security executive order. Then, on a grant from the Fund for the Republic (an offshoot of the Ford Foundation that emphasized civil rights and liberties), he and several other lawyers compiled the accounts in a volume called *Case Studies in Personnel Security*: dry legal summaries of ruined careers and lives. Politics was becoming this Washington bachelor's passion, procedural liberty his core belief; and in the summer of 1952—as the Democrats convened in Chicago to nominate their presidential candidate—he would fall in love politically for the first time.

When I was a boy, the name Adlai Stevenson was spoken around my house with an admiration bordering on reverence. He was a youthful crush neither of my parents quite got over—one of the mysteries that preceded my birth. I accepted him as one of the good guys, but I couldn't put him alongside someone like FDR. In fact, my parents' attitude baffled me. Since Stevenson never got elected President— worse, was beaten twice—what made him so great? This was before I learned the central lesson of my parents' political experience, which was to become my own: the lesson of defeat, honorable liberal defeat. Stevenson's greatness, it turned out, lay not in what he did, but in what he said and was. "Oh, his wit," my mother would exclaim, "his style, his elegance." These qualities meant nothing to me then, and so Adlai Stevenson was consigned to the category of grown-up things I knew I was supposed to appreciate but couldn't muster any feeling for, like tennis and *The Forsyte Saga*.

When the Democratic Party drafted this dome-headed, little-known first-term governor of Illinois in 1952, the nominee's reluctant acceptance speech electrified millions of young listeners and almost created a new kind of liberal politics, with a new constituency, the instant it was given. His very reluctance, which baffled and disgusted a seasoned pol like President Truman, made Stevenson attractive to idealists. "I have asked the merciful Father, the Father of us all, to let this cup pass from me," he told the convention. "But from such dread responsibility one does not shrink in fear, in self-interest or in false humility." What John Dos Passos wrote of Woodrow Wilson's "Peace without Victory" speech to Congress in January 1917 was true of Stevenson's Chicago acceptance speech in July 1952: his "leadership of collegebred idealists throughout the Englishspeaking world was assured from that moment." Like Wilson, Stevenson spoke in "glittering generalities" that soared far above the grubby playing field of conventional politics; better yet, he had a brilliant sense of humor, which Wilson, the Presbyterian schoolmaster, lacked yet desperately needed in the dark days of 1919.

Stevenson's program was unremarkable—a rather cautious, fiscally restrained continuation of the New Deal and the Fair Deal, muted support for civil rights and labor, internationalism, containment of

Communism, and condemnation of McCarthyism. He antagonized key elements of the Roosevelt-Truman coalition by, for example, refusing to call for the total repeal of the antilabor Taft-Hartley Act and by condemning equally racial prejudice and antisouthernism. He went out of his way not to play interest-group politics. "I get so sick of the everlasting appeals to the cupidity and prejudice of every group which characterize our political campaigns. There is something finer in people; they know that they *owe* something too." Moral high-mindedness was Stevenson's political signature, and it galvanized large numbers of the new postwar middle class who did not identify with any of the old voting blocs, ethnic, regional, occupational. The old populist rhetoric that filled my grandfather's speeches—talk of "the gilt and splendor of Fifth Avenue and the squalor and hunger of the slums"—no longer moved these newly prosperous Americans. President Truman, a former machine pol from Missouri, with his class-based appeals to Democratic voting blocs and his administration plagued by corruption, left them cold and even repelled (he only became a hero in the grave). The postwar middle class saw themselves as mature and free citizens, motivated by impersonal ideals, and they responded instinctively to Stevenson's vision of politics as a noble calling that rose above narrow group and class interests.

By the early 1950s, with the seemingly boundless prosperity brought on by a mixed economy and the welfare state, the old Marxist categories had given way to a new social theory, the theory of mass society. The questions it raised had less to do with justice and equality than with mechanization and bureaucratization, the loss of individual freedom to large institutions of control, social disorganization, political apathy—in other words, questions about the quality of modern life and of the individual in society rather than about the distribution of goods and power. The object of sociological concern was no longer "the forgotten man" of the 1930s—the Okie, the Alabama tenant farmer, the unemployed coal miner, the striking dockworker, the hobo. Now it was "The Man in the Gray Flannel Suit"—organization man, one-dimensional man. In the year of Stevenson's campaign, the sociologist

C. Wright Mills wrote that nineteenth-century liberalism, which had located reason and progress in the free individual, couldn't account for the psychic and social facts of the new economic age. "The seat of rationality has shifted from the individual and is now in the big institution. The increase of enlightenment does not necessarily wise up the individual. . . . This modern weakness and irrationality of the individual, and especially his political apathy, is crucial for liberalism; for liberalism has classically relied on the reasoning individual as its lever for progressive change."

Stevenson arrived on the national scene with an intuitive feel for these vague new phenomena and the moral longings buried beneath them. In presenting himself as a candidate who owed nothing to anyone, in appealing to the sense of individual obligation in a democracy and to the idea of politics as an almost spiritual calling above merely material concerns, he seemed to offer an old republican answer to this newly prosperous, psychologically uneasy America.

For this very reason, harder leftists distrusted Stevenson and the new politics he represented. Irving Howe, in the inaugural 1954 issue of his magazine, *Dissent*, which he founded to carve out a socialist margin between Stalinism and McCarthyism, wrote: "Stevenson was the first of the liberal candidates in the post-Wilson era who made no effort to align himself with the plebeian tradition or plebeian sentiments; Stevenson was the candidate whom the intellectuals, trying hard to remove plebeian stains, admired most."

So he became the candidate of the arriviste intellectuals who as likely lived in suburbs as cities, worked for large universities and corporations, did not think of themselves first as Jews or Protestants, craved what Howe called "that restrained yet elegant style of life which Stevenson himself embodied." But that life wasn't just witty conversation at cocktail parties. It was a life of "higher things." Two decades later the narrator of Saul Bellow's *Humboldt's Gift* captured its spirit: "If you could believe Humboldt (and I couldn't) Stevenson was Aristotle's great-souled man. In his administration cabinet members would quote Yeats and Joyce. The new Joint Chiefs would know Thucydides.

Humboldt would be consulted about each State of the Union message. He was going to be the Goethe of the new government and build Weimar in Washington."

And Stevenson's wit, often self-deprecatory, was enormously appealing to the sophisticated. "Every thinking person is on your side," an admirer once told him, drawing the bright line where Stevenson supporters thought it belonged. "That's wonderful!" the candidate responded. "But I need a majority." And that was just the problem. "Thinking people" were not a majority. Thinking of themselves as "thinking people," with all the implications of elitism and contempt, would keep them from being a majority. The wit itself would keep them from being a majority. It was considered "over the people's heads" (during the 1952 campaign the reporter Richard Rovere overheard a pro-Stevenson bus driver telling passengers, "I don't suppose the average fellow's going to catch on to what he's saying. But I'm telling you, this is just what I've been waiting for"). Stevenson's bald pate and the brain within it inspired the label that would mock a whole class of liberal intellectuals—"egghead" (his mentally ill ex-wife, punning on the musical *The Egg and I*, announced her intention to write an exposé of the marriage called *The Egghead and I*). To which Stevenson responded, "Eggheads of the world, unite! You have nothing to lose but your yolks!" Eisenhower, irritated by Stevenson's jabs, implied that there was something almost un-American about his brand of political wit. "Is there anything funny about the fact that [the Democrats] have fumbled and bungled away the peace and have even gotten us into a war in Korea?" But while the General floated benignly above the campaign, his vice presidential nominee, who had already smeared the careers of previous opponents with the tar brush of anti-Communism, went after the Democratic candidate along the low road.

Stevenson had known Alger Hiss when they were both involved in the birth of the United Nations. They were wellborn New Dealers and traveled in similar circles. At Hiss's perjury trial in 1949 Stevenson gave a deposition in which he stated that Hiss's reputation for "integrity, loyalty and veracity" had been good. As governor of Illinois he had also vetoed the state legislature's loyalty-security bill. And during the 1952 campaign he denounced the curtailments of individual freedom in a speech before the American Legion in New York. These principled stands were more than enough to win Stevenson—a hardcore anti-Communist—the inevitable brand of "soft on Communism." "Stevenson holds a Ph.D. degree from Acheson's College of Cowardly Communist Containment," Nixon liked to say. "There is no question in my mind as to the loyalty of Mr. Stevenson," he claimed in a nationally televised address, thereby raising it while pretending not to, "but the question is one as to his judgment." Stevenson, Nixon charged, had lost the public trust by "going down the line for the arch-traitor of our generation."

Stevenson despised Nixon with a passion that surprised friends who knew him for his gentleness. But, perhaps unwisely, he wouldn't stoop to retaliate beyond the selective use of irony, describing Nixon as "the kind of politician who would cut down a redwood tree, and then mount the stump and make a speech for conservation." So the battle line was drawn by Nixon himself. The innuendoes, the smears, the sham of fairness: in 1952 Nixon became a national hero to the Republican right and the man liberals most loved to loathe. The way the country divided on Nixon suggested a political and cultural split as deep as the one that opened when President Roosevelt in the 1936 campaign welcomed the hatred of the rich. But in 1952, the divide pitted educated liberals against middle Americans—and Nixon welcomed the hatred of the New Deal pinks, the State Department traitors, the Ivy League eggheads. Republicans suddenly found themselves with the populist advantage for perhaps the first time since the Civil War—the all-important right to define the elite and claim to speak for "real Americans." They even threw the taint of homosexuality into the mix, with the *New York Daily News* calling the divorced Stevenson "Adelaide." Joe McCarthy, the party's blood-stained wedge, added "pansies" to his diatribes against "punks and pinks."

In fact, women found Stevenson—bald and dumpy, but witty and attentive—rather attractive. He had a number of close female friends before and after his divorce—whether they were lovers is unclear—including Marietta Tree and Lauren Bacall. My mother worked for him in the 1952 campaign in Birmingham and in 1956 at Democratic National Committee headquarters in Washington, where the campaign was so amateurishly run that a little research into cost-of-living increases made her the resident expert on the subject. She once met Stevenson on a stop in Montgomery, Alabama, at which the following exchange took place:

NANCY HUDDLESTON: I'd like to take you home with me.
ADLAI STEVENSON: That would be very nice.

Female supporters coined the slogan "I'd lay for Adlai."

In the fall of 1952 my father, on leave from his law firm, had his first and last practical political experience as Assistant to the General Counsel at the Democratic National Committee. Years later, in 1972, at the height of President Nixon's popularity, he said, "I've always loathed that man, ever since 1952, when I was working at the Democratic National Committee. Believe me, anybody who was around in 1952 knows that that man is just not to be trusted." Nixon's name was spoken around the house with such utter contempt that my parents' other political enemies—George Wallace, Governor Reagan, George Lincoln Rockwell of the American Nazi Party—seemed relatively harmless to me. The source of this feeling wasn't Nixon's policies—in fact, he was fairly moderate throughout his career and really governed by no clear ideology—but his tactics: the contempt for fairness, the perversion of intellect, the elevation of winning to the highest virtue.

My father, in turn, was exactly the sort of man Nixon despised most: an Ivy League Jewish liberal intellectual, a moralist who talked in terms of abstract principle, one of the smug self-appointed "thinking people."

By the last days of my father's life, when Nixon was racking up a historic percentage of the popular vote in the 1972 election, it had become a lonely hatred. But in 1952 New Deal liberalism was still the dominant philosophy, and my father actually believed that Stevenson would win. He sat down to watch the Checkers speech, for which Nixon's frozen wife, Pat, had been hauled into the TV studio as mute testament to her husband's honesty, and rejoiced that Nixon had destroyed his own career—who could be taken in by such self-pity, such shameless manipulations? He didn't understand the public's mood. It turned out that a lot of people were taken in, including General Eisenhower, who embraced Nixon and said, "You're my boy!"

Two weeks before the election, my father wrote to friends on the West Coast: "Even discounting the professional optimism around headquarters, the latest reports from around the country look pretty encouraging. At the moment, though, we figure to make it without California." He exchanged letters with his friend and fellow attorney Warren Christopher expressing the same confidence. After all, the last time a Republican had won the presidency my father was three years old.

Stevenson took 45 percent of the vote. It turned out there were only 27,314,992 thinking people in America. By 1956, after four years of Republican rule, the total had shrunk by about a million. Stevenson's national political career was on its way out, and Richard Nixon's was launched; he would be with my father the rest of his life.

"In politics I grew up a loser," he said years later. "Adlai Stevenson took my virginity—twice."

My father and Bellow's Humboldt were on the wrong side of history. Postwar America didn't want to be Periclean Athens. It wanted the golfing general, prosperity, the new toy called television. Pax Americana wasn't interested in turning for guidance to a tiny class of statesmen-philosophers. The experience of political defeat, especially in the bitter 1952 campaign, marked my father for life. During the Depression and the war, the heyday of the New Deal, it had been possible for him to feel he was on the winning side. His estrangement from the political mainstream, the sense of being in a minority that was neglected when it wasn't despised, began in 1952, when he received his political education amid the hysteria of McCarthyism and the bland all-Americanism of Eisenhower. That campaign, now scarcely remembered, set the stage for so much that followed, in my family's life and the country's. In some ways the 1960s began in the

1952 campaign. It introduced the egghead as an unreliable political type. It drew an ugly line between intellectuals and ordinary people. It gave Nixon and the Republicans a set of code words that could be used to devastating effect. It replaced economic issues, on which Democrats had been winning for two decades, with social ones, on which Republicans would win for most of the next four. While the New Deal was implicitly accepted by the Eisenhower wing of the Republican Party, freedom of speech, patriotism, and toughness became the defining terms between the parties. Liberals—who had beaten the Depression and the fascists—were suddenly weak, soft. Stevenson became the model for a long series of unsuccessful candidates. He represented the liberal as loser.

The mystique of the loser hung over Stevenson for the rest of his career. I think it partly accounted for my parents' undying love. He was too good for America, too good for politics. In 1960, when a handful of Democrats tried to stop the Kennedy juggernaut by proposing that Stevenson be drafted one more time, Senator Eugene McCarthy of Minnesota—who, eight years later, would become my Stevenson, my loser—roused the Los Angeles convention with a stirring appeal: "Do not turn away from this man. Do not reject this man. He has fought gallantly. He has fought courageously. He has fought honorably. . . . Do not reject this man who, his enemies said, spoke above the heads of the people, but they said it only because they did not want the people to listen. He spoke to the people. He moved their minds and stirred their hearts, and this was what was objected to. Do not leave this prophet without honor in his own party."

The pathos! This good man, having accepted the bitter cup and then been denied three times! To lose with honor—to lose and be right—to lose on principle, because he would not sell his birthright for a mess of pottage—to lose and keep his soul—for all this, my parents never got over Adlai Stevenson.

In 1949 my father's mother, Lillian, after years of ill health, died of a stroke. The next year Abraham Packer married a woman who had been a close family friend, my step-grandmother Ann. Almost immediately he too suffered a stroke, and for the last three years of his life he was incapacitated, eventually unable to move or speak. He died in 1954. These events scarcely register in my father's letters at the time, or in others' memories of him, or in what he later revealed of himself. His parents died as noiselessly as they had lived. My father, not yet thirty, moved on.

Did he think he could escape them? Didn't he see that it would have been better to take stock of the immigrant Jews and the slaughterhouses and the strokes? Fifteen years after his father's death, his own stroke would awaken haunting memories. He would confess to friends that he was frightened of ending the same way as his father. And now it seems to me that the harder a son tries to flee the specter of a father, the less likely it is that he will ever be truly free.

CHAPTER 6

◆

Winds of Freedom

After Stevenson's defeat, my father went back to his law practice. He had strong political beliefs but not a political temperament. In what he once called "the Faustian struggle between power and knowledge," he was tempted by the former but inclined toward the latter. His mind was analytical, not strategic; his taste for the fray was undermined by his love of argument on the merits and ideas for their own sake. And something vulnerable in his character, a principled rigidity combined with a lack of resilience, made him unfit for the blows of the arena.

Scholarship was the natural home for his mind, and for the next three years he engaged in a long-distance flirtation with the Stanford Law School. In the summer of 1955 the university finally made an offer—and then very nearly canceled it. Political passions and rational habits of mind: these two forces that were to collide so destructively in the late 1960s dealt my father his first blow in the mid-1950s, in an obscure incident at the twilight of the McCarthy era that set the course for the rest of his life.

By the 1950s the Ford Foundation, its endowment swollen to several hundred million tax-free dollars by the bequests of Henry and Edsel Ford, had begun to exert a large influence on American society. Almost inevitably, this attracted the attention of anti-Communist inquisitors in Congress and the press. Grants for international development and the social sciences smacked of subverting the American way of life—in the name of the famously anti-Communist (and anti-Semitic) Henry Ford, whom Hitler called his "role model" and whose portrait graced the walls of the Führer's Berlin residence. Earlier in the century, private foundations had drawn critical scrutiny from the left, when Andrew Carnegie, John D. Rockefeller, and other industrial titans were suspected of trying to promote reaction and corrupt public officials while perpetuating their own wealth and power. Members of one federal commission even proposed that the Rockefeller Foundation be dissolved and its assets distributed to the unemployed who should have received company profits in wages.

In the 1950s suspicion about the motives of corporate philanthropy moved far over to the right—demonstrating not just how paranoid the leading anti-Communists of the period could be but also how comfortable the liberal welfare state and Wall Street had grown with each other. Twenty years earlier, Ford Motor Company operatives were assaulting union organizers at the Rouge plant in Dearborn, Michigan; now the company's profits were paying for the legal defense of conscientious objectors and community development in India. The conservative radio commentator Fulton Lewis, Jr., charged on his national broadcast that "the American people are paying more taxes to finance so-called scholars who work diligently to beat our brains and change our traditional way of life into something more Socialistic."

The Foundation had set up an autonomous offshoot called the Fund for the Republic, whose mission—to defend the Bill of Rights—guaranteed in the early 1950s that it would become controversial. Its president was Robert Maynard Hutchins, former president of the University of Chicago—bold, blithe, and afflicted with the superficiality of what would come to be called the knee-jerk liberal. Hutchins was made president of the Fund for the Republic partly to get him out of the parent foundation, and as he took the Fund into such dangerous waters as a study of the use and abuse of congressional investigations, the Ford Foundation drew back from its wayward child and announced that the founding grant of $15 million would not be renewed once the money was spent. The Fund for the Republic became, according to Hutchins, "a wholly disowned subsidiary of the Ford Foundation."

None of its grants drew more fire than the one that proposed, in the summer of 1955, to fund a study of the testimony of ex-Communist government witnesses, including Whittaker Chambers. The grant went to Stanford Law School, which was about to appoint to its faculty the young Washington lawyer who had worked on the Fund's loyalty-security case histories the year before and who would direct the new study.

As the hysteria of the McCarthy era burnt itself out, what would have been a routine academic hiring in another period became a political firestorm whipped up in part by the two Hoovers, Herbert and J. Edgar (an aging actress in a Stephen Sondheim musical sings: "I've gotten through Herbert and J. Edgar Hoo-oover / Gee, that was fun and a half / When you've been through Herbert and J. Edgar Hoo-oover / Anything else is a laugh"). The Hoovers joined forces with Fulton Lewis, Jr., to sound the alarm that New York Reds and pinks were going to use the cover of the innocent, palm-lined university out on the West Coast to whitewash Alger Hiss.

The collision involving Stanford, the Fund, and McCarthyism brought together the dominant political trends of the mid-century. It represented one of those moments when one worldview is visibly dying and another is taking its place; and yet the apparent victors turn out to have planted the seeds of their own undoing. The small drama of my father's hiring raised the large questions that came up over and over in the debates of the 1950s and that would return to plague Stanford and other universities a decade later: What is the role of intellectuals in society? Who is objective? What is truth?

Stanford was an unlikely setting for subversion. In 1955 the university was barely half a century old—founded in 1891 by Leland Stanford, a railroad baron and U.S. senator, on his 8,000-acre ranch thirty miles south of San Francisco. The university was to be a practical experiment in freedom of the mind: "hallowed by no traditions," according to its first president in his inaugural address, and "hampered by none." Its motto was "Let the Winds of Freedom Blow." This newness excited William James, who came out from Harvard to give a Founder's Day address and beheld an ecstatic vision of the American Arcadia, "as if the hills that close us in were bathed in ether, milk and sunshine." He titled his speech "Stanford's Ideal Destiny" and hailed Stanford's democratic egalitarianism: "no one superfluously rich, yet all sharing, so far as their higher needs go, in the common endowment . . . Eastern institutions look all dark and huddled and confused in comparison with this purity and serenity. Shall it not be auspicious? Surely the one destiny to which this happy beginning seems to call Stanford is that it should become something intense and original, not necessarily in point of wealth or extent, but in point of spiritual quality."

Yet exactly because it was new and traditionless, this sunlit utopia of the mind lying in a valley of orchards between the coastal hills and the bay was vulnerable to the personalities of its conservative founders and leaders. William James, even in the ether and milk and sunshine, ought to have anticipated this danger. As the man who introduced the French term "intellectual" to American discourse, he warned, "We 'intellectuals' in America must all work to keep our precious birthright of individualism, and freedom from these institutions. Every great institution is perforce a means of corruption—whatever good it may also do."

In 1900 Stanford—still a collection of dusty buildings and rough dirt roads amid the late senator's stables and paddocks and vineyards— became the site of the most notorious controversy over academic freedom of the time. By the 1890s newly rich capitalists with far more wealth and ego than education were establishing their legacies by endowing universities—Stanford, Chicago, Johns Hopkins—with unprecedented sums of money, in Stanford's case $24 million. And the donors wanted unprecedented control. Boards of trustees began to look like corporate directories. At the same time, the faculties included Populist professors on fire with the emerging idea that science could be applied to solve the social problems of industrialism. Tenure did not yet exist, and professors were expected to uphold their university's good name. To the plutocrat-philanthropists, support for William Jennings Bryan and free silver in the 1896 election was practically incompatible with this duty.

All through the 1890s, leading scholars and even college presidents were fired for anti-monopolist and anti-imperialist views. Populist writers became obsessed with what they called, in their conspiracy-mindedness, "the college trust." They saw the attempt to silence scholarly work as an inevitable result of the clash between wealth and science, with vested interest on one side and disinterested inquiry on the other. Truth, the Populists believed, was on the side of reform. "Free investigation," one of them wrote in 1901, "is all that is necessary to expose the rottenness of the existing economic system . . . But with an arrogance equaling that of the slave power, our plutocracy has issued its edict that the colleges and universities must fall into line. Hence the inevitable conflict."

Onto this battleground strode a radical Stanford sociologist named Edward A. Ross. A big-boned Iowa orphan with a chip on his shoulder, Ross was a brash speaker both in the classroom and outside, where his addresses sometimes drew several thousand listeners. During his years at Stanford he wrote one of the founding texts of American sociology, *Social Control* (1901), which grappled with the problem of order in a society increasingly torn apart by class interests. Eighteenth-century "sympathy" was too weak, Ross wrote, to control the social forces unleashed by industrialism. "If . . . society were founded upon sympathy, the enormous inequalities of lot and fate we see about us would be impossible . . . As well build a skeleton out of soft fibre as construct social order out of sympathies."

Ross thought that America's growing complexity required scientific planning, the expansion of state control, and with it the rise to prominence of a new class of elites, in possession of a "special knowledge" beyond the competence of the free public schools. Modern society could not be managed by citizen farmers and mechanics. A decade before Herbert Croly, Ross foresaw that the twentieth century would belong to the expert. The noun "intellectual" did not yet exist—it was just appearing in France at around this time, in the Dreyfus case, and was soon to be imported by James—so Ross had to reach for an Orientalism in describing the new class: "As higher education, claiming more and more years of one's life, widens the space between those who possess it and those who do not, and as the enlightenment of the public wanes relatively to the superior enlightenment of the learned castes and professions, the mandarinate will infallibly draw to itself a greater and greater share of social power."

But in 1900 the mandarinate's power wasn't great enough to save Edward Ross. Jane Stanford, the founder's seventy-two-year-old widow, had been lobbying for several years to have Ross relieved of his position because of his loud support for a silver standard and municipal ownership of utilities, his opposition to Japanese immigration, and his rumored remark that "a railroad deal is a railroad steal." And since the founding grant gave the widow virtually unchecked power, her remark to Stanford's president, David Starr Jordan, that "I must confess I am weary of Professor Ross" became university policy. Ross was forced to resign. The official reasons: he had violated the university's political neutrality by participating in Bryan's 1896 campaign (in the same year fifty Stanford professors had endorsed William McKinley), his character was suspect, and he had used slang in class.

Stanford became infamous as the university that fired a leading scholar because its patroness disapproved of his politics. Nine years later almost the same thing happened to an even more famous and more radical Stanford sociologist, Thorstein Veblen, author of *The Theory of the Leisure Class*. For decades Stanford lived in the chill of these two episodes, under the long shadow of a member of its first graduating class, Herbert Hoover.

In 1912 Hoover, grown rich as an engineer with a British mining firm, parlayed work for a California petroleum company into a seat on the Stanford board of trustees, which he quickly dominated. Over the next thirty-five years Hoover handpicked four Stanford presidents. It is safe to say that nothing important happened at Stanford between the world wars without Hoover's approval; his control extended to setting faculty salaries, a level of interference that no eastern university would have tolerated.

Yet Hoover did much to make Stanford a more serious university. He set up its business school and its first center for advanced study, in food research. Having saved much of Europe from starvation during World War I, he donated his vast collection of war documents to what would become the Hoover Institution on War, Revolution and Peace. He campaigned against social inequality and displays of luxury on campus. In some ways he had a progressive idea of the university as a center for research among leading scholars and equal opportunity without social distinction among students. By the time my father was appointed, Stanford was becoming just such a place—in part because it had stopped listening to Herbert Hoover.

For while he was trying to make Stanford great, Hoover came to see the university as his own. He took grave offense whenever the administration or faculty tried to do something against his wishes. Usually this involved a tendency toward political liberalism. Hoover, whose rise from poverty made him a strict laissez-faire individualist in the American Protestant grain, objected during the 1924 election to the "outbreak of Lafolletism [sic] on campus . . . Now I am perfectly aware of that well established form of blackmail on Universities called Academic Freedom. I am in favor of academic freedom in truthful statements, honest opinion and to competent men: But all the negitives [sic] of these freeze into our Universities under this form of blackmail." Hoover's notion of academic freedom never progressed any further than his writing ability, which had kept him on probation through most of his undergraduate career. Any pro–La Follette professor was either a fool or a liar and in either case had no business at Stanford. The test of a professor's competence and honesty was his closeness to the opinions of Herbert Hoover. This remained Hoover's view of objectivity to the end of his life.

His idea differed from the university's explanation of the Ross firing in an important way. Jane Stanford didn't hide the subjectivity of her motives, the fact that her objections to Ross were moral and political: "A man cannot entertain such rabid ideas without inculcating them in the minds of the students under his charge." Ross, however, wrapped himself in the mantle of objectivity, as if political views were simply founded on scientific knowledge: "It is my duty as an economist to impart, on occasion, to sober people, and in a scientific spirit, my conclusions on subjects with which I am expert."

Herbert Hoover, like Edward Ross, was a product of Progressivism and a man of science. And like Ross (and the other Populist critics of "the college trust"), he refused to believe that politics had more to do with passion than with science. The rather sinister implication of this "modern" idea was that no one could honestly disagree with him. Partisan politics cloaked as objective truth replaced morality as the standard for judgment.

Hoover's dogmatism only solidified in the decades to come. His presidency, according to a 1930 magazine article, transformed Stanford "almost into the condition of a Hoover province" in which "discussion of public policies or issues which could be remotely connected with the Hoover administration . . . dried up." But as President, Hoover proved as dismal a failure as the rest of his career in business and public office had been an unbroken success. When the world that had made him a millionaire collapsed in the Depression, he could only insist that prosperity was just around the corner. His scientism became an irrational ideology based on seemingly rational economic principles; the man who had fed postwar Europe remained impervious to data from his own hungry country, where the term "Hooverville" was coming into use. This was the Hoover of whom George Huddleston said in 1931: "[We] have a man in charge of the Government who is more interested in the pocketbooks of the rich than he is in the empty bellies of the poor."

Political defeat is always humiliating, but for Hoover it became a lifelong sore. Both his conservatism and his easily wounded sense of ownership of Stanford deepened, while the university for which he had such high ambitions stagnated as a country club of the California elite. Its football team won the Rose Bowl, its student life was dominated by fraternities, its faculty remained mostly mediocre. Ex-President Hoover became a petulant and meddling trustee. When 176 Stanford professors signed a petition in the summer of 1941 supporting Roosevelt's war policy, Hoover the isolationist commissioned his own poll to "prove" that the majority of the faculty were on his side. That same summer, his vanity and determination to leave his mark on Stanford achieved their fullest expression when the Hoover Library, housing his collection of war documents, was formally dedicated. On a campus of sandstone quadrangles where no building stood more than three or four stories, this 285-foot-high structure in concrete dominated the landscape like an oil derrick. You could never get away from the sight of it. When I was a boy, my friends and I oriented ourselves by the Hoover tower, climbed it, dropped gobs of spit from its belvedere. Its rigid vertical thrust and red-domed head inspired the nickname "Stanford's biggest erection." It begged to be mocked and we mocked it, but the tower is still there, Hoover's long humorless shadow.

After the war, the university spun increasingly out of Hoover's control. Under President Wallace Sterling, Stanford began to attract federal research dollars and scholars whose conservative political credentials were in doubt. Sterling himself, a smooth Canadian historian, had been vetted by Hoover and passed muster. On the subject of Communists in the academy he echoed most university presidents of the late 1940s and early 1950s by saying, "I doubt very much that a member of the Communist Party is a free agent. If he is not a free agent, then it would seem to follow that he cannot be objective. If he cannot be objective, he is by definition precluded from being an educator."

But who was a Communist? And what did it mean to be objective? These interrelated questions came up over and over in the controversies of the early Cold War, especially within academia. Hoover's positions are revealingly contradictory and show the crudeness of so much right-wing thinking in those years of Communist expansion abroad and liberal consolidation at home. On the one hand, he found more and more Stanford faculty to be politically suspect, including the new law school dean, Carl Spaeth. In every New Dealer he smelled at least a fellow traveler, and the Hiss case only confirmed his suspicion that the Roosevelt-Truman administrations were stained with Reds and pinks. Hoover continued to articulate his theory of free expression: "My conviction as to academic freedom is that when people claim immunity on the grounds of self-incrimination, they are as guilty as Benedict Arnold and Alger Hiss." As for his Hoover Institution, any deviation from the views of "the Chief" was intolerable. It had a clear mission, he wrote, "to demonstrate the evils of the doctrines of Karl Marx—whether Communism, Socialism, economic materialism, or atheism—thus to protect the American way of life from such ideologies, their conspiracies, and to reaffirm the validity of the American system."

On the one hand, then, Hoover couldn't abide the political bias of the increasingly liberal faculty; on the other hand, his own biases were clear. He wanted "documentary" studies that published "facts" about Communism—facts, however, that would serve the cause of "exposing the evil of ideas that have spread throughout much of the present world." It was exactly the trick he had pulled on "Lafolletism" in 1924: he demanded scholarly objectivity—meaning agreement with his own views.

Throughout the 1950s, as Stanford grew in prominence as a research university, Hoover's influence waned and his indignation waxed. This was the climate at Stanford and in the country when the Fund for the Republic decided to give the law school $25,000 to study the testimony of ex-Communists, to be carried out under the direction of the newly appointed Herbert L. Packer.

The testimony of relatively few people—Whittaker Chambers, Louis Budenz, and Elizabeth Bentley the most famous—was responsible for the whole concept of a domestic Communist conspiracy and the resulting frenzy of legislation, regulation, investigation, and prosecution; but none of it had ever been subjected to careful analysis.

The Fund's officers, in an internal memorandum, wrote: "It is not suggested that the aim would be to disprove the existence of a Communist conspiracy or a 'web of subversion.' The object would be to reduce to coldly factual statement what we have actually learned, or what a judicious mind may reasonably infer from the testimony of the key witnesses." At the same time, the memo focused on possible contradictions and gaps in the testimony, failures of congressional committees to follow them up, and the sum total of what had and had not been proved. If the Fund had a liberal political agenda, it was careful to leave no traces of one. In the summer of 1955 Robert Hutchins wrote to Dean Carl Spaeth that "under no conditions would the Fund consider interfering in any way with direction or control of the project."

The grant and my father's appointment were announced in the Fund for the Republic's annual report in August—and bicoastal hell broke loose. In New York on August 22 Fulton Lewis, Jr., began a series of national evening radio broadcasts about the grant that continued for over a month, some weeks every night. Lewis immediately decided that the study's purpose ("Study—my grandmother") was "to try to pick inconsistencies or contradictions or flaws in the testimony that has been given by the various anti-Communist witnesses at various times before various committees, with a view to discrediting that testimony and those who gave it." The purple mimeographed transcripts of these broadcasts that I found among my father's papers carry the odor of McCarthyism in decay. McCarthy himself had already been rebuked by Army counsel Joseph Welch and censured by the Senate — but as the power of accusation was beginning to wear off, the hunt grew all the more frenzied. In his broadcasts Lewis pursues trivia obsessively, scours every syllable for conspiracy. He impugns by epithet ("a so-called public service organization," "the ultra-liberal and very political-minded dean, Carl Spaeth"); by association ("[Spaeth] also made a great profession of his friendship with Alger Hiss, for whom he gave a cocktail party, I am told, in San Francisco after the war"); by reporting salaries, including my father's paltry $700 for his months-long work on the loyalty-security cases, and by reporting when salaries weren't disclosed; by appropriating the language of investigation ("informant," "inspection," "corroborate"); by announcing the failure to return phone calls. It all added up to a plot by "the controversial Dean" Spaeth and the Fund's "highly controversial" President Hutchins to use the good name of Stanford to disseminate left-wing propaganda, smear the ex-Communist witnesses, undermine the campaign against subversives in government, and elect Adlai Stevenson in 1956.

In Fulton Lewis, Jr.'s imagination my father was a young foot soldier carrying out the directives of committed ideologues. "How did Herbert Packer get into the picture," Lewis wanted to know on the evening of August 26, "a thirty-six-year-old Washington lawyer who is not even a member of the District of Columbia bar? What qualifies him to be making this survey? And what is his objective in making it, anyway? What legitimate end does he expect the survey to serve?" On a broadcast a few evenings later my father turned thirty-seven. In fact he was barely thirty. Most of Lewis' errors of fact went unacknowledged, but in a few cases where he was forced to correct himself on the air, even his own mistakes somehow confirmed that a campaign of misinformation, with all the earmarks of conspiracy, was abroad.

The real target of his broadcasts—the Stanford board of trustees—was meeting on the other coast, in San Francisco. "My report to you over this microphone last night," Lewis announced on August 23, "has stirred up some excitement among the guiding fathers of that institution." From his apartment in New York's Waldorf-Astoria Hotel, trustee Herbert Hoover was already working to convince the board to kill the appointment. He enlisted the help of J. Edgar Hoover, who sent "the Chief" a seventeen-page memorandum that gathered publicly available information about the Fund and the Stanford grant—a clipping service to a private citizen, a strange thing for the FBI director to provide.

"Carl Spaeth was very low in spirits Friday," the university secretary wrote Sterling late in the month. One of the key trustees, Lloyd Dinkelspiel, was leaning against the Packer appointment. Spaeth "was blunt to Lloyd in saying that any question of the objectivity of the research to be done, or the faculty judgment in selecting Packer, would be considered a slur at the faculty's integrity." Dinkelspiel wrote Sterling: "The study can have only one conclusion, which is well known to us all: That many conflicts will be found between statements at hearings and trials and subsequent statements . . . Do we then conclude that, the evidence being discredited, the concept of a communist conspiracy resting on it fails? Ergo, no conspiracy." Letters from alumni started peppering Sterling's office. "If you permit at all any Communist front research, such as I am listening to over Fulton Lewis, Jr's radio program, I refuse to consider entry of seven of my grandsons to your school," wrote Clarence T. Pullin, Sr. "It's time the garbage men visited all such universities who permit our enemies to hold forth in their insidious way. Shame on you—or—are you all loused up with the same brush?"

The university dug around to make sure there was no embarrassing material on my father. "Packer's background looks impressive here," the secretary wrote Sterling on August 25. "He has worked on the side of business in defending against antitrust suits. I hope the guy doesn't turn out to have been a member of Americans for Democratic Action or some such organization." By that standard, Arthur Schlesinger, Jr., and John Kenneth Galbraith would have had trouble getting jobs at Stanford. A security firm "could find nothing derogatory on Packer. The check is a 'dry well.' " After all, they were dealing with a liberal.

In the end, amid the threat of mass resignations by the younger law faculty, Sterling did what President Jordan had not done under pressure from Jane Stanford fifty-five years before: he overrode Hoover and convinced the board, in my father's words, "that I was an O.K. guy." The postwar meritocracy was at work: Stanford was engaged in a furious effort to make itself a top-notch university, and talent and academic independence finally seemed to count for more than influence. Still, a faculty committee was set up to monitor the young professor's study, and at one point Dean Spaeth even considered appointing an advisory committee of outside lawyers to consult—both of which my father found humiliating. But in his public statement announcing the appointment, Sterling implied that even liberals could be objective. "The University is concerned only that its faculty should adhere to those rigorous standards of independence of judgment, exact inquiry, and impartial evaluation of findings which have always motivated true scholars."

My father became a professor, as he later put it, "under sort of false pretenses," with the reputation of a radical politico and the bona fides of a witch-hunt victim. And for years afterward, whenever he published a book or article on a controversial subject, a memo would circulate through the inner coils of the FBI with a demand scrawled in the handwriting of J. Edgar Hoover: "What do we know of Packer?" "Well known to us for his leftist views and writings," came the answer. But the Stanford job was a cover for no political agenda. It suited my father's strongest abilities and urges. And his findings in the study of ex-Communist witnesses would defy the Cold Warriors' expectations.

In January 1956 he left his Washington law practice and headed West to start a new life—the rest of his life. On the way, he made a southern detour to visit a friend in Birmingham, Alabama.

In January 1956 my mother was thirty and, by period standards, very nearly an old maid. She had somehow lost her twenties—a stalled decade I never understood, since the stories of her youth were colored with dinner-table declamations, guerrilla combat with her four older siblings, underage smoking and drinking, joyrides and all-points police bulletins. But she spent the 1950s living at home, the girl who had lain awake waiting for her mother to come home now taking care of her intermittently warring parents at 2816 Rhodes Circle, on the south side of Birmingham—a city that was hardening and closing up with the early stirrings of civil rights.

At age eighteen, my mother underwent something of a conversion experience. Until then she had been the average enlightened racist, adoring the family cook and making fun of her speech, disliking individual acts of meanness and never giving the system of segregation a thought, keeping her mouth shut while her bridge partners joked about sending "them" back to Africa or Jerusalem. She spent her teenage years enjoying all the privileges of southern middle-class whiteness. But during her freshman year at Birmingham-Southern College she heard a story from a young man whom her sister Jane was seeing that changed her life. A group of his friends had been at a carnival in southern Alabama where a black boy, trying to grab the brass ring, came tumbling off a whites-only merry-go-round. The white youths set upon the boy and beat him to a pulp. When my mother heard the story, something in her broke. Suddenly, a black she *didn't* know personally became human to her. She wrote an essay about it for her freshman English class. And in the socially constrained and politically silent atmosphere of Birmingham, she tried to put this new insight into practice.

It wasn't easy. When she made a point of sitting at the back of the bus on her way to campus, the black passengers would get up for the white lady. When she spotted Birmingham's leading black attorney in a room off the county courthouse law library and approached him to discuss black participation in an upcoming election, he propped the door open with a chair so no one would imagine a rape in progress and the white lady couldn't claim one afterward. She participated in a series of secret conversations with students at a local black college, but since the purpose of the meetings was simply to show that they could take place, they soon ended. She became one of the first white members of the Southern Negro Youth Congress—"noblesse oblige," she dismissed it years later. She worked on behalf of President Truman's effort to make the wartime Fair Employment Practices Commission, which mandated equal opportunity in government defense contracts, a permanent body, but it was defeated by a Southern filibuster. She went to Memphis to gather information on the success of Negro policemen and met a white woman who had devoted her whole life to black causes, a woman as awkward and strange as such a woman at that time in that place was likely to be, with long, stiff, almost paralyzed fingers, a woman like Miss Habersham, the enlightened spinster in Faulkner's *Intruder in the Dust*. This woman invited the visitor from Birmingham back to her house, from which my mother departed with a deep sense of shame—for she knew she was not going to devote her whole life to black causes. She was not going to end up like this strange woman. She wanted to play bridge and date men and shop and read modern literature. Half the time she was congratulating herself for her efforts, the other half she was flagellating herself for their failure. She was a converted race liberal making personal gestures and tentative political moves in a city as segregated as Johannesburg, and almost as intimidating. None of it was enough; it could never be enough; it was doomed to fail.

"I could have thrown a bomb, or at least not enjoyed it quite so much," she once said. "My racial experiences are littered with shame."

(Years later, in the 1960s, the humid burden of Birmingham would follow her into the mild California sunlight, where she would try again to work out the problem of white liberal guilt, but in another context, with its own set of obstacles—not "Get up for the white lady" but "Sit down and listen, whitey!" And then it would become my problem, too.)

After the war she spent two years getting a master's degree at the University of Chicago, where her bridge partner and close friend (for in Chicago she found it possible to be real, and not just symbolic, friends) was a black man named Morteza Sprague, to whom Ralph Ellison would later dedicate *Shadow and Act*. When she went home on vacation, word had somehow reached Birmingham that she was engaged to marry a Negro.

In these years she didn't dare let her family know what she was doing. She didn't tell them about the black friends in Chicago or the Southern Negro Youth Congress. She and her father argued about almost every subject, but they avoided race—even in the summer of 1948, when the dissident faction of southern Democrats who called themselves States' Righters, but who came to be called Dixiecrats, held their national convention in downtown Birmingham's Municipal Auditorium.

By 1948 the South's brief love affair with the federal government—the liaison that ended George Huddleston's career when he turned against the New Deal—was over. Depression had begun the affair, and war had sustained it past its natural end. Class politics, played so surely by the charismatic Roosevelt, wooed the South from its old hostility to central authority and obscured the forces that were beginning to divide the Democratic Party. But once Roosevelt was dead and the war over, conservative opponents of the New Deal saw their opportunity to turn the region against Washington by singing the old, sure song of race, along with the new song of Communism. And the national Democratic Party made it easy when President Truman, going much farther than Roosevelt had ever dared, proposed in the election year of 1948 the most radical civil rights program since Reconstruction: desegregation of the armed forces, fair employment legislation, as well as national health insurance and federal aid to education. None of it passed the filibuster by Southerners of the President's own party. In Birmingham, Truman was mock-lynched from the balcony of the posh Tutwiler Hotel, with a sign pinned to the dummy corpse saying "TRUMAN KILLED BY CIVIL-RIGHT."

In the years after World War II, as civil rights became a liberal cause, the Democratic Party split wide open. It could scarcely contain both Hubert Humphrey and Strom Thurmond. For most of the century, the old Populist-Progressive opposition to moneyed interests had held the party together, even in 1928 when splinter movements against the Catholic and wet nominee Al Smith broke out across the South, with the backing of the Klan. But 1948 marked a watershed year for the South and the party. Broadly social issues, especially race, long submerged under economic interests, surfaced and started to break apart the liberal coalition, and it would go on breaking for the rest of the century. When class was the issue, liberals won. When social issues dominated, they lost.

The Alabama Democrats had more than just Negrophilic Northerners to worry about. The laborious work of the 1901 constitutional convention, which guaranteed a nearly all-white state politics, was imperiled by a 1944 Supreme Court decision and by the fact that the literacy and property qualifications were excluding fewer and fewer blacks. Three hundred dollars and the ability to read and write had become a rather porous sieve through which urban blacks were beginning to leak. So in 1946 the state legislature amended the literacy clause of the 1901 constitution to include an "understanding" of the U.S. Constitution, whose adequacy was left to the discretion of local registration boards. A black lawyer in Birmingham told me that when he first registered to vote in 1958, his detailed explanation of the Fourteenth Amendment left the white registrar so baffled that she had no choice but to sign him up. For most blacks, though, the revised law was enough to keep them out—until the cold March morning in 1965 when a column of protesters trying to cross the Edmund Pettus Bridge on their way out of Selma toward Montgomery were clubbed and gassed by mounted police, and Lyndon Johnson, having told the U.S. Congress, "We shall overcome," signed the Voting Rights Act five months later. By then, the Democratic Party had lost the South.

At certain moments a new social type, later to become so familiar that he seems to have been with us always, suddenly appears on the scene. An event that catches the spirit of its time provides him a platform, a way into public consciousness, and what historical forces have been desultorily concocting all along seems to appear out of nowhere. The States' Rights convention in Birmingham in July 1948 included a number of known southern types: bigots and racial ideologues (the author of *The Place of the Negro* and the author of *The Jews Have Got the Atom Bomb* attended), opportunistic local pols and party-boss·demagogues, spokesmen for Jeffersonian individualism (George Huddleston fell into this category), nouveau riche oilmen, and well-heeled industrialists. But these diverse classes and types now merged in the hybrid figure and rhetoric of the libertarian segregationist, the anti–New Deal, anti-Communist populist. Resentment of Washington among southern businessmen and politicians unhampered by patrician scruples bubbled up, and the flame that brought them to a boil was the first real prospect of civil rights progress since Reconstruction. Unlike during the Roosevelt years, large numbers of average whites, enjoying the emerging postwar boom, were now ready to listen. Race became the lever with which conservatives pried the South out of the New Deal coalition, and they did it in the name of Americanism.

"Right thinking people everywhere will rally to the cause," Alabama's ex-governor Frank Dixon exulted in his keynote address, "because the liberties of individuals are at stake in every state—in California, New York, everywhere—not in the South alone."

The Jeffersonian Populists of the 1890s and the Klan of the 1920s had, in utterly different ways, spoken for the economic interests of the working and lower middle classes. Both came to pose a direct threat to the rule of the state's conservative business establishment. But the Dixiecrat of 1948 was something new. He joined economic and social conservatism in a virulent mix. In 1901 horror of racial equality was a social convention. In 1948 it was a personal pathology, fused with hatred of federal intervention in the economy, dosed with paranoia and hardened by the new ideology of anti-Communism. To the Dixiecrat, Social Security and civil rights were part of a single government plot to destroy sacred individual liberties. Within thirty years, this view would become respectable Republicanism and help get Ronald Reagan elected.

Unlike the planters at the constitutional convention of 1901, the Dixiecrat had no authentic connection to an older way of life, and so he was defined most sharply by whom he was against: blacks, Jews, Northerners, New Deal bureaucrats, trade unionists, Communists. The Cold War raised the stakes on everything: the enemies were not just nigger-lovers or troublemakers, they were traitors. The smell of fear and betrayal that hung over Birmingham in July 1948 anticipated the smell of Little Rock and Dallas.

One could even say that the great realignment of the South, and the long decline of the Democratic Party from its Roosevelt-era heights, began in this unlikely gathering of reactionaries. A line runs from Strom Thurmond through Barry Goldwater, George Wallace, Nixon's southern strategy, the Reagan triumphs, and Newt Gingrich, to the Republican Party's current hold on the South.

The delegates were welcomed to Birmingham by a police commissioner and former baseball announcer, later to achieve world fame, named Eugene "Bull" Connor. For a day and a night they whipped themselves into an anti-Truman frenzy. Ex-governor Dixon declared that the national party "has sunk so low as to be willing to barter our individual rights for the votes of minority groups in doubtful states." Confederate flags and portraits of Robert E. Lee were raised around the floor; from the rostrum came more modern and less familiar terms like "federal gestapo" and "totalitarian state." Governor Strom Thurmond of South Carolina called the Fair Employment Practices Commission "the nearest thing to communism ever advocated in these United States."

At some point my mother looked in on the proceedings as a horrified visitor and wondered who her seventy-eight-year-old, Thomas Jefferson Democrat father had aligned himself with. That fall George Huddleston attended a meeting of Dixiecrat oilmen in Texas and came home muttering about the bad characters who had hijacked the cause of individual liberties. In November, Thurmond captured four southern states, including Alabama, where the Dixiecrats had managed the feat of keeping President Truman's name off the ballot. So my mother, who refused to vote for the Communist-supported Progressive Party nominee, Henry Wallace, had to sit out what would have been her first election. The next day she read with satisfaction the news of Truman's narrow win over Dewey. But the fault line between her father's Democratic Party and her own was beginning to open.

After 1948 my mother became less active in Birmingham's racial politics. She worked at a bookstore and started writing and publishing short fiction in a sharp-witted, rueful vein. She took care of her increasingly infirm father and ever-volatile mother, and dated many of the eligible men in Birmingham while approaching her thirties with no notion of marrying any of them. When the one man she fell for, an attractive and hard-drinking Chicagoan, proposed marriage, my mother turned him down and drove him off. He was a bad bet, and his seductive attentions threatened the control she had over her life. She might have missed another opportunity when her father's old political rival, Hugo Black, now a sexagenarian Supreme Court justice, asked her to come work for him in Washington. She declined; the woman who took the job soon became the second Mrs. Black.

In 1954 her father's old seat in Congress opened up and her older brother, George Jr., decided to run for it. My mother and Howell Heflin, later a U.S. senator, helped run the campaign. She wrote her brother's speeches, plotted strategy, and, having been a political animal since age three, turned her competitive juices to that form of warfare by other means. Over time she has worked on a number of relatives' and friends' campaigns, as well as on Adlai Stevenson's two. It's impossible for an election year to go by without my mother strategizing feverishly on behalf of the unknowing Democrats.

After her brother won, a group of prominent Birmingham blacks wrote him a polite letter. "We know how your sister stands on issues we care about, but we don't know your views." Her brother had inherited their father's name and freckled pallor but not his candor and independence. "I would not have run," George Jr. replied judiciously, "if I did not believe I could represent all the people of my district."

That would soon become impossible. Two weeks after he won the Alabama Democratic primary, in May 1954, the Supreme Court ruled unanimously that school segregation was unconstitutional. My grandfather surprised my mother when he remarked, "The South's been getting away with it for a long time, and it's about time we got caught." His career had fallen in the decades between the 1901 convention that eliminated blacks from Alabama politics and the civil rights movement that revolutionized the state and the country; he had been largely spared the ultimate test of political courage in the South. George Jr., less suited to such tests, tried hard to avoid them but never had a chance. His ten-year career in Congress would coincide exactly with the most turbulent years of the civil rights movement in the South, culminating in Birmingham police dogs and fire hoses being turned loose on schoolchildren in May 1963.

In 1957 the *Birmingham News*, the paper that had called George

Huddleston a Socialist and worse, ran a series of articles about the Highlander Folk School, an interracial center founded in Tennessee in 1932. Highlander had trained Rosa Parks in nonviolence for two weeks in 1954 shortly before she refused to vacate her seat on a Montgomery bus, and it was soon to become a training center for the Southern Christian Leadership Conference of Martin Luther King, Jr. It was at Highlander that King first heard a song called "We Shall Overcome" sung by Pete Seeger, a song he couldn't get out of his head afterward. The *News* articles accused the school of being a Communist front.

My mother wrote a letter of rebuttal, with "NOT FOR PUBLICATION" printed across the top. A week later her congressman brother called her up. "They're saying around the courthouse that the paper got three letters about those articles. One was from Martin Luther King. One was from Aubrey Williams"—a former New Deal official and outspoken race liberal from Montgomery. "And one was from you."

"I won't do it again," she said, and she didn't. Family loyalty counted for more than political principle. The letter was her last political act in Alabama.

By then she had already met a Jewish lawyer from Washington who had come through Birmingham to visit a friend on his way West to take a position at Stanford Law School.

In 1911 George Huddleston had sold his law practice to a Jew named Leo Oberdorfer. Oberdorfer's son Louis had been a lawyer with my father in Lloyd Cutler's firm (and would go on to become a federal judge in Washington). When Herbert Packer visited the Oberdorfers in Birmingham in January 1956, the dinner guests included Nancy Huddleston. She brought one of her regular dates. But she found this dark man from out of town—physically unusual in Birmingham WASP society—good-looking and intellectually formidable, and she spent most of the dinner talking to him. As for my father, according to his friend Warren Christopher in a letter he wrote my mother after my father's death: "He knew that he had found 'the' girl. Herb was never easy to please about girls or anything else, but he immediately recognized that you exceeded his exacting standards." The subject that occupied my mother and father that first evening at the beginning of an election year was Adlai Stevenson, whom they both fanatically supported and planned to work for.

My father went on to Stanford, where friends set him up with various single women. My mother continued her ritual dating. A few months after that first dinner, hearing that he was sick with hepatitis, she wrote him a sympathetic letter, and he responded. It took almost two years of phone calls and visits for these two fiercely independent thirty-two-year-olds to decide to marry.

Why, among all the possibilities, did my mother accept my father? Because he was brilliant, because he was undemanding, because she was suffering a years-long writer's block, and, perhaps, because he lived a long way from Birmingham. For my father's part, he had found a smart and attractive dynamo, free of "clinging femininity" and other reminders of his smothering mother.

When they finally set a date, Bertha Huddleston sat down to compose a letter on her husband's stationery. "Each and every member of the family (except the 88 year old) is delighted with the coming event of March 15th," she wrote her future son-in-law, "and we will always want you to feel like a member and we will certainly accept you as one."

When the eighty-eight-year-old learned of his youngest daughter's engagement, he refused to see her fiancé. He urged the date she had brought to the Oberdorfers' to head it off with a proposal of his own. He tried to convince his daughter that Herbert L. Packer of Washington, D.C., was marrying her for her money. "I haven't got enough," she answered. More to the point, he told her that if she married a Jew there would be hotels, clubs, places in the South and all over the country where the couple would not be welcome.

She knew that he was right, but she also knew that what he really wanted was for his last child not to leave him.

The man my mother married in her parents' house on March 15, 1958, was an emissary from the modern world my grandfather had never come to terms with. The place where the newlyweds were going to make their life together represented the future as much as Birmingham—by now known as "Bombingham," fearful city of the White Citizens Council, the Klan, and dozens of unsolved dynamite blasts in black neighborhoods—represented the sins of the past.

Their friends wrote out "Nomination speeches" and "Platforms," turning the wedding into a political convention in which the party nominates a ticket that is geographically, religiously, and sexually balanced.

> *We nominate Nancy to head the Liberals*
> *Where lime, ore, and coal are the minerals*
> *In independence she takes pride*
> *(At least before she becomes a bride).*
> *She attracts young men of high repute*
> *Tho' they sometimes part in grave dispute,*
> *For she loves to argue keen and strong*
> *And aims to right 'most every wrong . . .*
> *So we nominate Nancy to head all Liberals*
> *No matter where or what the minerals.*

"Nancy's Platform" proclaimed:

> *I'm a Yellow Dog Democrat*
> *I believe in peace and freedom,*
> *Freedom to be and say what I please,*
> *Freedom from any dull faculty teas,*
> *Freedom from family congressional restraint,*
> *Freedom to issue any complaint.*
> *Freedom to golf, to read, and to write,*
> *But not to stay in the kitchen all night . . .*
> *On matters domestic I have my convictions.*
> *Our budget and meals need cause us no frictions.*
> *Unbalanced they'll be, but I'll serve you for fare*
> *Intellectual hash, served medium rare.*

"Herb's Platform":

I stand firm for Democrats—Jackson and Wilson,
Jefferson, Roosevelt, and of course, Adlai Stevilson . . .
I shall also kick out J. Edgar Hoover
And if Liz Bentley speaks, I shall reprove her.
Loyalty oaths and such tommy rot
I denounce and decry right on this spot.
As for Freedom, I'm for it, since the beginner is,
Liberté, égalité, and things ejusdem generis.

The movie unspools in my head. They walk out the front door onto the porch of 2816 Rhodes Circle and duck under a shower of rice. My father has a carnation in his lapel, my mother is wearing a full-skirted gold dress and a borrowed mink coat. I feel no urge to stand up in the theater like the narrator of Delmore Schwartz's story "In Dreams Begin Responsibilities" and shout, "Don't do it! It's not too late to change your minds, both of you. Nothing good will come of it, only remorse, hatred, scandal, and two children whose characters are monstrous." No, the scene is too lovely and hopeful. They've sealed their own fates and mine, and I can't wish them to do otherwise. But it's strange, from my seat in the back row, to know so much more about what's to come than these two people who were younger then than I am now.

They made their lives out on the West Coast, where everything was new, at a university where tradition was weak enough to allow for an experiment in the unfettered mind. By the time my sister and I came along, California offspring of a Jew in name only and a lapsed southern Protestant, the air we breathed was bracingly pure secular humanism, clean of the lowland fog and smoke of any ethnicity or region or faith.

CHAPTER 7

◆

Golden Age

W ithin a few months of her wedding, my mother was thinking of asking for a divorce. She hated the hours and days she spent alone in their little apartment in Menlo Park while my father worked at the law school or went on trips out of town. She had left her hometown, where she had been one of the lesser stars, and her family, where her energies had gone into making life bearable for her parents, and now she knew no one and her energies had no outlet. She resented her dependence on this man to whom she'd joined her life; it humiliated her pride. And she was finding out that the man she had married didn't talk much. I once asked her whether he ever told her about his childhood, or whether they discussed the subject that couples of their education and class can't stop talking about today—their "relationship." No. "We talked about politics."

She wanted more, and her instinct was to demand. But when she tried to engage him he turned out not to be the sparring partner her older brothers had been. Instead he fell silent and withdrew and buried himself in his work. She had no one to fight with.

This was before men in general learned to talk and couples to "process." In my father's correspondence with both men and women from those years a sort of cocktail-party sparkle fizzes in every turn of phrase. "I hope that by now you are comfortably ensconced in the land of milk and honey, fully recovered from what I gather was the winter of your discontent." In a series of exchanges with Warren Christopher, the talk is all of Democratic Party politics and Broadway shows. "Speaking of plays did you see the Thurber original with Carol Channing on last Sunday's OMNIBUS. I laugh to think about it. That program has been quite satisfactory in the poverty of this town [L.A.], though perhaps not quite to your taste." The men do not know how to talk, while the talk of the women is witty with hidden sharp-cornered resentments. "Tim is screaming & I'm beginning to ooze sediment & it's nearly noon & I guess I'd better have a pint of sherry, get dressed, & feed the young." Dissatisfaction makes the women—their stationery monogrammed with curlicue initials—more interesting than the men. One friend's wife tartly annotates her husband's bland letter in the margins: "[He] was kind enough not to tell you about the recent 'firm' party at which I was conspicuous on a set of Children's swings. Just swinging." A few letters later she has left him. In the 1950s, with a child, it is a very brave or very reckless move, and the fizz is gone from her sentences—they have the abrupt rhythm of truth. "This just isn't the sort of thing that one does. I know. This may not be the way my life should flow. I know that this is what I had to do with my life. If I am mistaken I shall pay dearly. I may be wrong. Everyone that I know seems to think so . . . The life ahead that I can see will be most difficult. Perhaps I am not tough enough for it and may retreat from sheer physical exhaustion."

My mother never had to write such a letter. She got pregnant instead. And when my sister was born in March 1959, my mother fell in love with her and did what her mother had never done—accepted the marriage as it was and decided to make it work. A year and a half later I arrived. My mother began to write again and took a teaching position in the creative writing program. Her days filled and her life became purposeful.

But she was about to discover the flaw in the foundation.

By 1960 the study of ex-Communist witnesses was four years old. In 1955 the journalist Richard Rovere had predicted that it would take a research team three months. The Stanford Law School countered that the project could be completed by September 1956, which the Fund accepted. In the summer of 1956 Carl Spaeth wrote to Robert Hutchins asking for $30,000 more and another year. The Fund's vice president, W. H. "Ping" Ferry, again accepted.

On top of his law school duties, my father now found himself confronted with assembling and analyzing over 200,000 pages of testimony from congressional investigations, administrative hearings, and court cases. This mound of documents, left behind by the tide of an era already ebbing into the past, together with his own inclinations had changed the study's focus: from the credibility of Whittaker Chambers et al. to the process of fact-finding itself, from answers to questions. "The deeper I have got into the forest of hearings and trials in which these witnesses have unburdened themselves," he wrote in an interim report, "the more I have been struck by the incomplete and inconclusive nature of their testimony . . . If one theme runs through the many occasions on which these witnesses have testified, it is the inadequacy of the procedures employed to determine the 'historical truth.' "

If he had approached the task with as simple an agenda as Fulton Lewis, Jr., believed he had, then things would have been much easier. He could have hunted down every discrepancy, gap, and uncorroborated fact, feeling more energized, more vindicated by every find, and ignored a good deal of the rest. But his sense that the task demanded real objectivity and that the truth was an elusive thing drove him to read every page of testimony, and not just read but study, compare, cross-check. Without an ideological slant, he had only his powers of rational analysis. And the research was leading him to the conclusion that, for all the uncertainties in the vast pages of testimony, Alger Hiss was in all likelihood guilty of perjury and therefore espionage. Though nothing in the documentary record proves it to be true, he also felt— had felt from the start—that Hutchins, Ferry, and the officers of the

Fund, for all their hands-off protestations, wanted Hiss vindicated, and wanted it done while the public still cared. Now it was becoming clear that if the Fund wanted a quick and clean exoneration, it wasn't going to get one.

The burden of expectation, his scrupulous method, the scale of the labor, and his academic responsibilities began to paralyze my father.

On October 15, 1957, an officer of the Fund wrote: "Dear Herb: Where is it? Love, Hallock Hoffman." The answer came back, deceptively blithe: "A good claret takes at least five years. Is that any help?" In the files of the Fund for the Republic at Princeton's manuscript library, my father's note is tartly annotated by the pen of a Fund officer: "A. How long does it take a good lawyer? B. No."

A year and a half later Hoffman is writing again: "Some unreliable fellow told me that you had telephoned last weekend and announced that a progress report would be en route to us immediately. The only airplane crashes I have heard of have both been in Maryland. What is the problem?" My father's handwritten response now betrays a certain desperation. "Your quip about the plane crash had more relevance than I'm sure you intended. Two old and dear friends of my wife were killed in it . . . That, however, doesn't excuse my tardiness in answering your request for a report, nor would a description of my current work load—although it might arouse a measure of amused sympathy."

When the report finally arrived in November 1959, what my father later called "a failure of communication with the Fund for which I must bear the predominant responsibility" gave the impression that there would be no book-length analysis of the testimony—only an "Index-Digest" of abstracts. "This is execrable," Hoffman wrote in a memo to Ping Ferry. "What shall we do?" What Ferry did was fire off a letter to Carl Spaeth threatening to demand a refund. "I have just read Packer's report on the status of the ancient Testimony of Witnesses project entrusted to your institution. I just wanted you to know that, as vice president in charge of program, I am aghast."

The only document I have from this period that illuminates my father's mental state is a typed draft of a letter he wrote to Carl Spaeth, on yellow paper, self-edited in pencil, undated. It must have been composed in the last days of the decade. "As you know, I have had the feeling for a long time that people at the Fund, and Ferry in particular, saw this project from the outset as a means for striking a quick blow for freedom; and that they never quite reconciled themselves to our view that we could not lend ourselves to a partisan attack on the veracity of the witnesses or on the motives of those who used them. But suspecting that to be their reaction, all the more care should have been taken not to give them an excuse to air their disappointment on grounds irrelevant to the merit of what we were doing. My sense of guilt on this score is very strong." An additional sentence is crossed out: "I feel that I have failed you in a very crucial way."

My father goes on to propose a timetable that might salvage the project, but the letter ends bitterly. "This business has pretty well taken the joy out of my life for the present. I very much hope it won't have the same effect on you. It shouldn't. The fault, if fault there is, is mine."

Even this heartfelt confession to his boss at the law school, who had stood up for him in the midst of the hiring controversy, withheld the real depth of my father's anguish. In fact he was undergoing something like a nervous breakdown. He told my mother that he couldn't finish the book, that he wanted to quit his job and move the family to the beach, where, he rashly insisted, we would have enough savings to live on. The worth of his life had always been measured by achievement, and now it had all led to failure. He told her, "I imagine killing myself."

They were both thirty-four years old. It was the start of the 1960s. He had just received tenure; they were about to move into the modernist house they were having built on campus. They had a year-old daughter, and now my mother was pregnant again with me, and suddenly her husband was plunged into suicidal depression. The foundations of this new life turned out to be alarmingly weak.

In March they went to Alabama for George Huddleston's funeral. At my mother's old house my father depended on her so heavily that Bertha finally said, "Herb can't go to the bathroom without asking

Nancy," and she never shook the impression of her son-in-law's neediness. My father came back early to California in order to work, but his letters asked my mother to cut short her trip—he couldn't live without her. He wanted to tell his colleagues what was happening; she urged him not to, thought that he would never be trusted again. She responded to the crisis in the way she knew how, maybe the only way she could—by marshaling her energy, determining not to let her new family be destroyed, bracing her husband, helping him find an angle on his chapter about the ex-Communist Elizabeth Bentley. She saw what she was up against, and because she loved him and was frightened, she would fix it by force of character, would will him to persevere, the way she had tried to will her mother to come home sober. Having made up her mind to stay in the marriage, she would stake everything on its survival. But all the while she worried that she was bullying him.

I wouldn't have known any of this if she hadn't recently told me. It was one of the family stories that loyalty or shame had kept secret. I see it today as a dry run a decade early for the events at the other end of the '60s. I had once looked at those events as a random disaster, a tornado that chose our house to mangle. Now it seems that the parts had been assigned years before.

What if they had moved to a beach house in Santa Cruz? Is it even thinkable? My father never cared for the beach. He was useless outdoors. As far as I know, he never picked up a hammer in his life. He needed a book to read, work to do. What if he had just gone on leave from the law school, told Ping Ferry to take a cold shower, spent a year reading novels and listening to Mozart and playing with his two small children in the new house? What if my mother had said, "Of course talk to your friends. If they stop trusting you, then they're not real friends. Your happiness matters more than what people think. The only way for you to get through this is to let go for a while. We'll make do. You have to get those two hundred thousand pages out of your life." Would they have been better prepared for the much worse crisis that came later? Would our 1960s have ended differently? But it's impossible for me to imagine any alternative scenario. Given the limitless possibilities of revision, I can't change a single thing. All of it is fixed forever. I can't make my parents be anyone but who they were.

He saw a psychiatrist, and he forced himself back to work on the 200,000 pages, and after three or four months he came out of his depression. By the time I was born in August the delight on his face in pictures looks genuine. Two years later—six years after the original grant—*Ex-Communist Witnesses: Four Studies in Fact Finding* was published by Stanford University Press.

It must have been a severe letdown to Fulton Lewis, Jr., Herbert Hoover, and other partisans on one side or the other of what had been the most polarizing subject in postwar America—including, perhaps, Hutchins, Ferry, and my father's other benefactors at the Fund for the Republic. As a review in the *Carolina Israelite* said, "No one who believes Alger Hiss guilty will opt for Hiss' innocence after reading Professor Packer's book, nor will anyone who believes Hiss innocent realize Alger's painful guilt." The book's emphasis on the process of fact-finding rather than the truth itself was bound to seem pointless to anyone looking for ammunition to fight the Cold War. "While Professor Packer has written a conscientious and, in certain areas, an intelligent book," Nathaniel Weyl, himself an ex-Communist witness, wrote in William F. Buckley's *National Review*, "he suffers from lack of understanding of the world of Communist conspiracy . . . and a tendency to dwell on minor detail, neglecting the historically significant." "This is a disappointing book," another reviewer wrote, making the same complaint from the opposite side. "Pre-publication blurbs led one to expect an exposé of the use of government perjurers. But Packer has failed to make the most elementary judgments concerning the evidence he presents . . . It is time testimony of government witnesses was objectively evaluated."

What disappointed partisans of both sides was that every one of my father's conclusions—most importantly, that "the suspension of disbelief [toward Hiss] in which so many engaged for so long ought to be abandoned," but also that much of the witnesses' testimony remained uncorroborated or contradictory—was provisional. The book's main concern was "the pathology of fact-finding processes." Historical fact and truth were themselves difficult to secure, and the investigations of the McCarthy era, especially politicized congressional hearings, were deeply flawed instruments for doing so. Though the ex-Communists are found to be "largely convincing" witnesses, no comfort of certainty is offered anywhere—a result that no one but a rational, procedural liberal could want, and least of all those who, as my father said of the ex-Communists themselves, "appear to have forsaken one set of absolutes for another." In other words, it was exactly the kind of judicious book that Fulton Lewis, Jr., had predicted the study, being rigged from the start, could never produce.

Ex-Communist Witnesses didn't reveal my father's true feelings about loyalty oaths and congressional inquisitions. It focused on the weaknesses in the Communist hunts, not their viciousness. Unkindly viewed, his scrupulousness could be taken for timidity; but given his purpose, my father—who certainly would have wished Hiss innocent, if only to confound Richard Nixon—had to take a stance of strenuous objectivity: "As we now close the books on the Hiss case it must be with the consciousness that we have stopped far short of even so imperfect an approximation of 'truth' as the processes of law permit."

My father's life as a scholar, which had begun amid the muck of partisan politics, established itself on ground he held more sacred— the rational mind's ability to analyze fact and establish probability, if not absolute truth, which belonged to Stalinists and Republicans. His passion lay in reason. This was not the building block of a powerful political movement. Millions don't rally to the banner of Uncertainty. Procedural liberalism takes the individual in isolation; there is no class or community whose interests and desires it answers. It stands alone, like a man sifting through 200,000 pages without a hope of finding answers.

The Hiss-Chambers case never died (writing in *The Nation* as recently as 1997, Victor Navasky oddly enough cited my father's book in making one more attempt to vindicate Hiss). But by 1962 it had lost much of its heat and become a memory of the evil days alluded to in the book's dedication to Carl Spaeth, which quoted Virgil: *"Forsan et haec olim meminisse iuvabit"* — "Perhaps someday it will please us to remember these things." The new decade was creating a new climate, far more comfortable for liberals like my parents. On election night in 1960 my father leaned into the Zenith black-and-white television set, where a tortured smile was peeling Nixon's lips back from his teeth as he conceded to Kennedy and Pat stood blinking away tears, and he released all the frustrations of the 1950s, McCarthyism, Stevenson's two defeats, the Red-baiting that had targeted him, the ordeal of the witnesses study, his nervous breakdown. "Go ahead!" he exulted. "Cry!" His depression had lifted. He had a wife and two small children. The Democrats were back in power. And for the next decade his life, our life, would be the university.

From Birmingham in the 1890s to Stanford in the 1960s is a long way. But the scenes of my grandfather's and my father's careers have one thing in common: each stood at the center of the economic upheaval of its period. Birmingham epitomized raw industrialism, where wealth and power lay in minerals and pig iron and basic steel. Stanford was becoming the site of the postindustrial future. Already the electronics megalopolis now known as Silicon Valley was beginning to spread outward from the campus nerve center. The new source of wealth wasn't buried underground in coal, limestone, and iron ore deposits; human muscle wasn't required to extract and refine it. The new industry was knowledge — intellectual expertise — and already in 1963 the president of the University of California, Clark Kerr, estimated that it made up 29 percent of the GNP: "The university's invisible product, knowledge, may be the most powerful single element in our culture, affecting the rise and fall of professions and even of social classes, of regions and even of nations." The university became the knowledge factory. Its Morgans and DeBardelebens were the physicists and engineers who trained and in some cases taught at places like Stanford, thriving on a symbiotic relationship with government and business that seemed every bit as brilliant an arrangement as convict lease had been, only no one got killed, because the missiles stayed in their silos.

My parents were building a new life at ground zero of a revolution. They had settled in a state whose population increased by over five million during the 1950s, a factor of almost 50 percent. This explosion, which would make California the most populous state by the mid-1960s, had created not a new class structure as had the influx of immigrants to the eastern cities at the turn of the century, but rather the nearest thing in the United States to a classless society since the Civil War. Almost everyone was a recent immigrant here. Workers were paid well above the national average. The Japanese attack on Pearl Harbor galvanized the state's aerospace, shipbuilding, and electronics industries; the Cold War economy made California the nation's leading manufacturer of military hardware. Population pressure and the demands of this economy meant that a new public school had to be built every day, and back in the '50s and '60s, Californians were willing to pay for them. In the decade when I started school, the state spent over $2 billion on school structures and 40 percent of its annual budget on education. Its public school system was a national model, taking hundreds of thousands of California children all the way from elementary school to advanced degree. The GI Bill and the baby boom had created an enormous demand for higher education, and in the early '60s California expanded the number of campuses in the University of California system to nine, along with rapid growth in state universities and community colleges. For the first time anywhere, higher education became a mass product.

Tradition, class, religion, family, neighborhood, all the bonds that still identified and tied together and tied down Americans in places like Birmingham and New Haven, disintegrated in the dry western air. The concrete ribbons tying the long state together hadn't yet become choked with cars and road rage; they were called "freeways." There was more freedom, more money, more choice than anywhere else in the world. It wasn't Jefferson's utopia or George Huddleston's, and by the end of the 1960s it would look to much of the country like a nightmare. But if you were young and at least semi-educated and open to the new, California in 1960 could understandably be taken for an egalitarian democracy of swimming pools.

At the center of the California revolution—economic, social, cultural—was the university. In the determination of success, the postwar university became a monopoly power. To make it you had to pass through its gates. And no university has ever risen with more spectacular speed to renown and wealth than Stanford. It was young enough to see and exploit the forces that were transforming American society.

Because of Herbert Hoover's hatred of the New Deal, Stanford had largely missed out on the massive infusion of federal money for wartime research and development. Hoover had hoped that a partnership with business would raise the money that Harvard and MIT were receiving from Washington, but Bay Area industries were more interested in short-term profit than the benefits that scholarly research might bring in ten or twenty years. All this changed after the war, when an unsentimental and supremely self-confident electrical engineer named Frederick Terman, the son of the pioneer of intelligence testing Lewis Terman (who gave his name to my junior high school), became first dean of the School of Engineering and then provost of the university under Wallace Sterling. It took an engineer to see, as Terman wrote in a telegram while the war was still going on, that "war research which now secret will be basis postwar industrial expansion in electronics."

Unlike anyone else in higher education, Terman understood the future: that the success of the California economy would lie in defense-related technology, that the federal government would need research partners among a handful of universities, that this partnership would bring unprecedented money and opportunity to the universities shrewd enough to grasp them, that the "applied knowledge" it produced would in turn bring lucrative relations with the high-tech industries that would mushroom around the "cities of intellect." Terman called this new alliance of government, business, and university a "win-win-win" relationship, and in the two decades after the war he set about with astonishing single-mindedness to make it work at Stanford.

He succeeded so well that more than any other single person Fred Terman can be said to have created Silicon Valley.

Stanford's triumph had vast implications. Some of them took the form of violent eruption in the late 1960s. We're still reckoning with others today. "Win-win-win" meant the end of the ivory tower, the "community of scholars" that once kept its distance from the corrupting influences of power and money. Stanford and other leading universities now became "public-service institutions," deeply involved in social policy and private enterprise. They lost some of their intellectual independence in the bargain. Edward Ross's hope, expressed at the start of the century, that "other spiritual associations lying over against the state" would "redress the balance" of power concentrated in modern government now looked like a pipe dream. The universities were making themselves arms of the state. The individual scholar's loyalty shifted from the school to his grant-giving benefactor, whether a foundation or a company or, most often, a government agency. According to Clark Kerr, the only university-wide concern that occupied the attention of Berkeley professors was parking privileges. Acquiring the grants, running teams of researchers, exploiting the "knowledge products" that resulted turned professors into academic "entrepreneurs" and undermined the idea that the university was a community with a common purpose. In some cases scholars couldn't even discuss their work because it was classified by the Pentagon.

Terman encouraged these trends. He was a scientist, raised by his psychologist father to believe that nothing had real value unless it could be quantified. Like his father, he saw Stanford as a factory, dealing with "raw materials and with processes" and producing "something that is bought and paid for by the consuming public." Class size grew accordingly, in the interests of efficiency. As research and specialization became the measure of academic success, tenured faculty did less and less teaching about less and less. While competition among students to get into a place like Stanford and to do well there intensified (after the war Jews ceased being the only "greasy grinds"), undergraduate education suffered. Though he didn't go as far as the university secretary in calling for the abolition of the history department, Terman established a fairly ruthless regime in which departments had to justify their budgets by hauling in their share of federal patronage. It was survival of the fittest. Areas of study that didn't interest some funding agency were reduced or eliminated. Electrical engineering, applied physics, oceanography, biochemistry, and political science were cultivated, and they quickly made Stanford world-class; taxonomy, political theory, above all the humanities in general languished. Departmental power was reduced and the administration became swollen with new authority and bureaucracy. Insiders began to call the place Terman Tech.

In 1950 a strip of land on the southeastern edge of Stanford's enormous holdings was leased as an industrial park to electronics companies, many founded by Stanford grads, like Hewlett-Packard and Varian. This step toward the embrace of commerce proved fantastically successful, and by 1963, 42 companies employed 12,000 people on 700 acres of Stanford land. The companies hired experts trained in classrooms on the other side of California Avenue; the university received large contributions from the companies. Star professors worked both sides of the divide and benefited handsomely. No one seemed to mind that private individuals, private firms, and a private university were profiting from federal money. No George Huddleston stood up to defend the republican form of government and denounce special interests and special privileges. "The man and the dollar" was not the operative slogan of the postwar period. Blander, less pointed abstractions like "national security," "economic growth," and "academic excellence" justified the new arrangement as a kind of public service, even a form of patriotism. Terman himself believed that engineers like those at Stanford were eliminating poverty in America. "While the idealists, the social planners, the do-gooders, the socialists and others of their ilk . . . called for a better distribution of wealth," this hardheaded academic administrator told a group of engineers in 1956, men like those in his audience had already "solved the basic problem by making possible the creation of so much new wealth" that the social engineers were going to be put out of business.

Fred Terman was the perfect man for his moment. He was widely disliked by the faculty, especially those in obsolescent fields like classics and English. They regarded him as not just arrogant and heavy-handed but unimaginative, humorless, with his cold unsmiling face—incapable of seeing any value in the arts or any nuance in intellectual or personal life. Terman was the Gradgrind of the new university, and he kept an oversized loose-leaf account book in which the productivity of every professor was measured in class size and salary. His fanatical insistence on quantification dovetailed with the interests of the federal government and the academic trend of the 1950s, when the success of the physical sciences was being emulated in the study of man—in politics, in psychology, in sociology, even in philosophy—under the new rubric "behavioral sciences." These fields were heavily funded by the Ford Foundation and other private philanthropies looking for relatively uncontroversial ways to spend their money. The animating principle was "value-neutrality." Humanistic studies, if they were to have any credibility at all, needed to copy the scientific model: instead of asking ultimate questions of value, they needed to analyze human phenomena by means of numbers, which offered the only reliable method of establishing the truth. Ethical philosophers were phased out to make room for symbolic analysts; Machiavelli and Rousseau gave way to polling data; the heirs of Edward Ross and Thorstein Veblen became fellows at the Center for the Advanced Study of the Behavioral Sciences. "Objectivity," which had been claimed by the left and the right throughout the century, now lost every trace of ideology and fell into the hands of the academic experts—who meant "value-neutrality." Herbert Hoover spent these years complaining that his beloved Stanford was being overrun by liberals. It was partly true, but liberals and conservatives alike were muting their political views in number-crunching. Whether a response to the dangers of the McCarthy period—or a larger postwar intellectual trend, the idea that truth lay in "value-neutrality" may have had more far-reaching implications than anything else about the rise of the research university.

Not long ago, on a trip back home, I was walking in the cow hills above the Stanford campus. It was an October afternoon, and the grass was yellow from the long months without rain; by February or March the grass would be green and the earth dark brown. These hills had played a large part in the imagination of my boyhood. Rising between the campus and the Pacific Ocean, with their dirt trails and waist-tall grass and live oak, the hills represented a world of wildness. Though they sloped up only a few hundred yards from my house, they seemed miles away, almost inaccessible. The thought of stepping on a rattlesnake in the grass, as a school friend of mine almost did, was a terrifying thrill. Later, as a teenager I ran the steep trails to train for cross-country and came to associate the smell of dirt and dry grass with exhaustion and a parched-throat exhilaration. From the top you could take in the whole campus, a sea of red terra-cotta tile roofs, and the Hoover Tower, and the surrounding cities, all the way to San Francisco Bay. Those runs took me past the Dish, a huge satellite built up on the ridge. The Dish was an anomaly in the hills; nothing else was built there, or so it seemed to me then.

But on my recent October walk I entered a clearing of live oak and stumbled on two abandoned trailers bristling with broken antennae. Their windows were smashed and their doors ajar. Inside one I found, amid the leavings of rodents, several boxes of rusted metal the size of four-drawer filing cabinets. They were computers, dating from the 1950s, institutional green with big ungainly knobs and dials and needles. Nearby stood stouter black boxes that looked like radio transmitters. Forty years before, the trailers had been a cutting-edge communications station, the project of some academic "entrepreneur" with a Defense Department grant and a team of research assistants. The grant ran out, the project ended, the field of study moved onward and upward. No one bothered to dismantle the site and the trailers were left to decay. I had just begun to read about Stanford's history and here were some of the remains. Those abandoned computers evoked in me a strong feeling of the period in which I was born and received my early schooling—the ugly industrial design of the Cold War, the solemn voice-over of scratchy 16-mm fourth-grade science films, the faith in education.

I couldn't have expressed this when I was in elementary school, but I grew up believing in scientism and meritocracy. That is, I and the other children in my school, and children all over California, which had become the leading edge of the nation, were raised to think that the key to success was education, not money or birth, and the measure of educational success was testing, and the standard of success in testing was quantitative results. None of this had been the case in my parents' generation, let alone my grandparents', and it may well not be the case in my children's if I have any. But in some ways this belief was born at Stanford, where the elder Terman authored the Stanford-Binet IQ test, and which the younger Terman made the epitome of the postwar research institution.

By 1963 Stanford was one of six universities that received over half their operating budgets from federal patronage. That year Clark Kerr went to Harvard to give a series of lectures that were published in a soon to be famous and infamous book called *The Uses of the University*. In paying tempered homage to the postwar university—he was among the first to recognize what was new about it—Kerr coined the term "multiversity" to describe this loose collection of federally funded academic entrepreneurs, each working in his area of expertise. "This new phase can carry the American commitment to education to new heights of endeavor," Kerr said at Harvard. "It can enlarge the horizons of equality of opportunity. It can maintain and even increase the margin for excellence." In making his case for the multiversity, Kerr acknowledged that its elitism flew in the face of democratic sentiments. His answer went straight back to Jefferson—or to Kerr's version of him. "How may the contribution of the elite be made clear to the egalitarians," he asked, "and how may an aristocracy of intellect justify itself to a democracy of all men? It was equality of opportunity, not equality *per se*, that animated the founding fathers of the American system; but the forces of populist equality have never been silent, the battle between Jeffersonianism and Jacksonianism never finally settled."

So the rise of an intellectual elite was given the imprimatur of Jefferson himself. By an odd historical irony, Kerr's talks at Harvard mirrored and amplified a talk given twenty-three years before, in 1940, when Harvard's president, James Bryant Conant, made the trip in reverse to give the Charter Day Address at Berkeley. Conant's speech, published in *The Atlantic Monthly* under the title "Education for a Classless Society: The Jeffersonian Tradition," held up public schools as the means to democratize the unequal society that the industrial age had produced in America. The answer to class stratification was meritocracy and social mobility. "The requirement," Conant said at Berkeley, anticipating Kerr, "is not a radical equalization of wealth at any given moment; it is rather a continuous process by which power and privilege may be automatically redistributed at the end of each generation." This automatic redistribution could only be achieved by making education available to all: "that great gift to each succeeding generation—opportunity, a gift that once was the promise of the frontier." The frontier had ended at the Pacific and was now closed, but in 1940 Conant was speaking in the state of the future. If the new frontier of educational opportunity could be created anywhere, it would be in California.

The speeches of Harvard's Conant at Berkeley and Berkeley's Kerr at Harvard can be seen as bookends to the fantastic transformation of higher education that took place in the middle of the century, and a measure of the change. In Conant you hear the egalitarian liberal of the New Deal era invoking Jefferson to sanction education as the key to "a classless society." In Kerr you hear the corporate liberal of the Kennedy era invoking Jefferson to defend the new academic elite against the attacks of "populists." The following year, in 1964, those attacks came—and the populists turned out to be right under Kerr's nose. They were the Berkeley elite, and they were staging the first student revolt of the decade. In naming their grievances some of them used the term "multiversity"; it turned out to be a place where they felt more alienated than privileged. Kerr in his talk had anticipated "a minor counterrevolt" of the student " 'lumpen proletariat' " against a "blanket of impersonal rules for admissions, for scholarships, for examinations, for degrees." As it happened, the Free Speech Movement was more major than minor, and more revolt than counterrevolt—the first of a series of explosions that nearly destroyed Berkeley and soon spread across the bay to Stanford and then across the nation. By 1967 California's newly elected governor, Ronald Reagan, having seen enough, would relieve Kerr of the presidency of UC.

"Of all systems," Clark Kerr would say after being fired, "the meritocratic system may be the hardest to run and may set up the most strains."

I always think of the early 1960s as a golden age, though an essential feature of golden ages is that one remembers almost nothing about them. A dead orange cat buzzed by flies on a sidewalk remains my most vivid memory from the New Frontier and Great Society. Kennedy and Johnson were not exactly Aristotle's great-souled men, but they presided over an era of reform in which liberal intellectuals were no longer Stevensonian egghead pinkos and not yet Spiro Agnew's effete corps of impudent snobs. Instead, bringing knowledge and power into harmony, they were asked to put their minds at the service of social change. Whatever I've since discovered about the "best and the brightest," early Vietnam, the Kennedys' weakness on civil rights, the "other America," Cheever's suburban misery, and Sexton's mad housewives, has made little dent on my sense that it was a wonderful time in America. Convictions that are personal and impressionistic have nothing to do with historical knowledge and are far stronger. It doesn't matter that some of the associations date from years later. To this day the word "cocktail," the typeface of books circa 1964, the black-and-white pictures of serious forty-year-old men in black-rimmed glasses and thin ties, give me a feeling of extraordinary well-being: The world is in capable, grown-up hands. Good will prevail. LBJ is helping the Negroes in East Palo Alto, where my racially progressive parents have me enrolled for the summer at the Nairobi Day School, and where my best friend is a five-year-old black boy named Cookie.

My father never liked the Kennedys. He had distrusted both brothers ever since Jack, as a senator, maintained a prudent silence on Joe McCarthy's inquisition and their father pulled strings to get Bobby a job as an aide on the Wisconsin senator's committee. The McCarthy era was my father's litmus test for anyone old enough to have taken a position, and neither of the Kennedys passed. He saw them as tools of their father's ambition, opportunists rather than the idealists that violent death has made of their memory. He agreed, for once, with his late father-in-law, George Huddleston, who said in the last year of his life, "That bushy-haired Irish boy doesn't rate to run." When Jack, as President, and Bobby, as Attorney General, vacillated while Freedom Riders were assaulted in bus terminals and black children were terrorized by the Birmingham police, neither of my parents forgave them. The Kennedys, with their cold-blooded calculations ("I am obligated to carry out the court order"), were failing the great moral question of the 1960s as they had failed in the 1950s.

It wasn't the two good-looking Boston-born Harvard grads, but the big-eared vulgarian from the Texas hill country and Southwest Texas State Teachers College, Vice President Lyndon Johnson, who insisted to Kennedy's speechwriter Ted Sorensen: "The Negroes are tired of this patient stuff and tired of this piecemeal stuff and what they want more than anything else is not an executive order or legislation, they want a moral commitment that he's behind them. I want to pull out this cannon. The President is the cannon. You let him be on all the TV networks just speaking from his conscience . . . I know the risks are great and it might cost us the South, but those sorts of states may be lost anyway. The difference is if your President just enforces court decrees the South will feel it's yielded to force. He ought to make it almost make a bigot out of nearly anybody that's against him, a high lofty appeal, treat these people as Americans." And yet Kennedy remained—and remains—the liberals' darling, while Johnson may never be known for anything but Vietnam.

On its surface, the Kennedy administration was in every way congenial to people like my parents. Kennedy presented himself as the intellectuals' President, a Stevenson who knew what it took to win (vote theft in Chicago and Texas). This presentation was made on the level of personal style and rhetoric—a prickly, antinomian freelancer like Dwight Macdonald would not have been at ease in Camelot—but this was just the level on which a newly emergent and status-conscious class was most easily reached. The New Frontier began a confusion of intellectual life and style, money, and fame that is by now so complete we hardly see it as confusion. Twice before in the twentieth century, political power was open to reform ideas. But Progressive-era intellectuals like Randolph Bourne and even the well-connected editors of *The New Republic* remained outsiders, independent minds with quite radical notions for remaking American society. The New Deal brain trusters from Columbia and Harvard reached the highest circles of government influence, but they did so as individuals without obvious class interests, aligning themselves with workers and farmers against the status quo of business power. But in the Kennedy years the best and the brightest, within the administration and on its periphery, were practically anointed the new American elite. Entry into the Kennedy circles gave erstwhile eggheads and former freelance radicals purchase on a style of restrained glamour in the company of movie stars and famous singers and beautiful women, a cooler, more cerebral version of the experience that Hugh Hefner's empire was promising the readers of *Playboy*.

By the 1960s it was conservatives who were sounding like populists; liberals were making their peace with the new power centers in the universities and Washington. One writer of the period informed English readers that "American liberalism is an academic creed which flourishes hardly anywhere outside the schools and universities: perhaps its chief weakness." It was the Republican President Eisenhower who warned in his farewell message of a "military-industrial complex" and "the prospect of the domination of the nation's scholars by Federal employment, project allocations, and the power of money." But the Democrat Kennedy, in his 1963 message on education, hailed the new order as "aristocracy of achievement arising out of democracy of opportunity." No wonder sophisticated men like Arthur Schlesinger, Jr., and

Richard Rovere and Norman Mailer and Gore Vidal lost their bearings when Kennedy turned his detached but flattering gaze on them.

Here is how Christopher Lasch, in his 1965 book *The New American Radicalism*, described the American intellectual of the early '60s: "typically a graduate of an Ivy League college; he wore Ivy League clothes with the same casual authority with which he talked about books, wine, and women; he had traveled widely, mostly in Europe; he lived in a modern house filled with Danish furniture; his boys had long hair instead of crew cuts; his political opinions, like his other tastes, were vaguely unconventional and advanced; he was always questioning things the rest of us took for granted. In short, he was sophisticated." Lasch concluded, "The intellectuals, as a class, had achieved official recognition, affluence, prestige, and power, and something of the mentality that goes with them."

The portrait veers too far toward James Bond to fit my father exactly. I don't think he ever talked about women with casual authority—on rare occasions it was more with a clumsy enthusiasm; he hadn't traveled widely; though he wore tweed jackets and button-down shirts, at a slightly plump five foot six he had none of the bearing of an aristocrat and didn't aim for it. He was still too much the lonely Jewish boy. But he did know books and was beginning to know wine. Our house was modern; the furniture might as well have been Danish. By kindergarten my hair was "long." Taste and sophistication mattered to my parents, probably more to my wellborn mother than my lower-middle-class father. They collected prints and paintings by California artists like David Hockney and Nate Oliveira. When a family room was added to the house they had two floor-to-ceiling bookcases installed that opened like secret doors onto climate-controlled wine closets. Our coffee table was a three-quarter-inch-thick glass slab laid on top of a sculpture made of roughly wrought bronze that acted as the legs. My mother drank Dubonnet. The first movie I remember our family going to see was *My Fair Lady*, in 1964.

These cultural markers belong to the moment in the early '60s when people like my parents were beginning to achieve "official recognition." They match Lasch's portrait in the essentials. Coming across it reminded me of V. S. Naipaul's description in *The Enigma of Arrival* of leaving his native Trinidad for the first time at age eighteen to go to Oxford on a scholarship. The propeller plane shows him what he had never seen from the ground, "a landscape of logic and larger pattern . . . of clear pattern and contours, absorbing all the roadside messiness, a pattern of dark green and dark brown, like camouflage, like a landscape in a book, like the landscape of a real country. So that at the moment of takeoff almost, the moment of departure, the landscape of my childhood was like something which I had missed, something I had never seen." Lasch's picture showed me the world of my childhood from the air—as a world. The view made it seem narrower, but also more real. A child has no notion of being born into a certain historical time, into a certain social class, with its own tastes and desires and anxieties. A coffee table is the sharp-cornered object to be avoided on the living-room floor, not an emblem of the prestige and affluence of the new intellectual class. Decades can go by before you discover that, whatever efforts you might make to reinvent yourself, they must come against this backdrop. Here is the given.

When Robert Kennedy asked my father to serve on the Attorney General's Committee on Poverty and the Administration of Federal Criminal Justice, he contributed to its report calling for federally funded lawyers to represent poor criminal defendants. After a decade in the Eisenhower-Nixon wilderness, his talents were suddenly wanted at the seat of power. The worst prig would have felt gratified.

His area of specialization was becoming the criminal law, and he wrote about it in the spirit of the philosophers whom he'd read as a young man, John Stuart Mill and the Utilitarians. On every issue that was to become controversial during the 1960s, and remains controversial today—heroin, pornography, abortion, homosexuality, gambling, preventive detention, wiretapping—he put the burden of justification on the state for taking away the liberty of individuals. He was not a militant libertarian; he was enough a believer in the Utilitarian credo of the greatest good for the greatest number to recognize the interests of society, not just in protecting itself but in creating the conditions for public happiness. In the most influential of his four books, *The Limits of the Criminal Sanction*, he posed two models of criminal law—"due process" and "crime control"—and negotiated their competing claims. But in case after case, he argued for decriminalizing the so-called victimless crimes that did not meet Mill's famous test for depriving liberty: "The only purpose for which power can be rightfully exercised over any member of a civilized community, against his will, is to prevent harm to others. His own good, either physical or moral, is not a sufficient warrant."

Unlike *Ex-Communist Witnesses*, *The Limits of the Criminal Sanction* moved beyond analysis of data to propose a bold philosophical rethinking of the justification for punishment of crime. "We resort to it in far too indiscriminate a way, thereby weakening some of the important bases upon which its efficacy rests and threatening social values that far transcend the prevention of crime," he concluded. "It becomes inefficacious when it is used to enforce morality rather than to deal with conduct that is generally seen as harmful." The book won a prestigious triennial prize for legal scholarship, became a classic, and ensured that my father's reputation would survive him.

His skepticism about legislating morality was based on pragmatism as well as liberal principle. Between 1963 and 1968 crime rates in America increased by as much as 50 percent, and the illegal drug profits, the burden on the courts, the corruption of police tactics, the public's distrust of the criminal justice system, the crime surge itself were all partly due to the fact that America had made more things illegal than it could enforce. My father called it the "crime tariff" and compared it to Prohibition. In the experimental and hopeful atmosphere of the early 1960s, with the Warren Court handing down sympathetic decisions, this argument could be calmly made and seriously discussed. But "law and order" soon became one of the hottest political slogans of the decade, the battle cry of the growing middle-class revulsion toward demonstrators and dropouts that Richard Nixon would exploit so shrewdly in 1968. In the eyes of the "silent majority" the crime explosion became bound up with urban riots and campus disturbances, the smell of generational rot and national moral decay. The solution was to lock more people up. My father's utilitarian approach to criminal law, though widely praised in the legal field, became more and more a minority position, as it remains to this day, when the "drug war" has deprived over 300,000 Americans of their liberty, so that we can hardly build enough jails to house them.

But what's striking as I read his papers from the Kennedy and Johnson years is how often history then was on his side — on the side of reason, as he saw it, and of reform. The tone of his writings is quiet confidence: here is how rational people see these things, and sooner or later rationality will prevail. Reviewing the report of the Warren Commission in *The Nation* he found fault with part of its process but affirmed the result: "Only those who for whatever reasons of personal or political myopia cannot bring themselves to face reality will continue to think that the tragedy was proximately the work of more than one man and therefore ultimately the outcome of a conspiracy." A liberal Presbyterian magazine asked him to explain the difference between the sit-ins of civil rights activists and Governor George Wallace standing "in the schoolhouse door" of the University of Alabama to prevent the first black students from registering. Ten months earlier, Martin Luther King had addressed just this question from his jail cell in Birmingham, and his famous letter answered it on moral, even spiritual, grounds: "The answer lies in the fact that there are two types of laws: just and unjust," King wrote. "Any law that uplifts human personality is just. Any law that degrades human personality is unjust." But my father, the law professor, would not "venture into the deep waters of philosophic speculation about the moral justifiability of disobeying an unjust law." Instead the argument was narrowly legal: George Wallace's behavior was "lawless" defiance of a court order, while the sit-ins were testing the validity of local law by forcing it into the courts. If they continued after the courts ruled, then they would be just as illegitimate as Wallace's stand. "Primary reliance should be placed," the end of the article cautioned, "upon quiet and orderly processes of conciliation and negotiation to resolve specific civil-rights disputes."

Combatants on both sides of a revolution that transformed American society might well find the niceties of this argument irrelevant. They might point out that a legal scholar on a university campus thousands of miles from Birmingham couldn't begin to grasp the intensity of the passions and the enormity of the stakes. "Moral justifiability" was exactly what the civil rights movement was about. My father argued everything on the merits, but the answer might come back from both sides of the struggle: "That's easy for you to say. You don't know what it's like."

Here was the weak spot in my parents' wonderful new life. They could criticize, and in good faith, the administration's foot-dragging on civil rights law. They could deplore the university's myopic focus on research money at the cost of humanistic values. But they were inside the gates, comfortable there. Nothing real had to be sacrificed. They basically identified with that vague new thing just now beginning to be discussed in more radical circles—the Establishment. For this reason, they presented a tempting target to those who felt left out of the new liberal order.

One of them was my mother's brother George. Uncle George was a pale, redheaded, sweet-natured man whom I always remember smiling. He didn't share his father's relish for the lonely fight, had no interest in playing David. He lived by the political advice his father had offered without ever following it himself—"If you want to get along, go along." Neither demagogue nor dissenter, my uncle was badly equipped to deal with the revolution that swept through the South during his decade in Congress. When he talked about race it was in bland terms calculated to offend no one. A speech of his, "The Negro and the South," didn't mention political rights one way or the other, but instead described the disadvantages blacks faced as a kind of unfortunate historical accident and emphasized their need to acquire the skills that would equip them to play a vital role in the industrial economy. When the most violent klavern of the Birmingham Klan began phoning and telegramming his office, just a few months before Klansmen assaulted Freedom Riders at the downtown Trailways station on

Mother's Day, 1961, my uncle telegrammed back in the same spirit with which he'd answered the inquiry of black citizens after his election in 1954: he told the Klan to let him know if he could ever be of service.

In 1963 Martin Luther King chose to make Birmingham the scene of the civil rights movement's climax. In May of that year my uncle had the unenviable job of representing the city in Congress while schoolchildren were being herded into Bull Connor's police vans, threatened with snarling German shepherd dogs, and sprayed across Kelly Ingram Park by high-powered water cannons. Out of the long silence of oppression came a joyous explosion of singing, shouting black boys and girls. Segregation was crumbling in the most segregated city in America, the whole Jim Crow structure that the 1901 constitution had cemented in place was coming apart, and official Birmingham reacted with maniacal frenzy. The South's racial history was finally catching up with the Huddleston family.

No southern politician could hope to get reelected in 1964 unless he let his white constituents know where he stood on the agitators and the feds. So Uncle George had to defend the indefensible—not in the viciously racist terms of the demagogues of 1901; not as a matter of sacred rights as his father would have done; but in the neutral language of efficient city government. "Mr. Speaker, the police dog as an effective law-enforcement tool is a well-established fact. During the last six years there has been a tremendous growth of interest by cities using the dogs as an aid to regular law-enforcement officers. For more than a hundred years the London, England, metropolitan police have used police dogs in carrying out their duties. The record of the London police force and its K-9 corps is an outstanding one . . . Mr. Speaker, it has been proven in more than one city that the dogs have been especially effective in control of riots. By the wide use of dogs, one can readily see there is nothing remiss in the fact that the Birmingham Police Department has used police dogs in quelling the riots and demonstrations there."

But the whole country saw the pictures, and they were unforgettable, and Birmingham has never lived them down. In Stanford my mother saw them and felt grateful to have gotten out. For no white person in Birmingham, not even outspoken liberals like David Vann and Charles Morgan, dared to side with King's confrontational tactics in loosing children on the downtown streets to bait Bull Connor's men. The *Birmingham News* kept the story in its own backyard off the front page, later claiming that it wanted to avoid inciting a backlash of white violence. As a result, a large portion of Birmingham's white population hardly knew what was going on that first week of May. A woman I met recently in Birmingham, who had moved there from Ohio shortly before the demonstrations, told me, "It was happening in another world." But for the rest of the country, the events in Birmingham made the civil rights movement a matter of national conscience.

Thanksgiving that year found us all together at my mother's sister Jane's house in Swarthmore, Pennsylvania. For the holiday my uncle George, his wife, A. J., and their children had come up from Washington; Bertha Huddleston, now thriving as a widow, rode up on the train from Birmingham; and our family was spending my father's sabbatical year just down the street from Jane and her family. My earliest memories date from that year and include watching from a perch on my twelve-year-old cousin's shoulders in the middle of a huge crowd as President Johnson's green military helicopter landed with a terrific rush of rotary blades on the Swarthmore campus in the spring of 1964, where he received an honorary degree.

Johnson had just become President on the Friday before that Thanksgiving 1963. My grandmother took the news from Dallas hardest: "They'll blame it on the South!" she cried. Over the holiday weekend, nerves rattled by the assassination, the adults went into Philadelphia for dinner at Bookbinder's restaurant, where my aunt A. J. remembers an unpleasant argument breaking out in the corner booth between her husband and my father.

My father was making a case for the civil rights legislation that Kennedy hadn't lived to get through Congress. George, who would have to cast a vote on that legislation and see it enforced in his district, was defending the right of states and merchants to be free from federal intervention. At some point in the evening, his face brick red with rage, George snapped at my father: "You're just a knee-jerk liberal!" According to A. J., things between the two men were never quite the same again.

I would like to know what my mother was feeling during the course of that meal—torn between her love of a fight and her desire for peace, the competing claims of loyalty to her husband and her brother, the internationally reviled hometown she'd left far behind, her family and her conscience. But she can't tell me, since she has no memory of the argument having taken place. Maybe she repressed it. Or maybe it never happened. Memory is a function of character, and maybe the memory of my aunt, a woman not given to confrontation, exaggerated what would have passed at our dinner table for garden-variety political talk. Or maybe Uncle George went home and fumed about his liberal brother-in-law. But whether or not the two men fought that night, politics now divided the family.

A few months later, Johnson succeeded where Kennedy hadn't and brought sweeping civil rights legislation before Congress. My uncle found himself where his father had twice been, in direct confrontation with a President of his own party, and he resisted the Civil Rights Bill of 1964, trying to make it a matter of "man's right to hold, manage, and control the use of his property." But his deepest worry was reelection. Before the vote in the House, he was approached in his Capitol Hill office by a group of black leaders from Birmingham, urging him not to oppose it.

"I would lose my seat. It would be political suicide."

"We're not asking you to vote for it," the visitors said. "Just be absent the day it comes to the floor."

"What!" my uncle cried, well aware of the irony in what he was about to say. "And give up my right to stand for what I believe in?"

Unlike his father, he didn't go down on principle. He voted against the Civil Rights Bill to keep his seat and lost it anyway, to a conservative Republican named John Buchanan, who two decades later became the surprising founder of the liberal group People for the American Way. George Huddleston, Jr., was one of three Alabama Democrats to lose in the 1964 Goldwater Republican sweep of the South, which completed what the Dixiecrats of 1948 had begun and turned the partisan direction of southern politics 180 degrees for the next generation (on the night he signed the Civil Rights Bill into law, President Johnson glumly prophesied to his aide Bill Moyers, "I think we just delivered the South to the Republican Party for a long time to come"). None of the losers among Alabama Democrats was a race liberal, but George and the others had not been strident enough, and George had ridden a campaign train through the southern states with LBJ, who was now an archtraitor to his home region. Besides, in Alabama voters could pull one lever to vote the straight party ticket, and some of my uncle's personal friends had pulled the Republican lever for Goldwater imagining that George would be reelected easily.

Defeat was a greater shock to him than it had been to his father, and it sat even harder. My uncle was so bitter that he never again returned to his home state of Alabama until his body was brought back for burial in 1971. After years of working as a Washington lobbyist for an aerospace company and drinking heavily, he died of a heart attack at his office desk with the newspaper open to an article about the Attica prison uprising. All week, the sight of prisoners taking guards hostage had had him glued to the TV in a rage. He was buried next to his father in Elmwood Cemetery, in what by then had become a black neighborhood.

By 1971 the worm had turned for my father—he was in bad shape and so was his liberalism. But that Thanksgiving weekend in 1963 he could feel that history was bearing him out. Within a year all the strains in liberalism would make themselves felt. In August 1964 the Tonkin Gulf resolution let slip the dogs of the Vietnam War, and the old New Deal coalition soon split down the middle between hawks and doves. Later that month, in Atlantic City, the Democratic convention's failure to seat a black splinter delegation calling themselves the Mississippi Freedom Democratic Party marked the beginning of the end of the interracial civil rights movement. That fall, at Berkeley, the Free Speech Movement signaled the rise of radicalism among students against their liberal teachers. Those days of 1963 and the first half of 1964 were the high-water mark of my father's life. He was thirty-eight, my age as I write this.

The early 1960s were also, in my personal mythology, the golden age for my family—the more so for how thoroughly my memories before 1969 have been wiped out. In color pictures my father looks tan and healthy in the California sun, his hair longer on top, with a black summertime goatee. Holding hands with his pregnant wife, standing on the construction site of the new house, cooing over his baby daughter, clutching his baby son in both arms, he is smiling as never in pictures before or since.

I depend on photographs because I have not one real memory of my father in his health. I can't see him walking; I can't see his right hand holding a drink; I can't hear his clear, measured voice. When I was little, I'm told, he bathed me and read to me. In home movies he laughs, rolls his eyes, and makes faces as he pays bills; on a trip to the mountains he engages me in a snowball fight. But I remember none of this either. What I remember are objects around him: his pipes on a circular pipe stand, and the pleasant sharp smell of tobacco; his blood-red medicated shampoo and my sense of initiation into the mysteries of adulthood when he washed my towhead with it. And I remember, one day while he was away at work, trying to forge a letter from Stanford's President Sterling informing him that he was fired; when he came home he indulged me in the lie that he was fooled for a moment, before explaining with mild irony why it was unlikely that he would be fired, at least not in handwriting. Was I suggesting that he spend more time with his son?

In public, at work, he could be quick-tempered and often shot from the hip. When a colleague on a panel said something slighting about him, then afterward told him, "I don't know why I said that," my father answered, "Because you're just a son of a bitch, that's why." But he had no taste for domestic confrontation. I am told that he was a gentle, warm husband and father. His most consuming moments came in the quiet of his study, with a book. Not the sort of cruelly absent father thirty-somethings rediscover in therapy, but a benevolent, inward one, who left faint impressions that were erased as easily as footprints by the tide.

It didn't matter to me. He would have gotten in the way of my romance with my mother. In later years she liked to say, "I wasn't a very good mother but I was a damn good father." The father in her (who else but *hers*?) provided the beginnings of a moral education. Once, when I was no more than three and making a scene at the supermarket checkout line, my mother told the cashier, "Wait. I'll be right back." She carried me out to the car, sat me down inside with her, closed the door, and turned to address me. By this time fear had killed my bawling. "I don't embarrass you in public," she said. "Don't embarrass me." My record was far from clean after that, but I felt each transgression with a sharper bite of conscience than screaming or spanking would have achieved.

My parents managed the crucial thing of making my sister and me feel early on that our world was one of security and love. We were neither excessively indulged nor harshly disciplined. Our parents treated us like adults-in-training. This approach to child rearing was reflected in our vocabulary for the nether regions. "Passing gas is like hiccups in your rectum" went one of my early observations, and when I kept trying to lift a baby-sitter's skirt and the poor woman asked my sister what I wanted, she answered, "He wants to see your vagina, stupid." Our parents shaped my sister and me with respect but also a fairly heavy burden of responsibility, along rational lines. Santa Claus never made it into our household, nor the Tooth Fairy or the Easter Bunny. When I came home from a Christian friend's house talking about God, my mother said, "You know, we don't believe in God." I told her that at our house I didn't and at their house I did.

My mother wished that my father would involve himself more with the children, yet in trying to keep stress from pushing him back to the edge of a breakdown, she took most of the responsibility for child rearing on herself. And my father simply didn't know how to talk to a four-year-old about criminal law. Nor was he interested in sports. When I was slightly older, I began to receive an early intellectual training under his gentle questioning or else by listening to the adult conversations at our dinner table. But my ex-tomboy mother was the one who tossed the football with me, installed a basketball hoop, handicapped herself by playing Ping-Pong left-handed and whipped me anyway, spent hours with me in front of the RCA color TV watching the Lakers and the NFL and the Stanford Indians.

My parents were continually hosting dinner and cocktail parties or going out to them, leaving my sister and me with baby-sitters. I didn't feel neglected—I loved these occasions, loved seeing my parents dressed up, my mother wearing earrings and perfume. That my parents had their own separate adult life made me feel happy and, by extension, important. They were the family's connection to a world of glamour, the university, where grown-ups drank and talked their grown-up talk, and the best moment of a party at our house came when my sister and I were summoned from the TV room to say good night to the guests before going off to bed, and how glad the company seemed to see us, how the grown-up talk stopped as they turned to us, how much pleasure they took in this ritual of saying good night.

Our house—one story, H-shaped, plate-glass walls looking out on front and back patios with pine trees and a Japanese maple—was built on a one-third-acre lot in the middle of a field surrounded by similar lots on which other houses were going up. The street was a dead end no more than a hundred feet long, off another, longer dead-end street. This little neighborhood, part of the new faculty ghetto near campus (my father called Stanford's housing policy "tying the peasants to the land"), was the perfect place to be a small child. Cars rarely came down the cul-de-sacs. I walked by myself to kindergarten, a quarter mile away. Eighteen children under the age of ten lived in eight adjacent houses, within shouting distance of one another. Every family had a yard. On one side of ours were the Handys—an illustrator, his wife, four kids; on the other side the Eldridges—a gastroenterologist, his wife, two kids including the neighborhood bully; and two doors down the Liebermans—a statistician, his wife, four kids, the ones my sister and I were closest to. Our other neighbors were a historian, a physicist, an administrator (the men, that is; the women were all housewives). Every evening in summer one of the neighborhood children only had to ring a couple of doorbells and soon a dozen or more kids would be out on the street for hours of red rover or freeze tag. On July 4 we decorated our bikes in red, white, and blue crepe paper and paraded up and down the block; on Christmas we had a block party and went caroling house to house. It was a true community, and it took me years to realize just how lucky we were.

Stanford then, even in the midst of its phenomenal postwar rise, was still relatively rural. Large stretches of unused land, overgrown with yellow grass in summer or turning to marshy bogs in winter, brought the natural world right up to the fences behind our houses. One very dry summer, snakes came down from the foothills, looking for water, and a dozen turned up in our house and around the yard; lifting a maple leaf, I found a baby green snake curled up like a piece of string. The larger one that crawled up to the front door induced a more panicked reaction because my mother thought it might be poisonous; it met its bloody fate under my father's shovel, the only time I can remember him acting the role of paterfamilias around the house.

A reeky mudhole under a willow tree behind the Liebermans' house provided me every spring with an endless supply of froglets no larger than a nickel, which I collected—along with the black-and-orange caterpillars that become monarch butterflies—in Yuban coffee cans and brought home, only to watch them die in terrible numbers under my care. I was an overly sensitive boy and found animals a constant source of delight and grief. At least once a week one of the plate-glass walls around our house would shudder with a thud, and I would run outside to see if the bird that had just mistaken the wall for open air and smashed its existence against the glass was still quivering on the ground. The survivors ended up in a shoe box, where I would tend them carefully, looking for signs of hope as they made their pathetic attempts to beat their wings, until one morning I would peer inside the box to find a motionless creature with black sunken eyes.

When the university decided to build fraternity houses on the land behind us, our little world only became more exciting. The mounds of excavated dirt and the foundation trenches made ideal locations for war games, and we built our forts out of stolen wood and steel rebar.

I was in the middle of a splendid boyhood, on the country's most beautiful campus, in its most beautiful state. The red-tiled roofs, the smell of juniper and live oak in the foothills, the swarms of tadpoles that magically sprouted legs every spring, the games of kick-the-can with other kids on our dead-end street in the long, long summer evenings—the scene of my childhood was so idyllic that my whole adulthood sometimes seems like a corrective.

As late as 1968 the picture holds. Home movies show my father, my sister, and me collecting starfish on an overcast beach. But he's paler than in the earlier photos, and his body has thickened in the middle as if returning to boyhood plumpness. Never one to exercise much, he looks badly out of shape. His life has taken an irrevocable new course.

◆

Cults of Irrationality

I n 1966, I was stupid enough to become an administrator."

In the Faustian struggle between power and knowledge, my father's appointment as vice provost for academic planning skewed his public career toward the former at a moment when university administrators were about to find themselves thrust into the role of crisis manager, crowd controller, target, even hostage. Ten years before, he had been Red-baited; now he was about to be cast as a "fascist." While he held his liberal ground, American politics jolted violently under his feet.

The late 1960s became legendary in the time it took a photograph to develop in a vat of chemicals and flash across the wire, and the legend has only grown in the decades since, so that by now it's almost impossible to see those years fresh—the glare of attention has burned the color out of them. Say "Chicago" and you see a shirtless snarling young man at the front of a crowd of demonstrators giving you the finger. You've heard the story again and again, always somehow the same story, told by a twenty-year-old whom you admire or despise, identify with or reject. But my late '60s is two stories, neither legendary, not making history but made or unmade by it—one of a man in early mid-

2 2 1 ◆ Cults of Irrationality

dle age, his career peaking at a crisis, the other of a boy just becoming aware of the world beyond the tadpole bog.

"There are moments in history—Gershom Scholem calls them 'plastic hours'—when sentiments of hope spread across the globe," wrote Irving Howe, who found himself temporarily exiled to Stanford from New York just as things were warming up in the 1960s. "If there is a 'plastic hour' once in a rare while," he went on, "you surely don't want to spend it in Palo Alto." The '60s were slow to reach Stanford, but upon arrival they stayed a long time and brought both hope and destruction to Leland Stanford's 8,000 acres, so that by the burned-out end of the early '70s even people in Palo Alto felt they had experienced history.

Though there had been earlier tremors, the campus revolution began at Stanford on May 2, 1966, and it began as elsewhere in America—reasonably, with a tone of utmost earnestness. Early that afternoon on my mother's forty-first birthday, a mile away from our house, a group of students soon to call itself the May 2 Movement was picketing outside the president's office. They were about to become a problem for my father.

The students, and a few faculty, were demonstrating against classified research and the holding of Selective Service exams on campus. The American ground war in Vietnam was just over a year old, the draft was in high gear, and these students were pointing out the most obvious ways in which the university was lending itself to the war effort. Clark Kerr's multiversity, that loose collection of "academic entrepreneurs" standing at the "center of the knowledge process," the "focal point for national growth," had made itself quite vulnerable to this kind of attack. If universities were becoming the engines of a complex postindustrial society, intimately connected to government and industry, what happened when that society turned its energy to making war? On May 2, 1966, the picketers organized by the Graduate Coordinating Council's Academic Freedom Committee were not saying, "Tear it down." They were championing, in reasonable terms, the idea of the old-fashioned community of scholars. They seemed to have absorbed the meaning of the McCarthy years. In opposing classified research on campus, they were defending the university against politicization. "Such classification, imposed for purely political or ideological reasons," their statement said, "is a violation of one of the fundamental principles of academic freedom. The University is a place for free and open inquiry, for the disinterested pursuit of knowledge. Any violation of this principle must be resisted."

My father wasn't yet vice provost, still a member of the law faculty, but he was increasingly involved in university affairs. He had come to see that professors with their federal research grants might be advancing fields of knowledge in undreamed-of ways, but they were not acting as members of a community, and they were not asking the larger questions about values, which was the unique purpose of that community. The role of the independent intellectual was beginning to disappear between the grind of the "knowledge industry," which made academic work an engine of national growth, and the demands of the students, who would soon require that their education have political "relevance." As a result of the faculty's abdication, the administration had grown top-heavy and remote, and the word "alienation" was becoming a student mantra. My father's goal was to make the faculty more involved in university governance and undergraduate education. To that end he was serving on the Academic Council's Executive Committee, which put him on the front line in the events that followed the May 2 picket; and there he would stay for the next three years.

On May 21 Stanford was to be the site of a deferment exam held by the local draft boards for male students. The faculty's Executive Committee was to consider the question of classified research and selective service exams on May 24. But the student demonstrators wanted to stop the exam from being held at all, and on May 19 a hundred of them rallied around the fountain at White Plaza, in the middle of campus, epicenter of its antiwar activities. My father went to the microphone on behalf of the faculty and was introduced by a graduate student, who said civilly enough, "After he speaks we'll march." My

father promised the crowd "careful, rational, undemagogic consideration" of the question by the Executive Committee on May 24, but the
university would follow its normal procedures, which meant that the
exam would be held. This left the students far less than satisfied. One
of their speakers said, "The administration has been very adept in
promising rationality and saying 'no' to our demands." So "rationality"
now meant one thing to the students and another to the university's
representatives. To the latter it depended on accepted procedures; to
the former it had become an excuse.

Into this gap in perception and trust fifteen students marched, from
White Plaza to President Sterling's office, which they occupied for the
next fifty hours. Stanford's first sit-in was admirably restrained on all
sides. Students who were considering disrupting the draft board exam
decided not to. "The time for rhetoric about reasoned action is over,"
they said. "The time for reasoned action is now." Hardly a revolutionary appeal. As for the university, it sent in professors like my father,
who assured the protesters that the Executive Committee was about to
hold hearings on the very questions that had prompted the sit-in and
that it would "welcome the rational and considered expression of views
on these issues from all segments of the University community." He
reasoned with the students: "Unless you disbelieve these assurances,
there is no impasse. We urge you to terminate your defiance of University regulations."

Over the fifty hours of the sit-in the only real threat of violence
came from a crowd of drunken students—fraternity brothers and football players—who on the second night tried to storm the president's
office and throw out the protesters. My father was called away from a
dinner party, and together with other faculty he put himself in the way
and the threat ended.

The university simply waited the students out. Here is how a student chronology of the sit-in described its last hours: "As the police are
about to take our names, Professor Packer of the Executive Committee
enters with a reply to our letter to the Executive Committee. He states
that the Executive Committee could not get a quorum and so could

not make the request [that President Sterling attend a public meeting with them]. The individual members available would call for a public meeting but would not agree to ask President Sterling to attend it. We then ask Prof. Packer as a last-minute request if he personally would work for negotiations between [student body] president David Harris and the Executive Committee concerning ways of including students in that committee's decision-making on the Selective Service issue. We specifically inform Prof. Packer that this would almost certainly end the sit-in. He refuses."

A couple of hours later, on the afternoon of May 21, the students—grown to three dozen now—left the building in apparent defeat. The university's judicial process was already turning. But the students' parting statement augured what was to come in the next few years, when the numbers would be greater and the tone harsher: "We end by establishing the depth not only of this moral callousness and authoritarian decision-making, but of the utter unreason of the university which, instead of beginning a dialogue with students who come with just demands, turned a deaf ear and resorted only to policing power and punitive measures."

That autumn my mother fell getting out of a friend's car and bumped her right leg. She had just gone on the pill, and a long car ride kept the blood from circulating, and soon her leg developed a life-threatening blood clot. She went into the hospital for treatment, while at home my sister and I cut windows and doors out of empty Kleenex boxes, making little houses to take as presents. "Thrombophlebitis"—comical when I tried to pronounce it, a little verbal joke between my sister and me, but the word evoked my first apprehension that the world my parents had made was tenuous and could be taken away. For the time being my father was in charge, and I felt comforted by his trips back and forth to the hospital, his assurances that my mother would be all right. In a pinch, he was acting like a father. The illness made me aware as I hadn't been before that I loved both my parents, needed both. If my father was stricken with the fear of losing his mainstay, the woman who propped up his existence, he didn't show it to me, or I was too lost in my own low-grade terror and my usual haze of army costumes and animals to notice.

On a Thursday evening in November that year, my father came home late for a dinner party. The guests were sitting in our living room, and in between greeting them and fixing drinks he managed to pull my mother aside long enough to tell her what he'd just learned at a meeting with President Sterling. Sterling had gone to the board of trustees to name my father, whose prominence and stock had risen after the draft exam sit-in, as vice provost for academic planning. A member of the board—it turned out to be David Packard, of the Hewlett-Packard electronics company, later to be Deputy Defense Secretary under Nixon—had vowed to block the appointment. Packard, still fighting the wars of the 1950s, decided that the 1955 Fund for the Republic grant disqualified my father for an administrative job. He was too liberal to help run Stanford. Packard also couldn't have been happy with Sterling's choice for the number two job of provost to replace the iron-willed Fred Terman, who had finally retired—Richard Lyman, a sharp-tongued historian who had signed an antiwar petition. But the fight Packard chose was with Packer, and this time Sterling, who had defied Herbert Hoover when my father was appointed to the law school, hesitated to press the issue.

The fate of the appointment was unclear that night, and my father sat brooding over dinner while my mother kept their guests distracted. Between courses they huddled in the kitchen or bathroom, where my mother tried to keep him calm. The phone kept ringing, one colleague or another who had heard the news. My mother took it as a sign of a successful dinner party that the guests never realized their hosts were in the middle of a crisis. She liked to say that she was good at laughing in one room and crying in another.

Once they were alone, my parents sat together in the study and my father unleashed his hurt and anger. He was going to quit, he was going to call friends at Yale and Chicago and Penn to see about jobs—

he kept reaching for the phone, and my mother kept urging caution, just as she'd done in the midst of his crisis over the Hiss book. These roles seemed at odds with their public faces: she was the fighter with a quick trigger finger, he the thinker who considered every side of a problem. But when his hurt went deep enough, reason collapsed, leaving incoherent rage. "He wanted to hit somebody," my mother wrote her sister Jane, "and just could not find an appropriate object that wasn't self-destructive." She "had to restrain him almost by force, he was so deeply wounded and furious, saying he was a second-class citizen and he wouldn't work for a pusillanimous guy like Sterling." It's not that she didn't want to fight; in fact, the prospect of a fight overrode her misgivings about the job and what it would cost them in privacy and freedom. But she wanted to win the fight; my father wanted to lash out.

For the next few days, while the appointment dangled and Sterling temporized, my parents repeated the Thursday-night drama over and over. Crisis brought out the lines of veins running beneath the skin of their marriage. From day to day my father's work appeared to be their lifeblood, the source of money and meaning, the substance of talk at all those cocktail parties and dinners. "We know that's what Herb thinks," a colleague once said when my mother—by now a lecturer in the English department—expressed an opinion about university matters. When she went home furious and told her husband, he exclaimed, "I'll call that son of a bitch right now"—thereby missing the point. But when he was threatened, in the hot place in his brain where judgment couldn't reach, she turned out to be the one holding it all together—while his career remained the focus. And this role, a supporting role and yet the crucial one, entirely depended upon and yet peripheral, answering her need to be strong and yet leaving her own abilities unused, filled my mother with resentment.

"He can discuss with me the facts," she wrote her sister, "the way it will affect his career, his psyche (to some extent), the politics of it, and in short every way which does not affect me, which every way is nearly all. But since my part of it is altogether related to him and since we are constrained to be fully honest in re the effect on each other, then all that has to do with him, which is all, I can't discuss with him. So I can't really discuss any of it. If I did, I would fill Herb with anxiety and perhaps undermine his capacity to arrive at a sound decision." She went on bluntly:

> I just don't think he is tough enough to withstand the strain of making tough decisions, or of taking the disasters laid right to his office, or finally of not whistling in the dark, that is, being overly optimistic in order to avoid being panicked or at least anxious. In other words, I don't think he would be at his best as no one decision-maker, and also I think it would be very difficult for him; perhaps disastrous. So not being able to tell him straight out for fear of undermining his morale which is very dependent on me and also because I don't want to plain out hurt his feelings (he performs more happily when he is on top, no question) I have to lie a little about my reasons for . . . my reasons. . . . I let it out in measly undermining ways, like facial expressions, or tones of voice, which is pretty bad and anxiety-provoking to Herb.

My mother set all this down in great detail, in the six-page typewritten letter to her sister, using a carbon for the first time in her life. She wanted to hold on to the memory. Thirty years later, she gave me a copy of the carbon. So now I have this record, vividly written in the heat of crisis, one version of a moment in my parents' lives. At six I was far too out of it to sense the dynamic, the mood. For that reason I'm wary of letting the letter stand for the truth. Still, it's a more honest, self-lacerating account than one would expect from a woman whom the incident left feeling "very righteous and peculiarly strong, like Mt. Rushmore, unspeaking, taking it all, martyred." By 1966 she was not just an English instructor but also the author of more than a dozen published stories. In one that came out the following year, "Early Morning, Lonely Ride," a lawyer's unhappy wife picks a fight with her husband on a late-night drive home from a party among his friends: "She saw clearly, not for the first time, how she drove him to it, with her vanities and irritations, her untapped powers and her vast need for consolation." The story reads like a merciless what-if, playing out all the buried emotions of the vice-provost incident, with a wife who has no public function at all, acts not a bit like Mount Rushmore, saying everything, taking none of it. In these years just before the feminist awakening, ambition held a woman like my mother in check, somewhere between background and foreground. In earlier years she had lived politically through her father and her brother. In 1966 she still had to live mostly through her husband.

In the end the conservative trustee backed down; maybe it had all been a bluff. So the Fund for the Republic grant did not, as my father said, mark the end as well as the beginning of his Stanford years, we did not move to Chicago or New Haven, we stayed in Stanford, my father was "stupid enough to become an administrator," and he began the new job just as the student revolution was making itself felt along our stretch of the San Andreas fault. "I like flak," he would later say. "I thrive on it." But it wasn't true: his commitment to principle was firmer than his grip on life itself. My mother knew this better than anyone, and when he became vice provost she feared disaster.

Flak first came not from the student left but from where it had come in 1955—the right. But in 1967 it sounded ludicrous. "The rewards have gone to the political activists," the newsletter of the Winds of Freedom Foundation, a conservative alumni group, wrote of the Lyman and Packer appointments; they were nothing less than a threat to national security. My father's sins included not just the Fund for the Republic grant but opposition to the House Un-American Activities Committee, advocacy of civilian police review boards, and ACLU membership. "Is there really any necessity for the Berkeley disruptions to be repeated at Stanford?"

"Silly," my father told a reporter. "Professor Lyman and I are scholars. We were chosen for our tasks because of this—not because of political activity we might or might not agitate." By 1967 it was obvious that if students were going to repeat Berkeley at Stanford, they did not need to be incited by a forty-one-year-old law professor turned administrator; that, if anything, my father was going to become not their leader but their enemy.

It happened almost at once. His main task as vice provost was to chair a committee called the Study of Education at Stanford, or SES, which was embarking on a thorough reconsideration of the research university's purpose. By February 1967 the political atmosphere on campus had become so charged that even the selection of students to this committee became the focus of protest. The student body president was a young man named David Harris—soon to become famous as Joan Baez's husband and a draft resister willing to do jail time. On campus he'd been jumped by frat brothers who held him down and shaved off his long hair. Harris argued that student representatives to the committee should be voted by the student legislature. My father opened the committee to applications for spots that would be chosen by the administration with the advice of student body officials. To the academic liberal, it was a question of intellectual independence.

"The Steering Committee should not be viewed as representing any constituencies or interests," my father wrote in a letter to the *Daily*. "The wide range of issues that would necessarily be raised in the Study, the free and open kind of inquiry called for, made it imperative that the participants should approach their task with no external constraints. In particular, the idea of having members speak for THE student body, THE faculty, or THE administration, was foreign to the spirit of the Study. The time for 'political' scrutiny by 'constituencies' would come later when specific proposals for action emerged. The Study and those who are engaged in it would have no 'power' other than the persuasiveness of the ideas they put forward."

But to the student radical, it was a question of democratic rights. "Students are different people than administrators and faculty members and involved in that difference is a vision of the University strikingly unlike that of Mr. Packer and the man who appointed him," Harris wrote in the student paper. "No one man, however competent, is capable of choosing without the bias of his own position." Another student leader claimed that the student body "has a common interest . . . a group identity," and Packer hadn't explained "why the students don't exist as an entity. He wants to de-personalize the student body." Already the contours of the generation of 1968's most lasting contribution to American political thought are materializing: identity politics, the idea that "the personal is political."

Just as Fulton Lewis, Jr., had thought my father incapable of conducting an objective study of ex-Communist witnesses in the 1950s, in the 1960s David Harris thought that students chosen by my father would be captive to administrative interests, and that these interests existed in opposition to student interests. The archconservative radio commentator and the antiwar militant shared a suspicion of any claim to disinterestedness from a quarter they didn't approve of.

But my father was arguing against the very primacy of "interest" in debate and thought: what mattered, he said, was "critical intelligence." In the free marketplace of ideas, a disinterested sophomore could vanquish a disinterested dean. The distinction between the power of interest groups and the power of ideas was central to his notion of intellectual life, of fairness, of freedom. Now, of course, hardly any enlightened person even pretends to believe in objectivity. Almost everyone with a graduate degree knows that disinterest has been abolished and nothing exists except power and groups. But in 1967 the idea was up for grabs. And the tendency of student thought in 1967 was running against my father. Students were beginning to see power everywhere, and in my father they saw an administrator with his own—and the university's—interests to defend. "Is a non-political question one that the administration can decide by itself?" the *Daily* asked editorially. "Does an issue become political simply because students disagree with the administration's point of view or with the status quo?"

Over the next two years it would be impossible for my father to extricate himself from these arguments. And something in the *Daily* exchange, opening salvos in this war, makes my pulse beat a little faster. The tone of my father's letter is neither nasty nor patronizing— almost the opposite, he takes it all very seriously. This is no minor "miscommunication" between people who share the same beliefs. It's a matter of principle, his blood is up, and his letter's close raises the stakes for everyone. "Those who agree with Mr. Harris' reported exhortation in White Plaza that students should boycott the Study betray a preference for the irrationality of confrontation politics over the reasoned discussion of educational policies." The style of argument is East Coast, postwar blunt. To twenty-year-old baby boomers raised by Dr. Spock in upper-middle-class Hillsborough and Pacific Palisades it must have sounded harsh, and some of them concluded that this was a harsh man. An administrator more concerned with PR would have disarmed his student critics and softened his response under a light snowfall of conciliatory euphemisms and psychobabble. A more arrogant one—the retired Fred Terman—wouldn't have deigned to answer them in their paper at all. But my father loved argument, tended, as he said, to "shoot from the hip," and he dug in over principle. In this case it was reason versus irrationality. So he joined the fight in print and immediately made himself a lightning rod.

The Study of Education at Stanford was launched to answer the disaffection of students, but it never had a chance. Their revolution was moving too fast for reform by committee. In a sense Stanford was finally paying the bill for its entry into the ranks of elite universities. All the features of its rise to greatness—the multiversity made up of separate kingdoms of research specialties, the heavy dependence on Pentagon money, the embrace of "value-neutrality"—became battering rams in the hands of politicized students who often had no serious interest in what happened at Stanford, to knock down its sandstone walls. But if "value-neutral" research resulted in weapons and strategies that were being used to kill Vietnamese peasants, then a crude case could be made that Stanford was implicated in an immoral war. What did it mean to be "value-neutral" when radar developed in Stanford labs was guiding bombs that were blowing holes in rice paddies? Stanford put a scholarly face on a war crime, this thinking went—it was rotten at the core. Therefore any claim to disinterested pursuit of knowledge was a sham. My father answered that universities should never have abandoned values for statistics, and he hoped that SES would place liberal education and broad intellectual inquiry back at the heart of undergraduate life. But it was too late.

Like the Populists of the 1890s, the student radicals of the 1960s described the university as a handmaid of power — corporate power, state power, military power. But something important had slipped from the picture: unlike Edward Ross and the Populists, they no longer believed that scholarship was on the side of truth and freedom. Ross himself had foreseen and welcomed the rise of a "mandarinate" of academic elites. But to this latest generation of social rebels, the mandarinate had compromised itself at the slop bucket of federal grant money. Reason itself became the enemy. Reason strangled feeling, gave oppression cover, blighted the natural goodness of youth. And the political expression of reason, modern liberalism's use of government in the shaping of national life, was discredited. It had led directly, inevitably, to the war in Vietnam. Reform at home has often preceded foreign war: Populists championed the war against Spain, Progressives hailed World War I, New Dealers led the war against fascism. The universalist and humanitarian rhetoric of domestic liberalism easily inflates the airships of international crusades. LBJ himself proposed to the North Vietnamese something like a TVA for the Mekong River.

In their attacks on liberalism and big government, radicals began to sound like conservatives. The October 1966 issue of *Viet-Report*, an antiwar paper, made the case in terms that could have come out of William F. Buckley's *National Review*: "The Vietnam War has begun to expose for the first time the New Deal state machine as a huge, effective and tyrannical bureaucracy, inclined to set its own policies and ride rough-shod over those who oppose them. Is it not the same presidential government of the liberal rhetoric which once chased after 'robber barons' and which now pursues peace marchers and draft-age young men? . . . The Welfare State apparatus is a threat to our free institutions."

By February 1967 this analysis had reached the Students for a Democratic Society chapter at Stanford, in the way New Left ideology kept upping its own ante and discarding last month's position as shopworn and weak-kneed. When Hubert Humphrey came to speak at Stanford in the middle of the month, during the same week that my father and David Harris were tangling over SES, a flyer called on students to walk out on the Vice President. "Vietnam is the liberals' war," it announced. "This is the true fruit of American liberalism: in the name of freedom, genocide is practiced. DENY HUMPHREY A PLATFORM TO PEDDLE. HUBERT HUMPHREY IS A FRAUD—HIS LIBERALISM PHONEY." In this thinking, Vietnam and the burning cities became the last spasms of the New Deal.

A year before, in 1966, a Stanford student leader had said, "The University is a place for free and open inquiry, for the disinterested pursuit of knowledge. Any violation of this principle must be resisted." The students' goal was "to democratize the university." A year later, another leader—a veteran of the Free Speech Movement at Berkeley in 1964—said, "We're not talking about free speech. It's not a matter of discussion, conversation or debate that can change this society. It's force." In the aftermath of a student attempt to block the CIA from interviewing on campus, someone in the Stanford chapter of SDS imagined a surprisingly heartfelt dialogue between a professor and a student—the sort of informal document that captures a mood, a historical moment, better than a hundred manifestos. You can feel the pull of doubt and thrill on a mind trained for a profession by years of rigorous education in a competitive society and getting ready to throw it all away for the politics of the deed:

> S: Rights and privacy and these kinds of freedom are irrelevant—you old guys got to get it through your heads that to fight the whole corrupt System POWER is the only answer—we can't vote the CIA away, or do anything but use power and coercion to stop it.

> P: You've learned your lessons very well, haven't you? It's just that kind of righteousness and benevolent power-grabbing that

you hate in the CIA—personally assuming power to change something that is part of the government, but wrong and immoral in your view. It's not a very attractive group—the CIA—to me either, you know.

S: What's wrong with power? We need it—the whole colonialist-imperialist-capitalist-monopolistic free world is based on corruption and power! . . . You want a panel to cover all views and keep up the myth and fetish of an open mind and considering all sides of a problem. That's your way of life—no guts, no action, no strong beliefs you'll sacrifice anything for.

P: You don't know the difference between indecision or apathy, and careful rational consideration of the problem, its possible solutions, and their short- and long-range consequences. When I was in college I felt about action much as you. . . .

S: Well, you're not in college—but you are *in a college* and it's run by the System—big government, big corporations, lawyers, businessmen—the only people who have no voice are the students, the sweetly submissive faculty, and the greater Stanford community. You're still *in* it, but you don't realize it.

There's a superficial resemblance in New Left language, especially before it descended into its late phase of Stalinist-Maoist madness, to the antiauthoritarian streak that runs through American history all the way back to Jefferson. In an 1816 letter, Jefferson anticipated the early New Left's mantra, "participatory democracy": "Where every man is a sharer in the direction of his ward-republic, or of some higher ones, and feels that he is a participator in the government of affairs, not merely at an election one day in the year, but every day . . . he will let the heart be torn out of his body sooner than his power be wrested from him by a Caesar or a Bonaparte." When the Stanford SDS declared, "We see our force as a response to the force of concentrations of power—be they business or government," there's a strange echo of the Jeffersonian creed that was also George Huddleston's; in another context he spoke nearly the same words. My grandfather would have despised the 1960s if he'd lived beyond the decade's second month. And yet the ethos of the student activists at its best—the suspicion of institutional power, the vision of democracy as not just an arrangement but an activity, the hatred of hypocrisy, the moral passion, the emphasis on personal virtue—draws on the bloodline of American political character that in the eighteenth century was called republican, at the end of the nineteenth went under the name Populism, briefly joined hands at the beginning of the twentieth with socialism, and came to power in the decade of the New Deal—only to be denounced by George Huddleston in 1935 and by student radicals in 1967, not the fulfillment of their democratic desire but its perversion into a bureaucratic octopus. So in some very thin, surprising, and questionable ways the Alabama politician and the bearded student were closer to each other than either was to the academic administrator, made by the New Deal and the postwar meritocracy, who came between them.

But SDS was not the Agricultural Wheel or the Farmer-Labor Party. The student radicals lacked—rejected—the very basis of Jeffersonian democracy. They had no roots in any authentic community (if you follow the careers of SDS leaders, they seemed to turn up wherever the action was—Mississippi, Newark, Columbia, Chicago, Berkeley), and they had no interest in any authentic tradition. They willed their own society into being and called it the Beloved Community, but their brand of utopianism only increased their isolation from the rest of America. And they regarded tradition as a dead weight around the necks of the young, to be cast off with Dionysian joy and contempt. Jeffersonians like my grandfather believed that the small town and the farm with their narrow hidebound ways were the backbone of the republic. They believed that reason, the basis for self-government, lay in the humblest men. But the student radicals had other dreams in their eyes. If the frontier regalia, the jeans and boots and bandannas and back-to-the-land of the counterculture, seemed to reach back to an old and "real" America, it never really got past the point of symbol and gesture; nor did the proletariat mentality of some of the weirder sects that splintered off in SDS's fragmentation-grenade final years. And as for the humble members of society—Andrew Jackson's "farmers, mechanics, and laborers"—in the 1960s many of them were hard hats who wanted nothing more than to kick some longhair's ass. What the students were slow in realizing was that most of the country hated them. In California, Ronald Reagan's political career was launched in the 1966 governor's race largely because of this hatred; it only gathered fury over the next four years, and he rode it to reelection in 1970.

So the radicals faced, or rather did not face, an increasingly glaring paradox: they were convinced that a revolution was at hand in American society; no other revolutionary group, besides the Black Panthers, seemed prepared to get out in front of it; therefore it was up to the students themselves to become its vanguard—a revolutionary elite without a following. Never mind, they would force (to use an increasingly favored word) the rest of the country to go along. They would will their revolution—the power of mind! History would be made out of collective fantasy. But how could they be a revolutionary vanguard if they were not oppressed? After all, they were the best-educated generation in American history, in the middle of the longest peacetime boom, and the postindustrial future seemed to be theirs for the taking, right here in the Santa Clara Valley, where it was being hatched in a hundred research labs and technology firms.

The problem seemed insoluble until the students discovered that they were, in fact, an oppressed group themselves. They were cogs in Clark Kerr's multiversity, and once they got out they would become fodder for Lyndon Johnson's war. An SDS pamphlet widely circulated at Stanford was titled *The Student as Nigger*. Birmingham had come to Palo Alto! So well-educated young white people, who had gone South in the early 1960s to help poor black people get their freedom, now discovered that they themselves were not free. Moral activism curdled into revolutionary rage and antic theater. Being a nigger justified anything you did. It justified turning on the one community that gave you shelter and draft deferment, that protected antiwar protesters and hippies from the wrath of the larger public, that tolerated dissent and preserved intellectual freedom and depended on rational debate, and that for these very reasons was terribly fragile, so fragile that a hundred students could just about destroy it by themselves. They looked at the university and saw a monolith — "a big, automated institution," as my father himself said, "where one man sits at the top, pushes buttons, and makes things happen." But instead it turned out to be a community based on moral authority and ultimately built on sand, and in 1968 it began to come apart, and there was more than enough blame to go around.

As 1967 careened into 1968 my father was pushing himself hard on several fronts, as if the problems of the university and society had all come to depend on the exercise of his analytical powers. He was teaching a seminar at the law school. He was finishing his masterpiece *The Limits of the Criminal Sanction* (in August 1967 he put aside his administrative duties and went away for several weeks to get the book done in Santa Cruz, where during his breakdown, he'd fantasized about retiring). Most demanding of all, he was laboring on the massive education study, generating thousands of pages of recommendations from teachers and students on dozens of subcommittees, much as he had sifted through thousands of pages of testimony by ex-Communists a decade earlier. "The one sphere in which we need more rather than less activism," he said in a speech, "is in student participation in their own educational progress. I also think, although I could perhaps be utopian about that, that if there were more activism on that front, there might be less on some others." He was responding to crisis the way he knew how, through "reasoned discussion," but at a punishing pace, trying to reform the university before it was pulled down from within or policed from without.

In 1968 history would keep getting in the way.

On a Thursday evening in early April of that year I walked into the kitchen to find my parents sitting at the table with tears in their eyes. This was unusual, maybe unprecedented, and I must have registered alarm. A man had been killed, they explained. Did we know him? No. Then why were they crying? Because, they said, he was a good man.

So at age seven, just a few hours after his death, I heard about Martin Luther King for the first time. Learning that he was black, I associated the dead man with my second-grade teacher, Miss Prudhomme. She was a young, warm, elegant woman with very black skin and a round shiny face, and I was in love with her. At my insistence we'd had her to dinner not long before April 4, and Miss Prudhomme had said at our dinner table that this would be her last year at Escondido Elementary School; black children needed her more than white children. My mother tried to change her mind, saying that the white kids needed her too, needed her help to overcome their racial biases. Miss Prudhomme wasn't interested in that—white kids could deal with it themselves, and so could their parents, a few of whom had withdrawn their children from her classes. She said that black children needed to learn that black is beautiful, and when my mother tried to talk her out of this too, making the liberal and universalist argument that both whites and blacks should get beyond color, Miss Prudhomme rejected this as well. In 1968 this young teacher in a mostly white school was moving fast toward black pride and militancy. Of course this discussion was lost on me; I only knew that I didn't want her to leave.

So the night of King's death I thought that Miss Prudhomme would be very upset by the news from Memphis. I was distressed on her behalf and my parents', though not on King's, knowing nothing about him. Yet I was fairly alert to the plight of Negroes; the subject was much discussed in our house, in strong moral tones. I gathered that Negroes had been treated unfairly and we owed them something, and my way of grasping this fact was to feel sorry for them, much as I felt sorry for the birds that flew into our glass walls and that I nursed to death. My notion of justice amounted to a sympathy with the weak and a dislike of bullies, compounded by a dim awareness that we were more fortunate than others. I didn't see why this should be so—I'd done nothing to deserve to be more fortunate.

The summer before King's murder, the problem of Negroes entered my consciousness through a picture in a magazine of a black boy lying facedown on a street, one arm extended, blood pooling out of his head. His name—I still remember it—was Joe Bass, Jr., and his eyes were open and he was alive, with pellets from a policeman's shotgun in his head. Joe Bass, Jr., was a few years older than I; he had been shot in the middle of the Newark riot. I wondered how anyone could be shot in the head and survive, and I stared for a long time at this boy lying on the pavement with large patient eyes, like a wounded animal's.

Around this same time, my family was driving through San Francisco when we passed a black boy, again a year or two older, walking on the sidewalk with blood running down from a cut on his forehead. My father stopped the car, my mother rolled down her window and asked him what had happened and where he lived. Apparently the boy had been in a fight and someone had thrown a rock and hit his head. Then the back door on my side opened and the boy with the bleeding face got in with my sister and me. None of us children spoke to one another as we cruised by the chain-link fences and concrete playgrounds of the Fillmore District, San Francisco's black ghetto, and my father looked for the address. I remember the boy as frightened to be in the car with us, but my mother says he was cheerful, answering my parents' questions, pointing out the run-down house at the top of a flight of stairs where he lived. Probably I was the frightened one, but also curious—who was this strange bleeding boy to whom I had nothing to say? It was the first time someone my own age seemed so alien that the common bond of being boys meant nothing. I felt that he knew things I could have no idea about. I felt that his world was harder than mine. To be a black boy meant that sooner or later you were going to bleed from the head.

So at seven I was extremely race-conscious, but it was mostly an abstract awareness. I knew that when a white boy named Dirk Doss called a black boy "a piece of chocolate cake" while playing flag football, I was to tell him not to say that, and I did (but didn't think to ask myself what it meant that Dirk lived with his grandmother in a crumbling cottage and wore the same ratty shirt and dungarees day after day). I knew that the worst word you could say, worse than any four-letter word, was "nigger." I thought that, through no fault of their own, Negroes needed help (O'Neill Maloney, the only black boy in my third-grade class, needed help with his project on shrimps in San Francisco Bay, and I gave it to him). What I didn't feel, on a visceral level, was that Negroes were my equals. The fact that they needed help meant they were inferior, not by birth but as a matter of fact.

All this acute sensitivity to race that my parents bred in me (my mother, watching a couple of Deep South college football teams, would point out with emotion the hand of a black player laid approvingly on a white teammate's helmet) did not render my relations with black people natural and warm. In fact, it meant that the first and in some cases the only thing I noticed was their skin color.

From birth on, I had spent more hours of my life with our black housekeeper Willie than with anyone else except my mother and sister—long hours before I attended school or when I was home sick, lying around bored and trying to find some amusement, which often meant sneaking up on her and saying "Boo!" Whether humoring me or easily startled, Willie always jumped, then mock-reproved me. In a fit of sexual curiosity I once asked to see her breast, and she obliged me: I was startled and impressed by the color of her nipple. But on a somewhat higher level of consciousness I knew that Willie was less fortunate than we were and that this had mysteriously to do with her being black. Her husband didn't work and she had to support the three children and her little baby boy had a heart condition and they lived in the East Palo Alto ghetto across Bayshore Freeway. Once, this awareness led me to slip some pennies from my piggy bank into her purse, but she caught me. Black pride in its militant version never had reached Willie. Her main source of strength was Jesus; she also drank. But she wouldn't take my pennies.

Willie was hardly an equal either. She worked for us, she called my parents Mr. and Mrs. (I once asked my mother about this—it was Willie's choice, she said) while to us she was always Willie, never Mrs. Arline. But she held a unique place in my limited world. If my mother was more of a father, Willie was left to fill the maternal role, and when I wasn't suddenly mindful of her unfortunate situation I took her for granted and loved her. At five a boy named Cookie had been my friend, not my black friend. But three years later, by the day of King's death, Willie was the only black person I saw first as an individual. My parents' racial liberalism, in my mother's case steeped in white southern guilt, had soaked into me, leaving a silt of exhortations and taboos that I constantly felt but barely understood. I would never be racially innocent again.

The Monday after King's murder, Provost Richard Lyman, a British historian, read Wordsworth's sonnet to Toussaint L'Ouverture before a packed Memorial Auditorium:

> *Though fallen thyself, never to rise again,*
> *Live, and take comfort. Thou has left behind*
> *Powers that will work for thee: air, earth, and skies;*
> *There's not a breathing of the common wind*
> *That will forget thee; thou has great allies;*
> *Thy friends are exultations, agonies,*
> *And love, and man's unconquerable mind.*

Lyman had begun to pay tribute to Coretta Scott King when a group of sixty black students quietly walked onstage. While the others stood by with arms folded, some in sunglasses, Afros still at a modest 1968 height, one of the students took the microphone from Lyman and read a list of demands. It included increasing minority enrollment and employment and firing Associate Provost Robert Rosenzweig for mishandling a case in which several boys from East Palo Alto had been arrested for shoplifting at the campus store. The university had until the next night to answer.

My father welcomed the demands for affirmative action as a chance to do what he wanted to do anyway. The drama of King's murder could force the resistant trustees' hand. He went home from Memorial Auditorium, sat down at the typewriter in our study, and with characteristic focus and acuity wrote out the university's responses to the black students. He took the sheet of paper into the kitchen, where my mother was cooking dinner, and said, "He who has the written word leads the way." For the rest of the crisis he would be the university's key player.

The next day, Tuesday, April 9, my father and Robert Rosenzweig went for a walk with a young administrator named Wyman around the Inner Quad, the brick-paved heart of the campus lined with sandstone and terra-cotta buildings and arcades. Wyman had just gotten through telling Rosenzweig that he should keep his ego out of it and resign. Rosenzweig answered that principles were involved, not just ego. When Wyman left, my father and Rosenzweig kept walking in silence. Suddenly my father said, "It's really tough for us ambitious Jewish kids to know how to operate in a WASP world."

Neither of them ever referred to the remark again, nor did my father again mention Judaism in Rosenzweig's presence. But in this moment they were more than just besieged colleagues. They were Jews, still very much a minority in the circles of power at a major university, with their own burden of guilt and resentment, their combative instincts, their lack of social smoothness, their vulnerability, and it was hard to figure out where to make a stand, where to back down. Jews were often the hard-liners in universities during these critical years; they seemed to understand something about revolutionary romanticism that their WASP colleagues, readier to stroke students' raw feelings, did not. "I see very disturbing analogies in that kind of approach, that politics of the apocalypse, to what has gone on in democratic societies that have crumbled," my father once said. "The Weimar Republic is a horrible example of what can happen when people start thinking with their blood." The remark to Rosenzweig was my father's version of an arm around the shoulder, an offer of comradely comfort.

That night he was one of half a dozen university representatives who met with the Black Student Union on the roof deck above the bowling alley of Tresidder Union. A thousand students and community members and others looked on, including my mother. It was dark and tense on the deck, and the meeting nearly fell apart at the outset.

"Are you ready to respond to the first demand?" Kenny Washington asked.

My father said that he wasn't.

"The complexities can be worked out at a later date," the Black Student Union leader persisted, "but we must have some discussion on these demands now."

"This is not the atmosphere," my father said, "this is neither the time nor the place to discuss the points you've brought up. I've tried to give you a progress report. I'm sorry if that is not enough. We want to ·talk." While the university was in sympathy with most of the demands, he said, detailed answers would have to wait until a private meeting Thursday between university and student leaders.

Boos and hisses came from the crowd. Kenny Washington said, "I don't see the problem here. These are students. They don't bite. They have minds. I don't think it's at all unreasonable to talk now."

On the verge of confrontation, the meeting recessed. The six middle-aged white men were in a bind. They wanted to agree to most of the demands—because they thought the demands, for entry to the university and not its destruction, were just, because they had a collective bad conscience on racial issues, and because a man they revered had just been killed. But they didn't want to appear to be giving in, or turning over university decision-making to a group of students. A news photo shows my father, in white shirt and tweed coat and tie, leaning with the other professors and administrators over the speakers' table. His face is shadowed, but his posture shows the strain of the moment. It's like a huddle of political operatives during a crisis on the floor of a convention, one more emblem of the 1960s. He is clearly the point man. My mother was in the crowd, trying to see him, wondering whether the anger burning major cities across the country was going to make a target of her husband.

The meeting resumed, and my father outlined the university's general plans to recruit more black students and faculty and comply with fair employment practices. But he also said, "We're not going to fire Bob Rosenzweig. America suffers from too much scapegoating." There was applause, and my mother relaxed a bit. "To move a university, you have to move the people in it," my father concluded. "We think we ought to do these things because they are the right things to do."

Two days later, Kenny Washington emerged from a private meeting with my father and the others, flashed a victory sign, and told the waiting crowd, "They have met our demands."

Of all the shocks that hit American universities in that year of violence, 1968, and the violent years to come, the one that made the most difference in the long run was Martin Luther King's murder. The others now seem like utopian chimeras, bad dreams, goldfish-swallowing fads, tragic missed chances. But King's death, almost instantly, gave rise to aggressive affirmative action in recruiting and hiring, to black studies departments, eventually to other ethnic programs. For better and worse, it caused the only lasting change that student radicalism brought to the universities. The backlash came almost as fast, and keeps coming.

The following month, in May, it was the white students' turn. This time my father was on the other side.

The climactic event of my father's career began on Friday, May 3, 1968, when a five-man faculty board called the Interim Judicial Body (IJB) overturned the Student Judicial Council's decision and suspended seven students, SDS members, who had tried to block entrance to a CIA interview the previous November. Because two of the students were repeat offenders (they had sat in at Sterling's office in May 1966), their suspensions would carry over from summer to fall, stripping them of the protective covering of the student deferment and exposing them to the draft at the height of the war. That same day 150 students rallied at White Plaza, heard speeches denouncing the university's power over students, and marched to the president's office, which had been secured by plainclothes police, where my father ("Herbie Packer" student leaders had taken to calling him) and another administrator waited to receive their demands. These included reversal of the suspensions, abolition of the IJB, and creation of a student-dominated judicial body. The cause prompted an exhilarating surge of rage and confidence. The language became both juvenile and revolutionary, with the university cast in the double role of hapless parent and ruthless colonial power. It was, one student said, "the same discovery black people are making." The new cry was "Student Power."

By noon Monday, without a satisfactory answer from President Sterling, a core group of students was discussing not whether to sit in but where and how. The obvious place was the Old Union, surrounding a courtyard next to White Plaza, which housed administrative and student-service offices. But the university, anticipating the move, had closed the building and padlocked it from the inside, "in the vain hope," my father later said, "that burglary and forcible entry were offenses that Stanford students would be unlikely to commit." A handful of students jimmied open windows, climbed in, and liberated the front door with bolt cutters. Several hundred more poured into the Old Union, and the sit-in began.

Just a few days earlier, officials at Columbia had called in New York City police to clear students occupying half a dozen buildings. The cops had broken heads and stampeded down Broadway on horseback, and this disastrous end to the weeklong takeover was staring Stanford in the face. "We don't want the type of thing we had at Columbia," David Packard, the trustee who had tried to block my father's appointment as vice provost, said during a surprise evening visit to the sit-in. Violence, like Communism in the 1950s, was still considered foreign to innocent Stanford. But the students were daring the university to call in the (not very menacing) Palo Alto police. It became clear later that officials like my father were considering it.

The obscurity and complexity of a showdown's origins only intensify its escalation. Reactions overwhelm causes, each side feels free to claim its own genealogy, common ground disappears underfoot. Stanford's crisis had broken over an issue of university governance that almost no one understood. The events of the mid-'60s had made it clear that Stanford's old judicial code, dating back to the 1890s, was outmoded—too vague and too paternalistic to handle the kinds of nonacademic problems that the era of demonstrations presented. President Sterling had named a committee of students, faculty, and administrators to design a new judicial system, with greater student participation, and by May 1968 it had almost completed the job—but not in time to judge the CIA case and the sit-in that followed. This was left to the IJB, a temporary all-faculty body—and with students now facing suspensions and possibly the draft it was easy enough for the radical student leaders to discredit the decision's legitimacy, and by extension the legitimacy of all university decisions. The suspensions gave them an opportunity to lock the administration in a struggle that would polarize the campus. And although several votes in which thousands of students took part during and after the sit-in condemned its tactics by majorities of two to one, they also supported its demands. Here is a point that most recollections of the student revolution ignore: the majority of students remained indifferent; a large minority wanted reforms that gave them a greater share of control in their educations; and a small minority, intent on turning the university upside down, wanted to make those reforms impossible by using tactics that would radicalize other students. Within a year or two, administrators learned in a rather cold-blooded and Machiavellian way how to isolate the radicals, who were using the university for political purposes, and keep the liberal students focused on internal reform. But in 1968, at Stanford, these hard lessons hadn't yet been learned.

My father—liberal, libertarian, a dove on Vietnam—became over the next few days, along with Provost Richard Lyman, the university's most visible hard-liner, its sharpest-beaked hawk. In retrospect it's possible to see the mistakes he made, chief among them the mistake of speaking too plainly, too harshly, and the mistake of projecting a sense of siege instead of openness and conciliation. But the whole course of his life, the contour of his thought, had led him to this moment and this response. He was functioning less as an administrator trying to hold the place together by consensus than as an intellectual defending core values of freedom. As the university's information officer, Bob Beyers, who was on the scene of every disturbance in the 1960s, later told me: "There was very little community. That's what really mattered: to have people supporting you—even people who might disagree with you. The administration looks at the facts, they say here it is, this is what we're going to do. To a lawyer, to throw away the judicial procedure—forget it! Then you turn around and all of a sudden the community that's there is against you. Jesus, that's scary."

The sociologist Daniel Bell, who had tried and failed to mediate an end to the Columbia occupation, wrote afterward: "In a community one cannot regain authority simply by asserting it, or by using force to suppress dissidents. Authority in this case is like respect. One can only *earn* the authority—the loyalty of one's students—by going in and arguing with them, by engaging in full debate and, when the merits of proposed change are recognized, taking the necessary steps quickly enough to be convincing." A week after Columbia, where the assertion of authority had been so costly, my father and Stanford's other top administrators were loath to call on force, and yet they couldn't bring themselves to go in and earn anything while the students were using force. As a result, the administration became isolated during the crisis. And yet my father, like Bell, saw the university as a community. He had no other—had never had any other throughout his life—and he gave this community all his energy, much more than he gave his family, because he believed in the high importance of the life of the mind. Now, as he saw it, a group of morally righteous and intellectually shallow students were trying to destroy it.

Colleagues urged him to see the crisis in pragmatic and nuanced terms. A physiologist wrote a letter counseling him not "to worry about saving face . . . [but] to help well-meaning students escape safely from the self-made trap of their excesses." This professor was surprised upon visiting the occupied Old Union by the courteous reception and orderly manner of the students, and he wrote, "It is unfortunate, but understandable, that you and others with deep responsibilities for the continuity of our university abstract the real nature of the groups sitting-in under the pejorative term 'activist.' " A hematologist wrote my father, "I cannot comment on the issues of fact in the whole mess, for I am poorly informed on them, but I can comment on the feelings which can easily be identified in the students' reactions. They sense that the administration distrusts their abilities to self-govern."

But to my father courtesy and good intentions and feelings were really beside the point. Where some professors saw the Stanford community as a group of people who needed to get along, my father saw it as a set of principles that needed to be protected from threats. People's feelings were evanescent, fluid, sometimes flammable; abstract principles were more real, and in a pinch they were all you could count on. He had already lived through one period of mob rule and frightening populist passions and charges of elitism. Perhaps in 1968 he and men like him were reliving the unhappy years of the 1950s, when the independence and integrity of liberal intellectuals had come under assault from the other flank. "Study—my grandmother!" Fulton Lewis, Jr., had said then. "We will rationally discuss when we're equals," the students said now. "Until then, it's the streets." But to my father force was not a legitimate means of persuasion at a university, nor was mob rule. Only rational debate was legitimate.

By 1968 growing numbers of students no longer believed in it. Michael Novak, then a young religion professor, since converted to neoconservatism, told the sit-in, "Where one group has all the power, one must beware of appeals to reason." Steve Weissman, a veteran of the Free Speech Movement who became the key figure in the sit-in, said, "Force is very much part of the world, a fact of life. People who call themselves teachers had better stop trying to teach us out of that fact." The students no longer believed in the meritocracy of intellect that had gotten them into Stanford, because this meritocracy had gotten the country into Vietnam. Casey Hayden, wife of Tom, wrote an article for *The New Republic* called "The Question of Who Is Qualified." Those who claimed to be qualified to lead, by virtue of talent and training, were now utterly suspect.

The radical argument that Stanford was helping to fight the war was simplistic; attacking the one institution that protected radicals from public wrath was foolishly destructive. But if intellect itself was the enemy, the students had found the right target.

With the administration and the students so deeply mistrustful of each other, it was left to the faculty to solve the crisis. But the faculty was just waking up from its long federally funded sleep to discover that it belonged to a community whose survival was now in question. These academic entrepreneurs with their grants and research teams divided the world into departments. They had no experience and little interest in solving campus-wide problems. It took a pair of bolt cutters to show that the multiversity was a university after all. One of the sit-in's ironies is that my father had accepted the post of vice provost partly to make the faculty a more integral part of running the university, and to that end he had proposed an elected faculty senate. By May 1968 the senate was nearly a reality, but, like the new judicial body, it had not been born in time. When the sit-in began, the only decision-making body of the faculty was the Academic Council, nine hundred professors, most of whom had never attended a meeting. The Council left most decisions to its ten-man Executive Committee. On Wednesday, May 8, the third day of the sit-in, the committee presented the Council with a set of resolutions: President Sterling should rehear the CIA case; the new judicial body, giving students a larger though not dominant role, should be approved; students should now vacate the Old Union.

The Council meeting that afternoon was chaotic. Over five hundred faculty jammed Dinkelspiel Auditorium for hours of motions and amendments and votes, and it wasn't always clear that those voting were Council members (my mother, as a lecturer, wasn't on the Council and had to slip in to watch). But the crucial decision came in the first five minutes. A group from the medical school moved to table the Executive Committee's resolutions and substitute their own, including a blanket amnesty for the CIA demonstrators and those sitting in.

The committee's resolutions were shelved without any debate. Three and a half raucous hours and two amendments later, the amnesty passed on a narrow vote.

"And so the Council," my father said in a speech five nights later, "its mission of securing peace in our time accomplished, adjourned. Two hours later, the demonstration was over. The following evening the President and the Provost gave their reluctant acquiescence to the Council's action, as they had to do unless the University was to be plunged into a far more serious crisis."

On a yellow sheet of paper he typed up a three-paragraph letter of resignation. "I believe that the action taken by the Academic Council on Wednesday, May 8, has made the University ungovernable, in the literal sense of that word," he wrote. "The message is very clear and has already been understood by the students who celebrated their victory on Wednesday night: coercion pays. Confrontation politics will now become the daily routine of academic administrators. I want none of it."

He never submitted the letter. Instead, he poured all his bitterness at what he saw as the faculty's betrayal into his speech at a Palo Alto hotel, before the Stanford chapter of the American Association of University Professors, the body that had sprung up after the Edward Ross case to defend academic freedom. He stood at the podium, smoking a cigar, using it to gesture as scorn dripped from his words and he analyzed "The week that was." The audience included many of the colleagues who had voted to give in to the students' demands, and also my mother, sitting at a table by the podium, listening with pride, cringing, and wishing she could grab the cigar out of his hand.

"They thought they were saving the University," he said. "And by their lights, they succeeded—for a few days or a few weeks. By yielding to gross physical coercion they ended the sit-in. And they taught a lesson that is easily learned: coercion pays. What do they propose to do next time it is applied? They did not face that question. And that, I submit, is the height of substantive irresponsibility."

Someone asked him a question about the wisdom of this sort of legalistic thinking during a community crisis. My father's reply summed up his liberal philosophy in one sentence. "Procedure is at the heart of all liberty."

The speech shows him operating at the height of his powers, pulling no punches. The effort of control is enormous. The muscle of his mind is clenching again and again to squeeze reason out of rage. All the blood in his head is concentrated in the precision and force of language. Reading, I can almost feel the strain thinning the weak place in his cerebral artery.

The speech won him wide admiration and wider criticism. "Hardly what is needed now," sniffed the university chaplain. "Vitriolic," said the Stanford *Daily*, which called both the sit-in and the faculty vote "examples of participatory democracy at its best." For the rest of May my father was the lightning rod for all the voltage still flowing ungrounded from the sit-in. In his files from that month there are letters and replies that flew back and forth across the campus of what was after all a tiny community of people who saw each other every day, harsh attacks from the fathers of my school friends, from professors who lived in our neighborhood. By June, as the disastrous school year limped to an end, my father had begun to regret his tone. He sent the speech to interested friends around the country but tried to stop its dissemination around Stanford. He called publicly for an end to the "atmosphere of bitterness and recrimination. Many things have been said and done in the last two weeks that might perpetuate such an atmosphere. Few of us are guiltless in that respect. Certainly I am not."

He began to sound, for once, like an administrator, and he kept up the effort for the next year. But in a private letter to a colleague, he put the lessons of the sit-in in stark political terms. "Centrists like you and me and most other members of the Stanford faculty will be sitting ducks for the radical right unless we demonstrate our ability to distinguish between 'legitimate complaints' and illegitimate means of seeking redress for those complaints . . . If we believe that the university is not so corrupt that revolution rather than reform is needed, then we had better see to it that revolution does not become acceptable. That requires reform but it also requires the willingness to resist revolution."

A few months after the sit-in, in a Parents' Day speech on educational reform, he reflected more dispassionately on the "cult of irrationality" among youth—"a penchant for the apocalyptic that is profoundly disturbing to those of us who have staked our lives on the proposition that progress in human affairs depends upon rationality and self-restraint." He offered "the joys and the frustrations of intellectual analysis" as "the best anodyne against existential despair."

But this was 1968—the year of Tet, assassinations, riots, Paris, Columbia, Chicago, George Wallace, the new Nixon. Lyndon Johnson, the high liberal ambitions of his Great Society engulfed in chaos, withdrew from the presidential race and brooded about his fallen predecessor Woodrow Wilson "stretched out upstairs in the White House, powerless to move, with the machinery of the American government in disarray around him." Johnson feared that he too, like Wilson, would have a stroke. University administrators began to retire, quit, die of heart attacks, even commit suicide. Over the summer, a firebomb destroyed the office of President Sterling just weeks before his retirement, consuming the records of his nineteen-year presidency (the man chosen to replace him, a chemist from Rice named Kenneth Pitzer, was out of his depth from day one and left after a year and a half). As a possible target our house was fitted with exterior floodlights and an emergency phone with a direct line to the police. One evening, horsing around with my mother, I kicked the phone off the hook. A few minutes later my sister came into the room. "Mom, there's a policeman at the door and he has his gun in his hand." "Lady," the cop told my mother, "another ten seconds and I was going to blow the lock off the door."

In 1968 who could believe in rationality and self-restraint? Against existential despair and its fraternal twin, romantic primitivism, intellectual analysis was as weak as paper. And liberalism looked like the excuse of hypocrites who wanted to end the war but not the system that started it. As that year of apocalypse unfolded in a series of explosions, each stronger than the last, leaving the reasonable world in ruins, my father was battling his own existential despair. And it had become a matter of principle not to give in. To throw up his hands, surrender to

madness, appease the student radicals, vote for the Peace and Freedom Party, become a neo-con, weep, shout in rage, tear his hair—
these would be a betrayal of himself. In the face of an onslaught, he
had to stiffen and clench. The burner was turned to a high flame, and
the lid of his values pressed down on the boiling pot.

Nineteen sixty-eight was the year I discovered the wider world; it was
the year I discovered politics. All but oblivious to my father's battles,
barely aware of the turmoil less than a mile from our house, I became
obsessed with the history of presidents and the ongoing presidential
campaign. This obsession began in the mute stupor of the breakfast
table as, spoon in hand, I stared at the backs of my Cheerios boxes,
where pictures and biographies of American Presidents appeared in
sets of four. On the basis of this and other sources, I composed a presidential history heavily biased toward the Democrats and Lincoln, with
a special interest in the four assassinated Presidents, who appeared
together on the same box.

In my first effort at autobiography, written at age seven sometime
that year, my family barely makes an appearance; instead, I mark the
events of my life by American politics in the 1960s, grandly and often
inaccurately.

I was born to early.
Luckely I lived.
About two months later my mom named me. She named me
GEORGE. I didn't cry much. My sister was born earlier than
me. All this happened when Dwight D. Eisenhower was Presi-
dent. The year, 1960.
When I was three on November twenty second 1963 John F.
KENNEDY WAS MURDERED! A man named Oswald did it.
A week afterward the police were taking Oswald to a nother jail,
when a man named Jack Ruby shot Oswald because Oswald
shot Kennedy.

When I was five, Johnson was running for President against Goldwater. Johnson won. When I was six, Johnson was Anaugurated.

When I was seven, I voted for McCarthy.

I would have, a hundred times. That spring and summer of 1968, especially after a trip to Washington, politics became my passion and Eugene McCarthy my first hero. I wore a campaign T-shirt three sizes too large, composed speeches on the treatment of "Negreos" and the way to end the war, sent him letters of adoration and advice ("Get out of Vietnam and into Biafra") long after he had withdrawn into his famous sulk. Not coincidentally, he was my parents' candidate, too, heir to *their* hero Stevenson, dovish, witty—Nixon's opposite, flawed with a weak will. In a little essay I wrote about the looks of all the candidates, McCarthy became a benevolent protector touched with fatherly wisdom: "Eugene J. McCarthy has wavy gray hair. He has sad eyes but he is always happy. He has a nice smile. He has sort of long hair." As for the Republican nominee of 1968, I had fully absorbed my father's point of view: "Richard M. Nixon has big jaws. He has a long ski nose. He has a head shaped like a foot-ball." Combining my two main interests, I named a large green silkworm that I'd found in the backyard "Eugene J. McCarthy." The candidate was placed in a jar with fresh leaves and clean water, only to end up the next day in the same state as every other animal that came under my care, just three weeks before his namesake met the same fate in Chicago.

I predicted victory for McCarthy. Everyone we knew was for him— how could he lose? The Chicago convention left me thunderstruck, unable to comprehend the unfairness of it. But accepting compromise as the price of politics, I transferred my loyalty to Humphrey ("H. H. H. ISNT doing to well with the war. My dad doesnt think he is a very good man. But I do."). On election night I had to go to bed before the results were final. I woke up to the news of Nixon's razor-thin win and took my second blow in what was becoming a series that would last for most of a year (and then through most of my life). My parents blamed Humphrey's defeat on the liberals and radicals who had sat out the election or voted for Dick Gregory. Politics, with its personalities and drama, its thrilling Styrofoam hats and delegate counts and campaign rallies in the Stanford basketball arena, had suddenly become a source of intense pain. At eight I had no remedy.

In the shadow of all this precocious interest lay another kind of fascination: I was mesmerized by violence. The real drama of politics was death. The night of Robert Kennedy's murder after the California primary, I had a dream in which Eugene McCarthy was gunned down. It may be that my mother had woken me up to tell me about the shooting in Los Angeles and then I'd gone back to sleep with murder aboil in my unconscious. But in a sense I was already prepared for it.

In the way a younger child is frightened by monsters he can't get enough of, my political awakening was haunted by the assassinations of Lincoln and John Kennedy, then King and Robert Kennedy. I read about them in a state of absolute terror, going over every detail. In my parents' study there was a volume called *The Torch Is Passed*, a photographic narrative of the day of JFK's death put out by the Associated Press. This book became my dark secret. The knowledge that it existed, crimson and knife-thin on the shelf among world atlases, was enough to make me shudder whenever I was in the study alone—often enough, since I couldn't keep myself from staring at those black-and-white pictures that never lost their power to shock. The sunlit smile in the unbearable last moment, the blur of his hands clutching his throat, the shiny shoe sticking up over the seat. And later, Oswald under escort staring obliviously ahead as the stout figure of Jack Ruby rushes from the corner of the frame, snub-nose extended. In a home movie from 1968 I'm dressed like Lincoln, black beard and coat and stovepipe hat, sitting in a kitchen chair. Suddenly I mouth an explosion, grimace, and slump forward.

Apparently these horror films were rolling in my imagination throughout that year. My interest in presidential names and dates gave me a rational way to try to master events—I was my father's son after all—but disorder and death seeped into my mind and worked on me.

How much did this have to do with the pressure my father was under? An eight-year-old's parents are very important furniture, heavily depended on yet barely noticed. McCarthy was much more vivid to me than my father—he had an existence separate from mine, while my father was part of the background against which my boyhood was played out. Three decades later, I can see how the candidate became a stand-in and why his defeat wounded me so personally; how my parents' anxiety and the sense of siege in our house colored my new interest the red of assassination. Throughout 1968 I was simultaneously out of it and acutely aware, protecting and exposing myself, struggling to handle what couldn't be handled. People and things changed form, good and evil filled a single dream, adults offered comfort but turned out to be helpless, intellect sharpened but so did terror. The world opened and I fell in.

In January 1969 my father announced that he would leave his position as vice provost in June and return to teaching and writing. Two months earlier, campaigning on "law and order," Richard Nixon had been elected President like an unkillable vampire returning from the grave. Liberalism, the impulse that ran through American politics from the years of reform in the 1890s and the New Deal to the Great Society of the mid-1960s, had crashed in flames.

A week after the election, the Study of Education at Stanford published its ten volumes of recommendations for reforming the university. Just as the book on ex-Communist witnesses had been accused at the start of bias by the right but ended up giving little comfort to the left, the Stanford study, accused at the start of bias by the left, gave little comfort to the status quo. It urged sweeping reforms to democratize the board of trustees, replace the maze of required courses with small freshman seminars, redirect high-profile specialists back toward teaching and addressing "ultimate value questions," and give students more power.

"Not the kind of power that the SDS types are talking about," my father said, "but educational power, the power to have a voice in the formation of the educational policies of their institutions." It offered a more democratic vision of liberal education that tried to answer students' deepest grievances about the dehumanizing "system" and their deepest desires for meaning. But 1968 had almost doomed the study. And for my father it came too late.

"Students are niggers," one student wrote in the *Daily* magazine. "The Study of Education at Stanford proposes wooden floors for your cabins. I propose we abolish slavery."

"The effort that we've been making has come under very very heavy attack from radical, heavily politicized students," my father acknowledged. "And I think it's very understandable that that would be so. It's the old story of reform being the real enemy of revolution. They see these efforts to make the university more flexible and more responsive, but within roughly the existing framework, as terribly threatening to their desire to bring the whole structure crashing down."

"Reform Before Revolution" was the title of a PBS documentary shot by a crew that came to film the troubles at Stanford the week of Nixon's inauguration. Half the crew followed administrators, the other half radical students. But this was 1969, and the filmmakers became so polarized from each other's point of view that their work eventually aired on the same night as two separate films. The one on the radical students was called "Fathers and Sons"—I tracked down a copy from a former SDS member named Lenny Siegel who is still active in radical politics. I sat in a Stanford projection room and watched, in the reddish light of a badly faded 16-mm film, ancient-seeming images of Siegel and his SDS comrades confronting a nervously laughing President Pitzer outside his office (one student has a Pitzer mask over his head), crashing a meeting of the trustees, barbecuing with guitars at the beach, and kibitzing at all-night meetings, part strategy sessions, part encounter groups. "What does it mean personally for you to be a revolutionary?" "I was a liberal until last year." "Some people are my enemy," Lenny Siegel says. "David Rockefeller is my enemy. Kenneth Pitzer is my enemy." Siegel, lower middle class and Jewish, expresses resentment of the better-off radicals. One of them, David Pugh, is talking about his father. "He's very successful, a nice man. He doesn't have much faith in other people. He's very organized and rational. There's a clamp on emotions. There has been in my family—it's true of the upper middle, upper class. My whole personal liberation in terms of feelings has just been essential for me."

Fathers and sons, clamped emotions, the need to break free—did the revolution come down to this? The language was alien to men of my father's generation. For them, politics was a contest of ideas and power carried on in the public sphere. It had nothing to do, as far as they knew, with their private relationships to their fathers, their sons, and their feelings. Women are strikingly absent from "Fathers and Sons," as they were largely absent from, or subordinate in, SDS—but just a year or two before feminism would burst onto the scene with the slogan "the personal is political," young men were beginning to sound the same way.

David Pugh turns up in the other film, "Reform Before Revolution," as well—still talking about feelings. The week the filmmakers spent at Stanford was also the week in which the Study of Education at Stanford was debated at a mass indoor meeting attended by hundreds of students. "Take a quote out of the SES report," Pugh says from the speakers' table onstage (so many stages, so many speakers in those years). "'Think freely and think well.' That sounds awful good. Where's feel? We have plenty of people like McNamara and the brain trust in the Defense Department who think very freely and very well, and my God, how many people do they destroy? Somehow we've got to get back in contact with human values."

Three seats over, my father can hardly contain himself. Pale and exhausted-looking, he rolls his eyes, purses his lips, grins, and finally says, "Independent inquiry, critical disinterested scrutiny of what is going on in life, is a very specialized kind of function that either takes place within a university or it just does not take place. And for my money, which I think on the current market may be somewhat devalued, that's what the university is all about."

Questions from the student audience. What do things like freshman seminars matter when Stanford professors' research is going into F-111s and antipersonnel bombs?

"Are the issues involving the undergraduate education of this university so trivial that they simply aren't worth anybody's attention?" my father asks in disbelief. "If those of us in the university are prepared to give up on that job, then I think it's a very momentous and a very sad day for the human race."

(As he says these words, I accidentally put the video of "Reform Before Revolution" in super-slow motion. Suddenly, it looks like the Zapruder film. In the logic of the decade, a bullet is about to hit my father's head.)

The film ends in our living room. My father is interviewed sitting on the couch while Whiskers, our Siamese cat, keeps hopping on his lap in spite of my father's attempts to get rid of him. At one point he turns the conversation to David Pugh.

"He is in such total revolt against the rigid dry analytic overly scientific approach to human knowledge that he rejects the whole idea of thinking. He says, let's stop thinking and start feeling. Well, that's really tragic. The object has to be to bring the two into some kind of equilibrium."

And yet, as if mindful of his own need for equilibrium, he also speaks more charitably of the intractable problems that confront students in the 1960s. He almost begins to sound like a father, though not of his own son. "When I was Dave Pugh's age we were fighting a war that we believed in. It was the last of the just wars, maybe. But here Dave Pugh and his fellows are, seeing the country in a war that is totally unjustifiable, seeing the threat of nuclear destruction over us all the time—I think that's just made an enormous difference, and I can understand why people who have grown up in that atmosphere would feel a kind of apocalyptic sense of despair. If I were of their generation I might very well feel much as they do."

The interview captures my father as I imagine him wanting to be seen: criticizing students but also sympathizing with them, joking ironically, ranging over politics and education, rejecting both youthful nihilism and academic deadness, quoting "that really great humanist E. M. Forster who in *Howards End* said: 'Only connect the prose and the passion.' " In the film's last seconds he sits with his left leg crossed over his right. He is gesturing with his right hand. The eyes come piercing out of his shadowed face. And his voice—listening to it now, I have no memory of it, I can't recognize it as his: slightly nasal, measured, calm, and strong.

The program aired in April. My father watched it from his hospital bed, on a television that had been wheeled in by nurses. In mid-March, in the middle of the night, he had suffered a stroke from an occlusion in an artery on the left side of his brain. At the hospital, an arteriogram probing the blocked vessel opened a hemorrhage through the artery wall, causing another stroke that almost killed him. For a few days he lay in a coma while his life hung in the balance. And even when it began to seem that he would survive, the damage done was permanent: paralysis of the entire right side of his body. As he lay watching the articulate triumph of an earlier self, my father couldn't speak.

CHAPTER 9

◆

The Prose and the Passion

He came home a stranger in a wheelchair. When he was still in the hospital I spoke to him on the phone: at the end of what couldn't be called a conversation he said, in a moaning, ghostly voice, "Goodbye." I said goodbye, relieved to be getting off the phone, but he echoed himself, and again, and each time I tried to get away this terrible new voice drifted from the receiver: "Goodbye. Goodbye."

Ramps went up outside our house and inside, long black ramps with rails. We ate at a folding card table in the family room where access was easier: low-cholesterol chicken and fish every night. My father's right arm hung against his body, the useless hand curled rigid. He brought the food to his mouth with his shaky left hand. His thoughts now reached his tongue and stuttered out thirty seconds too late. When his frustration was unendurable, the curses exploded in thick choked stammers. Dinner became the sound of silverware.

The stroke put my father on my psychic map. From being remote, kind, reliable, and hardly a person at all, he became an indelible presence. I was aware of him all the time now, partly out of pity but mainly because I was afraid and careful to keep a distance. He seemed much less like a parent than a child, physically helpless, prone to sudden storms of anger or tears. Even when he learned to walk again, after heroic months of physical therapy, the metal brace that imprisoned his right leg, the ubiquitous cane, the clumsy rigid step, the electric golf cart he drove to school, the thick black beard he grew because shaving was so difficult and that soon began to gray—this strange new man never ceased to frighten and, I must confess, repel me. In pictures from the years after the stroke his eyes and mouth have a kind of vulnerable beauty that wasn't there before, with more feeling—warmth, despera-tion—as if the stream of blocked words was struggling to find a way out. But it wasn't beautiful to me then. I couldn't look him in the eye.

In the lifelong struggle of this most rational man to connect the prose and the passion, it was passion that ruled his last years.

My father and I are playing a military board game called Waterloo, in which divisions of troops are little chips that need to be stacked an inch or two high and moved from square to square. This game, our only source of father-son intimacy, seems designed to tax his mechani-cal skill to the limit, and from time to time he knocks over his troops or mine. Once, as he fumbles to stack the spilled chips, I notice that his French forces have crept a square closer to my Prussians. "You're cheating!" I tell him. How should he respond? Like a father, like his former self, coolly explaining the difference between trickery and mis-takes and suggesting that I give him the benefit of reasonable doubt? With wisdom and restraint, acknowledging that his illness is hard on all of us, that we need to pull together as a family? No doubt he would like to, but his emotions begin their gallop and trample him underfoot. "No I'm not, goddammit!" The game is over: he tells me I've ruined it for him. Later, my mother draws me aside and wearily asks me to be more sensitive.

"Your father is a great man," she says.

"As great as Abraham Lincoln?"

She nods, and I pretend to believe her.

I'm on a rooftop with two school friends, passing around an illicit cigarette. Tom Gann is describing what he admires in his father, and Marc Larrey turns to me. "What do you admire your dad for?" A booby-trapped question, and before I can think of something he follows it up with another: "For being a crip?" I start to sniffle, less out of real grief than the idea that this is expected of me. What I mainly feel is the shame of the word, the truth. Later Tom Gann tells me, "I'd've hit him," and my shame doubles: my father is a crip, and I won't stand up for him.

My father, mother, sister, and I are at a restaurant, demonstrating to ourselves that we are still a family. My father asks my sister and me for a lunch date at the faculty club in a week or so: an unprecedented invitation, and we both hedge, mumbling about being busy. "Do you prefer your mother so goddam much to me," he cries out, "that you won't even have lunch with me?" We try to mollify him, embarrassed that there might be a public scene, as if we aren't already conspicuous enough; and we both know it's true.

I am riding on an exercise bike that my father uses to build up his atrophied muscles. It runs on electricity, its handlebars attached to a metal stem that moves up and down at varying speeds. I try to get off with the machine still running and my heel catches between the stem and the seat, pinned there, the Exercycle crushing my Achilles tendon. I cry to my father for help. He's sitting across the room, immobilized, stamping his cane in a futile effort to get up. My mother comes to my rescue. Years later, I impute to myself the worst of motives: a desire, even in the midst of terror, to show him his helplessness, fling it in his face, punish him for it. I'm aware of the kinder interpretation, that I simply wanted a father, but the guilt that colors all these memories won't allow me to be convinced.

I come home from the basketball playground one evening after dark in the last year of my father's life, to see my parents sitting on the other side of the glass doors in the lighted kitchen, wearing sunglasses. I know at once that they've been crying, which terrifies me, so that the sunglasses have the opposite effect my parents intended for them. Instead of disguising their despair, they make it horribly, almost comically apparent, like ill-fitting wigs. In this sense the gesture perfectly represents the way my family has attempted to survive the thing that blew our old life to pieces: we refer to it as little as possible, while every moment serves to remind us, so that this tragedy we live with all the time has charged the house with tension and driven each of us into the separate rooms of our isolation. In home movies post-stroke, we hardly look at one another.

For twenty years after his death the stroke completely defined my father for me. He was nothing but impotent rage, desperate hope, misery, and a kind of vulnerable tenderness. But in the boxes of papers in my mother's garage, I discovered a separate life. During the months when he was pedaling the Exercycle and shuffling up the stairs, he was also writing articles and volumes of letters. The blue onionskin carbons are like facsimiles or ghosts of the life that seemed to have all but ended with the stroke. It was still going on, in private, in silence, on paper, away from the humiliations of conversation. And I knew nothing of it.

From a letter to a college friend: "Last spring, after I had quit being Vice Provost, I suffered a severe stroke, God knows whether as punishment or just as consequence. I am slowly but steadily recovering." The man I remember sounded nothing like that. The ironic stoicism is so superior to his paralysis, so determined to be unfettered by it, that I wonder if I knew him at all during those last years, and if, had I been able to recognize such a tone, we could have been father and son after all. Is it the letter or my memory that lies? Which man was he? Was he both at once?

I search his papers for signs of the gathering disaster. His first letters after release from the hospital are almost buoyant with hope for "complete recovery." "We are really going to come out of this perfectly all right—prevailing rather than enduring." A month later discouragement has begun to set in. " 'Under the weather' certainly puts it mildly. I am gradually, however, making it back." "My recovery is, as is customary in these matters, hardly 'complete.' My 'imminent return to law teaching' is still, I guess, problematical as of September. We continue to live in hope."

Less than two months after the stroke, using his left hand, he typed up these words on a scrap of paper:

Herbeert L. Packer, 807 San Francisco Terrace, Stanford
I am partially invalided my mind seems to be working much as it always did but I am somewhat disabled by the effects of a stroke which has affected my right side. How did all this happen and what was the progress of my illness?

He doesn't try to answer how all this happened. Instead, he documents in practical detail the various functions of his body. The most vexing is speech, regaining command of tongue, lips, breath, saliva. Someone—a speech therapist?—has written down sentences for him to practice:

I want my socks & shoes.
I want a drink of water.
I want to read the book.
I want my back scratched.
I want my wife and children.
I _____ approve of the student action at Harvard.
I am making good progress.

Yet even while he is learning to talk again, his career resumes. At the June commencement in Frost Amphitheater, pushed onstage in his wheelchair, he receives the award for service to undergraduate education for the Study of Education at Stanford, and an audience of several thousand gives him a standing ovation. He begins publishing work at an astonishing rate, in *The New Republic* and *The New York Review of Books*. In the vein of John Stuart Mill, he criticizes Nixon's harsh new crime policy and advocates the decriminalization of heroin. During the Vietnam Moratorium he argues against politicization of universities by the left and crackdown by the right. The voice is the same as before—sharp, reasonable—but there's now a tendency to reach judgment without quite as patient an argument as before. And as the months go by, some of his letters begin to seem out of control, crossing the line between tartness and incivility. "I have just yawned my way through your article," he begins a note to a sociology professor he apparently doesn't know; but to an old friend who's cautioned him about losing his temper and shooting from the hip, my father writes, "Since I got sick, I've had so much hostility floating around that it affects my work. Of course, I don't want to be a gratuitously curmudgeonly fellow."

And then there is a document titled "Notes on My Speech Therapy," one of the periodic attempts to record his progress:

After my stroke in 1969, I underwent speech therapy. The therapist was an inexperienced young lady who made up for her own lack of confidence by trying to assert herself into our relationship. Toward the end of our therapy, she insisted on giving me exercises in remembering series of numbers. I objected strongly to this because I did not think that remembering series of numbers was at all relevant to my condition. She also gave me some exercises in spelling words. One of those sessions occasioned the following incident, in which she is represented by the letter C and myself by the letter P:

C: Spell "banister."
P: B-a-n-i-s-t-e-r.
C: That is wrong: it has two n's.
P: I disagree. Look it up in the dictionary.
C: Well, let's just go on.
    (The dictionary gives the spelling as "banister," with "bannister" as an occasional alternative.)
C: Spell "barrister."

P: B-a-r-r-i-s-t-e-r. Would you like me to use it in a sentence?
C: Sure.
P: She broke her ankle sliding down a barrister.
C: That doesn't make sense to me.

I had remembered an old joke, which I used to get some revenge. The therapist did not understand that she had been one-upped. Shortly after this session, she phoned my wife and said that she would like to talk with her about my case. My wife, whom I had told about the preceding incident, went in and talked with the therapist, who complained that my attitude was not good. Shortly after this complaint, my wife and I decided to terminate the therapy.

The therapist did a competent job, but she struck out because she did not know how to "handle" me. That I would suppose was how she would put it. As a former patient, it still makes me bridle when therapists talk about "handling" people.

In the indignity of learning to speak again, he locked himself in a power struggle with poor C and outwitted her—to no avail. So he went home and told his wife, who at least provided a competent audience. Did she also want to tell him to let himself be "handled"—that these little contests were not going to heal his wounded mind? Later in the notes, he writes that a different speech therapist, along with a psychiatrist, "aided me to recover my self-confidence, to the point where I was able to speak extemporaneously before a large and critical audience." It wasn't really true—an impossible standard that would daunt someone in full possession of his faculties, the standard of his former self, the man he had seen on television as he lay paralyzed and speechless. He set himself tests he was bound to fail, returned to the classroom too soon and later apologized to his law students for the poor job done. "I have become progressively more silent," he writes at one point to his neurologist. "There is nothing I want more than to be able to communicate orally with people. That, if it happens, will be what I

would consider to be complete recovery from the effects of my stroke."
In the same letter he describes his new method of learning to speak
again, which includes "punishing myself by starting over again when I
don't breathe correctly." This method, he hopes, will give him back
his confidence.

The measured prose of these progress reports doesn't disguise the
killing effort to bring his mind and will to bear on his body, to free
himself from the prison his body has become, to understand "How
did all this happen?" In his letters he is forever recovering his self-
confidence. Each recovery means that he has lost it again; each time
he proclaims himself on the road to health there is a more desperate
edge; each recovery betrays months of despondency that the letters
don't describe. And no wonder—he couldn't bear to be what he was.

Not long ago my mother and I were looking through some of my
father's papers when she put her hand on a thick manila envelope
marked "Inter-Office Mail." It had been lying on the shelf untouched
for almost thirty years, but she knew at once what was inside, and she
groaned.

The envelope contained the half-completed manuscript of a book
he started writing after his stroke. Its subject was higher education. By
1970 books diagnosing the ills of higher education were pouring from
the presses. My father's contribution to the genre represented a sum-
ming up of the lessons he had learned on the front lines over the previous years, but it began with a cry of pain. For the first and only time
he was allowing himself to say: Look what they did to me!

"Shortly after I resigned my administrative position, I suffered a
severe stroke which left me partially paralyzed. In a sense, writing this
essay seems to have been an important part of my therapy and hence of
my recovery. I have tried not to be vindictive about the stresses which
contributed to my stroke. Yet, candor compels me to admit that the
psychic energy which fueled working out the theses in this book
derived largely from working through the frustrations that helped to

cause my stroke." And he named them: "the irrationality of certain students," "the romanticism of certain faculty members," "the pusillanimity of administrators," "the arrogant ignorance of trustees." One by one he fired off rounds at the tormenting specters of 1968. A few pages later, apparently satisfied, he declared: "Enough autobiography. This book is not an extension of these remarks. Now that I've made them, I feel, for the first time, free of their incubus."

But he wasn't free. The weight of the incubus lies on the whole manuscript, every page discharges irritation and anguish, the sentences aren't always clear, points are asserted and then claimed to have been proven. His most compelling ideas—getting rid of lifetime tenure, for example, as a spurious guarantor of academic freedom—gleam dully like headlights in a fog. The words read like those of a man who can no longer say exactly what he thinks. In the last sentence he seems to be paying an inadvertent tribute to himself. "There is an honored place in the recent annals of universities for those officers who, having endured much and having acted, did not survive."

So he gave these pages to his first and best reader. My mother saw at once that in their present form they were unpublishable. But she also saw the shadow of his former self struggling to emerge through the fog. She could have dispensed some patronizing praise and left him to find out later and in the most humiliating way that he had let himself down. Or she could have tried to find some gentle and supportive means of working together on it. But my parents were intellectual partners, and mutual respect as well as temperament sometimes brought out a fairly brutal honesty. When it came to prose my mother in particular had a hard time mustering the usual forms of insincerity. What's more, she thought she could do again what she'd done during his breakdown over Ex-Communist Witnesses—will him to get through the fog and fix the book. She wanted him to keep his passions out of it, to be more objective, to clarify his vision. He was, in a sense, thinking with his blood now, and she wanted him to think again with that great gift, his reason. So she typed up a letter that began: "About your book on education. Here is some very tough criticism. Duck!"

Seven single-spaced pages later, she concluded apologetically: "It's probably arrogant as hell of me to have gone on so lengthily about your book. My only justification is that over the years you've taught me so well what to think about universities and their problems that I can't help participating now in your thinking and organizing. No doubt I've overdone it."

The manuscript was never worked on again. Someone put it in the manila envelope, together with my mother's letter, where they both remained until she found them nearly thirty years later, with that groan of recognition.

This editorial heartache sums up the dynamic into which the stroke pushed my parents, from which there was no real escape. What had started with his crisis over the Hiss book was now thoroughly played out: my father had always depended on my mother, and now he depended on her completely. He needed her to tie his shoes, to carry his suitcase, to coach him on the Exercycle, to intervene with his children, and it was a terrible irony that he now needed her to edit his writings for rational clarity. Editing his conversation wasn't as easy. A rare dinner party went by without my father saying something explosive to one of his friends. When I went back home to speak to these men, every one of them recalled how hard my father was to take after the stroke, and yet how much they loved him, and every one of them, retired scholars in their seventies, wept in guilt and grief, as if they were still carrying the weight of all the things left unsaid, things men of their generation didn't know how to say. My father's only confidante was my mother.

She became the single parent in the house, strength to his weakness. When we played a board game as a family, my sister and I scarcely concealed our desire to be on her side and not his. And her power grew outside the house as well. She became an assistant professor and involved herself more than before in university affairs. She joined the battles my father had once led, and in place of his analytic powers she brought her own combative political intelligence, which had languished since her brother's campaigns. Her hatred of the "rads," whom she held partly responsible for her husband's condition, became quite intense. When violence was peaking on campus in early 1971, she wrote a letter to a colleague outlining how to defeat them. "Too great a squeamishness or too high-minded an attitude may, to put it apocalyptically, give us comfort on the way to the ovens. Which is not to say that we ought to stoop to lying, cheating, misrepresenting, breaking *their* windows, but it is to say that nothing should go unchallenged, unresponded to, that no means however trivial or seemingly undignified should go unused," she urged. "The essence of the counter-slogan is ridicule and reductio ad absurdum and we oughtn't to be above either." She sounded like a woman of political blood who plays to win, and who now felt more free to represent the family to the world.

My mother applied all her reserves of energy and will to the task of keeping the family afloat and my father's spirit alive and his work up to snuff. Sometimes in the fear of not pressing hard enough and all of us going under she pressed too hard. Then she lost her temper and he lost his courage and my sister and I kept out of the way. In my head I found ways to live somewhere other than home. My political obsession gave way to others—World War II, sports. My most acutely felt sorrow in the spring of 1969 was not my father's stroke but the Los Angeles Lakers, led by my injured hero Jerry West, losing yet again to the Boston Celtics. I avoided the few attempts either parent made to talk about what was happening at home.

In 1971 we took a trip through Europe: five months on the road, from Sicily to Norway, never staying in one place longer than ten days, my father hobbling up countless church steps. My mother spent a good part of the trip fuming over car problems and canceled reservations, alternately exploding at the family for leaving everything to her and making unilateral declarations of peace. My helpless father sank into depression and wept easily. The landscape outside the car was beautiful, the tension inside oppressive.

Within a week of our return in September my father was writing to a colleague: "If you catch a rather desperate edge in this exchange of correspondence you are right. It might do me some good to talk with you about this when you have a chance." Did the talk ever happen, or was it another lost opportunity? A few days later my mother's brother George died of a heart attack. She flew to Birmingham for the funeral, leaving the three of us alone. I remember a feeling of foreboding in those days, a sense that things were spiraling downward.

Not long after my mother's return, I was sitting at the kitchen table one morning when paramedics wheeled my father out of the house on a stretcher. His face was turned toward me: it had no color except in the lips. It looked to me like the face of a dead man—I thought he was dead. My sister and I were told that he'd had another stroke. There is a twelve-day gap in his correspondence, and when the letters resume he is thanking friends for their concern. Later he said, "Having gone through it twice, I just decided, goddammit, this stuff just can't kill me, so dammit, I better recover." For years the story of a second stroke held a comfortable place in my narrative of his decline. Yet when, twenty years later, in the week that I found his boxes of papers, I learned the truth from my mother—that the "mild stroke" was a suicide attempt— I wasn't surprised. It was as if I'd known all along, from the moment I saw his gray face on the stretcher: a face of annihilation beyond any medical condition. The truth of that sight stayed with me, existing unofficially alongside the other version. It was possible to "know" two contradictory things at once: one a rational explanation that made bio- logical sense and was easy on memory, family history, the need for public accounting; the other unconscious, dark, connected to assassi- nations and a sense of disaster, to the death wish, an unshakable con- viction I didn't know I had.

We like to think that the second kind of knowledge is the "truth," yet I sometimes find myself wondering whether I haven't misremem- bered what I learned two decades later: perhaps I have it wrong, there was no suicide attempt, I invented one to confirm an adult idea. This inability to accept one single version is bound up with my inability to give a final answer to the question of who my father was. Was he a man with a genetic flaw like a time bomb or fate that sooner or later had to destroy him no matter what any of us did? Or was there something brittle and remote about him, which, in the stress of events, caused a hemorrhage that didn't have to flow and drove him to a decision that he might have avoided if, for example, he had cooperated with C the speech therapist? Documentary evidence gives no more definitive an answer than fallible memory. The old account is as tenacious as the new. The one handed down to me won't completely yield to the one I've pursued on my own.

In early 1972 my father took on his last public battle. It was also the last spasm at Stanford of the years of sit-ins, firebombings, window smashing, and "Ho, Ho, Ho Chi Minh, NLF is gonna win!" Those years had gone on longer and more violently at Stanford than almost anywhere else—perhaps because Stanford had made itself so prominent and spectacularly successful an example of the postwar federal-grant university. Now the Vietnam War wouldn't end. The university wouldn't give in to demands that it sever every connection to war research. The students couldn't bend reality to their desperate and righteous will. So, by the logic of a self-proclaimed revolutionary movement determined to use the university as a lever to upend society, the failure of moderate tactics justified more extreme ones. When sit-ins failed, disruption of meetings, destruction of property, even a night of gunfire followed. Frustration led to escalation, and escalation led to isolation, and isolation increased radicalization, until half the windows on campus seemed to have been Xed with masking tape. One former Stanford radical explained the hallucinatory psychology of those years. "We saw ourselves as being the vanguard of a mass movement," she told me. "As stuff didn't work we kept getting a more apocalyptic view and we kept shifting in what we thought we had to do. That change, that despair over the efficacy of traditional liberal means, just meant that it was less possible for people to ignore what was happening."

By 1972 the mass protests of the mid to late 1960s had degenerated into violent underground factions. The dance of death exhausted itself in its own feverish energy. Richard Nixon, after contributing generously to the slaughter in Southeast Asia, was finally withdrawing the troops, and his popularity was at its zenith. Liberalism headed toward its worst defeat ever in the person of its latest avatar, George McGovern; a quarter century of liberals' status as believers in a despised minority creed had begun. And in this atmosphere of burnout and rancor, Stanford played out the last act in the drama that had contributed so much to my father's decline.

At the center of Stanford radicalism stood a young Melville scholar, former Strategic Air Command pilot, and convert to revolution named H. Bruce Franklin. During the 1960s he had switched one humorless dogma for another, replacing New Criticism with Communism, Cleanth Brooks and Robert Penn Warren with Stalin and Mao, making a brief stopover in 1965–66 as an ordinary nonviolent antiwar protester. Franklin was a particular type among New Left figures, the revolutionary with tenure, equal parts commissar, outlaw, and nerd. By the end of the decade he was the most influential leftist at Stanford, a professor in his mid-thirties wearing a blue work shirt, teaching "Hothorne and Mao-ville" and shouting at students half his age to bring the Stanford war machine to its knees. In the early 1970s he joined his Peninsula Red Guard with local Chicano members of the Brown Berets to form Venceremos ("We Shall Win"), a group theoretically devoted to armed struggle (the weapon of choice was M-1 carbines), but in fact more given to criminal activity and thuggish violence. Venceremos was, along with the Hell's Angels, a feared name in my childhood. H. Bruce Franklin's own name was uttered around our house with more loathing than even Nixon's.

Franklin was always careful not to participate in any of the violence himself, for his position as a tenured English professor (which made him my mother's departmental colleague) was seen as valuable to the revolution. It is also undeniable that the university was looking for an opportunity to get rid of him. The chance came the week in February

1971 when American troops invaded Laos and Franklin gave two speeches on the same day—one urging students to shut down the Computation Center, where war research was being undertaken; the other, that night, calling for "people's war" against conservative students and other counterrevolutionaries, which was followed by rampaging and serious injuries. The next day Richard Lyman, who had replaced the overwhelmed Pitzer as president the year before, fired Franklin.

Toward the end of the year a faculty Advisory Board heard the case. Franklin represented himself, decorating his table with a poster of Stalin and using the hearing to make more political speeches. But at an adjacent table, behind pictures of Groucho Marx and John Lennon, sat a young lawyer from the ACLU, which had entered the case on Franklin's side. The lawyer was Alan Dershowitz, who was spending the year as a research fellow at a Stanford think tank in the quiet foothills by the golf course above campus. A reluctant but righteous gunslinger fresh in town from the East, Dershowitz regarded the firing as a case of institutional hysteria and hostility to dissent, "since radicalism had not had any real history on the immaculately manicured lawns and palm groves of this most beautiful of American campuses." He seemed to be saying: You may have your Nobel Prize winners and your high-speed particle accelerator, but they don't make you a real university. It sounded like Harvard condescension, and after years of violence Stanford's thin skin and rattled nerves didn't take it kindly. "Mr. Dershowitz, the Harvard law professor," Richard Lyman said, "come to Stanford to save us all from sin." The case turned on whether Franklin's speeches constituted appeals to intellect, as Dershowitz argued, or incitements to action. In January 1972 the Advisory Board voted 5–2 to uphold the firing; and Stanford was finally rid of H. Bruce Franklin.

Was Franklin, as he presented himself in his 1975 autobiography, a latter-day version of Edward Ross and Thorstein Veblen—one more Stanford casualty of what the Populists had called "the College Trust" and the New Leftists now called "the military-industrial-educational complex"? As a doctrinaire Stalinist, Franklin himself had no use for academic freedom until that manipulable term could be turned to his advantage. His self-defense marked another stage in the decay of the idea of objectivity. "As the science of Marxism demonstrates," he wrote, "perception of reality is determined primarily by class relations to the means of production." Stanford was getting rid of him, he said, because its faculty depended on military and corporate funding.

Between the uptight university and the radical professor, Alan Dershowitz appeared to have seized the liberal high ground. He argued that nothing less than academic freedom was at stake. My father disagreed. To him, Franklin and not the university represented the real threat to freedom. He defended the firing in an article in *Commentary*, holding his breath through pages of careful legal reasoning, pages that came very close to his old intellectual standard, before letting out a tremendous sigh of relief at the end. "The Franklin era at Stanford is over," he wrote. "There is now an insistence on rational discourse. Free inquiry and the other values of academic life have been affirmed." But his conclusion was bittersweet, and indirectly quite personal. "The memory of that era, with its trashing, its arson, and its physical injury will remain in the minds of Stanford faculty members."

The article led to a tangle in the *Commentary* letters column with Dershowitz, who charged my father with pretending to give a disinterested account while being a very interested party. "I did not pretend disinterest," replied my father, for whom interest had always been secondary to reason. "How could I have when the last fifteen years of my life have been devoted to that institution?" Two law professors, one at the beginning of his fame, the other near the end of his life, arguing in the old style, the fist of polemic and passion gloved inside the claims of analysis. Four years earlier, the quarrel might have ended over our dinner table, neither side giving in but both perhaps conceding a bit of ground and affirming mutual regard over a bottle of the wine my father had collected. In 1972 there was no dinner. The conversation table at our house had become a place of defeat and despair. Dershowitz's quick wit would have been partnerless, and my father's frustration might have ruined the evening with an intemperate word and an ensuing bout of black depression.

As I weigh their arguments back and forth, all the while I have another response, which is to tell Dershowitz to lay off. "Leave him alone," I want to say, "he can't fight back," even though my father would never have asked such indulgence for himself or given it to someone else over a matter of principle. Between the prose and the passion, the article's author and the trembling figure at our dinner table, the man I discovered in boxes of papers and the memory this discovery intruded on, I can find no connection. One of them emerges at least even after a round with Dershowitz; the other is down for the count.

"Look, when I feel threatened, I just get very conservative," he told an interviewer in that spring of 1972. "I've felt very threatened by what's gone on at the University—not in a personal sense, just institutionally."

The interview marked, in a sense, my father's last public appearance. He proposed it himself, during one of his periods of restored confidence—the very last one—and everything in it betrays the shakiness of the recovery, including the question he suggested for openers: "What's a crippled guy like you doing on our faculty?" "I've only just really recovered," he said. "I thought about everything, including suicide. I had a real period of depression, but I think I'm out of it now." The interviewer pressed him: "Do you feel that because of your stroke you had difficulty communicating with your children?" "For a while," my father answered, "but now I find that barrier's been overcome. Actually, I'm happier now than I think I ever was."

My mother had a phrase that, since I never heard it from anyone else, as a child I assumed was our family's own: "whistling past the graveyard." In the interview everything seems out of balance: profane, vehement, even boastful, the public and private man come together in a combustible mix, the judgments of one set loose from restraint by the impulses of the other. In the following months he cast about almost manically for ways to keep the air in his balloon. He wrote an op-ed piece for *The New York Times* that was refused. He wrote to George

McGovern's campaign manager with advice, offering himself as "idea man and occasional speech writer," and got no reply. He arranged to give a series of talks in Japan, traveling by himself. Then, at the end of the summer, he canceled the trip. He canceled other engagements and projects. He wrote to friends that his health had taken a bad turn; in one letter he spoke of being "frankly too damned depressed to do anything affirmative." He was losing altitude fast.

It must have been around this time, in the late summer or fall of 1972, just after my twelfth birthday, that my parents called my sister and me into the family room. They had something important to tell us. "Your father can't work anymore," my mother said on his behalf, for he seemed unable to speak. They were trying to prepare us for the worst, but at that moment the words made no sense to me, since he was still driving himself to campus in his orange golf cart. At the same time, my parents' manner terrified me, and on some level I knew that this was the crash. I tried to buck him up, in a fatuous, let's-take-it-like-men way that makes me cringe at the memory. I thought this would be the brave, manly thing to do. I wanted desperately for *him* to be brave. My sister and I had been given a fact that was inexplicable, intolerable, and irremediable. Instead of my own grief, I felt an overwhelming desire to make my parents' grief go away. But they were saying that it wouldn't.

Throughout that fall I stayed out playing basketball as late as I could. In November, Richard Nixon was reelected in a landslide. On a Monday in December my father disappeared. He had left a note for my mother, his last written work, saying that he didn't know where he was going or what he would do, but that he loved her. It didn't mention his children. Two evenings later, as I walked up to the patio with a basketball in my hands, I saw my mother through the kitchen window let the phone drop. Her knees buckled and I ran to catch her. In her arms I cried, for her more than for the news she'd just heard—that her husband's body had been found by a maid in a San Francisco hotel room with empty bottles of sleeping pills in the wastebasket. I wanted physically to hold my mother up: one parent was gone, I couldn't lose the other. Then I went to my room and sat on my bed, where I began the process of removing my life from the death and escaping his fate.

Three decades on, I still don't know how to feel about the 1960s. In part I've never shed the idea I learned at home as a boy: that the 1960s screwed up my family, that Franklin and the radicals helped kill my father, that the students in their moral arrogance nearly destroyed a fragile and priceless institution. By the end of those years this idea had been made real enough to me in the sound of fire engines and the sight of smashed windows—even I wasn't able to remain oblivious to what was happening at the other end of campus. I spent a fair amount of those years being frightened of things. I was frightened of assassination. I was frightened of the Manson killings and wanted to know how close Los Angeles was to Stanford. The words "coed," "remains," and "Santa Cruz Mountains" appeared often enough in news stories that they became inextricable. I was frightened of drugs—a TV movie called *Go Ask Alice* convinced me that someone would lace my drink with LSD or heroin, killing me or making me insane—until sixth grade, when my first toke of marijuana had no effect whatsoever. I was frightened by several movies that my parents ill-advisedly took me to see, especially Z. The moment when the political leader is clubbed on the head, and the scene of emergency-room brain surgery, repeated nightmarishly, formed in me an unconscious connection to my father's stroke. I was even a little frightened of rock music. In fourth grade it was exciting to sit in the purple gloom of a black light and listen to someone's older brother's Creedence Clearwater Revival or Santana album, or *Let It Be*, but the guitars and lyrics also carried a threat of chaos. Violence was always just outside the door in those years. Basically I was frightened of death and of blowing my mind, which seemed like the same thing. In every nine- or ten-year-old there's a little moral dictator who dreads disorder and wants everyone to behave. In 1969 and 1970 his hands were full.

And yet, as I got a bit older, I began to wish I'd been born ten years earlier. I felt that I had just missed a great generational drama, the way someone born around 1930 would feel that he had been cheated out of the vast experience of the war. I had missed out on the energy, the music, the revolt, the communal passions of the 1960s. Born when I was, having seen the upheavals in part from the point of view of my parents, who suffered through them, I never had the chance to indulge in my own youthful and romantic plunge into excess. I had to be reasonable and good because the ones who came before me had been irrational and bad. I had to clean up after their fun instead of getting to have my own. And I was stuck with the political debris that their orgy had left behind. I grew up a liberal loser in a conservative age because they had decided to have a revolution.

So my attitude toward the '60s became one of resentment mingled with envy, and the interest only intensified over the years. Spending my childhood in a decade when history was almost instantaneous made me a lover of history. As I got older, events I'd lived through as a boy became layered in my mind with new transparencies. Altamont was one. At the end of 1969 the Rolling Stones gave a free concert at the speedway north of San Francisco. The Hell's Angels were hired to provide "security" around the stage, but they provided mayhem instead, and the day and night of violence and bad trips immediately became a convenient marker of the decade's end, Woodstock's dark twin, universal love turned to its flip side, death. At the time Altamont was one of the things that frightened me—the next day I read with horrified fascination (this had become my normal response to the San Francisco newspaper) the article about a young black man who pulled out a gun and was stabbed to death by the Angels. To this day "Altamont Speedway" sounds evil—speed, madness, murder.

But ten years after the concert, I sat in a college audience and watched *Gimme Shelter*, the documentary film that recorded it, and got caught in the fever of Mick Jagger strutting the stage as he sings "Sympathy for the Devil," and the zoned-out youths at his feet surging and staring and screaming and crying, and the Angels shoving and pounding bodies like the Chicago cops the year before, and then the climactic slow-motion stabbing, which the Stones replay in a film studio, yet another Zapruder film, maybe the decade's last. Watching with them, I felt no moral response but only the dark thrill of release — which ended as soon as the auditorium lights came on, returning me to the glamorless dullness of 1979, a shrill female voice still singing: "Rape, murder, it's just a shot away, it's just a shot away!"

Twenty years later, I rented *Gimme Shelter* on video and had an entirely different experience. It had become a period artifact, a historical drama whose outcome I knew in advance. I could follow the trail of significance, experience the Aristotelian emotions of pity and terror, from the distance that a work of art provides. The past is meaningful because it is past. In the middle of watching I suddenly thought: The weirdness of American history — from *The Man in the Gray Flannel Suit* to *Gimme Shelter* in fourteen years!

One event, three decades, three different takes, each replacing the last, and yet somehow all three remaining within me, in the complex entanglement of personal and historical memory, because I am no longer yet still am the person I was in 1969 and 1979.

"There is no bridge from the '60s," Todd Gitlin once told me. An early president of SDS, he's been both participant and chronicler, and yet he was letting me know that the decade did not build a future that a latecomer like me could inherit and use; I would have to make my own. The student revolution consumed itself and the world moved on. The university, which had seemed on the verge of implosion or overthrow in the last years of my father's life, within a short time looked stunningly like its old self again. Twenty years after naming the multiversity, Clark Kerr observed that Harvard and Berkeley looked basically the same in 1983 as in 1963. "The big research university is particularly impervious to structural change."

The radicals lost — but the liberals didn't win. Reform efforts like the Study of Education at Stanford, efforts to restore teaching and broad intellectual inquiry to their central place in higher education, hardly budged the research universities from their postwar march into heavily funded specialization, to the hypnotic drumbeat of Growth. Stanford became *the* example of the entrepreneurial university—hosting Super Bowls, devising a logo for the licensed application of products developed from its research labs, paving and building on every available square foot of dirt and dry grass, paying the head of the Stanford Development Corporation an annual salary of almost a million dollars, and finally making national headlines for overcharging the federal government on contracts.

"That's the real truth about American universities," Robert Rosenzweig, who had found himself on the firing line after King's murder in 1968 and later became president of the American Association of Universities, told me—"that they are embedded in great social forces. Today it's everything for sale. To a deplorable, to a discouraging extent, universities have bought into that."

The radicals got doctorates, joined English departments, and acquiesced in the careerism they had once reviled. The humanities became soft appendages to the sciences, the critical study of man a set of theories with a half-life of six months and a hermetic jargon imported from Europe. The radical desire to change society has been satisfied by an alchemical process known as "neo-Marxism," which has turned politics into the struggle over the syllabus. If the country can't be revolutionized, the curriculum can be. Meanwhile a handful of leading figures have ridden the wave to stardom, parlaying their celebrity into ever fatter salaries, cutting deals with large corporations, speaking the latest dialect of progressivism while sullen and underpaid teaching assistants take up more and more of the responsibility for undergraduate education. English professors have at last become full-status members of the multiversity: the humanist as operator.

And thirty years after student radicals declared it a cover for an oppressive power and demanded power of their own, what's become of reason?

Not long after discovering the boxes of my father's papers, I met a woman who gave me a partial answer. Her name was Janet Cooper Alexander. Twenty-five years before, as Janet Cooper Weiss, she had been a graduate student in the Stanford English department and a close associate of H. Bruce Franklin. She had fired up students at the Old Union sit-in in 1968, joined in the takeover of the Applied Electronics Lab in 1969, and eventually broke enough windows and shouted down enough speakers to get herself suspended for four quarters.

"I left with a lot of bitterness and never went back," she told me. "The movement seemed right to me and I was always glad I had been involved in the movement and willing to make sacrifices for those goals. But I wanted nothing more than to be a teacher of English in college, and I had prevented myself from doing that."

She spent several years in the Bay Area underground, first as a Venceremos militant, then with another revolutionary group organizing workers in the East Bay. And she began to wonder about the mentality of the movement and her role in it. An encounter with a Vietnam vet showed her that she had demonized soldiers—those who hadn't fragged their officers were baby-killers. Now she saw that they had been victims too.

"I guess I would say we should have been older so that we could have understood more about ambiguity and uncertainty," she told me. "We were very sure that we were right and weren't very prepared to entertain the possibility that we weren't. At the time we said objectivity was a scam. Now that I'm middle-aged I see the need for being able to consider that you might be wrong. In the East Bay a lot of people thought they were right and they were *crazy.* I thought: Well, I'm not crazy, but is it possible that I'm not completely right?"

These questions prompted her to go back to school for a law degree, and eventually to take a position as a professor of civil procedure at Stanford Law School, which is where I met her in her office.

"Now I guess I'm back to the traditional liberal values," she said with a slight smile. "In civil procedure there's something called neutral principles, which both sides can accept as being objectively valid. It's an old idea from the era when liberalism dominated. Now we all know that it's socially constructed. And I guess the idea that I've come to is that you have to act *as though* there could be neutral principles.

You can fine-tune the principles as you detect bias in them. But it's terribly important to act as if they exist."

Down the hall from her office at the law school is a faculty library called the Packer Room. Though it was dedicated in the 1970s, when I was still a teenager living at home, I had never visited it until I left Janet Cooper Alexander's office. On the wall of the Packer Room hangs a framed photograph of my father in his most characteristic pose, cupping his chin in his hand, listening with skeptical but intense attention.

Six months before he died, my father wrote me a long letter, flawlessly typed and signed "Dad" in pencil in his left-handed, childlike scrawl. It was a letter about sex and growing up, and when I received it from him, with dread, for (as he pointed out at the start) I had been evading this topic for months, its contents embarrassed me deeply. I didn't throw it away, though. I read it once and then put it in a drawer beneath my school binders, and I didn't look at it again. It was never mentioned between us.

Throughout my adolescence I was aware of its hidden presence in my room. The drawer gave off an odor of shame: not just for the sentences about masturbation and the "homosexual phase," but because it contained my only personal token of my father and so became a repository for all the shame I felt about him, about myself, about the connection he had tried clumsily near the end to create between us, about its failure. Still, I didn't throw the letter away. It was, I knew, "important," more so as time went on, a rite of passage in my life, a reminder of his.

When I was searching through the cardboard boxes in my mother's garage, I found the letter. Reading it for the first time in twenty years I came across these sentences: "Some day, when you have had your share of experiences, you will find another person whose happiness is just as important to you as is your own. Only by practicing the art of giving pleasure and learning that giving it means that you too receive pleasure will you really grow up. Love, which to me can be identified with what I have been calling pleasure, is the thing that matters most in life."

It's with these words that the letter ends. They came as a shock, for somehow I had managed to forget them completely. I remembered the letter as being full of sex; I remembered nothing of love, perhaps because at eleven I didn't grasp what the words meant, any more than I grasped my father's other life in articles and letters. It was as if he had appended them in the hope that I would reread them when I was older and that they would speak to me then.

Having tried for two decades to become someone other than my father's son, I now think about him all the time. Every year, I'm told, my face resembles his a little more. I have my cholesterol checked annually and wonder about a certain artery wall. And the famous legacy that suicides are supposed to leave their children seems to be my inheritance as well. On the night before a recent New Year's Eve, I was driving through downtown San Francisco, and something in the 2 a.m. menace of Market Street, the homeless men along the sidewalk, the shivering hookers on Geary, made me look for the address where my father's life ended. It was just outside Union Square, still a hotel but with another name. While the car idled I wondered how he'd spent his last day and a half. Did he clamber around Union Square? Did he stay in the room, changing his mind a hundred times? Did he bring something to read? Did he remember his own father, paralyzed and dying? I thought how lonely he must have been here, so far from us, from everything he'd ever known in his life. It was not at all the miserable dive of my imagination but a perfectly unremarkable hotel, with lace curtains drawn across the upstairs bay windows, and yet it represented absolute loneliness and despair, and I had to drive away.

My father shed his own inheritance—the family, the tribe, the sticky particulars of culture and place. Out in the golden West he lived in the sunlight of reason, trusting free man to solve his problems through the uses of mind. When the explosion came he had no fallback position and it hit him full in the face. Stricken, he was more available than he'd been, and at last he and I took notice of each other, but the hand held toward me was atrophied and curled. Love, "the thing that matters most in life," didn't have the power to save him. It was advice he couldn't live by—unless, by some dark logic, he decided that the happiness of others depended on his ceasing to exist. In either case, I wasn't consulted. "The only way to go through life," he wrote to me six months before he committed suicide, "is to find what work and love can mean. I'll devote another letter to work some day."

That day never came. Instead, the alternate scenarios crowd and clamor. If he had kept a picture of his parents on the wall. If he hadn't become vice provost. If we had stayed out of Vietnam. If he hadn't risen to the bait with the students in 1967 or the faculty in 1968. If he had spent more time with his children before the stroke. If I had been kinder. If he had taken up a hobby like left-handed painting. If he had had his breakdown at twenty like his hero Mill. If he had only connected knowledge and power, love and work, reason and rage. If his only faith, the liberal faith in man and man's mind, had gone from time to time past the graveyard without whistling and silent before the power of irrationality and blood.

"It is love," wrote Thomas Mann, "not reason, that is stronger than death." My father's letter suggested another life we might have had. By then it was too late, and I buried the words in a drawer. Twenty years later, wanting the connection I'd always shunned, I went in search of him, only to end with a letter I'd had all along, and the charge to find the meaning of work and love, to affirm life over death, without him.

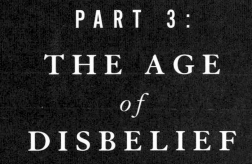

PART 3:
THE AGE
of
DISBELIEF

CHAPTER 10

◆

Free Ride

barely experienced my father's suicide. With all the will I could muster, on the evening of Wednesday, December 6, 1972, I checked out. Just as Eugene McCarthy's travails in 1968 mattered more to me than the turmoil down the block, just as the Lakers' defeat in the spring of 1969 felt like a worse blow than the stroke, his death failed to sink in. I would have gone to school the next day if my mother had let me. On Monday, my teachers' condolences surprised and embarrassed me. I wanted to slip into my seat without anyone noticing. When a guy on the school bus asked, with all the delicacy of an overweight thirteen-year-old who had flunked seventh grade, "Why'd he do it?" I answered, "I wish I knew," but even that wasn't really true. I knew, and didn't want to know. A family friend, a young law student, tried to play the role of older brother and probed my emotional state as we shot baskets. "How has it changed you?"

"I guess I have more chores around the house," I said, and glided off into my hook shot.

My mother was now solely responsible for the family's support. For the first year she turned inward in some welter of emotion that I had no interest in probing but whose terrific force I sensed in occasional storms of tears or anger. Protecting myself from her anguish and my own, I resisted any effort she made to get me to talk about the man who had disappeared from our lives. The most I would say was "I just hope you won't do anything like that."

She earned tenure as an associate professor and became director of the freshman English program and published her first collection of stories. She rented a room in our house to a succession of students. She became a visible and admired figure on campus, a number of her students turning into friends. Without ever proclaiming herself an ardent feminist in what was still the heyday of sisterhood, she set an example of independence to the young women who came within her orbit. My mother had disapproved of feminism in its first years in the late 1960s, thinking it would take energy away from the civil rights movement, which she considered more important. She herself didn't need feminism, she had believed. And yet throughout her life she had seen her star rise by attachment to a man's—her father in Birmingham, her husband at Stanford—before securing her own place through force of personality. In the 1970s she came to realize that some injustices were not as glaring as racism and poverty, that women—even privileged ones—were oppressed as women, and that she hadn't used her professional position to do enough for other women. She became a feminist almost as soon as she became a widow.

She was just forty-seven when my father died, and before long she had a few suitors, including a San Francisco doctor whose Mercedes impressed me more than his attempts at being my pal. But her new life would have been too compromised by the demands of a man of her generation. She said that no one would be able to replace my father. After a year or two the idea of remarrying seemed to disappear from her mind.

My father's death did change me—and its effect proved me in every way his son. The summer before he died, the summer of the letter about sex, my father had assigned me a reading list that was fairly daunting for a twelve-year-old. *Catcher in the Rye* was on it, and some

Frost poems, and a short history of the Civil War, and Kenneth Clark's *Civilization*, which I still haven't finished. *Julius Caesar* was the highlight. In response to one of the small essay questions my father gave me, I wrote that if I could not play Mark Antony I would want to play Brutus, since Cassius was too evil. He praised my effort, then explained the difference between evil and envy. His reply, of course, was typed—at the end of his life all his important messages for me came from the Smith Corona.

The summer reading list was my initiation into the high-ceilinged sanctum of my parents' study, the grown-up world of books and ideas. In December it became part of my father's legacy.

In the months after his suicide I became obsessed by the idea that I now had to read every book in the world, because my father was no longer there to assign me some and not others. This prospect sent my head spinning. Sometimes, lying on my bed, I would become aware of my thoughts as if I were reading them in a book and then imagine (I was taking a typing class at school) my fingers hitting the keys that spelled out my ideas as I thought them.

I needed order, and it came from an unexpected place—the list of titles on the back of the Cliffs Notes guide to *Julius Caesar*, which I'd bought for advice in staging a backyard theatrical. This black-and-yellow friend of delinquent college students became my highest authority on great literature, and the number of books that had to be read suddenly dwindled to about two hundred: *Ivanhoe*, for example, and *Black Like Me* (but not *Remembrance of Things Past*). I sat down and assigned myself four listed titles a month, calculating that by the age of eighteen I would have read everything worth reading.

Almost immediately I fell behind (the *Aeneid* was heavy going), but the list itself wasn't discredited by this failure—only I was. My father's death had warped my relation to books—a love affair ever since *Where the Wild Things Are*, when I walked around the house for days believing I was Max—into something systematic and compulsory. I anesthetized the part of myself that was alive to literature's capacity for shock, delight, terror. The simple telling of a story no longer held any value; now I had to master each book, which meant wrestling its theme down to a single sentence. This sentence was often buried somewhere in the text, and I would spend tormented hours digging it up—unless it was available on the Modern Library jacket, which, for example, told me that the theme of *Crime and Punishment* is that crime is its own punishment. Once I had the theme under control, I would underline the title on the Cliffs Notes list and move on.

It was as if, by plowing through the world's great literature, I could keep the world itself at bay and stop the spinning in my head.

Ideally, reading means getting lost. The process of surrendering and then recovering the self might be the essence of growing up: being exposed to an alien world and, instead of being broken down and destroyed, absorbing it, making it your own. But that year, the thought of losing myself was quite real and frightening. I might plunge into the depths of a book and never come back up. "If phantasies become over-luxuriant and over-powerful," Freud wrote, "the conditions are laid for an onset of neurosis or psychosis." He added, ominously, "Here a broad by-path branches off into pathology."

So I read and read, checking off titles and hoarding themes, without letting a germ enter my bloodstream.

It never occurred to me that I was handling the calamity exactly after my father's fashion, and in a way that brought me closer to him than I'd ever been while he was alive. By finishing the reading list that he'd started, I was turning the powers of analysis, the rational mind, on the unruly world in order to master it. I was trying to make reality bend to my ideas—the desperate act of a classical liberal.

No—it isn't completely true that literature lost its hold on me. Now and then, one of the Cliffs Notes titles would slip free of my mental vise and take over not just my imagination but my life in a way so extreme that it seemed like a symptom of the same disorder as my self-imposed reading list. *The Great Gatsby*, for example. When I was thirteen, the novel, and then the atrocious Redford-Farrow movie, made so deep an impression that for a few weeks I walked around junior high dressed in my own attempt at Jazz Age sophistication. In 1974 this involved a pair of white, wide-flared, high-cuffed double-knit polyester pants, a white two-inch patent-leather belt, a navy-blue polka-dotted shirt, a powder blue sweater vest, tan Hush Puppies, and a white Kangol golf cap. I briefly wanted to be rich and drive a Mercedes sports car and carry expensive leather accessories and express my personality in "an unbroken series of successful gestures," and since the lifestyle of a dandy was not exactly in sync with the values of my political education, the desire expressed itself through this total identification with a fictional character. But even if the figure I was cutting at school looked more like Malvolio than Gatsby, my classmates' mockeries were not enough to disabuse me; in fact, they confirmed me in my greater sophistication. Only my mother's unconcealed horror at the tackiness of polyester planted the seed that eventually undermined the whole concept.

At the same time, I was discovering an entirely different sort of literary pleasure. It had nothing to do with the rational education I was receiving at home and school, and it gave me the crucial intimation that ideas might be no match for the power of feeling. In the year of my father's death I also came up with my own secret reading list. It included *Story of O*, *Lady Chatterley's Lover*, and *Fanny Hill*. It involved researching key passages in *Fear of Flying* and *The Godfather*. The books originated, like all literature, in the study, but they ended up in the bathroom, where questions of theme never came up. There was nothing abstract about this reading. Instead of demanding impossible feats of self-discipline, it permitted brief escape from the confines of my other, classics-mongering self. Its satisfactions were easily available and quite concrete. It presented the same, limited, and always successful reading project every time. On the cover of *Story of O* a critic called the book "a total literary experience." I snickered at this piece of adult hypocrisy; my experience was something else.

But this reading was no longer the free ride of playing Max or Brutus or Gatsby. Children play, adults fantasize; and fantasy seems to carry a price. In his letter on sex, my father suggested that if I found myself doing this "once a day, or even more," I should talk about it with him or my mother. The suggestion seemed far-fetched, and the quota low. I carried out this secret reading like a criminal, pinning *Story of O* under my shirt as I made the dangerous journey from the bathroom down the hall back to the study, where I hastily returned "Pauline Réage" into the gap on the shelf (as, five years before, I had done with the book on JFK's assassination) and made sure her white spine was flush with those of her more respectable neighbors, to keep her (whoever she was) from betraying me.

In the summer of 1974, my mother took my sister and me to London. London meant ground zero of great books—half of the Cliffs Notes list came from London. But the literary experience I still remember from that summer involved neither Shakespeare nor Dickens.

My mother had a collection of contemporary short fiction called *The Naked I*, in which there was a story by Robert Coover called "The Babysitter," with a good deal of metafictional fantasizing about a teenage girl. The language performed its usual magic—too well, for one afternoon while my mother and sister were off doing something cultural, I accidentally stained the relevant pages of *The Naked I* beyond repair. The power of words to make us forget ourselves! In an instant the babysitter in the bathtub vanished, the book became printed text on a page, which I had just defiled.

Panicking, I smuggled the evidence out of the apartment in a brown paper bag and went hunting for a garbage can. Block after block, there was no garbage can. My package felt as if it was about to blow up or start wailing like an alarm. At last I spotted a Dumpster— but it stood on the other side of a high chain-link fence. I looked up and down the street, then flung the brown-bagged book and watched with amazement and relief as it sailed over the fence and landed inside. I turned to run.

"What did you just chuck in that rubbish bin?"

A few feet away, two enormous bobbies under blue helmets were staring me down.

"What did you just chuck in that rubbish bin?"

"A book," I murmured.

"What book?" The bobbies looked tense and angry. As in a nightmare, their arrival made complete sense.

"A book of short stories."

"Why'd you want to get rid of it?"

"I was finished reading it."

I could see that they didn't believe a word. One of them narrowed his eyes. "How do we know it wasn't a bomb?"

This was the summer of the Cyprus crisis. The rubbish bin stood near the National Bank of Greece, which the police suspected me of trying to blow up. I swore it wasn't true, while the burning in my cheeks betrayed my real crime. Silently I resolved to spend the rest of the summer pursuing themes from the Cliffs Notes list. The bobbies had provided a perfect lesson in the danger of "over-luxuriant" fantasy. Mercifully, they didn't order me to retrieve the evidence, but instead let me go with a warning about not chucking things into rubbish bins and running away. I slunk back to the apartment and waited for my mother to come through the door looking for her short story collection. But she never asked about it.

I grew up during the years of liberal defeat. Every fourth November a general election came along to confirm that the ideas on which my parents had raised me were discredited. Every presidential race offered a new victim in the line of liberal losers, each more hapless than the last on his way to the chopping block: McCarthy, Humphrey, McGovern, Carter (who, after winning one election, couldn't stop losing), Mondale, Dukakis. These years gave me the unconscious feeling that a liberal was a man in a wheelchair.

The faith of my ancestors was born two hundred years before me, in the century of Jefferson, in the philosophical creed of human liberty and self-government. A hundred years later, in my grandfather's youth, it found a plain raspy voice in Populism and fought the princes of wealth in the name of the common man. A half century after that, in my father's and mother's youth, it came to power in the modern state and made government activism its signature. A few decades after that, when I was a small boy, it ascended to the status of a cultural elite. Then, in a few short years, it ripped itself apart over the three great issues of the 1960s: race, war, and student revolt. It started out speaking for all mankind, and by 1972, when George McGovern was wiped out by Richard Nixon, it spoke for Massachusetts and Washington, D.C.

My inheritance was paid in a devalued currency. By the time I entered adolescence, liberalism seemed able to thrive only in the rarefied world of college campuses and eccentric city precincts.

A quick and partial list of some of the beliefs I was raised on:

- It's wrong to send rockets to the moon when we have problems on Earth that need money.
- Taxes should be higher for the rich and the "well-off." Complaints about high taxes are a sign of racism and mean-spiritedness.
- Government spending on everything but defense is good.
- American military actions are suspect. So is personal display of the flag. So is the presidency.
- The Cold War is a given, and permanent. So the point of foreign policy should be to shed as little blood as possible.
- Communism is bad, but not as bad as fascism. Just before our ill-fated 1971 trip to Europe we canceled plans to visit fascist Spain and Greece (I was taken to see Z as an object lesson), but Leningrad was eliminated from the itinerary only for logistical reasons, on the theory that things had gotten worse in countries under fascism but Communism had made socioeconomic improvements over what it replaced.
- As long as they don't hurt anyone else, people should be allowed to live their lives as they please.
- Abortion should be federally funded because black women will be the ones who can't afford to have one.
- Race is the biggest problem in America. Race, meaning black

and white, trumps everything else. Black claims on society are always valid. Black nationalism is regrettable in some ways but also necessary for group self-esteem. But integration is the ideal.

- In order of importance, second after blacks come the poor. The poor aren't poor by some fault of their own, nor is capitalism the root cause of poverty. They are simply the poor, and as such they deserve compassion and taxpayers' dollars. Welfare is organized compassion, therefore a good thing. A restructured economy is not on the table, and even the notion of the poor becoming productive working members of society isn't given much thought. They will always be poor—they will always deserve help.
- The most crucial social distinction isn't money but education. To be educated means that whatever your political views and income level, you have a set of cultural traits and tastes that make you someone who could sit comfortably at our dinner table.
- The working class and the lower middle class don't exist, except in cultural terms, as, for example, the people throwing rocks and screaming curses at the Boston school buses bringing black students to white high schools. They are the least interesting, least attractive people in America.

No system or principle holds the items on this list together, other than a vague imperative to help the weak and otherwise let people be. Yet they went as unchallenged as the virgin birth in a devout Catholic household. Since the values—compassion, tolerance, fairness—were so obviously good, the social policies weren't open to question. Some of these beliefs were little more than reflexes, in my case hereditary reflexes. Say "poverty" and a genetically programmed nerve called "government spending" twitched. Without my father to provide Socratic questioning and scholarly analysis of the issues, the brand of liberalism practiced around the house became moralistic and fiercely partisan. The day of Nixon's resignation speech was the happiest I'd seen my mother in years.

By the early 1970s, liberalism could claim to have secured a great many of the best things in American life: the eight-hour day, the end of child labor; widespread distribution of prosperity as a result of the postwar social contract among government, business, and labor; federal programs that had drastically reduced poverty in old age and broadened access to education; civil and political rights for blacks and women; greater social equality. Without liberalism, America would have been a much harsher country, less equal and less free.

But by the time I was growing up, liberalism seemed to have achieved what it could and stopped being a vital force for reform. It was becoming a set of fixed positions that went along with a certain way of life peculiar to a narrow social class. I reached none of my political beliefs on my own and was hard-pressed to justify them if challenged. And in Stanford they seldom were challenged.

My breakfast reading had progressed from the backs of Cheerios boxes to the submediocre San Francisco newspaper. I skipped the liberal columnists and ate up conservatives like William Randolph Hearst, Jr., and James J. Kilpatrick—their every line boiled my blood and proved me right. At fourteen I wrote an ode to Hearst in rhyming tetrameter couplets probably inspired by Pope, a sarcastic diatribe on all the major issues of the day—"What shall we do with troublesome blacks? / Hang 'em from trees, suspend 'em from racks?" Not even the quadrennial bad news from the outside world could shake me out of my complacency. Nothing confirms righteousness like defeat. The rest of the country just kept getting stupider and meaner. Someday, it would recognize its error and embrace our beliefs.

But every now and then some dissatisfaction would nag at me, a sense that our worldview might be vulnerable, a whiff of hypocrisy or contradiction. Once, during the Boston busing crisis (of course we were for busing; there was only a crisis because there were racists), I asked my mother whether she would allow me to be bused from my relatively good junior high school into one of the weaker ones. Probably not, she said—but education meant more to us than to people in South Boston. I choked on this explanation, and perhaps secretly she choked on it, too. One of the liberal ideas had run up against a personal prejudice, leaving scrapes on both—but the idea survived. I had uncovered a serious weakness in our position, yet I went on holding the position. It was too abstract, too untested, to be altered by a collision with reality.

One reality that escaped me and everyone else for years after was that 1973, a year dominated by stories like Watergate, Vietnam pullout, *Roe* v. *Wade*—in other words, by some fairly colorful fallout from the wars of the 1960s—was also the end of one economic era and the beginning of another. Nineteen seventy-three, the year of the oil crisis, ended the postwar economic boom, which had granted a generation the luxury of revolt. Nineteen seventy-three began a dreary age of stagnation and scarcity which would make revolt—serious revolt—much less alluring to people my age when we turned eighteen. Nineteen seventy-three was the year in which average wages began their generation-long decline. All the economic trends of the past two decades—the decline of American manufacturing under pressure from foreign imports, the growing inequality in wealth, the contraction of the middle class, the narrowing of opportunity—began in 1973. After an age in which the vast majority benefited from economic growth, the country was entering a new age of class division, not unlike the period of my grandfather's political career—and yet no class politics arose to meet it, no Populism or Progressivism or New Dealism. Unions were too fat and corrupt to bestir themselves. Liberals and conservatives went on fighting the cultural wars of the 1960s for decades.

By 1973 the kind of Americans my grandfather had once visited in their villages, broken bread with at their kitchen tables, and championed on the floor of Congress—working men who wanted fair treatment from business and government—had become the kind of Americans my family knew nothing about. They were "middle Americans," "white ethnics," "Democrats for Nixon," and quietly we feared and despised them, and knew that they hated us. They did not look like the oppressed miners and steelworkers of old Birmingham. They looked like Archie

Bunker. They owned two American-made cars and had bad taste. They were probably racist. Their sons were the kids who sometimes jumped me while I was biking through their part of town to junior high (the students at my elementary school, a five-minute bike ride from our house, had been almost all Stanford kids). They seemed unlikely liberal allies — and what's more, liberals no longer spoke their language or knew how to reach them. George Huddleston might have known, but he was long gone.

Busing, welfare, taxes, affirmative action, crime, patriotism — the majority of Americans turned against the liberal position on all the most controversial and divisive issues of the period. The decade of the 1970s was one long preparation for Reagan, the signs of conservative revival were everywhere, but even by 1978, when California's Proposition 13 passed in a landslide the year I graduated from high school, ushering in the national tax revolt, I still didn't see it.

Liberalism, the word that the early *New Republic* group brought over from England and gave its modern American usage, the word that Herbert Hoover tried and failed to wrest away from Franklin Roosevelt, began in the 1970s to acquire the connotations that have made it an epithet, a term of scorn and abuse, a word that dares not speak its name: the L-word. It was becoming known as the creed of the weak, the soft, the guilt-ridden, the hyperintellectual, the privileged, the out-of-touch, the hypocritical — all those who don't want to see the world as it really is.

During these years a novel appeared that spelled out this view in the obsessive detail of a sadistic (but not stupid) lunatic's nightmare fantasy. When *The Turner Diaries*, written by a Virginia physicist named William Pierce under the pseudonym Andrew Macdonald, was first published in 1977, no one noticed. Its meticulously recorded vision of a savage revolt by an underground Nazi brotherhood against multicultural America was too extreme to catch the imagination of an indulgent, self-absorbed age. For two decades the book was passed hand to hand among hard-core neo-Nazis. Then, in 1995, it suddenly surfaced to achieve a kind of cult infamy as the bedtime reading of

Timothy McVeigh in the months before the Oklahoma City bombing. By then, years of white backlash and antigovernment rhetoric and economic decline had made *The Turner Diaries* palatable to a sizable subculture of angry rejects and freelance desperadoes.

A truly crude piece of writing sometimes gives a clearer sense of the mental atmosphere of its time than more subtle and sophisticated work. The grotesque distortions of unchecked fantasy can sound like broadcasts direct from the political unconscious. Ten or fifteen years later, they emerge toned down as acceptable public speech. In the same way that the burst of utopian novels following Edward Bellamy's *Looking Backward* gives a strong sense of the late-nineteenth-century Populist mind-set, its optimism and its paranoia, *The Turner Diaries* reads like an exaggeration of the hatreds that would contaminate conservatism in the late twentieth. A passage describing liberalism could have been uttered, two decades later and mildly censored, on the *Rush Limbaugh Show:*

> The corruption of our people by the Jewish-liberal-democratic-equalitarian plague which afflicts us is more clearly manifested in our soft-mindedness, our unwillingness to recognize the harder realities of life, than in anything else.
>
> Liberalism is an essentially feminine, submissive world view. Perhaps a better adjective than feminine is infantile. It is the world view of men who do not have the moral toughness, the spiritual strength to stand up and do single combat with life, who cannot adjust to the reality that the world is not a huge, pink-and-blue, padded nursery in which the lions lie down with the lambs and everyone lives happily ever after.
>
> Nor should spiritually healthy men of our race even *want* the world to be like that, if it could be so. That is an alien, essentially Oriental approach to life, the world view of slaves rather than of free men of the West.
>
> But it has permeated our whole society. Even those who do not consciously accept the liberal doctrines have been corrupted by

them . . . Yes, the inability to face reality and make difficult decisions, that is the salient symptom of the liberal disease. Always trying to avoid a minor unpleasantness now, so that a major unpleasantness becomes unavoidable later, always evading any responsibility to the future—that is the way the liberal mind works.

The Turner Diaries' answer is to hang blacks and Jews from lampposts around Los Angeles. It inspired McVeigh to kill 168 people for the crime of being in a federal building. It isn't just a bad book, it's an evil one. Nonetheless, like many extreme fantasies, its violent cartoon picture of contemporary liberalism contains a glimmer of truth.

In the pink-and-blue, padded nursery of Stanford, the 1970s were like a long anticlimax to the high-drama 1960s in which parents and older brothers and sisters had played leading roles. My friends and I got to live out history as farce. What remained of the spirit of youthful revolt was basically drugs and pranks. When Nixon was trapping himself in the coils of his Watergate tapes, my friend Lewis Cohen and I sang "Jail to the Chief, he's a mighty motherfucker" and drew Xs one by one across the mug shots on his bedroom poster of all the President's convicted men, waiting for the day when the unindicted co-conspirator with the beady eyes would get his. The sordid language of Watergate entered our vocabulary with knowing snickers: ratfucking, Deep Throat, stonewall, dirty tricks, big enchilada, hush money—above all, impeach. Impeach the President! Nixon's father should have pulled out sooner! Watergate was a joyride (and how unfair it was that my father missed by just a few months his old enemy's slide into disgrace). No one could have scripted a better story line for early adolescence. My high school literary magazine ran a poem, after Ginsberg, that went: "Nixon, America / They don't rhyme at all / How can I write a poem / About such a jerk?" This alongside anarchic neo-Dylan verse that began with lines like "Yogurt round my toes goes / Plippety-plop."

The two poems basically expressed the same point of view, the view from a comfortable underground, where Kurt Vonnegut was saying, "So it goes," and back issues of *Mad* magazine were piling up and the worst thing you could be called was "conventional."

This wasn't organized political activism, it was a mood—premature cynicism against a backdrop of vaguely antiauthoritarian high jinks. Lighting a joint at lunchtime, going to an impeachment rally, or sneaking into Memorial Auditorium to catch a screening of Linda Lovelace doing her trick were equivalent acts of protest against—not really against the System, because the System had visibly broken down and was being hounded from all corners. But against something. Maybe just against. When my grandfather said, "No is always right," knee-jerk rebellion wasn't what he had in mind.

We thought of ourselves as the good guys, even idealists, somehow continuing in the footsteps of civil rights and antiwar marchers, as if a straight line ran from Birmingham and Selma through Columbia and Kent State to the subversive R. Crumb-like cartoons that littered the senior-class portraits in the yearbook. But our idealism was more assumed than available. On the one hand, I held the moral high ground on all the issues of the day, and on the other hand, I was a casual cynic. At home I kept the vigil on behalf of the poor and the blacks, and at school I took on the principal over a story—my own, published in the literary magazine I helped edit—that employed the phrase "fuck off." It was a story (loosely autobiographical) about a boy of roughly my fifteen years who throws up after swallowing too many tequila sunrises at a New Year's Eve party. I regarded its publication as an act of artistic and political struggle, a moment of existential self-definition. I might have even set the phrase off in its own tiny paragraph where it would be most conspicuous. The principal got complaints from parents, and I was called into his office. A copy of the magazine lay on his table; a moment later he walked in and gave me a look that said, "Don't tell me it was an act of artistic and political struggle. You were having fun—and now you're a pain in my ass."

We were having fun. Nothing needed to be built; the point was to laugh and mock until structures of power toppled over from sheer embarrassment. The Stanford Marching Band, having come a long way from the days when Herbert Hoover managed the football team, ridiculed Jerry Falwell during a halftime show, a giant marijuana leaf painted inside the tuba player's horn. As for the good society, we had it right there in California: well-funded, pre-Prop. 13 public schools, and a lax curfew. Basically, we had the New Deal plus '60s liberation. Nixon might be President, or Ford, or Carter, who made liberalism look like no fun at all (and wasn't much of a liberal), but we were right, and anyone who didn't see it that way probably didn't know what a reefer or a blow job was either.

If I think back to the mental world of my teens, what comes to mind is a Richard Pryor record, *That Nigger's Crazy*, which my friends and I listened to endlessly and secretly. In one routine, Pryor imagines the reception Nixon gets from the brothers when he arrives in prison. "Wha's happenin, Tricky Dick? Yeahhhh. We gonna see how tricky you are." Raised on Vietnam and Watergate and *Saturday Night Live*, how could we take politics seriously? Compare this early political education to my grandfather's—southern defeat, rural poverty, farmers' and workers' revolt—or to my parents'—Depression, government activism, war against fascism—and you begin to see how badly prepared we were to be responsible. But the choice for every generation is ultimately between taking politics seriously and letting power and wealth go unchecked.

Through junior high, high school, and college, I enjoyed an ideological free ride through a scenery of billboard slogans and low amusements—until, ten years after my father's death, I decided to get off and see what lay behind the fun house.

I passed through my teens doing, by all appearances, quite well, without noticing that I was split along several fault lines. There was the line between themes and stories, thought and feeling, reading and living. There was the line between inherited liberal reflexes that sometimes resembled ideas and social circumstances that rarely forced them to be tested against the world. There was the line between the fact of my father's destruction and the fact that I didn't want to face it.

Yet I followed him to Yale. Not the Skull and Bones, anti-Roosevelt, gentleman's agreement, shoe-exuding college that he'd attended as a local scholarship boy almost forty years before, but a Yale that was almost a third Jewish, almost half female, and majority Democrat. In my first week I watched the fallen liberal George McGovern debate Yale's own gift to conservatism, William Buckley, on arms limitation and felt the auditorium full of students leaning heavily toward McGovern. A week later, on the topic of affirmative action, an erratic black nationalist named Roy Innis was picked apart by a right-wing political scientist named Ernest van den Haag. I vividly remember two moments from that second debate. The first came before the formalities had even begun, when a group of black students rose in unison from their seats, started chanting "We are not debatable," and walked out of the room. A few moments later, the student representative from the Party of the Right went to the podium, preppie scarf draped around the shoulders of his sport coat, soda can in hand. He smiled, all smug contempt. He brought the can to his lips, tossed his head back, and downed the last of his soda. His fellow reactionaries in the audience cheered.

These two moments sum up the political atmosphere of my years in college in the late 1970s and early 1980s. Identity politics, that most enduring legacy of the 1960s, was coming into its own, and not just among black students. "Take Back the Night" had been institutionalized as an annual event. A radical lesbian magazine called *Aurora* began to publish articles collectively penned by CHAPS, or Chicks Against Pricks. In the arts the main creative energy seemed to belong to gay students. In my literature classes the required reading was Michel Foucault, and undergrads quickly learned to parrot his phrases about knowledge and power: "Humanism is everything in Western civilization that restricts *the desire for power.*" All the universals of the Enlightenment—the individual, freedom, reason, democ-

racy, equality, justice—burned to a crisp under the intensely magnifying stare of the French philosopher's square metal eyeglasses. Eigh-
teen-year-olds who the year before had been Ted Kennedy liberals
writing high school essays on the meaning of the blood imagery in
Macbeth transformed themselves overnight into poststructuralists and
neo-Marxists intent on showing that nothing had any meaning except
power. Any talk about emotion or ideas in literature was greeted with
knowing smiles. Our younger and hipper teachers had been students
themselves during the glory years. Now they had come back to make
their careers inside the institutions they'd tried to assault a decade
before, and they were building a whole curriculum out of David Harris' argument to my father that ideas reflected group interests and
objectivity was a myth of the powerful. Having failed to revolutionize
the university of their youth, they had returned to bore from within,
staging a subtler takeover by Ph.D. All the structures of governance
remained intact—in fact, pay and power were becoming more
unequal and hierarchical. But on the level of language and thought
they had seized control—and now *their* students, my classmates, were
adopting the new theory from France just in order not to be thought
stupid.

For two hundred years liberal politics rode the contest of universal
ideas to its greatest victories, while conservatism hunkered down amid
the narrow, local claims of tradition, including ethnicity and religion.
Now the two were once more trading places. Academic liberals under
the spell of identity politics were beginning to believe that what made
you right wasn't what you thought but who you were. Which, in effect,
justified that walkout by the black students from the affirmative action
debate: "We are not debatable."

And what about that self-satisfied speaker from the Party of the
Right? I had never seen such a creature in my life. They didn't exist in
egalitarian California. A young conservative in California was a used-
car magnate's junior-college daughter. But on the East Coast this
species of right-wing aristocrat had somehow survived the cultural revolution in sheltering habitats like Groton and Yale, still bearing the

distinctive markings of preppie scarves and condescending tones and even, in the more eccentric subspecies, bow ties and monocles. There was a group called the Rockingham Club where nth-generation Yale legacies and titled foreigners dressed up in tuxedos and drank champagne and yearned for a rigid class society. They struck me as anthropological curiosities, more than a little absurd. They had all the earmarks of historical losers. Yet I still remember the smile of that guy from the Party of the Right as he finished off the last of his soda. He didn't seem to think he was a loser at all. The woman who followed him, also from the Party of the Right, went on and on about upholding standards, which affirmative action made impossible. It sounded like pure snobbishness. Between the black walkout and the right-wing bores I lost my patience and didn't attend another debate during my years in college. It would be some time before I realized that the conservatives were picking up and claiming for their side the very concepts, valuable ones, that their left-wing opponents were busy discarding—merit, objectivity, universalism. By then the weirdos and throwbacks of the Party of the Right, scorned by the average blue-jeans-wearing Yalie, would be making policy in Washington as appointees of the Reagan administration.

Election night 1980, the first in which I cast a vote: I was walking across campus to watch the returns with friends when a former girlfriend stopped me and said that Carter had already conceded. The night was over before it began. The abruptness put me in shock; so did the realization that California's ex-governor, who had called for student demonstrators to be locked up, who had wished for an outbreak of botulism when the Symbionese Liberation Army was passing out free food to the poor in Oakland, who had said trees caused air pollution, who was so far right that his 1976 challenge to Ford seemed like a publicity stunt that almost worked, was going to become President. The beginning of the Reagan era left me speechless, and the bad news finally sank in. Politically I had been losing ever since the summer I turned eight, but in that moment I experienced defeat for the first time not as a mistake that would soon correct itself but as a condition that might be permanent—that might even make a kind of sense.

At Yale my father began to catch up with me. In all the conscious ways I kept my distance—didn't, for example, apply to live in his residential college, or join the clubs he had, or any clubs at all. My attitude toward Ivy League tradition was best expressed on the nights when my roommates and I got drunk at Naples Pizzeria and, staggering back to the dorm, stopped to urinate against the large heavy door of Scroll and Key or another of the secret societies that squat like Egyptian mausoleums around Yale's campus. I continued to work hard as a student, but a rebelliousness against expectation was rising in me. I moved off campus, carried an eclectic course load, and embraced the sexual and chemical freedoms that had been unavailable to my father.

Still, on some dimly tuned frequency I felt his presence. I fitfully attended services on the Jewish high holidays, without knowing why. I wrote a poem, after Joyce, about a father whose ashes drifted on a dark ocean. And one night, having ingested psychedelic mushrooms with some friends and climbed up into the belfry of the Branford College tower, I suddenly found myself crawling out toward the edge in the hallucination that I was fated like my father to end my own life. I stopped as soon as I realized what I was about to do, but the experience left me shaken and confused.

In the spring of 1982, age twenty-one, I seemed to be headed for graduate school in literature, to continue on the course I'd been following all my life. But at the last minute an instinct made me change my mind and jump off the track.

It might have been the instinct that made my grandfather, age twenty-eight in 1898, join the 1st Alabama Infantry to fight in the Spanish-American War, though he never got farther than Miami; the one that made my father, age eighteen in 1944, leave Yale on the early plan to join the Navy and sail off on a destroyer across the Pacific, where he saw six months of action against the Japanese. I wanted to test myself, have an adventure in the world, see what I was made of. Graduate school wouldn't do it.

But the military was never an option. It never even occurred to me to enlist. By the time I came of age the service was no longer the democratic leveler that joined Jewish intellectuals and southern farm boys in a common rite of passage into manhood. Vietnam, the end of the draft, and the volunteer army had turned military service into an employment agency for poor kids — one among many signs that America was becoming more and more divided along class lines. In 1982 for a son of the educated, liberal middle class like me to enlist in the armed forces would have been less likely than going to work on the railroad.

And yet the need for the experiences men used to find in the military — danger, physical discomfort, a break with home, camaraderie, commitment to something larger than personal ambition or pleasure — doesn't go away so easily. As far back as age seven or eight, my attitude toward war was ambivalent. I sometimes wore a peace button, and two raised fingers did not mean victory to me. I was deeply impressed by the flower poster that read, in childish handwriting, "War Is Not Healthy for Children and Other Living Things." At the same time, I was obsessed with World War II and could have told you exactly how many Americans died on Omaha Beach. My friends and I spent hours running around with plastic pistols, or setting up re-creations of the Battle of the Bulge with tiny lead tanks. Vietnam was wrong, but World War II, my father's war, was heroic. War wasn't healthy for us and other living things, but we couldn't think of anything as exciting. We had inherited one set of ideas and another set of instincts, and both made perfect sense.

When President Carter brought back draft registration in 1980 following the Soviet invasion of Afghanistan, there was a lot of agonizing among my college friends over the principle of resisting and the fear of getting caught. I found the latter more compelling and signed up, though I made sure to give my temporary address in Mobile, Alabama, where I was working as a summer intern at a federal poverty law office.

Needless to say, I never heard a word from the Selective Service, and my life's one gesture toward the military was lost in bureaucratic or postal oblivion—which was fine with me.

Going to Alabama that summer, the hottest in decades, was itself a kind of self-imposed test. On the scummy edge of downtown Mobile I rented a house with two black law students. One of them became my friend; the other hated his young white Ivy League housemate, providing an object lesson in the limits of liberal goodwill. I traveled by Greyhound to the rural counties north of Mobile and researched legal conditions in the poorest region of the country, where civil rights had barely left a trace other than a picture of the two Kennedys and King with the slogan "Three Who Set Us Free" that hung on the wall of an elderly black woman's shack. I interviewed the white probate judge of Monroe County, who told me that his colored and white folk got along just fine without outside help. The Klan was undergoing a revival in southern Alabama, and on dirt roads at night I wondered if local Klansmen were following me. I sort of hoped they were. It was my own personal Freedom Summer sixteen years late, an expression of some restlessness with my liberal and bookish comfort.

As graduation approached, the restlessness intensified. I had applications for study fellowships abroad that would never let me find out who I really was or whether I and my ideas would hold up in the world. At the last minute I decided to join the Peace Corps, and within three weeks of graduating I found myself on an airplane bound for Africa.

For a year and a half I lived in a cement house that shared a dividing wall and corrugated-iron roof with an African family of ten. The house stood alongside a potholed road where the village ended and the rain forest began. In the mornings I woke at dawn to the sound of a rooster crowing and women out on the road on their way to fetch river water in buckets and the eight-year-old girl from next door sweeping our dirt yard with a bundle of straw. In the heat of the early afternoon siesta I sat in my house trying to read while the rooster crowed and somewhere a child cried and the village slept. At night my neighbors' voices were hushed out of respect for spirits, and I kept my radio low as I listened to the BBC, or else I read by kerosene lamplight, while the frogs by the river raised a tremendous racket.

In Africa I taught English to classrooms of forty or fifty schoolchildren. I became close friends with an illiterate woman, the mother of the eight children next door. I attended a village trial in which the suspect, the woman's oldest son, was charged with stealing money and food and condoms from my rooms, and after his conviction I was told to watch while the elders took turns caning him. I drank a healing potion of charred leaf, schnapps, and rooster blood prepared by a fetish priest, the thief's grandfather. I traveled across the continent.

The Peace Corps was the most famous legacy of Kennedy-era liberal idealism. It belonged to the golden age of the early 1960s, when planeloads of smiling young men and women flew off to dig wells in Ghana and teach English in India, before Vietnam made every form of American involvement in the Third World suspect (the Peace Corps, after all, was an agency of the State Department). By the time I joined, two decades after Kennedy appointed his brother-in-law Sargent Shriver its first head, the Peace Corps had self-consciously dropped the trappings of Camelot. Under Reagan's director, a beer heiress and wife of a Republican Party contributor, volunteering was a job—"the toughest job you'll ever love"—that was supposed to demand technical know-how. English teachers were being phased out for small-business advisors. Naive college graduates would give way to more seasoned experts. This was the theory, anyway; in practice it wasn't easy to get engineers and agronomists to suspend their careers for two years of village life without running water or electricity.

Before leaving for Africa I had told people that my motives were not in the least idealistic, that I simply wanted an adventure, but this was only half true in a self-protective way. I wanted to go to Africa partly because of the race-consciousness bred in me from early on. Once there, faced with children who had guinea worm from contaminated water and students who knocked on my door asking for aspirin or employment and parents who begged me to educate their children in America and the mother next door whose life was endless drudgery, I felt the constant pressure to do what I could. I threw myself into the strange, humid, dull, intense life of the village. Because, of course, I wanted to do some good.

My role made it difficult to sustain the illusion. I was teaching English to peasant children who could barely speak the country's official language, French, in a school plagued by bureaucratic infighting and an irrelevant curriculum. I was living in close quarters, under constant scrutiny, with peasants whose culture was in many ways alien. Africa seldom made sense to me. Helping poor people on ground level turned out to be a lot more complicated than it had once seemed at a dinner table in Stanford.

The whole time, literally from the moment I set foot in Africa, a part of my mind stood aside and registered that something was wrong.

At first the wrongness located itself in my body. My tongue turned dry and prickly, and the heat dizzied me, and my pulse started racing so often that I took to checking it with two fingers on my wrist the way a diabetic habitually monitors his blood sugar. I had no one to talk to about these symptoms except myself, and in the cool early morning mist I went running to the next village and tried to think my way out of them. But they offered no explanation, I didn't know what they were symptoms of, and they wouldn't go away.

Some kind of panic had gotten into my blood. At times the faces of villagers, the people I had come here to help, looked like the carved masks sold in markets, with hatchet-shaped noses and slits for eyes, and I had to glance away while discussing the problem of drought. I had lost the layer of skin that comes between the world and the mind, and the smallest thing, a song lyric from a Police tape my sister sent me—"There's a little black spot on the sun today / It's the same old thing as yesterday"—had the power to crush me. In those moments time slowed to the pace of torture, every next second seemed dreadful, the only way out was suicide or sleep.

I began to feel that solitude, the long silent void of village days, was stripping away years of distractions and lies to lay bare the truth. The truth was that nothing meant anything. Everything I once valued sounded as hollow as the hot hours in the middle of the day when the crowing cock broke the silence like an insane herald of nothingness. Left to myself for weeks on end, I was completely unfit to handle this realization. I had gone out into the world to see what I was made of, and it turned out to be dried clay. Twelve thousand miles from Stanford's sandstone and terra cotta, the rational, moral world into which I had been born, and in which my own place was taken for granted, had crumbled.

I approached its disintegration in the only way I knew how, as an intellectual problem, and turned for help to the only familiar things at hand—my books.

I had packed them with the malaria pills and snakebite kit, the heavy load of my self-imposed Africa reading list, perhaps not the best books for relief from a mental crisis. They were lined up on the cement floor under a shuttered window that looked out on a papaya tree. In the early afternoons, while the village dozed in the peaceful sleep of the ontologically whole, I searched Kierkegaard's *Sickness unto Death* for the causes of my despair, underlining with one of the cheap Bics I passed out to my students. "When the enchantment of illusion is broken, when existence begins to totter, then too does despair manifest itself as that which was at the bottom." Mine turned out to be one of the most advanced forms—"the despair of willing despairingly to be oneself." According to Kierkegaard, I wasn't even a self—which was why I was in despair. He explained everything with dialectical beauty, and it made no difference. However hard I tried to embrace eternity and become a self, I continued to despair.

I put Kierkegaard aside and picked up Jung, and I found the archetype of the shadow, the antagonistic counter-self. "If we are able to see our own shadow and can bear knowing about it, then a small part of the problem has already been solved." I began to think that my problem lay in the period of my father's suicide—in all that had been repressed through things like reading lists. I thought that perhaps I had inherited the gene of self-destruction, and the only way to survive was to expose it to the light of consciousness. So I went back ten years and tried to retrieve everything.

But even as Jung explained the shadow, I noticed that it still rose with me every dawn, stood beside me before a classroom of African children, sat with me at night as I turned the radio to the BBC.

I went looking for my frightened self in fiction. In Conrad I read: "How can you imagine what particular region of the first ages a man's untrammeled feet may take him into by the way of solitude — utter solitude without a policeman — by the way of silence — utter silence, where no warning voice of a kind neighbor can be heard whispering of public opinion? These little things make all the great difference. When they are gone you must fall back upon your own innate strength, upon your own capacity for faithfulness." And elsewhere in Conrad (Conrad knew everything about me): "The truth was that he died from solitude, the enemy known but to few on this earth, and whom only the simplest of us are fit to withstand. The brilliant Costaguanero of the boulevards had died from solitude and want of faith in himself and others."

I read late into the night, and while the wick of my kerosene lamp burned down I entered the world of the imagination so deeply that for the first time since childhood I lost my way. Everywhere words led, down through the *Inferno*, into *Heart of Darkness*, at *A Bend in the River*, they mastered me with their suggestive power. The themes had finally escaped my brain and slipped into my bloodstream. And yet I got no relief.

The reading, of course, only deepened my solitude. The villagers I lived among were mostly illiterate, and anyway they didn't appear to have lost their sense of meaning. If I tried to explain what had gone wrong with me, they would have sent me to the old man who sliced open the shoulders of sick people and poured in the liquor of his medicine, which couldn't have helped any less than my books.

Toward the end of my time in Africa, I made a long trip by bush taxi to visit an American friend who lived several hundred miles away. This friend had found truth in Heidegger and radiated a tranquil wisdom even in 110-degree heat. I admired and envied him, and I wanted to find out what he knew about Being and whether I could get some of it.

For the two-day journey I brought along *Moby-Dick*. As I read, an

African in the seat in front of me kept turning around to stare. When-ever our eyes met, he laughed. Sometimes, after laughing, he said sim-ply, "*Yovo*," which means "white." As the miles and hours passed, and the landscape outside the window dried and flattened, and mad Ahab pursued the White Whale to the ends of the earth, and my fellow pas-senger continued to stare and find private amusement in my white-ness, I felt that I was journeying straight into "the heartless voids and immensities of the universe." My companions in the bush taxi kept up their chatting or sleeping or staring out the window or laughing at me—this destination was mine alone.

The only escape was into the book; but the book was no escape. It led me deeper, to the moment when Ishmael, having expounded on the "higher horror of whiteness," concludes: "Pondering all this, the palsied universe lies before us like a leper." In my copy, the page shows the ghost of a dog-ear. I had closed the book and tried to sleep. By the time we reached the hot little town by a muddy river and an outcrop-ping of rock, neither Heidegger nor my friend could do much to help.

In the end I left Africa six months early. In retrospect I wonder how I hung on for so long, but at the time quitting felt like failure. I was fail-ing others, especially the villagers, and I was failing myself. I flew home with a sense of doom. Apparently it was written across my face, for when I ran into a college friend on the street in New York a couple of days after getting back, he offered me fifty dollars. A great gulf seemed to have opened between us—between me and everything in my old life. I had returned to nothing solid or sure. I had no plans, no idea at all what to do. I would have to start over.

I went back to the house in Stanford for a month to figure out my next move. On one of my first nights home my mother and I were at dinner, tiptoeing around the subject of what I was doing back six months early, which neither of us knew how to talk about. Instead, falling back on habit, we discussed *Heart of Darkness*. My mother said that it was about the need for self-restraint: Marlow saved himself from

Kurtz's abyss by repressing his own darker impulses into work. I said that it was about the need to face the irrational and destructive forces inside you, and not bury them under a load of idealistic lies. Kurtz was a liberal, I said. That was why he became a killer. I argued bitterly, for we were talking about what I was doing back six months early, after all, in the only way we knew how, and the meaning of my experience in Africa depended on the meaning of Marlow's and Kurtz's. I wanted to make my mother see that her view, my parents' view, had failed me over there. The reading lists, the book-lined study walls, the Socratic dinner-table conversations, the correct positions on black people and poor people and student sit-ins, the whole life of reason—none of it had made any difference when I was sitting in a hot room in a cement house in Africa trying to hang on to sanity. At twenty-three I'd had my version of John Stuart Mill's crisis at twenty, when he found that "the habit of analysis has a tendency to wear away the feelings." My mother became uncharacteristically quiet at dinner that night. She must have sensed that more was at stake than literary interpretation.

Now that I was home again, in the cool evening of a California winter, everything about the house—my mother's cooking, the kitchen linoleum forever branded by hot oven racks from the time I was thirteen and had tried to put out a fire in a casserole pot, the creak of the middle hall step underfoot, the black support rails no one had taken down after my father's death, the clay masks on the family-room wall, the curtains in my bedroom, the high school yearbooks on the shelf, the sound of the mourning dove outside my window—none of it had changed, every inch of it was the same as before. The house seemed to say: this is real, not Africa, this is who you are, who you've always been.

I resisted its temptations. I feared the seduction of the familiar and comfortable life, for it had left me unequipped to deal with the alien. The past had failed me, and nothing would be the same again.

◆

CHAPTER 11

Winners and Losers

After a month at home I went to Boston, where I had some friends, and found a place to live and a job at five dollars an hour as low man on a construction crew. My old plan of graduate school and a career as an English professor lay on the scrap heap. It was the freest moment of my life.

Neither my father nor my grandfather had ever known such freedom. Under the pressure of financial burdens, social conventions, family duties, they had found their paths early, moved steadily upward, and never stepped off. But I wanted to get away from any ambition to succeed. I wanted work that would not involve my mind, that would put me in direct contact with the physical world. I spent my days tearing down old walls, sweeping floors, unloading lumber trucks, and loading garbage when the junk man came. For the first few weeks my unskilled hands were raw with cuts and splinters, so cramped at night I had to soak them.

There were two species of carpenter and our crew included both: union-card-carrying construction workers who read the tabloids at lunch, and ex-hippies who doodled design ideas on shim shingles. One guy called himself "the greatest Jewish carpenter since Jesus."

Subcontractors came and went, an even more varied group: the electricians were Jamaicans who fingered "de why-uh" to find out if it was live, the plumbers were gum-cracking lesbians, the painters Greeks, the plasterers Irish, the masons Italians, the Sheetrock hangers French Canadians. Twenty workers crowded a narrow town house on Beacon Hill, stepping over each other, slopping joint compound here and spraying sawdust there, dropping cigarette ash and knocking over cans of Coke, shouting three flights up over the blare of two radios, the shriek of the circular saw, the groan of the table saw, and the wail of the router that somebody's hammering was cracking the fresh plaster—and somehow the work got done, and done well, always a few inches from catastrophe. In the end reality is dust, and I went home every night with reality in my fingernails and tear ducts. I'd fall asleep exhausted, mentally sanding the same woodwork over and over. Then I'd get up at six to go back to the real work.

It was the spring of 1984. Boston, with the rest of the Northeast, stood on the verge of a real estate boom, and our crew was doing six-figure renovations of town houses for monied young clients in Boston's newly gentrifying neighborhoods. The Beacon Hill town house was a twenty-two-year-old's college graduation present. Another client had a picture in her bedroom signed with a sad marriage proposal by Robert Kennedy's son David, well on his way to death by drug overdose. We learned more about the clients than they ever imagined because even the ones who lived amid the ruins of a renovation didn't really register the workers. After a few days we became unofficial intimates, seeing clients in their underwear, overhearing marriages disintegrate, finding pills in the cabinets and dirty magazines in the attic—always privy to the nervous vanity, verging on panic, that overcomes people when they're sinking huge amounts of money into their shelter. The closer you are to the process of making visible things, the less you yourself are seen.

One day I was digging a drainage ditch in the backyard of a split-level condo. In every project there's a midpoint when the new face is almost painted on and yet some of the guts are still hanging out. We'd reached it on this job: the waste pipe, not yet connected to the sewer main, emptied into open air. The ditch where I worked was littered with camouflaged turds. As I dug, the architect arrived with his client for her weekly tour. They went inside over a plank spanning the ditch, and their noses wrinkled at the smell. A few minutes later, the tour apparently over, I heard the new European toilet flush upstairs. I just had time to fling my shovel and myself out of the ditch before fluid and soggy paper spewed over the mud where I'd been standing. Shortly afterward, the two of them came back out grimacing again, still puzzled about where the smell was coming from.

The client and her architect missed the waste pipe and me, and our connection to themselves, because they were caught in the dream of renovation. I'd been naive in imagining a job site like this as primordially "real." It turned out to be a place of massive illusion, where the idea of the thing was always worth more than the thing itself. What the carpenters built was only the mold into which others could pour fantasies of self and wealth. At the end of a job, after the chaos and the splintered wood and seven truckloads of garbage and two new coats of plaster and three of paint, after everything was destroyed and fixed and hidden, it sometimes seemed we'd never been there at all.

They brought us in to make over their lives. Whole areas of the city were being remade in this way, because enough people had the same idea in their heads at the same time. By common consent, an invisible pact, places once seen as slummy were now prestigious. During the time it took us to build decks outside a row of five identical prefab town houses in what one carpenter called "an Archie Bunker neighborhood," the price of each unit rose $60,000. On the riverfront, great lumps of condominium accreted like honeycombs. The water view was four inches wide, but the idea of water view went for $350,000. Molding came back in, and we transformed the opening between a client's living room and dining room into a Greek temple front, with columns, pilasters, entablature, and pediment. Surveying the finished work, our client turned to us and said, "Yeah, it'll enhance the resale value." This could stand as an epigraph to all my experiences in the residential building trade.

The bubble of consent surrounding the appearance of things—the agreement, say, that a kitchen renovation described by its designers as "a performance space entering the fourth dimension along the time-space continuum" should be worth a quarter million dollars—this bubble is hardly visible to people living within it. But Africa had pushed me outside for a while, and now everything back home seemed arbitrary and strange and even repellent. I felt like Gulliver returning from his travels to the company of human beings and finding that they stank. The year 1984 was one long American self-celebration, the year of the jingoistic L.A. Olympics and Reagan's landslide reelection on the slogan "It's morning in America." His popularity was at its absolute height. The cover of *Time* declared: "I ❤ U.S." Walter Mondale campaigned on the theme of "fairness" and was mocked in the press before being crushed at the polls. The country, which just two years before when I left for Africa had been suffering a severe recession and double-digit unemployment, was now in a spending-and-consuming frenzy.

Reaganism made commercial appetite a patriotic virtue. The unfettered individual, his taxes cut, his business deregulated, his responsibilities to society absolved, was king. Conservatism, which once cared about preserving the past, now sanctioned revolutionary change, and all the tokens of the future—mutual funds, computer software, foreseeable ownership of the White House—seemed to belong to the right wing. Reagan became the only President since Roosevelt who could articulate a utopian vision, but it wasn't FDR's utopia. Appropriating John Winthrop's speech to the Massachusetts Bay Company en route to the New World, Reagan called America "a shining city on a hill," in which unleashed individual self-interest would somehow create the beautiful and good community.

At the speed of American life, a whole generation of consumer goods and cultural trends—the VCR, the car phone, the words "yuppie" and "politically correct"—had sprung into existence while I was gone. I got dizzy in department stores and on shopping streets. The automatic teller machine, invented in my absence, overwhelmed me the first time I stood before one — it fit my African neighbors' idea of American wealth, a plastic totem and an incantation of numbers producing a drawerful of dollars, magical riches. "Do you need more time?" the screen kept asking until I pressed "Cancel" and hurried away. I felt as much a stranger on Beacon Hill as I had in Africa.

Having failed in Africa, I wanted to drive my guilt home by refusing to succeed in America. I simplistically divided the world into winners and losers. You had to choose sides, because one person's win meant that someone else lost. I belonged among the losers, and it almost seemed as if my life depended on this new insight. If I let myself be lured back into the old comfortable way, back to the winning side, what happened to me in Africa would happen again and this time I wouldn't survive.

I hated and feared money, physical comfort, consumer gadgets, men in power ties, the news from Washington and Wall Street, our construction clients and their architects and the glass-block walls and copper roofing and cherry floors we installed for them. I couldn't have my hair cut without calculating how many months' income of an African peasant I'd just spent. I agonized over which bunch of bananas to buy, opting for the one with smaller fruit because I could get more bowls of cereal out of it. I drank cheap piss-water beer even though I hated its taste. I refused to buy a fan in the heat of summer. Having figured out how to use the auto teller, I never withdrew more than $10 at a time. My $5.50 an hour (after a raise my second month) covered all my expenses. Even at the time I knew it was ridiculous, that I was making myself suffer to no one's benefit. But some inner logic was working itself out in a complicated, self-defeating, inexorable way.

From my first day in Boston I noticed the men, and a few women, who idled on benches in Boston Common or lined up at night outside a Lutheran church near Harvard Square where the sidewalks were thick with panhandlers. The homeless were just beginning to register on the national radar screen as a new social problem (Reagan and his Attorney General, Edwin Meese, suspected that most of them chose their fate). Psychologically I was drawn to these "losers," and I started working one or two nights a week in the church basement, doling out spaghetti and sauce onto paper plates and then sitting with the guests while they ate and trying to elicit their stories. Most were all too happy to talk, and I listened for hours and then went back to my room and filled notebooks with everything I'd heard. Down there among the unemployed, the alcoholic, and the lost, I found some relief from the sense of dislocation that pursued me in normal society aboveground. I wasn't one of them, but I felt like it.

The shelter had twenty-five mattresses, and whenever the number of guests exceeded this (every night during winter), a lottery was put in use. Once you'd spent a night, you were "presigned" and had rights to a bed for two weeks, as long as you abided by the rules (no weapons, drugs, booze, or violence) and arrived by ten o'clock. If you came in at three minutes past, you were out in the cold, "unpresigned." After two weeks the "presigned" had to reenter the lottery and draw numbers for a bed. Once a month there was an "amnesty," when the slate was wiped clean and everyone went back into a general lottery.

A guest's life at the shelter revolved around these two-week and one-month cycles, lulling stretches of security broken by random chance. This rather complicated system favored the regulars, the ones who knew a bed could be secured with half a day on laundry detail. Someone wandering in off the street one night could easily conclude that the rules were designed to cheat him. So the shelter managed to reflect the society that the guests had left behind up the basement stairs: it set up a hierarchy of insiders and outsiders, enforced it by rules and incentives, and periodically leveled them all with sheer luck.

It was easy to label the guests individually, but as a group they defied stereotype. There were middle-aged alcoholic men, out-of-state drifters, bag ladies, runaway teenagers, vets, young jobless blacks, ex-grad students, ex-cons, the evicted, the laid-off, a few men who woke up at 4 a.m. for minimum-wage day labor, a few crippled, a few crazy.

An unemployed construction worker just out of jail for drunk driving had found his apartment ransacked, leaving him nothing but the clothes on his back. A soldier back from Germany with an eye socket full of glass from a jeep accident was waiting for his first check and had dropped out of culinary school when his money ran out. A Namibian dissident had dropped out of the university and was risking deportation. Some, like him, were tight-lipped about their circumstances. Others spun endless lies, like the lame Willie Nelson look-alike who'd fished with Hemingway at Key West, stormed Iwo Jima, taken part in the Bay of Pigs, and served time in Castro's jails. Others tantalized themselves with the great apartment that was about to come through, the lawsuit against a landlord that would net a million. But the obvious fact of lacking a roof made it hard to disguise reality. The alcoholics in particular came up with point-blank self-appraisals that made you flinch. "I worked for a few days, and a little man was sitting on my brain saying, 'You've got some money—now get the water.' I started drinking with the dough, and next thing I knew it was two weeks later and I was out in St. Paul."

A common lot threw people together who might otherwise have avoided or hated each other. A half-crazy poet, son of wealthy parents, brought an exhausted bag lady her plate. An Irishman and a black played Ping-Pong for money after dinner. There were quarrels and insults every night, but they had more to do with shower rights than civil rights. Conventional prejudice seemed absurd. In spite of the shelter's rules and hierarchies, homelessness was an effective leveler.

"The lower strata," one homeless man told me, "it gets seductive." A scrupulous watchdog from the Reagan administration could have pointed out how each of the shelter's guests brought his fate on himself. There were not many pure victims among them. A woman's welfare check was cut, she didn't limit her expenses, back rent piled up, an eviction notice was served, and suddenly she found herself on the street. Or a hard drinker lost his job as a surveyor, was finally given the boot by his wife, went in for laboring, and couldn't scrape together a deposit for a furnished room. The shelter came at the end of poverty and mistakes that led to more mistakes, each compounded by the bad luck that haunts you when your income hovers around $10,000. The welfare woman and the surveyor didn't "choose" the shelter. In a city where rents were going up six times faster than welfare allowances, and where three-quarters of those eligible for subsidized housing could find none, the shelter chose them. Life in the booming cities on a low income had become a high-wire act. Most of the people who ended up there had taken one or two false steps.

But if anyone could have ended up as a Reagan anecdote, it was Joe Corcoran. The night I met him he looked like an Irish hiker: about sixty, with white hair and three days of whiskers, wearing oversized khakis and boots.

"I'm a bit of a dark sheep in the family. I was a hotel clerk, not going anywhere. So I took early retirement. I was paying $230 a month for a place but Social Security brings in only $300 and I just hated seeing so much of it soaked up by rent. It seemed the proper thing for me to go out onto the streets. Or I go to the Cape. Sometimes I spend the whole day in the public library reading James Bond novels. They're quite good, have you ever tried one? I can see you're an educated fellow."

In his slightly pained formality you could hear the voice of a desk clerk at a two-star hotel. He looked furtively at the people gathered in the church's back entryway, waiting to be admitted down into the basement, and he lowered his voice. "You know, some people here aren't normal. I stay clear of them. The lottery system is a good idea— makes them fend for themselves a little. Otherwise you get these people who just stay here night after night and don't want to leave. You can see I talk too much."

He smiled, and launched into a story about taking the train out to Vegas to meet a friend, wandering around the gaming tables and making, then losing money, falling asleep in hotel lobbies and being roused and told to leave. He finally got on a night train back East without ever finding the friend. Narrowing his eyes, he spoke of passing through time zones on the train and losing his sense of time and realizing it was unimportant. "You lose old patterns of thought, old worries—time, money." He tugged at his baggy khakis, leaned toward me, and murmured, "It's a comedown. But one gets used to everything."

At the shelter Joe Corcoran was eccentric. A disabled vet named Jim was nearer the center of homeless experience. He dragged his burly frame around on a pair of metal crutches. One night he lowered himself onto the top step of the entryway and began speaking, in a working-class Boston accent, to no one in particular. Noticing I was listening, he addressed me.

There was no small talk. He'd been in Vietnam, he said, and in the past two years his body had been falling apart: his legs had weakened, he was losing sensation in his feet and hands. Lowering his voice, he said, "I think I may be dying. Last month I was in the VA. They wanted me to stay three nights but after that they were gonna kick me out and I didn't want to lose my bed here. So I didn't sign nothing or take no tests. I did tell the doc I was feeling suicidal—which I was. I get three hundred a month but I'm almost through it after twenty days."

He smiled like a boy putting the best face on a fight with a bully. "But I've got a friend who might be able to get me a room cheap on Dana Street. So I could get outta here."

"Then you could go to the VA," I suggested. He shrugged. The government wasn't well loved by the homeless; the thought of the room on Dana Street cheered him up more. He rambled on, oscillating between his body's decay and the small things that left room for hope, like the bars in the Combat Zone that let you stay until 3 a.m. during winter and gave out free Coca-Cola. Eventually he confided his real plan.

"If I can save enough money from my checks till October," he said, "I'm going out to Hawaii. I'm going to lie in the sun in goddam Hawaii."

That night Hawaii seemed a long way off. The temperature had dropped close to zero, and when a college student came upstairs to call off the names of the presigned, six men and two women were left standing in the entryway. They drew for three beds. A Chicano boy, an old Irishwoman, and the man who had told me that "the lower strata, it gets seductive" won. But the Chicano announced he had a place to stay with friends and gave his number to Jim the vet, who could hardly believe his luck. As the Chicano went out the door, the hard-luckers got a gust of the Arctic air that awaited them.

Everyone would get dinner from downstairs before being turned out. The shouts and scraping chairs below sounded positively homey. At first none of the losers spoke.

"I think it sucks," a black kid suddenly said to me. "You all are cheating me. Why'd you let them in and not me?"

I was startled to realize that I was the one who stood for authority in the entryway. I had vaguely imagined myself to be on their side, almost one of them. I tried to explain the rules but got lost in the maze. He interrupted me. "I think it's fucked up. No, I don't want your subway money. You folks treat the homeless like they're shit, just bags you can toss out. You're as bad as the other places—man, to stay in one place I gotta act like I'm drunk, another like I'm crazy, here I gotta have a diploma or something."

By now he was laughing—not naturally, but in staccato bursts. Plates came up, the old woman smilingly buttered a slice of bread, a man in a parka with a furred hood chewed quickly and glanced around like a hyena expecting predators to challenge him for his food. A Portuguese carpenter was still staring at the scrap of paper with its losing number. He crouched beside me and started whispering.

"My wife told me that's it, to go. I drink, I can't work no more. I know I can't last on these streets! You're a carpenter, right? I did finish carpentry, and if you can do finish you can do rough, you know? Twelve bucks an hour. No!" he cried, hitting his forehead. "Bang, bang, something isn't right here." Apologizing, he begged me to do something.

The carpenter's thick black hair was streaked gray. His large capable hands and handsome face gave the impression of a family man, a provider. But the baritone voice was dissolving into a tremble. A skilled craftsman, he couldn't believe what was happening to him. And perhaps because he more than anyone else in the entryway wasn't supposed to have ended up here, the carpenter won my sympathy and made me uneasy.

On my advice he agreed to take the subway to the airport and sleep at the Eastern terminal. He made me go over the directions three or four times, and eventually I drew a detailed map of the subway, as if he were being sent behind enemy lines. The black kid decided to go along. They looked each other over, opened the door, and disappeared into the frozen night.

Finally the man in the parka swallowed the last of his prey and gave me a suspicious look from under the furred hood.

"I ain't staying here," he said.

"It's not a bad place."

"I don't like living like a head of cattle. I've been on the streets three years, I ain't afraid. Russian officers on the Mongolian border sleep outside without sleeping bags, did you know that?"

And he went out.

Whatever conspired with poverty—sickness, alcohol, mental disturbance, failure, age, bad luck—to turn someone out on the streets and down into a shelter was close enough to the path of normal life so that anyone who saw and heard would squirm. Most of the homeless I met were articulate and self-conscious about their situation, but self-consciousness didn't seem to help. It didn't help them to see that their days were wasted in boredom, obsessions about money, food, and weather, and the idle slouching through streets that was the unmistakable sign of disgrace. For Joe Corcoran homelessness may have brought a temporary mystical release, but most found themselves turning as sour as forgotten milk. Once that began, it was harder to resist the seductions of the lower strata.

For several years I worked at various shelters and heard dozens of stories. The lower strata seduced me—not as politics or sociology, for I didn't translate what I heard and saw into larger terms. I didn't have the policy answers and didn't particularly care about them. The existence of large numbers of homeless people in the big cities—as many as 50,000 in New York alone—bothered my conscience, but I didn't volunteer out of a sense of indignation. I was looking for the comfort of discomfort. The homeless shelters bore out the thoughts that had gotten into my blood in Africa and come back with me: that life deals mainly in suffering and injustice, that anyone who succeeds has compromised himself at someone else's expense, that the way to live is by embracing failure. I wanted to be on the side of the losers because it was realer, truer, and therefore better.

At some point during those years I ran into an acquaintance from college who was attending law school, a way station on the road to greater things. At Yale he had been locally famous as a conservative writer for the campus paper—his column was called "Juvenilia," or "Youthful Writings"—and, with his necktie and briefcase and skills at condescension, as a recognizable member (though a Jew from Toronto) of the aristocratic right wing that would come back from the dead under Reagan. When I won the freshman humanities prize he took an interest in me despite my liberalism and paid a courtesy visit while I was laid up in the infirmary with a bad case of flu. He would go on to make a name in print and broadcast journalism as an apologist for radical laissez-faire economics and a kind of high-Tory moralism on social issues, with an attitude toward the poor of contempt mixed with noblesse oblige: get rid of the welfare state and they would have to clean up their lives, emulating the behavior of their industrious and charitable betters. One of his radio commentaries expressed disapproval of the freedom with which people like bank tellers and schoolteachers called him by his first name rather than "Mr. Frum."

When we met up in Boston in the mid-1980s, we had arrived at opposing worldviews: I thought that money and virtue were incompatible, while he took them to be synonymous. He was amused by the uses to which I was putting my college degree, especially by the time I spent at shelters in the company of "your droolers." In his eyes I was going down a path of inscrutable perversity. In mine he epitomized the world of success in which I'd once held citizenship. His sudden appearance reminded me of where I had once been and was now supposed to be, at just the moment when I was beginning to worry about the strange direction my life had taken. It was not an auspicious reunion.

Nonetheless, he needed a new bookcase for his Beacon Hill apartment and hired me to build him one. I made it out of birch and assembled it in his living room one night while he was out at a Republican function. A week went by with no word. I wondered if he didn't like the bookcase—but I had also sensed from the moment I took the commission that going to work for him had changed something fundamental between us. The relationship had become hierarchical. Eventually an envelope came, with a check, which bounced, and a terse note informing me that the wood and fasteners I'd left behind would be thrown out if I didn't claim them. We were no longer equals as we'd been in college and he now felt obliged on principle to treat me in a different way, which is to say, badly. The next check, sans note, cleared, and I didn't hear from my old acquaintance again for a dozen years, until he published an op-ed piece in *The Toronto Sun* attacking a political essay of mine in *Harper's*. "I remember him vividly," he wrote, "a keenly intelligent, earnest boy, almost universally liked. We all expected him to go on to great things: to become a famous writer or perhaps a crusading politician. Instead, he vanished off the face of the Earth after graduation."

In truth, you are never nowhere, even if where you happen to be is Africa or a construction site or a homeless shelter. But the question of my vanishing wasn't a simple one. I knew that there might have been better uses for my time, with a larger impact on the world, than spending two months trying to find an apartment for a homeless Haitian woman and her three children. I still harbored desires to achieve something and was well aware that they were not being realized. And maybe escaping the winners' camp was driven partly by a fear of failure. A defeatist impulse that probably went back to my father's illness and death seemed to have me in its grip. My mother must have felt a ghostly shiver of his depressions—of the time when he was blocked on the Hiss book and wanted to quit his job, move to the beach, or kill himself. She worried, sometimes aloud, that I was drifting aimlessly. I was afraid she was right, and for a while every phone call ended up making me angry.

Half-consciously, I was trying to work out a new relation to the society in which I had grown up knowing my place and my beliefs; what had been handed down to me no longer seemed adequate to what I had experienced. The task wasn't simply personal, not just a matter of my own post-Africa alienation, but generational as well. I enjoyed the freedom and suffered the curse that my father and grandfather never really did. They had entered careers and institutions that put them at the center of events, their public roles determined, their convictions fixed, and neither of them ever seriously seemed to doubt what he believed. But in the aftermath of the 1960s, I was trying to sift through the ruins of liberalism—to seek and choose a new mode of politics rather than live out the one I was born to.

For a few years in the mid-1980s, my not very satisfying response was the construction site and the homeless shelter. But after four years of finish nails and paintable caulk and lower back pain and dust, I ended my career in the building trades, knowing that I wasn't a real carpenter. Around the same time, I stopped going to the shelters. The hopelessness of the stories had worn me out; and I was faced with the fact that I was only an interloper.

Instead, I began to write. I wrote about what happened in Africa, trying to make sense of it. Becoming a writer gave me a way to synthesize where I had come from and what I had experienced with what I still wanted to achieve. It expressed a condition of both freedom and skepticism. Unlike my father and grandfather, I would float along the edges of my own age and survey the landscape from that vantage point. In 1988 I published a book about my time in Africa; from then on I made my living from writing and part-time teaching.

I bought a new car and got married and returned to the soft embrace of the middle class. But I never completely lost the feeling of those first months back from Africa. What I thought might not have changed a great deal (I continued to vote for Democratic candidates, who continued to lose) but how I thought did. I'd been knocked out of my place, and the correct opinions no longer mattered without a human face behind them; abstract reason guaranteed nothing without experience. Even after I reappeared on the face of the Earth from Africa or the lower strata or whatever region of my mind I had vanished to, the beliefs of my forebears didn't look the same again. But what was there to replace them?

◆

Twilight of the Gods

Nineteen eighty-nine was a bad year for utopia. In Europe the twentieth century's dream of universal brotherhood, which had become the century's nightmare of total state power, collapsed in the ruins of the Berlin Wall. This was a good thing for the citizens of East Germany, Poland, Czechoslovakia, etc., who were liberated from a tyranny that only a few years before had seemed eternal. But it also meant that the idea of brotherhood, the idea of equality, the idea that human beings could through rational free will and collective action make their society more just—somehow these too seemed to go down in the concrete rubble of Berlin. The only ism left standing was capitalism. The god that didn't fail was the invisible hand of the free market. For better or worse, it became the one true faith.

By 1989 American liberalism was in no condition to raise any new idols. It had never been a visionary creed, always most successful—in Progressivism, in the New Deal, in the civil rights movement—when its ideals made practical accommodations with American life. But by 1989 liberalism had become both rigidly, almost theologically abstract and hopelessly compromised. It had two faces: the pious frown of a sensitivity-training consultant scolding a roomful of university officials and the slack grin of a Democratic congressman having drinks with a lobbyist. In Washington liberalism was a corruptible political party, and around the country it was a philosophy of intolerance and fragmentation. What it utterly lacked was popular energy. It excited no one, moved no masses to action, inspired no crusades.

In the election campaign of the previous year George Bush had made it officially unspeakable — the L-word: a minority creed of rapist-coddlers and flag burners and pornography purveyors and other elitists who were out of touch with "mainstream American values." The candidate tarred with this hideous identity, Michael Dukakis, governor of the state I was living in and a perfectly decent man, provided the crystalline image of liberal weakness when, during one of the presidential debates, a journalist asked him demagogically whether he would oppose the death penalty even for some hypothetical criminal who had raped and killed Dukakis' wife, Kitty. "I don't see any evidence that it's a deterrent, and I think there are better and more effective ways to deal with violent crime," Dukakis answered reasonably. "We've done so in my own state, and it's one of the reasons why we have had the biggest drop in crime of any industrial state in America." The bleeding-heart liberal was now a picture of bloodlessness, unable to express the most basic emotions. And so 1989 saw the inauguration of the fifth Republican administration in six tries, dating back to that January of 1969 when Nixon raised his hand to take the oath of office and my father gave his last healthy interview. By 1989 it was difficult to believe that there would be another Democratic President in my lifetime.

Anyone of my generation who wanted to translate liberal feelings into action was dealing with some formidable obstacles. One obstacle was the unattractiveness of the available movements, leftovers from the 1960s. The specter of my childhood had spawned two political heirs: pacifism and identity politics. The high drama of anti–Vietnam War demonstrations had given way by the 1980s to the ritual theater of protests against intervention in Central America. There was something automatic and mindless about these protests, even when the cause was just. As soon as the U.S. military turned its sights on some wretched corner of the world, a lonely and mostly graying band of protesters appeared in public carrying signs, chanting *"El pueblo unido no más será vincido,"* singing Pete Seeger songs, holding silent vigils.

The importance of style in political movements is underrated. Songs, clothes, tone of voice, even physical looks will attract or repel potential recruits regardless of the legitimacy of a cause. Left-wing style in the Popular Front 1930s, following orders from Moscow, went grittily native. "Communism Is Twentieth-Century Americanism" was the slogan, embodied in overalls, Jeffersonian rhetoric, Woody Guthrie songs, Henry Fonda as Tom Joad in *The Grapes of Wrath*. In the 1960s, the New Left came to cultivate a style of extreme effects, defiant of mainstream values and yet, in the manipulation of publicity and calculation of the power of images—especially violent ones—typically American.

Since the 1960s, the style of protest has been rigid, inward, and self-consciously symbolic. The more time I spent around the anti-intervention movement (you didn't have to be a pacifist to dislike the dirty wars fought by U.S. proxies in desperately poor little countries), the more bizarre and alien I found it. English words were spoken with Spanish accents. Public die-ins amused passersby without persuading them of anything. Six decades earlier, in 1928, George Huddleston had taken to the floor of the House and denounced the Coolidge administration's military expedition to suppress the Sandino movement in Nicaragua. He put his argument in patriotic terms: "Every man must know that America cannot exist as an imperialism abroad and a democracy at home. It cannot continue as 'the land of the free and the home of the brave' with its foreign policy under the dominion of a military autocracy. We cannot hold here at home that governments derive their just powers from the consent of the governed and yet in foreign countries ruthlessly deprive the people of their right of self-government." (In the 1980s *The New York Times* ran an op-ed article that quoted my grandfather's speech in making the case against the Reagan administration's war on Nicaragua.) But the point of the anti-intervention movement often seemed to be to antagonize the sensibilities of ordinary Americans. The movement was divided into "affinity groups" with portentous names like "The Black Sweaters"; meetings were governed by "consensus," which meant they dragged on for hours and ended not by majority vote but in the soft coercions toward an artificial unanimity of two or three "facilitators," who made it morally impossible to "block consensus." After one long night in detention with my *compañeros*, I felt more sympathetic with the Boston police, who at least were trying to be reasonable. Politics reduced to a series of dramatic gestures is a sign of powerlessness and probably of weakening conviction. It wins few converts, especially in its anti-American versions, and it ends by focusing on the self-expressive and virtuous satisfactions of its participants. During one protest, a friend of mine asked the antiwar priest Philip Berrigan whether he thought they could win. "No," Berrigan said, "but we'll save our souls trying."

The reigning left-wing ideology of the past two decades has been the identity movements—black, Hispanic, female, gay, deaf, and others—that fall under the term "multiculturalism." But beyond wishing them success in their struggles to find a place in the sun, there's not much an outsider can do to belong meaningfully. The point of identity politics is that other people *don't* belong. As these movements increasingly obsessed over "difference," elevating particularities of birth to a quasi-mystical status that determines political and all other choices, they rejected the ideas of universal humanism that have underlain liberal politics since the eighteenth century. This in turn made it impossible to win over a majority of Americans to any unifying program. "Diversity" as a hardened dogma (rather than a justified struggle for equality, which was how it began during the civil rights years) gave us the spectacle of full-scale war over English department hirings and a fragmented, unstable Democratic Party: on the whole, not a very promising direction for a political movement to take. And as mainstream liberals embraced diversity and abandoned their historic claim to speak for mankind against the privileged few, the claim fell into the hands of conservatives. Liberals used terms like "group interest" and "decentered knowledge"; conservatives spoke of reason, virtue, freedom, and responsibility, when what they really meant was "tough luck." Ten years on, the smug bastard with the soda can seemed to have won the debate.

Nineteen eighty-nine also saw the beginning of a recession. Today, after nearly a decade of soaring Dow indexes and unprecedented growth with low inflation and unemployment, when hardly anyone talks about poverty, it's difficult to remember the period that made the bland corporate term "downsizing" into a dirty word. Things happen so fast in America and leave so little trace that the recession of the late 1980s and early 1990s now seems as remote as the 1973 oil crisis. But a decade ago, for the first time in postwar history, upper-middle-class Americans suffered the brunt of an economic blow, and the cultural effect was jarring. Large-scale white-collar layoffs suddenly made people who had thought they were safe in suburbs and corporations feel vulnerable where they lived and worked. Unemployed executives shopped their résumés around to dozens of firms, only to be told they were overqualified and overaged, laid-off machinists delivered pizzas, downsized middle managers worked in visitor guide booths on interstate highways, support groups formed for depressed out-of-work engineers, houses went up for sale at a loss, twenty-five-year marriages fell apart. A new kind of book appeared—confessions of the downwardly mobile. The press and Hollywood discovered the angry white male. In *Falling Down* Michael Douglas played a laid-off aerospace worker whose status anxiety turns him one very bad day into a serial killer using military-grade weaponry on immigrants, minorities, women, and other targets of his rage.

Journalists and politicians suddenly figured out what had been happening economically since 1973: manufacturing jobs were disappearing, wages in the new service jobs were low, foreign competition threatened not just blue- but white-collar security, inequality in incomes was growing, the professional and upper-class elite were walling themselves off from the larger society's decline inside gated communities, with private schools and private security. The postwar dream of an ever-expanding middle class seemed to have busted. The middle class was eroding.

While working on a magazine article in depressed, blue-collar Lowell, Massachusetts, I met a man who had lost his job as a teamster in a produce warehouse when the supermarket chain was bought out by a Los Angeles investment firm. Jeff Surprenant received me in the kitchen of his small apartment next to an interstate, to which he and his wife and three children had moved after his severance pay ran out. He was resting between two fourteen-hour night shifts as an emergency medical technician, a job he liked but which paid him $6.50 an hour—almost $10 less than he'd made loading trucks. The family had fallen from the working class into the widening pool of the working poor; it was an extravagance to go out one night a week with the kids to Chuck E. Cheese. Sitting in his long johns at the kitchen table, Surprenant still seemed stunned and helpless in the face of the turn his life had taken two years before. "The company never approached us," he said. "That's what hurt. Guys would have taken a five-dollar-an-hour cut. We were all willing to give. But there were never any negotiations, just 'We're shutting down.' "

After several decades of politics based on identity and culture, the country discovered the politics of class. Or rather rediscovered it, for class politics had dominated the scene throughout my grandfather's career and, really, throughout the period between the Civil War and World War II. In one way or another those decades pitted the worker against the boss. The great story for half a century and more was industrialization, its effects on society, and the shocked middle-class conscience's response. The New Deal reforms and the postwar boom seemed to settle the class question. The economy became mixed; the state took responsibility for the poor, the sick, the old, and the young; national spending policy kept the business cycle from swinging too wildly. Wages rose, and workers became consumers. After World War II national elections were won and lost not on class but, broadly speaking, social issues: domestic Communism, patriotism, civil liberties, crime, "quality of life," government corruption, family values, and above all the overriding postwar obsession with race. When economics proved decisive (for example, in Reagan's crushing defeat of Carter), it had nothing to do with class. The economy was presented as a sort of national weather pattern: what was good was good for everybody, the same with what was bad. "A rising tide lifts all boats": this Kennedy cliché defined our political economy for half a century after World War II. For the first part of that period it generally favored the Democratic Party. But when the 1960s injected some virulent social arguments into the culture, Republicans exploited them brilliantly and ruthlessly, and the worm turned.

In 1973 things started to change again. What industrialization did between the Civil War and World War II, postindustrialization has been doing since that year—creating a newly hierarchical society, with ever-widening distances between winners and losers—but it only registered on the screens of opinion makers with the recession of the late 1980s and early 1990s (working-class people had known about it a while longer, but reporters no longer talked to them). Around 1989 economics became political again, and class politics reappeared after decades of dormancy. But liberals were too distracted by identity politics, demoralized by the Reagan years, softened by their own class privilege, consumed with private life, indifferent to politics itself, to know what to do.

So two things happened that year, and together they formed a paradox. On the one hand, capitalism stood triumphant around the world. The great ideological war of the twentieth century was over, and free-market democracy appeared to be the only idea left standing with a viable future. It was, one writer claimed, "the end of history." On the other hand, Americans began to notice that the country's wealth and power had become more and more unequal. The end of the twentieth century was beginning to resemble the end of the nineteenth: a period of explosive technological change, business domination, cheap wage labor, and two uninspired, intellectually dead, legally corrupt political parties. Corporate control over state politics helped spark the Populist revolt in the early 1890s, but as the 1990s began there was no coherent public response to corporate control over national politics. Within a couple of years Ross Perot would appear — an incoherent response from the corporate sector itself, whose popular following soon evaporated.

What had changed in a century? Among other things, this: a hundred years ago, free-market capitalism had challengers — several overlapping movements in which large numbers of people believed. Populism expressed the faith of farmers and small proprietors in the sovereignty of the common people and their suspicion of concentrated wealth, and it looked to the federal government for support. Progressivism gave the same set of concerns a middle-class, modernizing, science-minded set of answers. And socialism, transplanted from Europe by immigrant workers and a handful of intellectuals, found fertile soil in the big cities and labor unions for its more thoroughgoing attack on capitalism itself. These three movements together laid the groundwork for the Roosevelt revolution and the modern welfare state. Their power lay not just in programmatic content but in their ability to command belief. They were alive in people's minds and hearts — they had the vigor to move millions to action and provide a check against the juggernaut of industrial capitalism as it remade American life.

By 1989 nothing like that existed anymore. So I had to improvise.

Joining the Boston chapter of the Democratic Socialists of America in 1989 was like converting to Catholicism at the height of the Reformation, or coming out as a flat-earther during the Enlightenment. The whole world, from Poland to Ghana, was moving in the other direction, ridding itself of outdated political fantasies and waking up to the wonders of market capitalism. Democratic socialists could rightly claim that they had been among Communism's bitterest enemies from the start, knowing firsthand its ruthless methods. Still, they couldn't escape its taint.

Why did I make such a quixotic decision? No one sat me down and convinced me of a theoretical truth. I didn't come across some lines in *Das Kapital* and, like the young Augustine opening the Bible at random, see my destiny there on the page. When I joined I couldn't have said exactly what socialism was, and I still can't. In fact, I found that even for party veterans the contours of the future were extremely, perhaps fatally, vague. Having seen the failure of nationalization and central planning in both Eastern and Western Europe, they were casting about for new models of "worker self-management" and "market socialism," seeking to enlarge the control of workers and consumers over corporations that had grown immensely powerful, while defending unions and the welfare state against the conservative drive to gut both. The term "economic democracy" was invoked to suggest that rather than expanding state power, socialism would extend individual freedom from the political to the economic realm.

"I am now inclined to think the case for socialism must be made increasingly on moral grounds," one of the national leaders wrote. Another simply described socialism in terms of "kindness." But it had not been so different earlier this century, when large numbers of working people across the country believed that socialism was America's future. Most of its adherents were driven by motives no different from mine. That is to say, they became socialists out of objection and hope.

What I objected to in 1989 was the idea that plant closings and bought political representation and the Disney Corporation and Boston's 5,000 homeless exemplified the best of all possible social arrangements. What I hoped for was a different one, in which America would become something like the classless society that it has always pretended to be, or at least in which the management consultant and the warehouseman felt as though they inhabited the same country and lived by more or less the same rules.

In Africa, in homeless shelters, in my travels as a writer, I had seen enough poverty to know that it was systemic, not personal, a result of vast global forces more than individual failings. I also knew that volunteerism mixed with welfare-state liberalism kept poor people poor while making middle-class people feel a bit better. I wanted to join my

effort with others' in an organization that didn't accept the corrupt status quo of Democrats and Republicans. I went looking for the just society in a shrinking organization of fewer than ten thousand people that
called itself "the left wing of the possible."

"I didn't know there were any more democratic socialists," a friend
said, as if he was talking about California condors. But I knew they
weren't extinct. I had seen them at rallies, with their sign bearing the
old fist and rose of the Socialist International. A number of things
made the socialists attractive. They didn't cultivate weirdness or the-
atrics. They were genuinely open to discussion. They had an international network, with parties in power in several European and
Caribbean countries. They claimed intellectually serious members as
diverse as Meyer Schapiro and Cornel West. They had a long tradition—mostly of failure, but not completely. During the earlier part of
George Huddleston's career, socialism really did represent the left
wing of the possible. Though he rejected the label whenever it was
applied to him, he didn't run from it, and on a number of occasions he
found himself allied with or offering tribute to one of the handful of
Socialists in Congress. The Socialist Party's candidate Eugene Debs
drew almost a million votes in the 1912 presidential election against
Wilson and Teddy Roosevelt. In that year eleven socialist weekly
papers were published in Oklahoma alone. Child labor law, the eight-
hour day, Social Security, in fact much of the New Deal originated in
socialist thought.

But after the October Revolution in Russia, the Communist International drew off thousands of American socialists and sullied the
remainder with crimes committed in the much-abused socialist name.
By the time my parents came of age politically, the Socialist Party had
broken apart through schisms and had been Red-baited into a tiny core
of loyalists. Anyone born after 1920 was only going to become a socialist quixotically or hereditarily. If my father had been born five years
earlier and raised in New York, he might have. As it happened, the
word was never uttered in our house—it wasn't on the political map.
But without the tough economic critique of socialism, our liberalism

was vulnerable to the charge that it took people and politics in the abstract, failing to connect interests and passions with the realities of class and power.

In a way, socialists belonged to the oldest American political tradition of all, the one to which my grandfather belonged: the eighteenth-century republicanism of Jefferson, which held that democracy could not remain vital when too much wealth and power fell into too few hands, and that freedom and equality depended on each other. The issues that concerned me preoccupied the democratic socialists as well: economic inequality, between the West and the rest of the world, between the privileged few in America and the rest of the country. Their short-term goals were practical, focusing on unions and electoral work. The basis for their larger critique was humanistic, moral. Mercifully, this wasn't a sect or a cult.

In fact, the reigning mood on "the left wing of the possible" was irony. The style was understatement, deflation, self-mockery: a low-key Götterdämmerung. We held forums on the topic of "How Dead Is Socialism?" Our T-shirt proclaimed, "Socialism in my lifetime"—wistfully and half jokingly, like the bumper sticker that says, "My other car is a Mercedes." When the word "comrade" turned up, it always wore an affectionate smirk. One member, Comrade Mike, knew the entire history of left-wing sectarianism in the twentieth century, and he would tease the rest of us with hyperbolic analogies. "You know, Comrade George, as newsletter editor you hold what Lenin said is the key to party power." Or: "Comrade Guy is moving toward right deviationism. The politburo should consider a purge." No one was ever "purged." We had anti-abortion Catholics, orthodox Marxists, and liberal Democrats. As editor of our newsletter, the *Yankee Radical*, I published anything that came in—terrible poetry, pseudonymous rants, arguments for abandoning the "S-word." "Comrade George," Comrade Mike would mock-exhort me, "more Leninist discipline!"

The organization acquainted me with the pathos of left-wing activism in twilight. It was marginal, pedestrian work, based on the eternal postponement of gratification: three-hour board meetings in a narrow room in a church basement; a two-year fund drive to buy a used computer; a snowbound forum on the Canadian left, whose announcement reached most of the membership too late because the nonprofit mailing wasn't sorted properly. The word "Sisyphean" is mis-leading, since we never pushed our rock anywhere close to the top, but it's a fair evocation of the enterprise.

Sometimes, at a forum or board meeting, I would look around at the dozen or so souls who had ventured out into the cold on a week-night and wonder what made us do it. Why did we spend our lives on this stuff? Some were very old—gentle white-haired couples who sel-dom said much but turned out regularly, so inured to failure after half a century of it that they looked fairly content. No socialism in *their* life-time; might as well have some coffee and pull up a chair. For them, and for younger members of their temperament, the organization pro-vided the comfort of belonging, a mix of social club, night school, and church group. They seemed to me examples of Keats's negative capa-bility—able to go on being and believing without any certainty to sus-tain them.

But most members under fifty still nursed restless ambitions. They got up and demanded that we "define a sharper vision," as if vagueness were all that stood between us and triumph. At one meeting a former New Leftist who worked for the city government announced that all the socialists in Boston could fill Fenway Park. Why weren't we reach-ing them? We should launch a recruitment drive, reorganize, hire a staff person! And yet, year after year, our ranks dwindled; the evenings spent phoning snappish people who barely seemed aware that they were still listed as members brought in less and less money; the board exhausted itself trying to stay alive so we could endure another year of fund raising so that we could stay alive . . . like some ancient organism mindlessly perpetuating its own existence.

The truly ambitious almost inevitably drifted away. As soon as a member had his doctorate or got a political job or began speaking on NPR, we would stop seeing him at meetings. Before its fragmentation in the 1930s, socialism provided an outlet for talents and drives, but in the 1990s no one was going to get ahead through us. Our core mem-bership was characterized by rare decency and intelligence; among

the most durable we could count state legislators and union organizers. But there was a contingent of people who seemed to have nothing
else going on—marginal, odd, with a whiff of paranoia about them.
One member was apparently normal in all respects except that he had
an overly loud voice, and somehow this seemed linked to his being a
socialist. Another insisted on writing her name in all lowercase letters.
And what did they see in my face? Maybe just joining made us odd.
Maybe oddness made us join. In friends, I might have found these
peculiarities trivial; in comrades, I was hyperalert to every asocial quirk
and twitch, for they implicated me. And this seemed to defeat the
entire enterprise. I was supposed to be feeling solidarity with my brothers and sisters, and instead I was noticing that someone's navel was
exposed.

I never got used to our middle name, never overcame a chronic
and shameful sense of embarrassment. Whenever someone said, "As a
socialist I . . . ," it made me feel as if I had joined a 12-step group:
recovering capitalists. What could it mean to call yourself by a name
that has passed not only into popular disrepute but almost out of contemporary speech? It means either (1) you're old enough to have been
around when it was a living, breathing idea that animated people
around the world; (2) you've studied economic and political theory
and have some hypothetical proposals for worker self-management; or
(3) you have a good heart. In any case, the word didn't travel well
between our airless little office and the outside world.

This was brought home to me most vividly on the softball field.
The forerunner of our organization was the Democratic Socialist
Organizing Committee, or DSOC, which had picked itself up from
the ruins of the Socialist Party ("the defeated remnant of an already
defeated remnant," its founder, Michael Harrington, called it). So our
team was the DSOX, with the fist and rose stenciled across our jerseys.
Once, when we were playing the Shattuck mental hospital guards, a
team of large-bodied sadists who liked to take opponents out in the
base path, I let a pitch go by. "Strike," their catcher muttered. "High
and inside," I said. He answered, "Maybe in *Moscow*." There wasn't
time before the next pitch to tell him the history of the anti-Stalinist

left and how *our* brand of socialism had nothing to do with Moscow. This was just before the fall of Communism; later, teams responded more with amusement or blank stares than with contempt. But there's no real answer to being laughed at.

Whenever a new team joined the league there would always come a moment when I was playing third and their third-base coach would ask in all innocence, "What does the D in DSOX stand for?" "Democratic," I would answer. "We're a political group." Sometimes she was willing to leave it at that, but if absolutely pressed I would tell her our full name and then get into my crouch before she had a chance to ask anything more. Even a team called Peace Action felt a right to snicker. Between the pacifists and the socialists, play was especially aggressive. The softball games provided my most intense moments in the organization, which suggests something worrisome about the limited appeal of rational discourse and a cooperative model for society.

Our left fielder, a cabdriver named Glenn, launched a campaign to attract more mainstream people to the organization. Our old recruitment brochure put us at a disadvantage: printed on red paper, it was highlighted by the recurring phrase "We Are Democratic Socialists . . ." So we designed a new brochure on white paper that affiliated us with Thomas Jefferson and portrayed us as champions of the ordinary beleaguered American against the likes of Donald Trump. Glenn kept a stack in his briefcase, but the brochures somehow failed to win new recruits. Deciding that the problem lay in the word "socialism," he launched a new campaign to change our name. This plunged us into months of meetings, with arguments and counterarguments in the *Yankee Radical*. Glenn's proposal came before our national convention, where it went down to defeat in committee. So we remained the Democratic Socialists of America. Some members argued that our middle name was the only identity we had.

From the walls of the Workmen's Circle meeting room, grave, bearded, Yiddish-speaking socialists stared down on us. Their pictures haunted me with a sensation of unworthiness. How could we—laboring through another sparsely attended forum on the latest crisis in foreign policy or the organization's mission and vision, before repairing to a local bar for nachos and beer—carry the torch that had once been the light of hope for millions? We were linked in solidarity with great names, and one of them was still alive when I joined. I had written for Irving Howe's magazine, *Dissent*, and revered him as a writer and an intellectual. But there was something daunting in his politics, the kind he'd been practicing since Truman was President. His elegiac and severe voice, which after a lifetime of defeats qualified nearly every assertion, made a terrible demand: we had to "grapple with fragments of a tradition," he wrote in *Socialism and America*, while engaging "with the needs of the moment, struggling for betterment in matters large and small, reforms major and modest." At the same time he insisted on the importance of keeping alive an idea of "utopia," which he described in an article just before his death as "run[ning] like a bright thread through American intellectual life . . . a claim for the value of desire, the practicality of yearning—as against the deadliness of acquiescing in the 'given' simply because it is here."

So we had to be passionate and sober, pragmatic and visionary, skeptical and resilient. We had to endure our own insignificance without the prospect of a millennium. It was a very hard faith.

At least Howe's mix of dyspepsia and utopia came out of a period, the 1930s, when socialism meant something more than Victor Berger Night, our holiday beer-tasting fund-raiser named after the co-founder of the Social Democratic Party and first socialist congressman, to whom my grandfather had paid tribute upon Berger's retirement from the House. I read Howe's 1982 autobiography, *A Margin of Hope* (which offered, as always, some hope but more margin), and wrote him to express my envy of his radical youth. He wrote back (he always did; it was part of the faith), "Since you know what I'm going to say, what can I say? Only this: We have to make do with the best we can. We all know DSA isn't what it should be . . . but we have to stick it out for the long haul. Yes, some passion would be good, but the passion of the 30's was often of the wrong kind . . . We have to stick to it as long as we can."

He had known my parents when he was a visiting scholar at Stanford, during the year of my father's agony at the end of the 1960s, and when my father died he wrote my mother a letter. "I felt that it was the mere play of circumstance that kept us from being good friends—distance," Howe wrote of my father. "I felt always a strong admiration for him, and it seems so unjust that he should have been denied the years that should have been his." His letter ended with almost the same tone and message that he used with me twenty years later: "There is in these matters nothing finally to do but bear them—and yet, how easy to say and how hard to do."

I first met Howe in the mid-1980s when he accepted an article of mine for *Dissent*. It was characteristic that he gave me his home number and told me to call collect if I wanted to discuss the article. A few weeks later he was lecturing on Emerson at Harvard, and I went to hear him. What I remember best about the lecture was his allusion to what Emerson called some human or divine principle of leveling. "I have spent my life looking for that principle," he said in a voice that mixed cultivation and Bronx, "and I must confess that so far it has eluded me."

Afterward I went up, my self-serving eagerness somewhat dampened by the brilliance of what he'd just said, and introduced myself. "You're Herb Packer's son?" this tall white-haired man said. Behind lenses, his eyes moistened. "It gives me an eerie feeling to see you standing here."

It gave me an eerie feeling to see him sitting there. He was enough like my own father to fit the part of father figure—Jewish, intensely intellectual, driven by work, a bit remote. But there was also this difference, that Howe was connected to a movement, and this movement in turn connected him to historical events, to organizations around the world, to a magazine, to a community of like-minded people, to a passionate cause. In other words, he was a socialist, while my father had been a liberal, without the bloody history, the utopian future, the international brotherhood, the quarterly magazine. In a way I felt that this was why Howe had survived into his seventies. I only saw him once a year or so and never for more than an hour, but it was his respect I wanted more than anyone's, and he became the nearest thing I've ever had to a mentor.

I once heard him speak at a DSA national convention. The Berlin Wall had fallen that week. A few months before, the organization's founder and chairman, Michael Harrington, had died, and whether the organization would meaningfully survive his death was a real question. Howe, stooped and white-maned and weary, gave a gloomy, chiding speech in which he told the gathered democratic socialists that they had two years to reconstruct their organization, two years of hard work to turn themselves into the experts on social policy, the tireless activists and writers that Harrington had been, or else DSA would become a collection of nice, irrelevant people who liked to get together once a year or so. Then he took questions. I had one. I pointed out that socialism had been in decline since before I was born—since before *he* was born. Why did it have only two more years to decline?

"You know," Howe replied with a sly smile, "I ask the same thing about myself. You decline, and decline, and then one day you just stop."

Three years later he stopped, and the bright thread frayed a little more.

Every year I announced that someone else would have to put out the newsletter. But no one came forward, and I would find myself doing it for another year. This was my contribution: calling Comrade Tom on Wednesday to remind him that I needed his article on post–Cold War foreign policy by the weekend; then Sunday evening trying to lay the thing out on a borrowed or rented Macintosh; a trip to the printer, who was always angry about something and sounded like a Limbaugh dittohead but whom we were stuck with because there were no other union printers left in Boston; and then a long evening of folding and labeling with the other diehards, hoping that the membership got the mailing in time for our next forum on single-payer health care.

We moved out of our small office near the train station to an even smaller corner of a room near Fenway Park. Then we moved again, to a desk in a Cambridge church basement. Each time we moved, we had to haul halfway across town boxes and file drawers loaded with multiple copies of reasonable and enlightened position papers on the Panama Canal and the Reagan tax cuts. During one move, I put down the box I was carrying up a flight of stairs and started to laugh. The failure of socialism was killing my back. Then I thought of throwing out some of the papers. But that would have meant more work, and there would have to be a discussion first.

Still, I couldn't bring myself to quit. One voice told me that the flame had died out and I was wasting my years; another told me that quitting would be a betrayal of—something . . . the just society, a century of belief, Irving Howe, my "comrades." There's an odor of opportunism in such calculations. It's difficult to be an American and not worship success, to accept a permanent place on the losing side. The Lost Cause of my grandfather's South and the "No is always right" of his politics sound a strange minor chord in the national victory song. Sometimes I suspected that in Howe's and others' stoicism the lonely dissenter was made into a fetish, his chore glamorized. Having been brought up to lose in politics, I might even have shared this fetish (the honor of noble defeat in such company!), but I didn't care to spend my whole life in the margin. I wanted to be on the side of history at least for a while, and when Clinton was elected in 1992—the first Democratic President since I was eight years old if you don't count Jimmy Carter, which is easy to do—I and others in the organization wondered if the moment hadn't come.

One member wrote in *Dissent* that the new President was quite possibly "a stealth social democrat." This suspicion became increasingly difficult to entertain, but when you've spent your adult life with your eyes trained on the long distance, vision suffers. These dilemmas aren't easy to negotiate. You don't want to be seduced into vulgar accommodation; you don't want to stiffen into an opposition that's indistinguishable from death.

Our hard-earned irony sustained us and also crippled us. Ardor has seen generations of revolutionaries through seasons of obscurity and, worse, has fostered the delusion that they were the vanguard of historical necessity. The Maoist cashier sits behind the register of Revolution Books waiting for the dictatorship of the proletariat to arrive, like the shtetl Jew who's hired to keep watch for the Messiah and who, when asked how he can tolerate the low pay, replies that at least the work is steady. We had no messianic delusions. We kept our faith at the pace of gradualism, helped defeat a state tax rollback, joined a picket line of hospital workers. But anything that burns low and slow risks going out. And one winter evening, as a board meeting bogged down over the question of roast chicken versus Indonesian noodles for our Debs-Thomas fund-raising dinner, I looked at the faces of my comrades around the table and knew I was going to leave them.

"Our solidarity is not great enough," Isaac Rosenfeld wrote in "The Party," his 1947 story about his generation of socialists. "Again I should like to feel it strong about me, embracing us all with a love that is not in politics."

An organization becomes its own reason: what its members have in the end is one another. Maybe this was why we exhausted ourselves trying to prolong our existence for another year: we didn't want to lose what bound us together. Thinking back on the oddities and futilities, I also remember the bonds. I still send in my dues and sometimes ask myself whether I should go back. Unbelievably, what I miss most are the meetings.

The longing persists—call it socialism, community, the Beloved Republic. For Irving Howe it was "as needed by mankind as bread and shelter." Orwell felt the same way: "[E]specially since the French Revolution, the Western world has been haunted by the idea of freedom and equality . . . Nearly everyone, whatever his actual conduct may be, responds emotionally to the idea of human brotherhood."

We are learning to live without the word. Born in the eighteenth century, did the idea die in the twentieth? Or has it only been suppressed, deformed in our time into the motivational speaker, the cyber-community, the fact that we all watch *Who Wants to Be a Millionaire* at the same hour? In the age of capitalism's triumph over every other ism, we see its excesses, we might even object to its injustices, but we no longer have anything to set against it. For seven years I labored in the ruins of an idea that had once been associated with giants—Eugene Debs and Big Bill Haywood and Mother Jones—an idea that had once had the power to attract millions. No idea has risen to take socialism's place—and yet it's clear how badly Americans could use one. Every year wealth and power grow more concentrated, the blessings of the unregulated market less equal. But we've had to accept it as inevitable, like continental drift or tooth decay. The irony is that just when we need a serious challenge to global corporate capitalism, the old beliefs are discredited and the energy for new ones spent. People all over the world now cling to personal hope in the market's power to change their lives without a larger collective hope of transformation. If we're going to be saved, we will be saved separately, at a profit.

The end of the socialist idea, which endured for almost two centuries, has not been much remarked on in this country, where it never burned as brightly as elsewhere. But taking that idea in its broadest sense, as a vision of human brotherhood and a just society, we are all the poorer for its death. With nothing to replace it, each of us is left alone to acquiesce in the given—or else find the will to answer in a new way the old question: What are we to do?

◆

CHAPTER 13

Birmingham Dreams

I like to believe that Birmingham will one day become a model in southern race relations," Martin Luther King wrote in 1963, "that the negative extremes of Birmingham's past will resolve into the positive and utopian extreme of her future; that the sins of a dark yesterday will be redeemed in the achievements of a bright tomorrow."

Birmingham is an unlikely place to go looking for utopia. To most of the country, the city ceased to exist after the spring of 1963, when Bull Connor turned the dogs and fire hoses on black children and my uncle George defended it all in the House of Representatives. The instant the pictures were snapped (a *Life* photographer named Charles Moore took the most famous ones) Birmingham was branded in the heat of the flash, and again four months later in the dynamite blast at the Sixteenth Street Baptist Church. People in Birmingham, even— especially—those who regret its history, still say, "If it just wasn't for those pictures . . ." Because no one who thinks of the city can think of anything other than those pictures.

What's happened off-camera since 1963 is that Birmingham has joined the American mainstream, and the American mainstream has joined Birmingham. Birmingham has a black mayor, a rotting urban core, and an economic gold rush in the white suburbs—a prosperous Sunbelt metropolis, devoted as ever to the gaining of wealth but without the harder edges of its notorious years. In a sense, Birmingham has become a picture of the American future—which might make it an even unlikelier candidate for utopia than the industrial hell of the early century or the bigotry showcase of the 1960s ever was.

I didn't go to Birmingham in search of utopia. I went, several times over the last couple of years, in search of George Huddleston. And yet each time I went down there I kept meeting people and hearing stories that made Birmingham seem a place of strange dreams and dreamers—as if all the horrors that defied American optimism, convict lease and the Robert E. Lee Klavern No. 1, the labor wars and race hatreds that gave everything ugly about America its ugliest face, had incubated a counterspirit that couldn't thrive in a more rational and progressive city. It showed up like a fever in people's eyes when they called a vacant urban lot "sacred ground" or used the word "broken" as a term of admiration. It caught the voice of a man named Dennis Johnson, a former crack addict and van driver for Health Care for the Homeless, when he described how he moved to Birmingham from Cleveland with his girlfriend and her five kids, proposed marriage, confided his addiction to her, and in a matter of hours found himself living in the Jimmie Hale Mission. "When I hit this city I didn't have anybody to fall back on, nobody to go to," he told me, his eyes burning. "It was the best thing that could ever happen to me. I knew there had to be a reason for being in Birmingham. When I became homeless I had to put myself in someone else's hands."

This counterspirit is not concerned with a change of laws or social structures so much as a change of heart. It is at bottom religious, and as we became acquainted it put a quite direct challenge to me and my liberalism.

Birmingham invented white flight, a black activist told me, and you can literally see it from the air. As your plane circles for landing, the city's grid of streets and avenues stretches flat along the east-west rail-road lines for miles in all directions except south. There, Red Mountain, the exhausted iron-ore ridge that once provided minerals for the pig-iron and steel mills, rises up from the city's South Side. The mills are exhausted, too, their smokestacks rust along the train tracks, their furnaces and chutes stand idle, and the Sloss-Sheffield Mill on First Avenue has been turned into an industrial museum. Even Vulcan, god of fire and the forge, is exhausted, his 55-foot, 100-ton statue that has loomed over the city since 1938 now closed to visitors, threatening to fall from its pedestal, in desperate need of repair. The ridge of Red Mountain marks the dividing wall between the city and its southern suburbs. To its north is Birmingham, now over 60 percent black, its schools over 90 percent black. South Side, where my grandparents lived, where my mother spent twenty-one years in the house on Rhodes Circle, is mostly poor-white and black; for years the deteriorating house was posted for sale.

Take a drive around Birmingham and you see decay on an extravagant, almost picturesque scale. The old workers' cottages of Ensley—once a white section, now all-black, where Tennessee Coal and Iron, later U.S. Steel, had a huge mill—seem to sag with the humidity, roofs caving in, front porches crumbling. Across the city in Woodlawn I drove along streets behind the railroad tracks where the houses were so overgrown with trees and vines that I assumed they were abandoned until I noticed a white man standing in a front doorway with his arms crossed, returning my stare. Downtown: a few corporate towers, a glass extension to the public library, a civic center, and the University of Alabama in Birmingham with its huge medical center; also, shuttered theaters and department stores (the ones the 1963 protests desegregated) and a general air of abandonment. The whole area empties out at 5 p.m. weekdays, and on weekends there's a melancholy heaviness downtown. Each time I walked over to Kelly Ingram Park, the battleground of the 1963 demonstrations was populated by an integrated scattering of winos stretched out on the grass near commemorative and not very subtle statues of police dogs and water cannons and black children. "His dream liberated Birmingham from itself," says the tribute beneath a statue of Martin Luther King, diagonally across from the twin cupolas of the Sixteenth Street Baptist Church. What Birmingham seems to have been liberated into is ordinary urban neglect.

But south of the city, "over the mountain," a suburban boom is in full swing. In the 1960s, after the civil rights battles were largely over, the dynamiting of churches and houses ended and the dynamiting of Red Mountain began. A hole was blasted in the iron-ore ridge, and a highway was built through it heading south out of the city, and thousands of whites poured down into towns with names like Vestavia Hills and Cahaba Heights. Between 1960 and 1990 Birmingham went from 40 to 60 percent black while its population shrank by 75,000. During that period the five nearest suburbs over the mountain grew by the same number—with a black population of about 3 percent. Every time I return to Birmingham and drive the corridor of Highway 280, another hilltop development is going up. "The Summit: A Grand New View of Shopping—51 Days to Go." This is one of the fastest-growing areas of the South, and people are moving here from all over the country. Suddenly poor benighted Alabama is offering the good life for those who can pay—far cheaper than on either coast, and without the stain of Jim Crow. Shopping malls and corporate headquarters and country clubs and subdivisions and Protestant churches keep spreading southward along 280 like an oil spill, all the way out of Jefferson into Shelby County, where the Appalachian chain peters out and where George Huddleston once bought 50,000 apparently useless acres of scrub-pine hills.

I went to Birmingham looking for my grandfather, but he was hardly to be found. No government office or street had been named after him, no monument put up, no plaque declaring, "He didn't bring home much bacon but his oratory confounded the forces of plutocracy and imperial power." No one in Birmingham had even heard of him— sixty years was too long ago for anyone except highly political octogenarians and surviving family members. The Birmingham Public Library had managed to lose a part of his memory when one of the scrapbooks compiled by my grandmother and donated for microfilming by my aunt A. J. disappeared. And his papers were long gone. A quarter century's life in national politics had left not one single piece of physical evidence, except the granite gravestone saying "George Huddleston 1869–1960/Member of Congress/1915–37." I imagined him lying with a tight-jawed, open-eyed frown, next to my grandmother's and Uncle George's graves in Elmwood Cemetery, which is surrounded on all sides by the streets and shacks of a black neighborhood.

If George Huddleston's legacy lies anywhere, it's not in downtown Birmingham or Elmwood Cemetery but out in those scrub-pine hills down in Shelby County, where he's made a posthumous contribution to his family's and his country's future.

He had bought the land when he retired from law practice in 1911, with no apparent purpose other than to be lord of his own domain, his Jeffersonian fifty-acre constitutional allotment multiplied by a thousand. After his defeat in 1936 he sold all but 4,000 acres and used the proceeds to buy several downtown buildings for rental income to live on (there were no congressional pensions in those days). With the remaining land he did exactly nothing, except on weekends he drove along his dirt roads and looked at his pine trees and took in the vistas of ridgelines through the humid haze. He allowed hillbilly squatters to live there, including an old woman who kept a pack of semi-wild dogs. Characteristically, my grandfather gave Dog Woman the legal right to stay on the land until her death. This meant that when the land finally came under development, thirty years after George Huddleston's death, cemeteries all over Alabama had to be checked for proof that his sole legal tenant was dead and title to the land clear. Unfortunately no one knew her real name, but a relative was finally tracked down who was willing to confirm that Dog Woman had indeed passed on.

When development came, it happened full-bore. By the time I started visiting Birmingham, George Huddleston's land was well on its way to becoming "Highland Lakes, an Eddleman community." An Alabama developer had gone into partnership with the Huddleston family and was building hundreds of houses in the pine and oak woods around four man-made lakes stocked with bass. These houses had grand arched entrances and gleaming kitchens with walnut cabinets, and they were selling for three or four hundred thousand dollars, and the business and professional classes of Greater Birmingham were starting to buy them up. My grandfather's useless acres had turned into the area's hottest piece of real estate a half-hour drive from the city (which had given the developer a concession on sewage). At the end of the entrance road off Highway 280, formerly a rest stop and scenic overlook, stood a twenty-four-hour security booth. This was my grandfather's legacy, his children's and grandchildren's inheritance, the potential source of my own children's education. The "little Bolsheviki" had bequeathed to the future an upscale gated community.

No matter that George Huddleston, in his frayed shirtsleeves, would have taken one look at the showy homes under construction in "Highland Glen" and "Highland Manor" and spat, "Quit posturing." No matter that most of his children and grandchildren, even in politically inhospitable places like Albertville, Alabama, kept calling themselves liberals and trying to act that way (one of my cousins said that George Huddleston's progeny accounted for half the remaining white liberals in Alabama). No matter that Highland Lakes was, the excess of its architectural styles apart, an ecologically sound and picturesque development, or that a sizable fraction of home sales were going to black buyers. It was just one more irony that my grandfather's property should be developed progressively in every way except class. The people buying lots on his land were the people who had tried to have him beaten in 1918. This was the face of American prosperity at the end of the twentieth century: racially tolerant, environmentally conscious, and determined to wall itself off from the low-paid countrymen who cut its grass and wait on its tables and look after its children. If you want a picture of what Christopher Lasch called "the revolt of the elites," you only have to visit Highland Lakes, or the hundreds of communities like it going up all over the country.

I went to Birmingham looking for my grandfather and instead I found a moral irony.

On visits I stayed at the suburban house of my aunt Alice Jeanne, whom everyone calls A. J. She had been one of my mother's best friends in high school, and through my mother had met and married my uncle George. After his congressional defeat in 1964 George refused to set foot again in the state that had dealt him such a blow, but he was taken back there to be buried in 1971 and A. J. decided to return home with their three children. In Washington they had been a cocktail-partying political couple, but within a few years of widowhood my aunt became a born-again Christian.

"George, the New Deal failed," she said to me within hours of my arrival, smiling serenely as we sat drinking lemonade on her back terrace and discussing her former father-in-law, "because we humans are a fallen race."

In the mornings I would go downtown to study microfilm at the Birmingham Public Library, and she would go out with her Bible and a bottle of mineral-rich juice to pray with the afflicted—for she was considered by other Christians to be a healer, a prophet of sorts. In the evenings we would sit up late in her living room and talk about the family and Birmingham and the New Testament and Christ. Her shelves were lined with Christian videos and books with titles like *Year 2000: Victory or Defeat*. On her coffee table was a magazine called *Media Bypass* with articles on "FEMA: Blueprint for Tyranny" and the Vince Foster killing. In the last election she had voted for the candidate of the U.S. Taxpayers Party. "Christ was a socialist," I would say to provoke her. But politics was not my aunt's real interest. Her definition of justice was "the total working out of the will of God." She had two interests: her family and her faith. There had been a special connection between my aunt A. J. and me since the summer I worked at the legal-aid office in Mobile and, on a visit to Birmingham, defended her daughter Nancy's honor when her date ignored her at a debutante ball. Almost twenty years later, A. J. was still maternally loving and still quite naturally concerned about my salvation.

I held out little hope for making the leap of faith. All the years of rational training at home had killed the nerves that might have been receptive to religious stimuli. There have been times in my life when I wanted to believe in God, any God, but couldn't bring myself to do it; it would have meant lying. You can't will belief any more than you can will love. Still, I see the appeal of believing that everything happens for a reason, including death. In places like the Deep South, where I feel like an infidel in Mecca, I'm quite susceptible to this appeal. And as I listened to A. J., I began to sense that she and her worldview had something important to tell me—not necessarily about divinity, but about humanity.

She had left the modernizing, liberalizing Episcopal Church ("They're all going to hell anyway") and joined a small splinter congregation in the working-class suburb of Fairfield, run by a militant anti-abortion crusader named Jim Pinto. Once she even spent three hours in a city holding cell after protesting outside a clinic; later she left Operation Rescue when its protests turned ugly. The breakaway church was filled with the Holy Spirit, and its faithful were poor blacks and whites and a few suburbanites like A. J. who wanted the Charismatic experience—speaking in tongues, laying on hands, being "slain in the spirit," things I couldn't begin to understand—and couldn't get it in places like Mountain Brook. She attended similar services elsewhere in Birmingham and even at a revival house that was catching fire down in Pensacola on the Gulf Coast. For purely spiritual reasons—she had no use for the social gospel—she was joining groups of racially and economically mixed Christians, in the heart of the old segregated South, that her secular and liberal relatives knew nothing about.

One night A. J. and I watched a cable television feature on the life of George Wallace. The movie ended with a scene partly based on truth but also embellished: one rainy night in Montgomery, Wallace, out of power, in a wheelchair and despairing, tells his driver to stop outside the Dexter Avenue Baptist Church—Martin Luther King's old parish, a spiritual fortress of the civil rights era. The all-black congregation falls silent as the ex-governor, who once declared "Segregation now, segregation tomorrow, segregation forever," wheels his way up the aisle and turns at the altar to speak. What he says essentially is: Forgive me. And they do. They forgive him because they are Christians. And the choir bursts into "Amazing Grace," and as the congregation sings, Wallace wheels his way back down the aisle, and black hands reach out to shake his white hands, and on the sofa next to me my aunt A. J., whose husband had opposed the 1964 Civil Rights Bill, was singing, "I once was lost but now am found," and there were tears in her eyes.

I felt the strangest pang of envy. I couldn't have articulated it at the time, but what I discovered in that moment was the moral force of the evangelical tradition. This force is not based on a human idea of justice or rights, but on love, divine love. It appeals to emotion, not reason. It has no faith in man's ability to work out his own destiny and all faith in God's plan. It has existed in America since the beginning, a kind of countertradition to the one that stretched from the Enlightenment and Jefferson forward into the twentieth century, the liberal tradition that my grandfather and parents believed in. Jefferson himself edited the Gospels into a moral argument called *The Philosophy of Jesus* and regarded most Christian sects as imposing "artificial systems" of belief ("the Trinity, original sin, atonement") onto a man he called "this benevolent Moralist." He dismissed the "bigotry and fanaticism which have so long triumphed over human reason" and predicted that "the present generation will see Unitarianism become the general religion of the United States." In fact, Unitarianism was being crushed under the wave of the evangelical movement known as the Second Great Awakening. Jefferson the rationalist couldn't grasp its emotional power; but Jefferson the author of Virginia's "Bill for Establishing Religious Freedom" indirectly made it possible.

Aunt A. J. was the family's only link to that countertradition—to "Amazing Grace," a song written by an English slave trader named John Newton, who found God aboard a slave ship in a storm during the Atlantic crossing and became a minister. The story and the song are the reigning texts of evangelical Christianity: the conversion experience, the prostration of self ("a wretch like me"), the surrender to God. The Second Great Awakening of the early nineteenth century (the First took place in the mid-eighteenth) made religious revival a social force, especially in the South. Evangelicalism was a movement of the common people, and weeklong camp meetings in the woods gave the humble participants an emotionally charged sense of community as brothers and sisters in Christ, based on equality before the Creator without social hierarchies:

Of rich and poor the difference what?—
In working or in working not
Why then on Sunday we're as great
As those who own some vast estate.

In the South there were integrated meetings of poor whites and blacks, until southern evangelicalism turned respectable and established authority co-opted it. Eventually the white southern Baptists split off to form their own denomination in explicit defense of slavery. The southern evangelical turn toward the slaveholding social order had long-term consequences, both theological and political. White southern Christianity became less rebellious, less critical, more willing to leave matters in the hands of God and the temporal powers, more focused on sin than on mercy. But in the North the abolitionist movement was evangelical in origin; and a century later the black civil rights movement drew on evangelical Christianity for its songs, its imagery, its communal passions and moral arguments. King himself constantly mingled the liberal democratic and evangelical Christian creeds. "If we are wrong, the Constitution of the United States is wrong. If we are wrong, God Almighty is wrong!"

These days, evangelical Christians in places like Birmingham talk about a Third Great Awakening. Revival meetings are breaking out all over the South. These Christians are reclaiming the biracial mantle that southern evangelicalism dropped early in the nineteenth century, and they are doing it with amazing energy. They use words like "brotherhood" that no one else dares to utter. Through Christ, they believe, every social division can be overcome. Evangelical Christianity was an unlikely movement to investigate after my years in democratic socialism: two venerable belief systems, they seemed to be polar opposites. One looked to history and society for its explanation of human problems, the other to divinity and the soul. One took people as a mass, the other "one by one from the inside out." One shared certain fundamentals with liberalism, the other was foreign to it. But what they had in common was this: both were essentially morality tales, exceptions to the dominant American story of materialistic individualism. Both offered what Americans at the end of the twentieth century glaringly lacked and fitfully craved: a vision of community.

Perhaps because I sensed that my own liberal tradition had at some point during my lifetime run out of moral energy, and that the worst thing in this situation would be a closed mind, and the best might be exposure to an utterly alien world, I was willing to follow the stirring that night at A. J.'s wherever it led.

It led through a looking glass that reversed all the usual political expectations, into a handful of Birmingham's 1,300 churches (which fill sixteen pages of the Greater Birmingham Yellow Pages), into its most notorious housing project, and then back up to some of the more violent streets in Boston, and finally onto the National Mall in Washington, where almost a million men converged to make some very public promises, and where this particular road ended for me.

In 1974 a twenty-year-old black man from the Birmingham projects named Gerald Austin, whose mother had raised nine children on welfare, who had lived through school desegregation, whose street name was "Bull," who hated white people, and who had a job at Texas Instruments in Dallas, was getting high with a group of friends and working on a high-tech device that would allow drug-carrying planes to elude the border patrol's radar, when God hit him with a blinding light. It was the kind of "conversion experience" you hear about all the time in evangelical circles. Austin had "an immediate change in my heart," he told me, toward white people and toward God. But it took another sixteen years, and a successful career in corporate sales, before he met a white lawyer from Louisville named Tim Ritchie and decided to start an interracial church in what Martin Luther King had called "the most segregated city in America."

The New City Church was a utopian dream that seemed on its way to becoming a reality until it ran up against human limits. White families from Kentucky and North Carolina and rural Alabama moved to Birmingham and joined middle-class and poor blacks to form what its members called "a family." In a downtown former bank building they dedicated their lives to Christ and, following Christ, to working with tenants of the city's largest and bleakest housing project, formerly all-white, now all-black—Metropolitan Gardens, on the northeastern edge of downtown, housing 3,000 tenants in the country's poorest zip code. The church people "discipled" crack dealers and crack addicts and welfare mothers, they tutored the children, they opened a coffee-machine repair shop that employed ex-cons, they prayed together, and they raised large amounts of money from the city's richest corporations and most conservative suburban churches. It was an "intentional community," in the jargon of the evangelical movement, and an intense one, and it overturned a number of my assumptions about religion and politics in our time.

Start with Tim Ritchie. By the time I met him—in Boston, where he was earning a master's degree in public administration—he had spent most of the 1990s working with the black poor in Birmingham. So it came as a mild shock when, several conversations into our friendship, he described himself as a conservative Republican. Sandy-haired, freckled, soft-spoken, before cofounding the New City Church he was a lawyer in Birmingham's most right-wing firm, defending anti-abortion cases. He served on the Alabama commission that helped dismantle the state welfare system. But tenants at Metropolitan Gardens spoke of him as a brother. "I said to myself, this is a broken man,"

Angie Williams told me—meaning a man whom Jesus had emptied so that the spirit of God could pour in (Jesus broke her on November 20, 1995, and nine days later He broke the father of her child, a former crack dealer who'd just been sprung from jail). White liberals—it was possible to find them in Birmingham, but they seemed isolated and beleaguered—talked about Tim Ritchie and the New City Church as a front for insidious conservative political forces. But this is just the kind of argument for which the evangelicals have a sharp answer.

"I have found that religious conservatives in Birmingham are much more willing to engage in this hand to hand, one to one," Ritchie told me. "At least they're trying. The liberals really just want to send a check. Or they want to change a structure. And I'm telling you, changing a structure is not going to do it by itself. You have to change a heart. The only way to change a heart is you have to walk with them. And I have found that the religious community is more willing to walk than liberals are."

To Ritchie, the evangelical awakening stood not in opposition to the civil rights movement but as an extension of its desire to "change the world for Christ." The "first push," in the 1950s and 1960s, was liberal and political. The "second push," around the election of Reagan in 1980, was conservative and evangelical. I had never considered Martin Luther King and Ronald Reagan as spiritual brothers; and perhaps Ritchie doesn't either, for he's as critical of conservatives—including the Christian Coalition—who are lured by materialism and fail to walk the walk, as he is of armchair liberals.

White southern evangelicals have a lot to answer for. Not only did their churches fail to oppose slavery and segregation when it mattered, they gave theological benediction. When northern white liberals were marching and getting beaten up and sometimes killed alongside southern blacks in the early 1960s, Southern Baptists and Methodists and Presbyterians were justifying the regional caste system or maintaining a prudent silence. In the past few years they have tried to atone. The Southern Baptists, America's largest Protestant denomination, officially apologized for their historical racism, and it was the pastor of the sprawling Shades Mountain Baptist Church outside Birmingham who led the move. The evangelical men's movement called Promise Keepers made "racial reconciliation" a major theme. It was somewhat galling for me to be told by Drayton Nabers, CEO of Protective Life Insurance, friend of my aunt A. J., fellow Charismatic, and benefactor of the New City Church, that conservative Christians had been right about everything except race, and now that they were getting race right, too, secular liberals were left with nothing to call their own.

"Apart from God, give me one reason why I shouldn't be able to mistreat blacks if I want to," he told me in his large office, whose picture windows looked out on the fountain plaza of Protective Life's vast glass corporate headquarters off Highway 280. Racial reconciliation "is the Christian thing to do. It is so clearly the mandate of Christ's teaching." Nabers voted Democratic until McGovern; he had once thought that Johnson's Great Society would end poverty in a generation. "I really vote to this day—and you're going to laugh, George—on which party is best for the poorest. Liberalism is a disaster for the poor. And what one needs to be happy in this world are habits coming from a strong family and discipline instilled since childhood, and that has been destroyed for the poor."

In the world of urban evangelicals it began to seem less strange to find the daughter of Birmingham industrialists, whose entry into politics came via the 1980 Paul Laxalt for President campaign, running a job-training program for welfare mothers. It seemed less strange to meet a young man like Breck Withers: son of a white Kentucky preacher, he read an article in *Urban Family* magazine about an inner-city black minister in Boston, had a "conversion experience," sold his lawn-care business in Lexington, uprooted his wife and three children, and moved a thousand miles to join the minister's church—and still votes reliably Republican. Evangelicals explain their work in terms of the individual and the change of heart. What matters is being willing to "walk the walk." As Rev. Eugene Rivers, a black Pentecostal minister working with gang members in Boston, put it to me: "My thing is, you need God over the long haul or you ain't gonna make it. You've got liberals suffering from compassion fatigue because they're exhausted. You ain't got Jesus, you ain't getting up at six in the morning." He looked at me pointedly, though not accusingly. "There are no liberals in these trenches."

For the time being, I was prepared to suspend my doubt about whether you really did need to be a conservative evangelical to get up at six and do what Tim Ritchie and Gerald Austin and Breck Withers and Eugene Rivers do. I was interested in them because they possessed something undeniable, often missing in people with the best will in the world, something that can't be summoned on demand: vitality. Their belief gave them the energy to persist in the face of daunting experience.

Except that they don't always persist. They're human, and there's such a thing as evangelical fatigue, and it seemed to have struck the New City Church in Birmingham. White families were trickling away in noticeable numbers. What had begun as a utopian community dedicated to "Reformation Restoration Reconciliation" became a 750-thousand-dollar-a-year operation with a strong—some said autocratic—leader in Gerald Austin, placing a heavy emphasis on discipline and sins like teenage pregnancy and drug use. The devil was ever-present at a place like Metropolitan Gardens. Kenny and Angie Williams kept using the word "Enemy," and when I finally asked whom they meant she said incredulously, "Aren't you acquainted with him?" But a white church member told me that white families were beginning to feel "like missionaries" at the New City Church.

It turned out that racial-unity-through-Christ was hard-won and could be lost again. What one member called "the trump cards of race and religion" could turn any personal dispute, professional disagreement, or theological debate into a matter of racism and blasphemy. "You think you know, but you don't know what it's like," black members could tell whites. "It's turning into a black church," white members could tell blacks. But most of it went unsaid, in the imperative interest of family unity and Christian fellowship. The effort to create a community of believers seemed to build in its own demise. Austin's authority was partly based on the authenticity of his experience—he knew what kind of discipline residents at the housing project needed, because he'd grown up in one—but it couldn't be questioned without a rift. The white families were leaving, and the church was undergoing a financial meltdown. Corporate donors had moved on to other charities, the church had saddled itself with a huge mortgage, and it was delinquent on property and withholding taxes. One of my visits coincided with this crisis. God might have changed Gerald Austin's heart toward white people in 1974, but he was still a black man living in the American South, still must have felt he had much to lose and little to gain by trusting this white writer from out of town, and he avoided me as if I were an IRS agent—even seemed disturbed that I was talking to members of his congregation.

So I decided to go to church. I went downtown one Sunday with my aunt, who was a friend of the Austins. There were about a hundred people in the sanctuary on the ground floor of the New City Church, a dozen of them white, including four families. I felt vaguely sinful for counting. Everyone around me, including my aunt, was swaying and singing, "This is the day that the Lord has made, I will rejoice and be glad in it," and I was taking a racial census. I was thinking instead of feeling. My human brain seemed opposed to the will of the church. I was certain to be discovered and cast out.

Then Gerald Austin came to the pulpit and faced the congregation—a bearded, tall, imposing man in a suit. His voice resonated through the sanctuary.

"Last Thursday we learned our teenage daughter is pregnant. And it rocked our world. It's not the pregnancy that matters but the sin, the fornication, the sex outside marriage. Our hearts are broken. I stand here a broken pastor, a broken man of God."

His wife stood alongside him looking truly heartbroken. She too spoke, saying she'd rather not bring out their dirty laundry but it was necessary to be honest with the family of the church. The daughter was brought forward along with her boyfriend, both staring down, and the microphone was passed to them and in barely audible voices they confessed their sin and asked forgiveness, the girl crying, the boy looking stricken.

Grandmothers came to the pulpit, and children, and then members of the congregation including whole families, and soon the entire church except A. J. and me and a few others were gathered around the Austins, hugging and kissing and blessing the girl, and someone anointed the seed in the name of Jesus, and Austin said, "There will be a baby. We don't believe in abortion or any other 'alternatives' as the world calls them," and the girl was smiling through her tears, and the boy still looked stricken.

While I was still reeling from this drama, which in a matter of minutes had covered the distance from righteous anger and disgrace to acceptance and love, visitors were announced. With dread I got to my feet alongside my aunt. People came over to shake my hand and thanked me for coming and urged me to come back. Benevolent warmth shone on their faces. I felt what I always feel at such moments in a church—gratitude and shame. I had witnessed the power of a tiny Christian community to judge and humiliate, and its power to forgive and embrace. Brotherly love was extended unquestioningly to me, a white stranger who had been allowed to witness the public airing of a private crisis; and I felt like an imposter.

On the northeast corner of downtown Birmingham, City Block 27 is surrounded by a freeway overpass, an old stone church now occupied by Birmingham Health Care for the Homeless, and the brown two-story apartment blocks misleadingly named Metropolitan Gardens, the city's worst public housing project, where mothers don't let their children play outside for fear of gunfire. Block 27 was part of the right-of-way for the Red Mountain Expressway extension, connecting Highway 280 to the interstate that goes to the airport, so that suburbanites arriving from out of town could drive home over the mountain in a straight line without having to circumvent downtown. But tenants objected to having the expressway built through their homes, and the city's black mayor backed them, and so now 280 makes a little jog east around Metropolitan Gardens. This jog left Block 27 vacant and overgrown for several years, until a Birmingham millionaire bought it from the state in 1995 for $377,000 with the idea of turning it into a utopian village.

Jimmy Rushton is a son of the family that founded Protective Life Insurance, a bachelor in his sixties, and a self-described "social reject." He is slightly built, hunched over, squinting through glasses as if life is a perpetual blur. He hardly seems to be living in the physical world; his apartment, say those who know, is a health hazard. When he talks, he seems to be hesitating to use up too much oxygen. Despite the soft southern accent you feel as if you're listening to a character from a nineteenth-century Russian novel, like Prince Myshkin, Dostoyevsky's "Idiot." "He is constantly dealing with ultimate things," a friend of his told me. "Fatal." According to this friend, Rushton—whose family included war heroes and business tycoons and trustees of Birmingham-Southern College, my mother's alma mater—was "never successful at anything in his life."

One day, at the rock bottom of his existence during his forties, when he felt he had utterly failed everyone, including his parents and God, Rushton had a nervous breakdown. "I let go of everything for ten or twelve seconds, or twenty seconds, or however long it was," he told me as we stood in the sunlight on the sidewalk outside Metropolitan Gardens. "And I didn't fall off the end of the earth. There was still ground to land on. And I realized if you let go of everything there's still solid ground under existence, very solid. I saw God with the awful burden I'd let him carry, and God was going down over the horizon like the sun. But then God appeared on the other side of the world behind me, without the burden. And I thought: This is wonderful. And if it's true for me, it must be true for everyone in the world."

It wasn't, strictly speaking, a Christian vision; he isn't an orthodox believer of any kind. "No sandals, no toga, no beard—and I was glad, really, because it seemed universal, it didn't just happen to me but to us."

After that, Jimmy Rushton seemed to figure out what he wanted to do. His moment of enlightenment had made the millionaire failure feel that all human beings, especially the lowest, were his brothers and sisters. It didn't occur to him that people living in a place like Metropolitan Gardens could be any different from him. "I wanted to work with people defined as the hard-core unemployed. Because I figured they had exactly my mentality, exactly my limitations. And I had managed my way through the worst of that, and I figured if I could do it anybody could." He had dropped out of architecture school without ever finishing his thesis, but now he decided to write one on his own. It was called "A Planned Mutual-Support Village Community," and it envisioned all the other social rejects, addicts and homeless and mentally ill, living and working and playing and getting help in a Rushton-financed world within the larger, harsher world of Birmingham.

But once he bought Block 27, his "sacred ground," he scaled back his dream: the vacant lot would house centers for child care and the elderly, shops, job-training offices, a teaching restaurant, small-business enterprises, an auditorium, and a community garden. It would provide everything that residents of Metropolitan Gardens—a place that almost everyone else, including the tenants themselves, wanted to shut down and leave behind—needed to help one another lead productive lives. The mission was to "transform the community of Metropolitan Gardens into a neighborhood characterized by strong families, intellectual and educational development opportunity, economic vitality, spiritual strength, safety and beauty." Half a dozen blocks from the New City Church, another utopian vision was incubating.

But it was clear when I visited that the "Planned Mutual-Support Village Community" was having trouble being born. Rushton's foundation had a staff of six, including a recovering drug addict, a retired social worker, a former Reagan-Bush volunteer, and Tim Ritchie, who had left the social-service arm of the New City Church to become Rushton's executive director. But Ritchie moved on, and Block 27 remained an overgrown lot with a small vegetable garden at one end. The job-readiness program was training half a dozen young mothers on welfare how to dress for a job interview and keep their tempers around a boss, but a good deal of the instructors' energy was going into finessing conflicts with the clients themselves. The staff of the New City Church, which had been working with the people at Metropolitan Gardens much longer and with an entirely different theological system ("obedience under duress," Jimmy Rushton called it), seemed to regard the white and wealthy newcomers on their turf as amateur do-gooders. A vision of universal human connectedness and five million dollars weren't enough by themselves to create a new community.

Two years later, when I went back to Birmingham and drove past Metropolitan Gardens, Block 27 was still a vacant lot.

In my travels with urban evangelicals and other dreamers, a sort of chicken-and-egg riddle kept coming up. Over lunch in Cambridge, Tim Ritchie put it this way: "Structural change is no good if you don't have change of hearts; change of hearts are no good if you don't have change of structures." In his essay on Dickens, George Orwell wrote almost the same thing: "Two viewpoints are always tenable: The one, how can you improve human nature until you have changed the system? The other, what is the use of changing the system before you have improved human nature?"

Talk of changing hearts is often heard by liberals as the smug sanctimony of the comfortable, making themselves feel virtuous while keeping their incomes steady. But the change of hearts isn't pious hypocrisy. A system of laws and institutions decays if the people living in it feel nothing for one another. The main political thought of the urban evangelicals I met is that the laws and programs of the federal government have not created justice because they left the human heart unchanged. Liberalism failed because it relied on human reason instead of faith. My father's politics could not explain why people should care about one another. Two centuries after Jefferson, the evangelicals were offering their own version of "sympathy": the way to transform the world is to transform people's hearts with the love of God. Law can force a department store to let black people work there, but law can't force the white store owner to love black people. "But if you believe," Drayton Nabers, the corporate CEO, told me, "that a brother, white or black, was created by God in God's image with a soul, then an entirely different ethical construct comes about and it is only that construct that is going to save Western society."

No one was talking about getting rid of civil rights law, but most evangelicals were prepared to reject the main insight of twentieth-century American politics, that the federal government must intervene to alleviate suffering where people can't help themselves. Instead, they believed, the government has destroyed true community in the name of a forced community of taxation and entitlement. Welfare is everyone's favorite example. Aid to Families with Dependent Children was a minor piece of the Social Security Act that my grandfather had voted against on states' rights grounds. Originally intended to help widows and their children, as illegitimate births soared in the 1960s welfare became the prime conservative example of wrongheaded big government and liberal do-goodism destroying the family and undermining the work ethic. In Alabama, AFDC didn't provide much incentive to do either, paying out $164 a month for a mother with two children, second lowest in the country. To survive on welfare in Alabama, everyone involved in the system said, you had to lie. Yet people spoke of it as a form of slavery. When he finally agreed to talk to me, Gerald Austin, who had grown up on welfare, said, "I despised welfarism and the evils of welfare—the servitude—the attitudes of my mother and the people in the agency."

In these terms, welfare reform is emancipation. As it happened, I was in Birmingham the year after the Personal Responsibility Act was signed into law with a stroke of Bill Clinton's pen. I had a chance to see up close the early response of a range of people—evangelicals, businessmen, social workers, and those on welfare—to the most drastic change in domestic legislation since the 1960s, maybe since the 1930s. In Alabama the welfare rolls had already been cut by half. The end of the federal guarantee seemed like a test case for the riddle about the change of structure and the change of heart. In theory, once you got rid of a bad government program, you would be able to see the human heart at work. All the compassion that welfare had stunted would flourish. People would help the poor out of love, not because of a federal mandate. And out of this effort a true community would have a chance to grow.

There was one problem: everyone admitted that churches like Gerald Austin's and private organizations like Jimmy Rushton's could never pick up the slack that the government had let slip. And the state was barely spending half the federal money it had received for welfare-to-work programs. "Alabama's just not really the state where you'd want to develop model social programs without some kind of federal supervision," a man in social services told me dryly. "We still have kind of a harshness toward helping other folks in our personalities." This meant that by and large the poor would be on their own. Opinion differed whether this was a good thing. Poor people themselves, at Metropolitan Gardens and in other neighborhoods, all basically told me that some people would be helped by being put to work, others would be hurt.

Take the example of Lee Sanders, and what she understated as her "dilemma." On a sweltering September afternoon I visited her sparse one-story house in the black neighborhood of Ensley, in the shadow of the old U.S. Steel plant, where she was looking after the six of her nine children who still lived at home. Her husband, once an employee at U.S. Steel, had long since abandoned the family for a heroin habit, sending Lee and her children into a free fall from lower-middle-class security to near-desperation. The fall accelerated when, four months before my visit, she received a letter from the Alabama Department of Human Resources saying that her check was being cut off under the new welfare rules. In spite of prior warnings she was completely unprepared. At forty-four, she told me, she suffered from high blood pressure, blackouts and headaches, and felt "confused—I'm looking at you and I see you but you're like in a haze." She spoke softly and pleasantly and with candor and a trace of understandable self-pity. There was something placid and passive about her that made her seem too beaten down to go back to work now, regardless of whether her health would allow it. Her social worker was counseling her to apply for disability as a last resort.

We talked for two hours as her younger children came and went, and she was affectionate with them and they were polite and playful. "See, I got something to live for. I want to see my kids all grow up, good jobs, married—I want to see all of 'em, I want to see her walk and get her diploma. This is my dream. All of 'em. Nothing comes before my kids." Had welfare made her "dependent"? Quite possible. It was a mean and corrupted system, and the women themselves hated it with a passion, and anyone whose liberal conscience was soothed by its existence didn't know the score. Yet I wondered why society demanded more of Lee Sanders than this: that she raise her kids with love and care.

"People like that would like you to feel sorry for them. She needs to get her a job, even at McDonald's."

I met LaTashia Tubbs, the speaker of this unsentimental assessment, in the job-readiness class that Jimmy Rushton's staff was holding at Metropolitan Gardens. Tashia was half Lee Sanders' age, had one-ninth the children, and was as combative as Lee was phlegmatic. She had grown up in the nearby industrial wasteland of Bessemer, home-town of my grandmother Bertha, who used to complain about the effect on houses and front yards that black families like Tashia's were having in her old neighborhood. Tashia didn't care for Bessemer her-self, and when an apartment opened up at a project with the bucolic name of Metropolitan Gardens she jumped at the chance. "I said: That sounds like a wonderful place!" She quickly discovered other-wise, and after three years there she felt trapped by the violence and inertia. She enrolled in the job-readiness program hungry to start her own housecleaning business for suburban homes and buy her way out of the projects. She had no interest in going to work for anyone else; a job as a motel maid had ended badly when she ran into authority prob-lems with her boss. But the class, according to one of the instructors, was teaching her to control her temper—even on the day I visited, when Tashia's baby had a fever, and she was checking her beeper every minute for her mother's call, and in two days she would attend the funeral of an aunt gunned down in a drive-by.

Tashia's pragmatism was bracing. She expected nothing from the father of her baby, had no interest in marrying him. "I'm young, I have my whole life in front of me. I might meet another man. We can't get married in these projects. I want something of my own, that I can fix up like I want." Her concept of welfare-to-work had nothing to do, though, with shame or self-respect or "personal responsibility." She simply wanted more than the $137 monthly check could get her. She wanted a bed for her baby, a living-room set, wanted to be able to walk into a store and buy what she saw. This was her idea of freedom—this, and getting out of Metropolitan Gardens.

LaTashia Tubbs seemed as ideally suited to leave welfare for work as Lee Sanders seemed disastrously unready. The Rushton job-readiness class was teaching the young women things like business etiquette and dining skills. They were enumerating short-and long-term goals and talking about how hard it is to know oneself. "All of you know you can get a job," one of the instructors said. "But do you want to get a job that's fulfilling? That will change your life and give you the kind of financial return that will make your life better? None of this minimum-wage stuff."

But here was the rub that complicated even a prospect as promising as Tashia's: the fact that, even with unemployment in Birmingham low, wages remained at poverty levels. The Central Alabama United Way released a worksheet that itemized expenses for a single mother of two who went off welfare and took a job at minimum wage. With her loss of benefits and the additional burden of housing, transportation, child care, and health care costs, her yearly income would fall five thousand dollars short of her expenses. For her to meet minimum needs, her wage would have to be $10.35 an hour—out of the question for everyone in the room at the job-readiness class and for most of Birmingham's welfare mothers. Add to this that all the jobs were being created over the mountain in the suburbs, many poor women had no car, greater Birmingham had a primitive bus system, the Alabama constitution of 1901—the one that disfranchised blacks—made it almost impossible to raise income taxes, and a regressive sales-tax initiative stood little chance of passing. So how would the women get to the jobs?

In other words, the change of heart envisioned by welfare reform advocates—dignity in the former recipients, charity from the public, a renewed sense of community in everyone—ran up against fairly resistant structures. Some of the same people who were preaching racial reconciliation through faith in God had no interest in changing those structures. When I suggested a $10-an-hour minimum wage to Drayton Nabers, he suddenly sounded less like a Charismatic Christian than a life insurance executive. "It would cost jobs. The current system does create social problems, but it's essentially fair and has created a higher standard of living than ever before. George," he said, "there is no alternative." He could imagine a nationwide spiritual transformation, but he couldn't imagine a minimum wage higher than $5.15 an hour. Those left behind without welfare checks or viable jobs would have to count on help from neighbors and churches. White evangelicals can continue to work for racial reconciliation, and the end of the welfare entitlement might actually make this easier to achieve. But that leaves the old issue of class unsolved—the issue that Alabama Populists raised a hundred years ago, that dominated my grandfather's career, and that has returned at the end of the century with a new face of injustice and no remedy in sight.

Even the sense of community (as favorite a word among evangelicals as among certain liberals of a public-spirited stripe), which supposedly was destroyed by federal giveaways, seems unlikely to flourish with welfare reform. The women in the job-readiness class had no interest in staying at Metropolitan Gardens. Their ideal was self-sufficiency outside the hell of the city. They wanted their own businesses and homes. They wanted to send their children to private schools. They wanted the American right to withdraw from social problems and exercise purchasing power. They wanted to become individualists. Jimmy Rushton was providing the training for them to abandon the very place where he envisioned a "planned mutual-support village community."

Ken Dupree escaped Birmingham with his wife and two daughters when the New City Church helped this black family find a house in a lower-middle-class, mixed-race suburb called Midfield. He had been a good student and star athlete in high school and college. Then he became a crack addict, and the drug consumed his life. He told me the story as we sat in the stands of old Legion Field and watched a night football game between two black state universities. One night, in a housing project controlled by Bloods where Ken had gone to buy, he fired a gun at a dealer who had "yanked" him—sold him too little. "I was crazy," Ken said. Gang members came after him shooting and chased his car until he got free and drove over the mountain into the safety of white Homewood. He parked and sat behind the wheel looking down at the city with his heart pumping madly and realized he would now have to drive home to his wife and kids as if nothing had happened.

Ken's addiction, which led to numerous periods in jail, became the concern of the church as publicly as the pregnancy of Gerald Austin's teenage daughter. He credited God and the church, especially Austin and Ritchie, for his recovery. Now, what this thoughtful and talented man wanted was to read his Bible every morning before dawn, leave his eight-dollar-an-hour job at a hardware store, start his own lawn care business, educate his daughters at home, and worship at the New City Church. And, to consecrate the new life, he would be traveling with other church members to Washington, where an evangelical men's organization called Promise Keepers would be holding a rally called Stand in the Gap: A Sacred Assembly of Men.

A month later, on October 4, 1997, I was sitting on the grass of the National Mall under an unseasonably hot sun next to Ken Dupree and a few others from the New City Church. All around us were the green T-shirts and baseball caps of hundreds, maybe thousands, of Alabama Promise Keepers who had driven up all night by the busload, a large minority of them black men. And the state's delegation in turn was engulfed on all sides by three-quarters of a million Christian men, filling the Mall north and south to Pennsylvania and Constitution avenues, a mile west back well beyond the Washington Monument and east to the speakers' stage just in front of the Capitol—men sweating, rehydrating, snacking, regrouping, wending their way to the port-a-johns, reading New Testaments distributed in the hundreds of thousands, praying, singing, facing godlike Jumbotron screens set up every hundred yards down the mall, hearing hours and hours and hours of sermons and songs.

"Why are we here and why are we not here? Is it to demonstrate political might? No. Is it to demonstrate masculine strength? No. Is it to take back the nation for our faith? No. We have come to demonstrate spiritual poverty, that Almighty God might influence us. We come not as protesters to this city to declare our rights. We come as sinners to declare our wrongs."

Thirty-four years later, in three times the numbers, it was the anti-March on Washington. And yet Martin Luther King haunted the day. "Thank God Almighty, we are free at last!" he had cried. "Obey God's law," the Promise Keepers enjoined. The rally's slogan came from a passage in Ezekiel (22:30) in which God says, "And I sought for a man among them, that should make up the hedge, and stand in the gap before me for the land, that I should not destroy it: but I found none." At the other end of this green public space, from the steps of the Lincoln Memorial, King had asked America to make good on its eighteenth-century promise of freedom and equality—to redeem the "bad check" it had written to black people. His imagery mixed religion and democratic secularism, but the content was political, an appeal to man, not God. His dream was "deeply rooted in the American dream." Today, a long procession of speakers was telling the men to forget politics, abandon human pride, prostrate themselves before God. "We are facing a catastrophe. The future of our country will not be determined at the ballot box. The future of our country will be determined in the prayer closet."

I spent the day floating in this ocean of believers like an insoluble speck of consciousness. I wanted to dissolve but couldn't. I had flown down to Washington hoping for an exalted experience. I wanted to be transformed, but on my own terms: human terms. I did not want to accept Christ as my savior, but I wanted to be part of a great mass of men of every color, from every corner of the country, joined together in a flicker of community.

In Birmingham I'd spent hours talking with Ken Dupree, but it was only on the morning of the rally, when I met him and another young black man named Cedric at the Vietnam Memorial, that I worked up the courage to confess.

"I'm not a Christian."

They were reassuring.

"Promise Keepers is about morality, not Christianity," Ken said.

"It's about being a good person," Cedric said.

Two white men from New Hampshire across the aisle on the little commuter plane flying down had said pretty much the same thing (they used the word "lifestyle"). Steve had a fire-alarm installation business; Bob excavated foundations. "My marriage was going down-hill," Bob told me. "I was working too hard, drinking too much." His friend Steve brought him into a group of men at church who counseled him, watched over him, held him accountable. Now Bob washed the dishes, read to his kids, and attributed the survival of his marriage to Promise Keepers. These two guys were buddies, and they treated me like a buddy too. It was like men's group therapy. Women's groups were protesting the rally as a Trojan horse for right-wing, antifeminist politics, but Steve and Bob were in no position to take back America for Jesus or put their wives in servitude. It was hard to see what anyone could have against them.

But maybe my seatmates from New Hampshire and my friends from Birmingham were just being nice to me. The night before, the group's founder, Bill McCartney, a man with all the single-minded drive and severe personal limitations of a college football coach, had told Ted Koppel on *Nightline* that unless you were a born-again Christian, you would feel uncomfortable at the rally. And as the day wore on, the sermons and the hymns, the T-shirt announcing "Darwin Is Dead and He Ain't Coming Back" and the one saying "Hang Out with Jesus, He Hung Out for You," the conservative political groups passing out literature on the fringe of the crowd, the videotape featuring a man asking forgiveness for allowing his girlfriend to have an abortion, the sun beating down, the name Jesus Christ repeated until, like all repeated words, it sounded like nonsense—as the day wore on, I began to feel uncomfortable.

There was a program for every Promise Keepers rally, and it was time to move from sins of sexual impurity to sins against the family. The men around me were kneeling in postures of abject submission, bottoms in the air, faces in the grass, murmuring confessions while the speaker led them: "I have sacrificed my family on the altar of machismo, selfishness, greed, power, pleasure, and personal ambition. O God—I need your help." The men had taken out their wallets and were clutching snapshots of wives and children, and the sight of those faces had many of them in tears, including Ken Dupree. They were deep inside themselves, each one alone in a vast crowd, confronted with some apparently terrible pain.

And then came the time for racial reconciliation. A black minister spoke of the 1963 March on Washington and reminded the crowd: "But four months earlier Martin Luther King sat in a Birmingham jail cell. He wrote a letter that expressed his disappointment in the white Christian church and its leadership." Next to me a short stocky blond fellow from the New City Church grunted assent. "Woe to you religious leaders because you tithe and offer sacrifices but neglect justice, especially for your brothers. Today we must do what the church failed to do thirty years ago. King brought us to rejection of racial prejudice—but rejection without repentance."

What followed was a strange display of Christian multiculturalism. One after another, representatives from every ethnic group got up to ask forgiveness for the group's sins: blacks for their hatred and bitterness, whites for their arrogance and greed, Indians for allowing themselves to become pitiful, Hispanics for making their religion more cultural than spiritual, Asians for their aloofness, Messianic Jews for forsaking their true destiny as Christians. Even a deaf Christian got up and signed. Every speaker was accorded the utmost respect, and when the black one spoke the white men around me from Alabama wept. This multiculturalism, though, didn't end in "diversity" or a rainbow or a patchwork quilt. These men had a principle of unity, a universal, and it was Jesus Christ. Not socialist solidarity or the rights of man or liberal humanism. It was the opposite of humanism. They were brothers in Christ, and the Alabama whites—not just urban missionaries like the New City Church contingent, but suburbanites in golf shirts from archconservative Briarwood Presbyterian—were looking around for a black brother to hug, and the outnumbered Alabama blacks were circulating to make themselves available for a cross-racial embrace. I watched Ken Dupree lean over a seated old white man who looked, in his overalls and straw hat and long gray beard, the picture of a southern cracker—and this man received Ken's offering with such ferocity that the two of them nearly toppled to the grass. I didn't know if I was seeing the fulfillment of King's dream or a moment of cheap sentiment, but I was moved. I didn't know if Ken's and Cedric's hug made me a brother, too, or just an undercover spy, but I was moved.

Then I got bored. On and on it went, hour after hour, Jesus Christ Jesus Christ Jesus Christ. I resented the incessant fervor, as if the point were to fill every second so we couldn't have any stray mental activity. I wanted to talk to my companions but talking was impossible with one bodiless voice after another exhorting us over the public address from every direction and nowhere at all. As my estrangement deepened, I let my thoughts untether from the grass of the Mall and drift over the crowd, over Constitution Avenue and the Smithsonian, down to the Tidal Basin and the Jefferson Memorial, where these words are carved in marble: "I have sworn upon the altar of God eternal hostility against every form of tyranny over the mind of man." And I thought of George Huddleston, my Jeffersonian grandfather, who spent twenty-two years in the domed Capitol building directly in front of me just behind the speakers' stage—who based his whole life on a belief in human dignity and man's ability to govern himself. There was to be no transcendent moment for me today, only passing encounters with ordinary human decency among virtual strangers.

By evening the Mall had a littered, straggling, post-rock concert look. I said goodbye to my Birmingham friends and walked toward the Jefferson Memorial as the sun went down over the Potomac—too late, it had already closed. Groups of teenagers heading home chanted at each other across Washington streets: "We love Jesus, yes we do, we love Jesus, how 'bout you?" I caught the last commuter flight back to Boston—clear, rational, tired city, where the chill of autumn hung in the air and people avoided eye contact on the subway.

CHAPTER 14

◆

Past Is Prologue

A week ago I turned thirty-nine. In a few months the century will end. So will the millennium, but that fact means nothing to me and I've grown to hate the word. The cord of history connecting me to the reign of the Carolingian dynasty doesn't exert much pull. But I can feel the pull of 1900. A line begins with J. P. Morgan on Wall Street and the Russian Jews on the Lower East Side and the Tennessee Coal and Iron Company in Birmingham and the Alabama constitutional convention, and this line runs forward and sideways and back, through a torchlight parade during World War I and bathtub gin and a miserable marriage and the Public Utility Holding Company Bill and the smell of slaughterhouses and all the books in the New Haven Public Library and the Pacific sun beating down on the destroyer *Bailey* off Zamboanga and the dour Gregory Peck of *Gentleman's Agreement* and the Dixiecrat convention and dome-headed Adlai Stevenson with a hole in the sole of his shoe and Fulton Lewis, Jr.'s nightly broadcasts and a wedding couple on a Birmingham front porch and a glass-walled house in the dry California air and a jar full of caterpillars and childish letters to Eugene McCarthy and a student sit-in and a speech with a cigar and a burst blood vessel and an unhappy dinner table and five Republican wins and a village in Africa and a homeless shelter in a church basement and a meeting room in another church basement and three-quarters of a million men worshiping Jesus on the National Mall, to this moment as I write.

The line that connects all these various things within a single century looks as erratic as Jackson Pollock's drips. But lately, having summoned the past, I've felt its pull hard. These people I know intimately or not at all, the obscure and the famous; these events that took place down the hall from my bedroom or decades before I was born; these places scattered in Alabama and California and New England—their collective weight gives the line's tug a strange urgency. And now that I'm coming to the end of my story, I don't know how to answer it.

It's not so hard to find a pattern in history, or in someone else's life, especially someone dead. But at ground level my own life and times look like a random mess, pieces from ten different puzzles, a dozen stories started and interrupted without a middle or ending. What holds it all together? What are the larger themes? Where is the trajectory leading? Why this road and not that? How can so many different impulses and pursuits amount to anything as coherent as a story? How can I justify the way I've lived?

In the fall of 1992, as the Democrats were finally closing in on the White House, I played and replayed a videotape biography of Lyndon Johnson that had aired on PBS. In the last minutes Johnson collapses under all the disasters of 1968—Tet, assassinations, riots, his withdrawal from the presidential race, the Chicago convention, Nixon's victory. "The liberal impulse that went back to the New Deal is challenged," a commentator says, "and what you get beginning in '68 with Richard Nixon's election is an era of conservatism. And the irony is, Johnson presides over the extraordinary achievement of liberalism, reaching its zenith, reaching its heights, and then within three years' time plunges to its depths, from which it still hasn't recovered in the year nineteen hundred and ninety." Johnson in morning coat and pinstriped pants walks down the Capitol steps with a wan smile creasing his face. Behind him, Nixon descends toward his inauguration with his jaw in the air and eyes skitting from side to side. Then LBJ is clutching hands in a crowd and waving goodbye as he boards Air Force One for his final trip home to Texas. "He was the last soldier in the New Deal war."

In the fall of 1992 I watched those last minutes of tape dozens of times. They made me think of my father. I felt the loss of him as never before, but now that the Democrats at last had a hope of victory there was also somehow the chance of a reconciliation.

The night before the election, I dreamed that I was watching the returns, waiting for the moment when Clinton would be declared the winner, a moment that held the promise of so many wrongs redeemed, so many burdens removed. But at some point I stopped paying attention to the TV screen, and when I looked back the announcement had already been made. So I missed my chance at deliverance and now I would never get it back. This dream turned out to be prophetic, for the next night as I was sitting on the edge of the sofa and Clinton's electoral college total was nearing 270, ABC's Boston affiliate cut away to local returns, and when Peter Jennings came back on-screen the magic number had already been reached, history had happened without me to witness it. I desperately wanted to be part of that moment, out of superstition or narcissism; otherwise it wouldn't be quite real, and I would have to go on carrying the load of loss for another quarter century.

Needless to say, Bill Clinton turned out to be a badly flawed vessel into which to pour such hopes and meanings. But even though the moment of truth had eluded me, for a few weeks after that election night in 1992 I felt as if I could let out a breath I'd been holding since the election night in 1968 when I had to go to bed before Nixon's win was announced. We find our fathers where we can.

Suddenly I wanted to know mine again. I wanted to share the good news with him, and to find out what had gone wrong a quarter century earlier for him and his politics. By some odd emotional alchemy that only lasted for a short time, public defeat and personal loss were made tolerable, even redeemed, years later by a presidential election.

When I went home at Christmas, I discovered those cardboard boxes that had been moldering untouched for twenty years in a loft in my mother's garage. I stayed up nights for a week reading everything they contained, hundreds and hundreds of pages, like an archeologist sifting through a tomb filled with treasure. The tomb contained my father in his health and his sickness, and it gave him back to me as much as the dead can be given back. Those boxes of papers brought the past to life and set it to rest. I spent most of the 1990s, the Clinton years, my thirties, looking into what came before. And what has it left me with?

For every answer the past offers, ten new questions arise. The old answers are never enough. Every generation faces a conflict between inherited ideas and current conditions. For George Huddleston and his generation, the conflict set Jeffersonian values of freedom and equality against the modern fact of big institutions and centralized power, and he never resolved it. For my parents and their generation, the New Deal and the civil rights movement seemed to answer every important question, until a reaction set in even in the hour of victory that pushed them back on their heels or flat on their backs. One generation tried to be Jeffersonians when it was no longer really possible; the next tried to be New Dealers when another era had already begun.

My generation (What is a generation? The average interval between parents and children? Thirty years? A group with shared social and historical attributes? Does my generation begin with the year of my birth, or end there, or straddle it? And what significance does any of these markers have? Does my generation only exist relative to me, or is it a historical entity? I want it to be a historical entity, because that's the way I've seen the age of my grandfather and my parents, and that's the kind of argument I'm trying to make here. Common ideas, values, conditions—these arrive in historical generations. So I will call my generation those who came of age in the aftermath of the 1960s, who didn't fight for but took for granted the social welfare system and the rights movements and the cultural revolution, who have had more experience of government's failure than its success, who grew up hearing the word "liberal" used as a term of contempt) — my generation has a different kind of conflict. We have no Jefferson and no New Deal to set our compass by. We have the 1960s — but the 1960s failed to produce a set of ideas that would be a guide and obstacle to those who came after. The decade of the 1960s was more than anything else a mood: an extremely powerful mood, as powerful as five hundred thousand voices or a bomb, but like any mood, short-lived. It came along and changed forever the lives of those who lived through it, including mine at age eight. But it didn't leave behind a viable worldview.

So our conflict comes down to this: We don't have the equivalent of Jeffersonian democracy, ending with the New Deal, or New Deal liberalism, ending after the 1960s, with which to navigate our own time and place. We don't have a political philosophy, even an unconscious one, to play the role that parents play: to be the given, the inheritance, the background we live our lives against, revolt from, come to terms with, and make our own. Instead, we have confusion, fatigue, disbelief — and the unprecedented freedom that underlies them.

To act politically you need to believe that political action can achieve something. The children of Vietnam, Watergate, and the Ford-Carter doldrums are more likely to believe that organized politics is a sham. The counterexample of protest politics offers more illusion than substance, a swig of elixir that turns rancid when the world goes on as before. The dramas of the '60s have distorted the years since with a false image, for in most cases marching and shouting slogans are completely inadequate to bring about lasting change. But the idea of patiently building a coalition over the years and slowly turning public opinion your way through rational persuasion and electoral struggle has little appeal when you've never seen it work and you're predisposed to cynicism.

The industrial struggles of the early twentieth century gave my grandfather's generation the social psychology of the crusader, prone to great, oversimplifying passions. Depression and war made my parents' generation pragmatic and repressed. But the generation that came of age in the aftermath of the '60s has acquired a psychology of

defensive contempt and free-floating anxiety. Any urge toward affirmation we undermine with irony as reflexively as flinching. The ardent
language of my grandfather—"We must hold on to the old Americanism of justice, liberty, and equality"—and the rational language of my
father—"The joys and the frustrations of intellectual analysis are the
best anodyne against existential despair"—embarrass us. Words like
"liberty," "equality," "justice," "brotherhood," "humanity," "progress,"
"reason"—the vocabulary of liberalism for two centuries—are now
impossible to utter without a smirk. Our mind-set is expressed in the
deflating, quasi-professional jargon of the Clinton years: "spin," "trian-
gulate," "on message," "focus group," "disconnect," "dysfunction."

Clinton's presidency combined policies carefully designed to win
the support of the prospering middle class with a reliable diet of personal exposure. He asked very little of anyone except welfare recipients, essentially telling the public: I will protect your interests while
you pursue your fortunes and pleasures and I pursue mine. An ad I saw
in *The New York Times* a couple of years ago sums up the hybrid political thinking that has prevailed under Clinton. It was a full-page spread
for Dewar's scotch, and it said: "When you realize you're still a liberal,
in a conservative-lower-my-taxes sort of way."

When the Reagan revolution was at high tide, it seemed like a total
repudiation of the 1960s. Reagan himself and his conservative movement blamed everything from the national debt to infanticide on the
liberal attempt to engineer equality and the youthful philosophy of do
what you will. Too much government and too much counterculture:
this was the two-pronged conservative attack, and it proved enormously
successful, signaling the beginning of the end for the postwar welfare
state and its social contract between government, business, and labor.

But today we can see that the country only bought half of it. Cut my
taxes, fine. Deregulate business, let the airline price wars bloom, chip
away at the welfare state, no more handouts. But I want the right to
abortion, divorce, sexual experimentation, trashy music and movies—
private happiness on my own terms. No one's going to tell me what I
can and can't do with my own time. Freedom is the bottom line in

America: freedom to earn, freedom to spend, freedom to start a new life. There was no total repudiation after all. It turned out that the 1980s completed what the 1960s began—the economic half of Reagan's revolution was continuous with the cultural half of the '60s revolution. They were both about freedom, and they both won, and we're living with the consequences.

Bill Clinton consecrated the marriage. He reined in both sides toward a soft center that called for "personal responsibility" and protected the more popular entitlements. He delivered booming markets, middle-class social guarantees, and continuous scandal, and he became the first two-term Democrat since FDR. Throughout his presidency liberals criticized him for not attempting enough, lacking backbone—true enough, but liberals owe Clinton a large debt. He took away the stigmas that had plagued them for years. It now sounds hollow when Republicans recite the old accusations of being soft on crime and welfare, of fiscal irresponsibility, of taxing and spending. Government is less distrusted than it has recently been, and after years of deficits it is now free to do more. Under Clinton the word "liberal" itself lost its cutting edge as a political weapon: in the 1998 elections Republican ads targeted a number of Democrats with mind-numbing repetitions of the word, and all the Democrats won. After a thirty-year run, conservatism has played itself out, and Clinton shrewdly helped it to its demise. We may well see liberalism's revival as a self-proclaimed political creed. The question is what liberals can now do with the opening—whether, psychologically and morally, they are capable of seizing the political moment.

Clinton began his first inaugural address by saying, "My fellow citizens"—stirring words, after so many years in which self-interest was elevated to a national virtue—but the Clinton decade has made private life sovereign for a generation that never had a collective experience of civic engagement. In what way are we citizens? Where has the energy, the time, the talent of people under forty-five gone? Into careers, family, entertainment, finances, bodies, self-improvement, self-expression—anywhere but public life. The action is in computers, on Wall Street, at the new sushi restaurant, the personal growth work-shop, the health center. The same restless, idealistic middle-class peo-ple who used to sign petitions and march on behalf of Temperance or woman suffrage or civil rights or peace now enroll in writing programs, where they work on their memoirs (and where I teach them). The impulse to do good outside one's immediate circle usually finds a local and specific outlet, in soup kitchens and literacy programs, not in larger causes with ideological affiliations, which are widely mistrusted. I see all this in my own life, in where and how I spend my time— instead of doing any organized political activity these days, I tutor high school students in inner-city Boston.

Recent American literature reflects this triumph of private life. The writing that has had the greatest influence in the past two decades, that thousands of students at dozens of programs have tried to imitate—the short stories of Raymond Carver and Ann Beattie, the novels of Anne Tyler and Richard Ford, the memoirs of Frank McCourt and Mary Karr—is a breakfast-table realism, focused inward on marital com-plaints, childhood troubles, alcohol, sex, general self-loathing and dis-satisfaction. Read the *Best American Short Stories* collection over the past twenty years, or the National Book Award–winning novels, and you would hardly know about the white backlash or the culture wars. The whole idea of a common social reality against which individuals follow their private destinies has disappeared from literature. When a contemporary novelist attempts to do what John Dos Passos did for the first three decades of the century and get down the unwritten history of American life, the result is likely to be a work of ambitious incoherence like Don DeLillo's Cold War novel *Underworld*. Dos Passos' readers brought to *U.S.A.* a shared idea of the history his characters were living out. They had a common language for it. DeLillo can't count on his readers for the same thing. The work of the most daring younger writ-ers who have tried to move past the realism of private life is too bur-dened with knowingness and sophisticated cultural irony to achieve a compelling vision, even a harsh one, of contemporary America.

It's not as if we have no politics. In some ways we have too much.

We grew up with the cliché "the personal is political." It originated in the late 1960s, among women who were pointing out that the kitchen and the bedroom are scenes of power struggle, inequality, injustice, etc., and that even men with the right views on the war turned oppressors with the lights out. It was an important insight, but it also blurred two realms that need to be kept distinct if either is to mean anything. The phrase has metastasized until everything becomes political, including paper bags and dog food—which is almost the same as nothing being political. Politics has to retain something of the original Greek *polis*, the city—the affair of public life, something citizens do, not are. Politics cannot save anyone's soul or answer the existential questions of human life. Expect salvation or the end of personal troubles and politics will disappoint until it grows hateful and you will reject it in favor of a variety of self-cultivations. When it merges with private life, one or the other gradually disappears. The result is either totalitarianism or triviality. When private life goes, you're left with Nazi Germany or Soviet Russia. When public life wastes away, you get Clinton's America.

What if the large movements of history are behind us? What if the great causes lie in the past? 1917, 1933, 1963, 1968, 1989—years that resonate like these might not come again for a long time, and given the amount of human suffering they represent, maybe we should all breathe a sigh of relief. Maybe the job of politics now is to manage our hard-won freedom and prosperity. For that, we won't need visionaries but technicians. Instead of Roosevelt declaring, "Divine justice weighs the sins of the cold-blooded and the sins of the warm-hearted in different scales," we have Al Gore making a campaign issue of lost luggage at airports. Liberalism could just declare victory and retire from the field, while a horde of consultants moves in to keep the books and volunteers to smooth the rough edges.

Perhaps we no longer need and should learn to live without the soaring voices of Debs and King, with their utopian talk of brotherhood and dreams. Perhaps it's a romantic yearning, or an enfeebled nostalgia, or even a reactionary impulse, to look back over the century as it ends and wish for a replay of its dramatic struggles on behalf of the disfranchised—workers and poor, blacks and women—in the name of humanity. The looking back might itself be a bad omen. My grandfather began looking back "to around 1820" just when history was rushing past him in the 1930s. Liberals of later generations have been looking back to the 1930s or 1960s ever since the election of Richard Nixon. You look back when you feel out of key in the here and now. It's not necessarily a sign of health.

Go searching into the past and as much as you find, you also find you've lost. Some of it you lose in the act of looking, because you're looking. In the summer of 1998, when all my belongings sat in storage in a friend's basement and I was out of town, a week of rain raised a flood in the streets of Cambridge when the storm drains flowing into the Charles River backed up. My cardboard boxes, with papers I'd removed from the boxes in my mother's garage, got soaked. A hundred books drowned. And the scrapbook that my mother had put together after my father's death was water-damaged. Newspaper clippings, diplomas, bar certificates, Navy documents, and photographs got wet. By the time I returned and dug out the scrapbook, a green mold was growing on its brittle twenty-five-year-old pages.

I took it north of Boston, to a document conservation center whose vats and air dryers occupied the fourth floor of a former textile mill. I sat in a conference room with the conservator—a woman in her forties, short salt-and-pepper hair and Central American earrings, an air of former hippiedom and professional sympathy. With delicate fingers she peeled the rippling, stained newsprint away where it had stuck to the moist glue backing on the opposing page. "Mm-mm. Oh shit. Come on, sweetie, that's it," she coaxed a letter from my father to the *Stanford Daily*. I winced like a parent watching a bandage being stripped off his child's wound.

The conservator turned a page and a black-and-white portrait of my father came unstuck: darkly bearded, the vulnerable post-stroke eyes, but the face blotched with missing patches of ink that had been transferred to the facing page. The conservator turned another page and the photograph that also hangs in the Packer Room of the Stanford Law School appeared—but this one was slashed diagonally with white stripes as if someone had dragged fingernails across wet ink.

"Your father's a mess."

Staring at his mutilated face, I realized that my hand was cupping my chin just like the man in the picture.

The conservator closed the scrapbook and looked at me gravely. "The first thing you're going to have to accept," she said, "is that there's going to be some loss."

Each time I go back to California, the scene of my childhood looks less recognizable. Silicon Valley has glazed everything in an unreal wealth that fills Stanford parking lots with luxury imports, replaces downtown Palo Alto's sports shops and variety stores with restaurants serving twenty-dollar ravioli, builds software mini-empires along the industrial wastes of Bayshore freeway. Onetime nerds and heads came to my twentieth high school reunion reincarnated as Microsoft millionaires. The idea born half a century ago in the minds of Stanford engineers has made my hometown the shiny capital of a new Gilded Age.

My mother and I talk on the phone once a week. These days we talk about her father and mine, the election of 1928, the election of 1968, and the election of 2000. She plots strategies and wonders how to get word to the Democratic candidates. The excesses of campaign spending, the cynicism of the media, the triumphalism of the Internet, the "moneygrubbing" of her former employer, Stanford University, have left her disenchanted with the end of the American century. Retired and in her seventies, she sounds more and more like her populist father.

If anything connects the three generations of this story, she does: daughter, wife, mother. Over the years there has been some loss, and yet the fire for politics never really went out. Seventy-one years later, she is still in some ways the three-year-old girl who marched around Washington with an Al Smith button and announced with a swagger, "I don't like old Hoover."

In looking back these last few years, I've gained or recovered fragments of my family, fragments of history, and tried to assemble them into a coherent story. The effort has brought a sense of closeness to the past, to people dead before I was born as well as to people I've known all my life. It's shown me how little is really new, and how even with so much freedom to live my life as I please, a great deal was already fixed at birth. It's made life a little less narrow, a little less lonely. It's restored to me a part of myself—for as anyone approaching forty ought to know, none of us authored ourselves.

But what this effort cannot do is tell me how I or we ought to act, now and in the future. Nor can it give any meaningful inspiration to act. That has to come from one's own age, and from within, or else it's just sentimental fantasy.

Over the past few years a flurry of books has appeared offering cures for liberalism. One prescribes a limited but activist government; another an egalitarian nationalism; others an affirmation of democratic universalism, a revival of civic republicanism, a program of economic populism, or a judicious mix of autonomy, diversity, and solidarity. I agree with every one of them, even when they contradict the others or are self-contradictory. In political philosophy anything seems possible, so in the reading such books can be completely persuasive, but afterward they tend to melt away like daydreams in the afternoon heat, leaving you struggling to remember the verbal formula that had been so reassuring just an hour ago.

These books approach liberalism's decline—or the left's, or democracy's, or America's—as a philosophical problem, a flaw in the concept. Retool the basic structure, remix the ingredients, a little less individualism, a little more community, a little less race, a little more class, and you'll attract a majority of Americans to your intellectual side as you build the next reform movement. It's true that political ideas have fateful consequences (*Ideas Have Consequences* was the title of a 1948 conservative manifesto by Richard Weaver). When the Democratic Party embraced the federal welfare state during the Depression, it became a majority party with a coalition that took some key constituencies away from the Republicans—blacks, prairie progressives, large parts of the northern middle class. When the Democrats embraced civil rights in the 1960s, they began their journey back toward minority-party status, losing many of the working- and middle-class whites, North and South, that had made up the coalition's backbone. My grandfather's career ended in the first case, my uncle's in the second.

In the preface to his 1950 book *The Liberal Imagination*, Lionel Trilling wrote: "In the United States at this time liberalism is not only the dominant but even the sole intellectual tradition. For it is the plain fact that nowadays there are no conservative or reactionary ideas in general circulation." Echoing Mill on Coleridge, he went on to claim that this was a bad thing for liberalism, and that liberals needed conservatives to be smart in order "to keep our ideas from becoming stale, habitual, and inert." Fourteen years later, in the debacle of Barry Goldwater's presidential campaign, conservatism appeared to have expired politically as well as intellectually. Read the history written in the 1960s and you find that conservatism is presumed dead—the only choice is between the liberal establishment and its radical antagonists.

By the end of the following decade, Ronald Reagan was President—and he won with a program that went straight back to the ruins of Goldwater '64. In the intervening years, conservatives and neoconservatives had been hard at work in magazines and universities and think tanks laying intellectual dynamite around the foundations of the welfare state. Once a year through the 1960s and 1970s, William F. Buckley met with a group of fellow conservatives, funded by the estate of a millionaire named John Gaty, at a bank in Wichita to plan a right-wing revival and distribute their benefactor's money to conservative causes. Even corporations, notorious for their tunnel-visioned focus on the bottom line, understand the importance of ideas enough to pour money into pro–free market think tanks like the Olin Foundation and the Cato Institute, which in turn have bankrolled the careers of a whole generation of conservatives. Perhaps some combination of private philanthropy and union money should be pooled to set up a think tank for the other side, wealthy enough to blunt the flow of books and papers proving that poverty is caused by bad genes and bad habits, or that hundred-million-dollar executive compensation packages are in the country's economic interest. And not just blunt the flow: come up with ideas and arguments that will rejuvenate liberalism as conservatism was rejuvenated after Goldwater's defeat.

The right has shown that ideas matter. If Lionel Trilling were alive today and updating the preface to *The Liberal Imagination*, he would have to admit that liberalism needs more self-confidence than self-criticism. I read the new cures for liberalism when they appear, hoping for not just enlightenment but encouragement. And once a month, I go to New York to meet with a group of writers, editors, academics, labor activists. It's not as self-consciously solemn or grand, certainly not as well funded, as John Gaty's beneficiaries. We sit around the kitchen table at one member's apartment, eat take-out Chinese food, and hear a presentation on some key issue of the day: education, foreign intervention, impeachment. Some of the discussions are forgettable, some contentious, some truly illuminating. No one in the group has any power, political or economic, beyond the force of ideas. We're neither shaping the agenda at next month's White House meetings nor laying the foundations for the next century's political philosophy. We have no estate to distribute. Expectations are modest—and yet I always go home feeling a bit let down.

The problem with the books that offer cures for liberalism, and the problem with the monthly group in New York, is that the battle for ideas is only part of the battle. Ideological muddles usually begin in a crisis of faith. You can make a convincing case that smaller class sizes would improve education. You can make a convincing case that no one who works should be poor. Still, little or nothing happens, in society or in yourself, because the deepest impediments aren't intellectual but psychological, even existential. They lie in the will and the imagination.

The main problem of our time is the loss of belief in collective self-betterment. If anything connected the worldview of Jefferson's age to

Franklin Roosevelt's and Martin Luther King's, it was the idea that human beings, relying on their own capacity for reason and goodness, could make their world more free and more just: in Jefferson's words, "to show by example the sufficiency of human reason for the care of human affairs." Historically, this belief has depended on confidence in the instrument of our collective will—government. Who can deny that we've lost that confidence, and the underlying belief in human agency and a shared destiny? We're left to put our faith in God and the market, a pair of invisible hands.

One response is: just as well. If we're no longer called upon to dream large dreams, make large sacrifices, and commit large errors, that might be a sign that the really difficult questions of freedom and justice in this century have been resolved and we're now living in the footnotes. We're free to pursue our private destinies without the distraction of public struggles—isn't that what people all over the world long for? To be left alone by history?

Yes . . . but people want, or need, other things, too, and the triumph of private life comes at a psychic cost. Just as I'm not entirely a creature of comfort but also have a conscience that nags me even if I've just had dinner and am lying peacefully on the couch watching a baseball game, I'm also not entirely a private soul who will do anything to escape public obligations and commitments. Part of me feels some connection to other people even when I don't behave that way. I might walk past the homeless woman as if she doesn't exist, but I know she exists. I might not give her anything, but I'm not happy about it. Most people feel tugged by a sense of responsibility. Nor is it only a weight around their necks, for they also want to be part of something larger than their own lives, and suffer a feeling of moral emptiness as they withdraw another $50 from the ATM or spend another two hours online at the computer. This desire is as real as the urge for physical comfort or the hunger for success. When it goes unfulfilled, a kind of unhappiness sets in.

Every few decades, an internal clock goes off and moral restlessness wakes the American middle class from its slumber, filling it with a fierce energy that, for a short time, is a force to be reckoned with. In these periods of reform, comfortable people cease identifying, as they normally do, with those above them, the wealthier and more success-ful, and focus their sympathy instead on those below them, the poor and outcast whose voices have begun to make themselves heard. In the early 1900s, after the defeat of Populism, a whole flock of educated men and women shook off the complacency of the Gilded Age and invaded city slums looking for social ills to bring to light and remedy. In the 1930s another generation, economically squeezed by the Depression and haunted by the shadow of fascism, identified with striking workers and the unemployed and went to work in Washington or joined the Communist Party, or did both. In the 1960s college stu-dents—the most privileged generation in history, as Richard Nixon and others reminded them—revolted against the soft consumer society in which they'd been reared, embraced the movement of southern blacks for freedom, and then, ignited by the war, tried to remake their world, starting with the universities.

In each case, this middle-class moral zeal produced excesses and worse. The Progressives in their self-righteousness had no patience with the apparent chaos and ignorance of urban immigrant ways—the com-munal squalor, the alcohol, the political machines—and they were too easily satisfied with half measures that eased their outraged consciences without changing the structures of injustice. Some 1930s radicals went the opposite way, lost faith in reform, and in the name of justice were prepared to replace American democracy with a system of tyranny. In the 1960s, students became disgusted with their own liberal moralism and began to imagine themselves a revolutionary vanguard of the oppressed, with disastrous consequences.

Depression-era reform was triggered by an economic event—the stock market crash of 1929. But the Progressive years and the 1960s were both preceded by a period of comfort and drift, vague unease, fit-ful dissatisfaction with prosperity and the hollow forms of democracy. The unease could claim no real ideological content or political vehi-cle. It expressed itself diffusely in works of literature and sociology and religion, in youthful rebellion, adult hand-wringing and soul-searching, talk of sin and shame or alienation or meaninglessness, a growing sense of rot underneath the successful surface of American life. It originated in that sacred American unit, the individual, in a sense of entrapment by forces beyond one's control that kept one from acting in accord with desire and principle.

There's nothing automatic about these recurring bouts. If they were as dependably regular as the thirty-year swings that Arthur Schlesinger, Jr., proposed in *The Cycles of American History*, then the decade of the 1990s would have seen an outpouring of social investigation, pamphleteering, crusades, protest, legislation, and ideological excess. Instead, the century has ended in a period marked by celebrity scandal, journalistic voyeurism, technological domination of everyday life, ideological emptiness, and a presidential election that illuminates no sharply contrasting visions.

And yet, beneath the surface complacency of the soaring Dow and the plummeting crime rate, it feels like a time of fragile confidence, rattled whenever some alienated schoolboy or angry loner with an automatic shoots up a playground or office building. The main forces shaping our national life don't appear to be under any rational control. Chronic underlying ills go untreated because no serious government policy or aroused citizens' movement exists to address them. We endure them with the self-contempt of a man who can't stop overeating even though his joints are swollen with gout and his face keeps breaking out.

If there's any historical recurrence going on today, any distant mirror, we might find it by going back a hundred years to the turn of the last century. Two interrelated features of our time, one political and the other economic, would be immediately familiar to a visitor from the other end of the century, the Populist and Progressive era. First is the system of legal bribery by which our elected officials reach office. Year after year bills to curb the flood of private money going to political parties and campaigns creep their way through Congress. Year after year polls show substantial public support for reform of a system so corrupt that even an organization of businessmen, finally tired of being shaken down, has begun calling for change. Yet no bill ever passes, and the public seems to feel that if the campaign finance laws are changed then lobbyists and contributors and politicians will find ways around them. No defender of the current system has ever been punished with the loss of his seat. The popular attitude isn't indignation so much as resignation.

Meanwhile, for a quarter century the economic trend has been toward greater stratification and inequality, with a steady hardening of class lines and narrowing of opportunity. Almost half the country's wealth is now concentrated in the hands of 1 percent of the people. At the top end, Sandy Weill, co-CEO of the financial services giant Citigroup, received a $167 million compensation package in 1998— 5,566 times the average bank teller's salary, in a year when the company laid off 10,000 workers and its economic performance was subpar. The wealthiest 2.7 million Americans have as much after-tax money as the bottom 100 million. In a period of unprecedented growth and prosperity, the annual median family income, adjusted for inflation, has increased by just $300 since 1989. Though incomes at the lower end are rising for the first time in a quarter century, the gains barely begin to offset the enormous disparities produced by the postindustrial economy.

Of the nation's fourteen million poor children, a third have parents who work. The working poor have become a normal feature of the booming new economy, a key element of its success in raising productivity while keeping inflation low, and absolutely necessary to shareholders' profits.

By now these trends toward unequal distribution of wealth and power are well known. Most Americans see them as injustices. Most Americans don't know what to do about them. There are policy proposals: a variety of national campaign finance reform bills and state ballot initiatives; a substantial increase in the federal minimum wage to, say, $8 an hour; "living wage" campaigns in cities like Baltimore, Los Angeles, and Chicago, and on college campuses, which require city contractors or university employers to pay $2 or $3 above the fed-

eral minimum; indexing of executive salaries to the lowest-paid workers at a fixed rate, from the current average of 419 to 1 down to, say, the
1980 level of 42 to 1; labor law reform that would allow workers to
form unions without the constant risk of being fired.

A hundred years ago, a Populist newspaper in Alabama called the
Troy Jeffersonian wrote: "In this country of undeveloped resources, rich
in endowments of nature, no man should go idle who wants work.
Under a proper distributive system no man who works should be
poor." This principle is so central to Americans' self-ideal that the
growth of the working poor represents a quiet revolution in our political economy, as demoralizing as the open cynicism of the campaign
finance system. Either we have to revise our core ideas about equal
opportunity or we have to find a more "proper distributive system."

Ever since Jefferson, a persistent strain of American thought has
held that great disparities of wealth and power are dangerous to the
republican form of government, and that when these disparities
become entrenched in favored classes and passed on across generations, the threat is all the greater. In other words, the distribution of
wealth and power and opportunity affects the quality of democratic citizenship, the fabric of civic life. If the ideal of equal opportunity is
mocked by vast inequality of result, Americans will lose their stake in
the country's fate.

By the beginning of the twentieth century, industrial America had
become so grossly unequal that a great debate broke out about the
nature of democracy and the philosophy of the two parties. The
decades of liberal reform that followed created the first middle-class
majority in history. Now, at the turn of a new century, that middle
class is shrinking as we slide back toward the money-driven hierarchical society in which my grandfather began his career. If he came back
as a Democratic member of the House and took a look around, he
might feel tempted to quote his own words from seventy-five years ago
and say that America "cannot be a truly democratic nation if, typical of
its life, is the gilt and splendor of Fifth Avenue and the squalor and
hunger of the slums."

Today the contrasts are less striking, the pain spread more diffusely and subtly. Instead of the Alabama miner, his face blackened by coal dust, we have four-job families living in the suburbs, steelworkers turned security guards employed in strip malls, home health care workers taking six buses a day, $7-an-hour sandwich makers on upscale shopping streets. Instead of Andrew Carnegie sending in Pinkertons to break the Homestead steel strike, we have Bill Gates's empire of temporary workers without benefits. Economic forces today are as distant and complex as globalization. Moreover, the old humanistic language is dead, and the belief that something can be done has grown weaker. Intellectually and morally, we are less equipped to deal with the worst effects of capitalism than my grandfather's generation. People with the best will in the world feel thoroughly enmeshed in the current arrangements and powerless to do more than express a vague wish. Without a vehicle for reform and a belief to sustain it, the trends overwhelm anyone's individual effort, like the flow of winds or tides, and we seem able to imagine no alternative to the world as it is.

And yet, with our endless talent for experiment and hope alongside our vast material comfort, we will have a more just society as soon as we want one. Throughout American history this desire keeps rising to the surface, often at the unlikeliest moment. There's nothing inevitable about its appearance, but neither is it impossible. The liberal impulse didn't die around the time of my father's stroke. It still beats somewhere under our skin.

♦

Note on Sources

This book owes a debt to two scholars who raised the writing of history to a literary art, Richard Hofstadter and Christopher Lasch, and in particular to Hofstadter's *The American Political Tradition*, *The Age of Reform*, and *Anti-intellectualism in American Life* and Lasch's *The New American Radicalism*, *The Agony of the American Left*, and *The True and Only Heaven*.

I have also depended for facts, quotations, and historical understanding on these sources:

Chapter 1: *The Portable Thomas Jefferson*, ed. Merrill D. Peterson; *The Life and Selected Writings of Thomas Jefferson*, ed. Adrienne Koch and William Peden; Gordon S. Wood, *The Radicalism of the American Revolution*; Drew R. McCoy, *The Elusive Republic: Political Economy in Jeffersonian America*; Michael Sandel, *Democracy's Discontent*; E. Merton Coulter, *The South During Reconstruction, 1865–1877*; C. Vann Woodward, *Origins of the New South, 1877–1913*; Edward L. Ayers, *The Promise of the New South*.

Chapter 2: Ethel Armes, *The Story of Coal and Iron in Alabama*; *The Survey* magazine, January 6, 1912; Ronald L. Lewis, *Black Coal Miners in America: Race, Class, and Community Conflict, 1780–1980*; Robert David Ward and William Warren Rogers, *Labor Revolt in Alabama: The Great Strike of 1894*; *Official Proceedings of the Constitutional Convention of the State of Alabama*; William Warren Rogers, *The One-*

Gallused Rebellion: Agrarianism in Alabama, 1865–1896; Sheldon Hackney, *Populism to Progressivism in Alabama*. I am grateful to James Goodman, author of *Stories of Scottsboro*, who gave me a copy of the ACLU confidential report on Scottsboro, and to Diane McWhorter, who generously allowed me to read pages from her book about Birmingham in manuscript.

Chapter 3: Sigmund Freud and William C. Bullitt, *Woodrow Wilson: A Psychological Study*; *The Philosophy and Policies of Woodrow Wilson*, ed. Earl Latham; *The Priceless Gift: The Love Letters of Woodrow Wilson and Ellen Axson Wilson*, ed. Eleanor Wilson McAdoo; Woodrow Wilson, *State Papers and Addresses*; Gene Smith, *When the Cheering Stopped: The Last Years of Woodrow Wilson*; John Dos Passos, *Mr. Wilson's War*; Randolph Bourne, *The World of Randolph Bourne*, ed. Lillian Schlissel; Charles Forcey, *The Crossroads of Liberalism*.

Chapter 4: Edward S. LaMonte, *Politics and Welfare in Birmingham, 1900–1975*; Drew Pearson, *More Washington Merry-Go-Round*; Arthur M. Schlesinger, Jr., *The Age of Roosevelt* (*The Crisis of the Old Order, 1919–1933, The Coming of the New Deal*, and *The Politics of Upheaval*); Walter Lippmann, *Interpretations 1933–1935*; Arthur Krock, *Memoirs*.

Chapter 5: Dan A. Oren, *Joining the Club: A History of Jews and Yale*; Leonard Dinnerstein, *Antisemitism in America*; *Anti-Semitism in American History*, ed. David A. Gerber; *The New American Right*, ed. Daniel Bell; Porter McKeever, *Adlai Stevenson: His Life and Legacy*.

Chapter 6: Dwight Macdonald, *The Ford Foundation: The Men and the Millions*; Frank K. Kelly, *Court of Reason: Robert Hutchins and the Fund for the Republic*; George H. Nash, *Herbert Hoover and Stanford University*; Kenneth O'Reilly, *Hoover and the Un-Americans: The FBI, HUAC, and the Red Menace*; Ellen W. Schrecker, *No Ivory Tower: McCarthyism and the Universities*; William D. Barnard, *Dixiecrats and Democrats: Alabama Politics 1942–1950*; Glenn Feldman, *From Demagogue to Dixiecrat: Horace Wilkinson and the Politics of Race*.

Chapter 7: Clark Kerr, *The Uses of the University*; Paul Goodman, *The Community of Scholars*; Andrew F. Rolle, *California: A History, 2nd ed.*; Rebecca Lowen, *Creating the Cold War University: The Transformation of Stanford*; Michael Davie, *California: The Vanishing Dream*; Richard Reeves, *President Kennedy: Profile of Power*.

Chapter 8: Todd Gitlin, *The Sixties: Years of Hope, Days of Rage*; Paul Berman, *A Tale of Two Utopias: The Political Journey of the Generation of 1968*; *Revolution at Berkeley*, ed. Michael V. Miller and Susan Gilmore; *Confrontation: The Student Rebellion and the Universities*, ed. Daniel Bell and Irving Kristol; Nathan Glazer, *Remembering the Answers: Essays on the American Student Revolt*; Robert Dallek, *Flawed Giant: Lyndon Johnson and His Times 1961–1973*.

Chapter 9: Alan M. Dershowitz, *The Best Defense*; H. Bruce Franklin, *Back Where You Came From: A Life in the Death of the Empire*.

Chapter 12: Todd Gitlin, *The Twilight of Common Dreams: Why America Is Wracked by Culture Wars*; Irving Howe, *Socialism and America*.

Chapter 13: Paul Hemphill, *Leaving Birmingham; Encyclopedia of the American Religious Experience, Vol. II*, ed. Charles H. Lippy and Peter W. Williams; Benjamin Schwarz, "What Jefferson Helps to Explain," *The Atlantic Monthly*, March 1997.

I also benefited from research at Harvard University's Widener Library and Lamont Library, the Boston Public Library, Stanford University's Green Library, the Stanford News Service (with thanks to Karen Bartholomew), the Pacific Studies Center (with thanks to Lenny Siegel), Princeton University's Seeley G. Mudd Library, and the Birmingham Public Library (with thanks to Anne Knight).

◆

Acknowledgments

Thanks to those relatives and friends in Alabama and California who helped me along the way by answering questions, offering thoughts and memories, and providing shelter—especially to A. J. Huddleston, George Huddleston III, John Chiles, Mary Chiles, and Jane Aaron.

Thanks to my agent, Kathy Anderson, for her enthusiastic editorial work and for placing this book with the ideal editor. Thanks to Jonathan Galassi for the intelligence of his questions and the warmth of his support. Thanks to Lorin Stein for ushering the book through.

Thanks to Nancy Packer, who withheld nothing from this book, including a generous response when it was done.

Thanks to those who read the book in progress and improved it with their critical judgment and advice: Gloria and Bill Broder (who first suggested a three-generational story), Todd Gitlin (whose conversations with me were crucial throughout the writing), Gordon Harvey, Mark Melnicove, Askold Melnyczuk, Ann Packer, Liam Rector, Becky Saletan, and Naomi Wax.